As the
RABBIS TAUGHT

As the RABBIS TAUGHT

STUDIES
in the
AGGADOS
of the
TALMUD

Tractate Megillah

translated by
Dovid Landēsman

commentary and notes by
Rabbi Chanoch Gebhard
and Dovid Landesman

JASON ARONSON INC.
Northvale, New Jersey
London

Library of Congress Cataloging-in-Publication Data

As the rabbis taught : the aggados of the Talmud / introduction, translation, and commentary by Dovid Landesman.
    p. cm.
    Adaptation of: Shi'urim be-hagadot Hazal : meha-Talmud ha-Bavli : 'al pi 'Ein Ya' akov : Masekhet Megilah / ba-'arikhat Avraham b.R. Yitshak Vinberg, Hanokh b.R. 'Ozer Gevhard.
    Includes original text of Ein Ya' akov, Tractate Megillah with English translation.
    Includes bibliographical references.
    ISBN 1-56821-949-0
    1. Ein Ya' akov. Megillah. 2. Talmud. Megillah—Commentaries. 3. Aggada—Commentaries. 4. Aggada—Translations into English. I. Landesman, Dovid. II. Shi' urim be-hagadot Hazal. III. Ein Ya' akov. Megillah. IV. Ein Ya' akov. Megillah. English.
BM516.E433A8   1996
296.1'2507—dc20

96-1864

Manufactured in the United States of America. Jason Aronson Inc. offers books and cassettes. For information and catalog write to Jason Aronson Inc., 230 Livingston Street, Northvale, New Jersey 07647.

With heartfelt gratitude to

Mr. Sonny (Ben Tzion) Kahn

a most generous supporter of

Torah causes, who founded the

Kollel and Beit Midrash "Beit Hashem"

in his parents' home in Bnei Brak,

where lectures on the

Aggados of the Talmud — Ein Yaakov

are delivered in memory of his late father

Eliyahu ha-Kohen

son of Yaakov and Miriam

זכרונם לברכה

Dedicated in honor of

Eli and Esti

ט״ו בשבט תשנ״ה

Boaz and Aliza

ט״ו בשבט תשנ״ו

... שכל האילנות היוצאים מכם יהיו כמותכם ...

TABLE OF CONTENTS

THE FOURTH CHAPTER

BIBLIOGRAPHY OF SOURCES AND COMMENTARIES

מהמהדורה בעברית

בס״ד   ט״ו מרחשון תשנ״ג

הנני להעריך את העבודה ויגיעה הרבה שהשקיעו הני תרי צנתרי דדהבא, מיקירי קהילתנו הק׳ הרה״ג חנוך גבהרד והרה״ג אברהם וינברג שליט״א, בחיבורם הנחמד על אגדות חז״ל במסכת מגילה. אנו מקובלים שכל העומק שבאגדות הש״ס לא יתגלה רק בביאת הגואל בב״א, אבל על דברי תורה נאמר ועליהו לא יבול וכ״ש פשטות דברי חז״ל בלי להבין עומק עומקם, ויש בהם פרד״ס - פשט, רמז, דרוש וסוד. הרבנים הנ״ל טרחו להבין לנו את עומק הפשט ובזה סללו לנו מסילה בהבנת דברי חז״ל הקדושים. את חיבורם עשו בעיקר עבור אלה שעדיין לא נכנסו ללימוד הגמ׳ היטב, וע״כ דברי חז״ל באגדות חז״ל תמוהים בעיניהם. אבל לתועלת יהי׳ לכולנו ללמוד להתבונן ולחפש דרך ישרה בהבנתם.

הנני לברכם שתצליחו לעורר להתבוננות, ובפרט בדברי חז״ל העמוקים מאד מאד.

כעתירת

שלמה זלמן אולמן

רב דקהילת משכנות יעקב

קהלות יעקב בני ברק

ב״ה

לרוב טרדותי לא אוכל לעיין בחיבורים חדשים, אבל את זאת ראיתי שעשו המחברים החשובים עבודת הק׳ לשם שמים להועיל בעיקר להמתקרבים לתורה להבין דבר ולחבב להם קדושת התורה - ע״כ ראויים לשבח - וכל מי שדבוק לדברי חז״ל בהלכה ובאגדה - ונכנס לעומק דבריהם אשרי לו - וע״כ הריני מצטרף לדברי הג״ר שלמה ז׳ אולמן שליט״א רב ק׳ משכנות יעקב.

על זה בעה״ח

מצפה לרחמי ה׳

שמואל הלוי וואזנר

רב ואב״ד ור״מ זכרון מאיר

בני ברק

Our Sages teach: If you wish to know the One Who Created the World, learn *Aggadah* (the non-legal sections of the Talmud). In *Aggadah* there is historic narrative at a deeper level, perspectives on Providence, human character, Exile and Redemption, the secrets of G-d's relation to His world, and the character and destiny of Israel. For a variety of reasons, the Sages often presented their views through veils of metaphor and parable — not only as protection from unfriendly eyes — but also to simultaneously instruct the learned and saintly, as well as the ignorant and simple.

On the major compendium of Talmudic *Aggadah* — *Ein Yaakov* — many commentaries have been written. But for this generation a novel work was needed — one based on reverent faithfulness to our Sages' teachings, but one speaking in the idiom of our time for the growing army of new students of Torah who have no access to the available works in the field.

Finally, a dedicated and gifted Torah scholar, R. Chanoch Gebhard, has authored such a work, and he has been blessed by an equally dedicated and gifted translator and adaptor, R. Dovid Landesman.

As an initial indication of the promise entailed in the work, the *Aggados* of the Destruction from *Masechet Gittin* have been prepared for separate publication. The undersigned has been genuinely and positively impressed by the quality of the work of both author and translator. May the edification and inspiration of this first part of the planned series reach the many who seek the guidance of our Divinely inspired but mystery laden *Aggadah*. May our Sages — from their heavenly abode — view this work as a testament of honor to their teachings.

הכותב והחותם לכבוד התורה ולומדי׳

נחמן בולמן

אסרו חג שבועות תשנ״ג

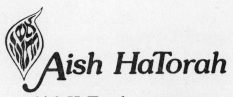

Aish HaTorah

Aish HaTorah	אש התורה
World Center	המרכז העולמי
At the Western Wall	ברחבת הכותל המערבי

בס״ד

Jerusalem

10 Cheshvan 5756

There have been, thank G-d, many translations of the books of our heritage including the Talmud and commentaries on the Talmud; and that is wonderful to enable those who have not been fortunate enough to have acquainted themselves to read and understand the original.

With Rabbi Chanoch Gebhard's work we have a wonderful opportunity not only to see the world of the *Aggadah* of the Talmud, but to be taken by the hand by a talented deep scholar and shown how to question and answer and understand the *Aggadah* in the footsteps of our traditional methods of study.

Fortunate indeed are those who have found Rabbi Gebhard as a guide.

Rabbi Noach Weinberg

Rosh HaYeshiva

יתברך **ה**יוצר **ו**ישתבח **ה**בורא

It is with a profound sense of gratitude to God that we present this work to the public. Based on the text of EIN YAAKOV, the classic compendium of Talmudic *aggados*, this work is the second volume — and the first full tractate — in a new series designed to provide the English reader with at least some of the means to help him understand the *aggadic* material included in the Talmud. Many serious students, including those with a broad background in Torah study, find the *aggados* difficult to comprehend because of language difficulties, or a lack of familiarity with the style and mode of presentation of the materials. Regrettably, some students simply skip over these materials when studying *gemarra* and fail to avail themselves of the opportunity to be enriched by their contents. It is to them that we dedicate this series and add our sincere prayers that these works prove to be a source of enlightment and a springboard to deeper and more comprehensive learning.

The *aggadic* material to be included in the volumes of this series is drawn from the ROMM edition of EIN YAAKOV. A number of editorial decisions have been made regarding the method of presentation. In the project's initial stages, it was felt that the translation of the *aggados* should be presented on a phrase by phrase basis. Doing so would allow the student/reader to absorb the material in the same fashion as it would be presented in a classroom. Moreover, this type of format would be especially beneficial to those whose difficulties were in translating the texts. However, when we showed sample galleys using this type of layout to a number of people associated with the project, the overwhelming response was that the layout — though potentially valuable — seriously affected the material's readability.

The decision was therefore made to present vowellized segments of the *aggados* followed by an English translation. The translation itself should be sufficient to enable the reader to understand the material on the most basic level. To assist the reader in mastering the text, the segments have been broken into short paragraphs so that one can easily refer between the Aramaic and English texts.

The footnotes are an integral part of the translation and, aside from providing sources and cross references, include comments and information designed to give the reader a somewhat deeper appreciation for the material than would be possible from reading the translation alone. The commentary offers the reader an even broader picture of many of the issues touched upon.

Because the original EIN YAAKOV is not bound by the צורת הדף — the traditional page presentation of the Talmud — we felt that it was not obligatory that we do so. However, to enable the reader to quickly locate specific materials should he choose to use this work with a *gemarra*, the relevant folio numbers appear as a header on even-numbered pages. Additionally, the page breaks, as they appear in the Talmud, have been included in the appropriate places within the English translation.

EIN YAAKOV was compiled by R. Yaakov Ibn Chaviv who fled the Spanish Inquisition and settled in Salonika. It was there, over a period of some twenty years, that he devoted himself to collecting the *aggados* that appear in the Talmud *Bavli* and *Yerushalmi* and writing a commentary to them which appears in most editions under the title HA-KOSEV.

There are many textual differences between the *aggados* that appear in the EIN YAAKOV and between the parallel versions in our editions of the Talmud. Moreover, the author sometimes omitted materials from one tractate when the same *aggadah* appeared elsewhere in the Talmud. At times, and for reasons that we do not know, the author included purely halachic material within the compendium.

In translating the *aggados*, we have strived to achieve consistency with the syntax and style of the Talmud without sacrificing readability. At times, these efforts have caused us to deviate from strict adherence to the rules of English grammar. We did so because we felt that it was of paramount importance to translate as literally as possible, for the Sages were quite meticulous in choosing their words. However, realizing that complete fealty to Talmudic sentence structure might make the material awkward, we have taken minor liberties in translating. The translation of Scriptural references often deviates from the literal or accepted meaning of the verses, for it was our intention to enable the reader to understand the Talmud's use or exegesis of the specific verse. Where the exegesis of a verse is dependent upon the meaning or vowellization of a word or phrase, the methodology is explained in a footnote.

To assist the reader in fully understanding the material, additions have been made both to the text and to verses. These have been placed in square brackets and have been set in a slightly smaller type size to emphasize that they are not part of the original material. When the Talmud only cites part of a verse, we have often included additional parts so that the intent remain clear. In these cases, square brackets have also been used but the type size remains constant. The name of God is spelled out in the commentary as befits Torah literature. God is used as a translation for י-ה-ו-ה and Lord as a translation for אלקים. The contemporary convention of using Ashkenazic consonants with Sefardic vowels has also been adopted.

It is our distinct honor to serve as the vehicle to introduce the English reading public to the commentary of Rabbi Chanoch Gebhard of Bnei Brak. Rabbi Gebhard's lectures in EIN YAAKOV — delivered under the auspices of ARACHIM — have won him a well deserved reputation as a master in the field. His students have found his lectures to be a masterful blend of profound insights and simple *p'shat*. The range of sources which he has used in compiling his commentary, in conjunction with his *chavrusah*, Rabbi Avraham Weinberg, bears eloquent testimony to his scholarship. We have taken liberties with his commentary so as to meet the specific needs of the English audience and have included many additional notes and comments that do not appear in his Hebrew work. Thus, any shortcomings or mistakes should not be attributed to him.

No work of this scope could be undertaken without the active encouragement and assistance of others. I am deeply indebted to Rabbi Nachman Bulman of Yeshivas Ohr Somayach who, through the years, has made himself freely available to me for questions, discussions and review. It is a great honor to have merited the opportunity to "pick the brains" of one of contemporary Jewry's most profound and original scholars and I offer him my profound gratitude for his time and incalculably valuable suggestions and criticisms. May God grant him and his *rebbitzen* good health and the strength to continue their many educational endeavors.

It is customary at this point to thank one's wife and family for the sacrifices and support that allow a writer to pursue his interests. I lack the means to express the thanks that I owe them. Instead, I offer a prayer that God grant them His abundant bounty in the merit of these works and may they be accepted as an effort להגדיל תורה ולהאדירה.

Dovid Landesman
Kfar Chassidim
Shevat 5756

Note: As we prepare additional volumes in this series, we would be most appreciative of your criticisms, comments and suggestions. They should be forwarded to POB 1405, KFAR CHASSIDIM, ISRAEL 20450.

Studies in the Aggados of the Talmud
based on the text of Ein Yaakov

מסכת מגילה
Tractate Megillah

רצונך להכיר
את מי שאמר
והיה העולם -
למד הגדה,
שמתוך כך אתה
מכיר את הקדוש
ברוך הוא
ומתדבק בדרכיו
ספרי, עקב מ״ט

Do you wish to know He who said and the world came about? Study the *aggadah*, for through it you will recognize the Holy One, blessed is He, and cleave to His path.
Sifri, Ekev 49

TALMUD

אָמַר רַבִּי יִרְמְיָה, וְאִיתֵימָא רַבִּי חִיָּא בַּר אַבָּא: מְנַצְפַּ"ךְ, צוֹפִים אֲמָרוּם. וְתִסְבְּרָא?! וְהָכְתִיב: "אֵלֶּה הַמִּצְוֹת", שֶׁאֵין נָבִיא רַשַׁאי לְחַדֵּשׁ דָּבָר מֵעַתָּה? וְעוֹד, הָא אָמַר רַב חִסְדָּא: מֵ"ם וְסָמֵ"ךְ שֶׁבַּלּוּחוֹת, בְּנֵס הָיוּ עוֹמְדִין? אִין, מֶחֱזָה הֲווּ, מֵידַע הוּא דְּלָא הֲווּ יָדְעֵי, הֵי בְּאֶמְצַע תֵּבָה, וְהֵי בְּסוֹף תֵּבָה. וְאָתוּ צוֹפִים וְתִקֵּינוּ פְּתוּחִים בְּאֶמְצַע תֵּבָה, סְתוּמִים בְּסוֹף תֵּבָה. סוֹף סוֹף, וְהָכְתִיב: "אֵלֶּה הַמִּצְוֹת", שֶׁאֵין נָבִיא רַשַׁאי לְחַדֵּשׁ בָּהֶם דָּבָר מֵעַתָּה? אֶלָּא שְׁכָחוּם, וְחָזְרוּ צוֹפִים וְיִסְּדוּם.

TRANSLATION

[2b] R. Yirmiyah said, and some maintain [that the opinion is that of] R. Chiya bar Abba: מְנַצְפַּ"ךְ — [the final letters ם, ן, ץ, ף and ך which replace the regular forms of the letters מ, נ, צ, פ and כ], were introduced by the Prophets.[1] Do you really maintain this opinion? Does the Torah (*Vayikra* 27:34) not state: *These are the commandments* [i.e., only the Torah itself can establish a practice as being binding by Torah law, which means] that [even] a Prophet may not establish a new practice now [i.e., once the Torah was given]?[2] Moreover, R. Chisda said: The letters מ and ס in the tablets [i.e., in the Decalogue] [3a] remained in place by virtue of a miracle?[3] Indeed, [the letters ם, ן, ץ, ף and ך] were already existent [at the time that the Torah was given. However, although these letters were known], they did not know which [form of these letters was to be used] in the middle of a word, and which [form was to be used] at the end of a word. The Prophets came and declared that the open forms [מ, נ, צ, פ and כ] would be used in the middle of a

---

1 - The use of the term צופים — *seer* — for Prophets is based on the verse in *Yechezkel* (3:17): *I have made you a seer for the house of Israel*, and on the verse in *Yirmiyahu* (6:17): *I shall establish seers upon you*.

2 - Thus, how could the Prophets have introduced new letters on their own?

3 - The verse in *Shemos* (32:15-16) states: *and the writing on the tablets went from side to side ... [the words were] engraved upon them.* According to tradition, the letters on the tablets were engraved through the entire stone. Thus, the letters ס and ם which are completely closed, could only remain in place through a miracle. Otherwise, the middle of the letters — not being attached to anything — would have fallen. The Talmud points out that this tradition proves that the final ם was already known when the Torah was given. Thus, the opinion that it was introduced by the Prophets is difficult to support.

word and the filled forms [ף ,ץ ,ן ,ם and ך] at the end of a word.[4] The [initial] question remains unresolved, for the verse states: *These are the commandments*, [and the implication is] that a prophet may not introduce a new practice once the Torah was given [and thus, how can one maintain that the practice of using the final letters at the end of a word was first established by the prophets]? Rather, it was forgotten [i.e., the practice of using the final letters only at the end of a word] and the Prophets reintroduced the practice [but did not establish it on their own].

COMMENTARY

Why was it necessary for the Prophets to reintroduce the practice of using the final letters at the end of words? Was it not possible to determine their proper placement simply by examining the Torah scrolls that were in use?

Tosafos[5] points out that Amon, King of Judah, burned the Torah scroll kept in the *Beis ha-Mikdash*. Thus, there was no authoritative scroll that could be used as the basis for establishing the proper use of the final letters. *Rashi*[6] writes that the authoritative scroll was destroyed by King Achaz.

Ritva is of the opinion that the proper use of the final letters was forgotten after King Yoshiyahu buried the ark containing the tablets and authoritative Torah scroll written by Moshe.

According to *Yefeh Mar'eh*, at the time of the destruction of the first *Beis ha-Mikdash*, the people feared that their Babylonian captors would defile the Torah scrolls. They therefore purposely omitted the final letters in the scrolls taken with them into captivity so that they would be considered less sacred. As a consequence, subsequent generations had no basis for determining the proper usage of the end letters. At the end of their exile, when it once again became possible to openly write Torah scrolls, it was necessary to turn to Chagai, Malachi and Zechariah — the last of the Prophets — to determine when regular letters were to be used and when final letters were to be used.

Interestingly, the Talmud speaks of the letters כ ,פ ,צ ,נ ,מ whereas the

---

4 - *Chasam Sofer* points out that there never was a question regarding which forms of the letters were to be used at the beginning of a word. What had been forgotten was whether the end forms of the letters were to be used in the middle of a word or only at the end of a word.

5 - ד"ה ועוד האמר רב חסדא.

6 - מלכים ב' כב:ח ד"ה ספר התורה.

alphabetical sequence is ‎מ, נ, צ. ‎כ, מ, נ, פ, צ. *Tosafos* points out that the form ‎מ, נ, צ,
‎פ, כ is a an acrostic for ‎מן צפך — *from Your seers*.

TALMUD

וְאָמַר רַבִּי יִרְמְיָה, וְאִיתֵימָא רַבִּי חִיָּא בַּר אַבָּא: תַּרְגּוּם שֶׁל תּוֹרָה, אוּנְקְלוּס
הַגֵּר אֲמָרוֹ מִפִּי רַבִּי אֱלִיעֶזֶר וְרַבִּי יְהוֹשֻׁעַ. וְשֶׁל נְבִיאִים, יוֹנָתָן בֶּן עֻזִּיאֵל
אֲמָרוֹ מִפִּי חַגַּי זְכַרְיָה וּמַלְאָכִי. וּבְאוֹתָה שָׁעָה נִזְדַּעְזְעָה אֶרֶץ יִשְׂרָאֵל אַרְבַּע
מֵאוֹת פַּרְסָה עַל אַרְבַּע מֵאוֹת פַּרְסָה. יָצְתָה בַּת־קוֹל וְאָמְרָה: מִי הוּא זֶה
שֶׁגִּלָּה אֶת סְתָרַי לִבְנֵי אָדָם? עָמַד יוֹנָתָן בֶּן עֻזִּיאֵל עַל רַגְלָיו וְאָמַר: אֲנִי הוּא
שֶׁגִּלִּיתִי אֶת סְתָרֶיךָ לִבְנֵי אָדָם. גָּלוּי וְיָדוּעַ לְפָנֶיךָ שֶׁלֹּא לִכְבוֹדִי עָשִׂיתִי, וְלֹא
לִכְבוֹד בֵּית אַבָּא עָשִׂיתִי, אֶלָּא לִכְבוֹדְךָ עָשִׂיתִי, שֶׁלֹּא יִרְבּוּ מַחֲלוֹקוֹת
בְּיִשְׂרָאֵל.

TRANSLATION

And R. Yirmiyah also said,[7] and some maintain [that the opinion was that of] R.
Chiya bar Abba: The Aramaic translation of the Torah was said [i.e., authored]
by Onkelos the convert[8] according to the tradition [passed on by] R. Eliezer and
R. Yehoshua. And [the Aramaic translation of] the Prophets was said by Yonasan
ben Uziel[9] according to the tradition [passed on by] Chagai, Zechariah and
Malachi. At that time [i.e., when Yonasan ben Uziel publicized the Aramaic
translation], the Land of Israel shook [throughout its entire area[10] which is] four
hundred *parsah* by four hundred *parsah*. A Divine voice was heard to say: "Who
is this who has revealed My secrets to mortal man?" Yonasan ben Uziel stood
up and said: "It is I who has revealed Your secrets to mortal man. It is obvious

---

7 - Having quoted a statement of R. Yirmiyah, the Talmud continues with another of
his statements even though there is no direct connection between the two subjects.

8 - A nephew of Titus who lived at the time of the destruction of the second *Beis ha-
Mikdash* — see *Gittin* 56b. Acording to the *Yerushalmi* (1:9), the translation was
written by Aquilas. *Korban Edah* maintains that Aquilas and Onkelos were the same
person. Other commentators maintain that the *Yerushalmi* is referring to the Greek
translation of the Torah written during the reign of Ptolemy Philadelphus (Talmai) —
see page 62.

9 - Hillel's greatest disciple who lived approximately 100 years prior to the
destruction of the second *Beth ha-Mikdash*. *Maharitz Chayes* points out that the
Targum Yonasan to *Chumash*, printed in editions of the *Mikraos Gedolos*, should not
be ascribed to Yonasan ben Uziel.

10 - See *Rashi*, ‎במדבר יג:כח.

and known to You that I have not done so to increase my own prestige, and I have not done so to bring honor to my father's household. Rather, I have done so for Your sake, so that misunderstandings not increase among Israel."

COMMENTARY

Why did Yonasan's Aramaic translation of the Prophets cause the Land of Israel to tremble? Furthermore, why was Yonasan ben Uziel criticized for having revealed God's secrets to mortal man? It would seem that he should have been praised for having provided the people with the means to better understand the depth of the prophetic messages by translating them and adding explanations.

Tosafos Rid answers that once the Prophets were translated, people no longer had to apply themselves diligently in their studies. Yonasan ben Uziel's translation lessened the effort necessary and he is therefore criticized. Nonetheless, though the Aramaic translation can be faulted for having made study simpler, can it not also be seen as having made a qualitative contribution by allowing people to increase the amount of material they studied as well as a quantitative contribution by enabling more people to understand?

The Talmud teaches an important lesson regarding the proper approach towards Torah study. When faced with a choice between diligent effort and between material covered, the former is preferable. Mastery of Torah is dependent primarily upon the extent of the effort one makes. *Chazon Ish*, in a letter to a young student, wrote: *The concept of diligent Torah study is not measured solely by time, but depends upon the effort expended in studying. An hour spent in diligent study is preferable to many hours spent in simply reading material.*

Faced with the criticism, Yonasan ben Uziel pointed out that the translation had been made so as to prevent misunderstandings. Living in a period when the people faced persecutions that prevented them from devoting substantial time to study, Yonasan was concerned that the political and physical difficulties would lead the people to forget the Torah. He therefore undertook to publicize the translation so that the people would understand the true meaning of the Prophets. In doing so, he prevented misunderstandings. *Rambam*[11] notes that R. Yehudah *ha-Nasi* was motivated by the same considerations when he committed the *Mishnah* to writing.

---

11 - הקדמה למשנה תורה.

TALMUD

וְעוֹד בִּקֵּשׁ לְגַלּוֹת תַּרְגּוּם שֶׁל כְּתוּבִים, יָצְתָה בַּת־קוֹל וְאָמְרָה לוֹ: דַּיֶּךָ. מַאי
טַעְמָא? מִשּׁוּם דְּאִית בֵּיהּ קֵץ מָשִׁיחַ.
וְתַרְגּוּם שֶׁל תּוֹרָה, אוּנְקְלוֹס הַגֵּר אֲמָרוֹ?! וְהָא אָמַר רַב אִיקָא בַּר אָבִין, אָמַר
רַב חֲנַנְאֵל, אָמַר רַב: מַאי דִּכְתִיב: "וַיִּקְרְאוּ בַסֵּפֶר, בְּתוֹרַת הָאֱלֹהִים מְפֹרָשׁ,
וְשׂוֹם שֶׂכֶל, וַיָּבִינוּ בַּמִּקְרָא". "וַיִּקְרְאוּ בַסֵּפֶר בְּתוֹרַת הָאֱלֹהִים", זֶה מִקְרָא.
"מְפֹרָשׁ", זֶה תַּרְגּוּם. "וְשׂוֹם שֶׂכֶל", אֵלּוּ הַפְּסוּקִים. "וַיָּבִינוּ בַּמִּקְרָא", אֵלּוּ
פִּסְקֵי טְעָמִים. וְאָמְרֵי לָהּ: אֵלּוּ הַמַּסוֹרוֹת. שְׁכָחוּם וְחָזְרוּ וִיסָדוּם.

TRANSLATION

He [Yonasan ben Uziel] also wanted to reveal the translation of *Kesuvim*. A Divine voice was heard and said to him: Enough! What is the reason [i.e., why did the Divine voice prevent him from revealing the translation of *Kesuvim*]? Because it [*Kesuvim*[12]] contains [i.e., has allusions to] the end [of time when] *mashiach* [will come].

Was the *Targum* of the Torah said [publicized] by Onkelos? We see that R. Ika bar Avin said in the name of R. Chananel who said in the name of Rav: What is the meaning of the verse (*Nechemiah* 8:8): *And they read in the book, in the Torah of God, explicitly and with full comprehension and they understood the reading*. [The phrase] *And they read in the book, in the Torah of God* — this refers to the text; *explicitly* — this refers to the *Targum*; *and with full comprehension* — this refers to the [traditional construction of] sentences; *and they understood the reading* — this refers to the [traditional] cantillation [which serves as punctuation]. And some say, this [the phrase *and with full attention*] refers to the vowelization. [According to the manner in which the Sages explained the verse, we see that the *Targum* was already extant before Onkelos?][13] [The explanation is that] they forgot it [i.e., the *Targum*], and they [Onkelos based on the tradition passed down from R. Eliezer and R. Yehoshua] reestablished it.

---

12 - *Rashi* (ד״ה קץ המשיח) explains that the Talmud is referring specifically to the Book of *Daniel*.

13 - Since the reference is understood to be to the traditional Aramaic *Targum* of the Torah, the fact that it is mentioned in *Nechemiah* indicates that it was known well before Onkelos.

COMMENTARY

The Talmud[14] records that Abba Chalafta once went to visit R. Gamliel in Tveria and found him reading the *Targum* of the Book of *Iyov*. Abba Chalafta reminded R. Gamliel that his grandfather, R. Gamliel *ha-Zaken*, had ordered that the work be buried and not publicized. This would seem to suggest that there was a known *Targum* to *Kesuvim*, despite the fact that Yonasan ben Uziel had been told not to publicize it. *Tosafos*[15] explains that the *Targum* on *Kesuvim* was passed down orally — in fulfillment of the injunction mentioned here not to publicize it — until the time of the late *tannaim*, when it was written down.

Rav's quotation of the exegesis of the verse from *Nechemiah* makes it clear that the *Targum* to *Tanach* was already known in Biblical times. The existence of an oral *Targum*, prior to those publicized by Yonasan ben Uziel and Onkelos, would also seem to be suggested by the *Mishnah*[16] which refers to the role of the *meturgamen* — the translator — who would translate the Torah reading for the benefit of the congregation.[17] It is clear from *Rashi*[18] that this translation was recited by heart rather than being read from a written version.

TALMUD

מַאי שְׁנָא אַדְּאוֹרַיְיתָא, דְּלָא אִזְדַּעְזְעָה, וּמַאי שְׁנָא אַדִּנְבִיאִים דְּאִזְדַּעְזְעָה? דְּאוֹרַיְיתָא – מְפָרְשָׁן מִילֵּי. דִּנְבִיאִים – אִיכָּא מִילֵּי דִּמְסַתְּמָן, וְאִיכָּא מִילֵּי דִּמְפָרְשָׁן. אִיכָּא מִילֵּי דִּמְסַתְּמָן, כְּגוֹן: "בַּיוֹם הַהוּא יִגְדַּל הַמִּסְפֵּד בִּירוּשָׁלַיִם, כְּמִסְפַּד הֲדַדְרִמּוֹן בְּבִקְעַת מְגִדּוֹן". וְאָמַר רַב יוֹסֵף: אִלְמָלֵא תַּרְגּוּם דְּהַאי קְרָא, לָא הֲוָה יָדְעָנָא מַאי קָאָמַר, בְּעִידָנָא הַהִיא יִסְגֵּא מִסְפְּדָא בִּירוּשְׁלֵם כְּמִסְפֵּד אַחְאָב בֶּן עָמְרִי, דְּקַטְל יָתֵיהּ הֲדַדְרִמּוֹן בֶּן טַבְרִימוֹן בְּרָמוֹת גִּלְעָד, וּכְמִסְפֵּד יֹאשִׁיָּה בַּר אָמוֹן, דְּקַטְל יָתֵיהּ פַּרְעֹה חֲגִירָא בְּבִקְעַת מְגִדּוֹ.

---

14 - שבת קטו.

15 - שם ד"ה ובידו ספר איוב. Interestingly, while *Tosafos* specifically writes that the *Targum* on *Kesuvim* dates from the time of the *tannaim* "and not like those who say that the *Targum* on *Kesuvim* was written by R. Yosef," *Rashbam* (commentary to *Shemos* 15:2) seems to ascribe the *Targum* on *Iyov* to the *amora*, R. Yosef. *Otzar Yisrael* quotes a responsa from R. Hai Gaon regarding the source for the *Targum Yerushalmi* (also known as the *Targum Eretz Yisrael*) in which R. Hai writes: "We have no tradition as to its authorship."

16 - מגילה ג:ג

17 - See quotation from *Rambam* on page 264.

18 - שם ד"ה ולא יקרא המתורגמן.

TRANSLATION

What is the difference [between the *Targum* of] the Torah [where] the land did not tremble, and the *Targum* of *Nevi'im* where it did tremble?[19] [The *Targum* of] the Torah [did not cause the land to tremble, because its] words are explicit. [But the *Targum* of] the *Nevi'im* did cause the land to tremble because some [of the meanings] of its words are explicit and some are hidden. For example, [the verse (*Zechariah* 12:11) states:] *And on that day, the eulogy held in Jerusalem will be great, like the eulogy of Hadadrimon in the valley of Megiddo.* R. Yosef said: Were it not for the *Targum* on this verse, I would not know what was being said![20] [The *Targum* explains the verse as meaning] and on that day the eulogy in Jerusalem will be great like the eulogy said for Achav, the son of Omri, who was killed by Hadadrimon ben Tavrimon in Ramos Gil'ad, and like the eulogy for Yoshiyahu, the son of Amon, who was killed by Pharaoh, the lame, in the valley of Megiddo.

COMMENTARY

The Talmud uses the example drawn from the Book of *Zechariah* as a means of illustrating the difference between the Torah and *Nevi'im*. Though the words of the Torah can also allude to sublime or esoteric meanings, they can always be literally explained. The words of the *Nevi'im*, on the other hand, do not necessarily have meaning on the literal level, as the example from the Book of *Zechariah* indicates. The verse can only be understood by using the *Targum*, who explains that the Prophet was referring to two separate instances: the murder of King Achav by Hadadrimon in Ramos Gil'ad (see *Melachim* I 22) and the murder of King Yoshiyahu by Pharaoh in the valley of Megiddo (see *Melachim* II 23:29).

Vilna Gaon explains that the verse in *Zechariah* is referring to the symbolic slaying of the *yetzer ha-ra*.

---

19 - I.e., why was the publicization of the *Targum* on *Nevi'im* more earth shaking than the publicization of the *Targum* on the Torah?

20 - I.e., since there is no mention in the entire *Tanach* of a eulogy held for a Hadadrimon in the valley of Megiddo, had Yonasan not explained the verse, we would have no means of understanding the reference.

Having made reference to the fact that Yonasan's *Targum* was based on the tradition which he received from the Prophets Chagai, Zechariah and Malachi, and that he refrained from publicizing the *Targum* on *Kesuvim* because of the allusions to the coming of the Messiah in the Book of *Daniel*, the Talmud now proceeds to describe the greatness of these four Prophets.

TALMUD

"וְרָאִיתִי אֲנִי דָנִיֵּאל לְבַדִּי אֶת הַמַּרְאָה, וְהָאֲנָשִׁים אֲשֶׁר הָיוּ עִמִּי, לֹא רָאוּ אֶת הַמַּרְאָה, אֲבָל חֲרָדָה גְדֹלָה נָפְלָה עֲלֵיהֶם, וַיִּבְרְחוּ בְּהֵחָבֵא". מָאן נִינְהוּ "אֲנָשִׁים"? אָמַר רַבִּי יִרְמְיָה, וְאִי-תֵּימָא רַבִּי חִיָּא בַּר אַבָּא: זֶה חַגִּי זְכַרְיָה וּמַלְאָכִי. אִינְהוּ עֲדִיפֵי מִינֵּיהּ, וְאִיהוּ עָדִיף מִינַּיְיהוּ; אִינְהוּ עֲדִיפֵי מִינֵּיהּ – דְּאִינְהוּ נְבִיאֵי וְאִיהוּ לָאו נָבִיא הוּא. וְאִיהוּ עָדִיף מִינַּיְיהוּ – דְּאִיהוּ חֲזָא וְאִינְהוּ לָא חֲזוּ.

TRANSLATION

And I, Doniel, saw the vision, but the men who were with me did not see the vision, but great trembling siezed them and they fled to hide (Daniel 10:7). Who were these *men*? R. Yirmiyah — some say that it was R. Chiya bar Abba — said: It is [a reference to] Chagai, Zechariah and Malachi. They were superior to him and he was superior to them. They were superior to him, for they were Prophets and he was not a Prophet. And he was superior to them, for he saw the vision and they did not see the vision.

COMMENTARY

Rashi[21] explains that Doniel was not a Prophet in the sense that he was not given a message to transmit; however, he did have prophetic vision. *Eitz Yosef* points out that it would seem that *Rashi*[22] retracted, for he does not count him as one of the forty-eight Prophets referred to in the Talmud.[23] *Ramban*[24] holds that the ability to perceive angels or see a vision which others cannot see should not be taken as constituting prophecy. *Rambam*,[25] on the other hand, maintains that prophetic vision and prophecy are one and the same.

21 - ד"ה אינהו נביאי. See also *Maharsha* to *Sanhedrin* 93b, s.v. ומנלן.

22 - דף יד. ד"ה מ"ח נביאים.

23 - See page 147.

24 - Commentary to *Bereishis* 18:1, s.v. וירא אליו.

25 - *Moreh Nevuchim* 2:45.

TALMUD

וְכִי מֵאַחַר דְּלָא חֲזוּ, מַאי טַעְמָא אִיבְּעִיתוּ? אַף עַל גַּב דְּאִינְהוּ לָא חֲזוּ מִידֵי,
אֲבָל מַזְלַיְיהוּ מִיהָא קָא חֲזִי. אָמַר רָבִינָא: שְׁמַע מִינָּהּ, הַאי מָאן דְּמִיבְּעִית,
אַף עַל גַּב דְּאִיהוּ לָא חֲזִי מִידֵי, מַזְלֵיהּ חֲזִי. מַאי תַּקַּנְתֵּיהּ? לִיקְרֵי קְרִיאַת־
שְׁמַע. וְאִי קָאִי בִּמְקוֹם הַטִּנֹּפֶת, לִינְשֹׁף מְדוּכְתֵּיהּ אַרְבַּע גַּרְמִידֵי. וְאִי לָא,
לֵימָא הָכִי: עִזֵּי דְּבֵי־טַבְחָא שְׁמֵינֵי מִינַּאי.

TRANSLATION

If they [Chagai, Zechariah and Malachi] did not see the vision, what is the reason that they trembled? Even though they did not see the vision, their ministering angel[26] did see the vision. Ravina said: From this we can learn that if one is siezed by trembling, even though he has not seen anything [which would cause him to tremble], his ministering angel has seen [something]. What should he do? He should recite the *Shema*? And if he is standing in a place that is filthy [where prayers may not be recited]? He should move four *amos* away from that place.[27] And if not [i.e., if he can't move], he should say: "The goats in the slaughterhouse are fatter than I am."

COMMENTARY

The soul and the body, although they function on two different planes, coexist and share use of the sensory organs.[28] Thus, while something may be invisible to the physical eye, the spiritual eye might still see it clearly. The ability of the spiritual eye to perceive is dependent upon the stature of the person. A parallel to this concept can be drawn from radio transmissions which, given the proper equipment, can be transformed into physical sounds that the physical ear can hear even though they are intangible. Daniel was judged by the Talmud to be greater than the three Prophets in that his spiritual essence could perceive the vision, whereas the three Prophets could not, the presence only being detected by their ministering angels.

Moreover, a vision detected by the ministering angels, though unperceived

---

26 - See *Rashi*, s.v. מזלייהו.

27 - By moving away, he can avoid the danger posed by the demon, in accordance with the Talmudic dictum (*Rosh Hashannah* 16b) משנה מקום משנה מזל — *when one changes his place, one changes his fortune.*

28 - See *Sha'arei Kedushah, Sha'ar* 1.

by the person's soul, can still effect him — hence, the trembling of the three Prophets. If the person is of great stature — e.g., Chaggai, Zechariah and Malachi — he realizes that his trembling is a result of his spiritual essence having been exposed to a level of prophecy.[29] But when the trembling — which has no logical or physical explanation — occurs in someone of lesser stature who lacks the ability to attain any level of prophecy, its source must be from the world of evil and impurity.[30] Ravina therefore said that when this occurs, one should recite *Shema*, for by declaring his recognition of God's total and sole dominion, he can free himself of the influences of these evil spirits.

Ramban[31] explains that the goat which was sent to Azazel on Yom Kippur[32] was given as a source of appeasement, as it were, to the destructive forces which God — in His infinite wisdom — created in the world. The statement that "the goats in the slaughterhouse are fatter than me" should thus be understood as a reference to the goat sent to Azazel on Yom Kippur; i.e., the person seized by the trembling should admonish these evil spirits, reminding them, as it were, that God has granted them their place and they should therefore leave him alone.

TALMUD

תַּנְיָא: כֹּהֲנִים בַּעֲבוֹדָתָם, וּלְוִיִּם בְּדוּכָנָם, וְיִשְׂרָאֵל בְּמַעֲמָדָן, כֻּלָּן מְבַטְּלִין עֲבוֹדָתָן, וּבָאִין לִשְׁמוֹעַ מִקְרָא מְגִלָּה. מִכָּאן סָמְכוּ שֶׁל בֵּית רַבִּי שֶׁמְּבַטְּלִין תַּלְמוּד תּוֹרָה, וּבָאִין לִשְׁמוֹעַ מִקְרָא מְגִלָּה. וְקַל וָחֹמֶר מֵעֲבוֹדָה, וּמָה עֲבוֹדָה שֶׁהִיא חֲמוּרָה, מְבַטְּלִין, תַּלְמוּד תּוֹרָה לֹא כָּל שֶׁכֵּן.

וַעֲבוֹדָה חֲמוּרָה מִתַּלְמוּד תּוֹרָה? וְהָכְתִיב: "וַיְהִי בִּהְיוֹת יְהוֹשֻׁעַ בִּירִיחוֹ, וַיִּשָּׂא עֵינָיו וַיַּרְא, וְהִנֵּה אִישׁ עֹמֵד לְנֶגְדּוֹ, וְחַרְבּוֹ שְׁלוּפָה בְּיָדוֹ, וַיֵּלֶךְ יְהוֹשֻׁעַ אֵלָיו, וְגוֹ' וַיֹּאמֶר: לֹא, כִּי אֲנִי שַׂר צְבָא ה', עַתָּה בָאתִי. וַיִּפֹּל יְהוֹשֻׁעַ אֶל פָּנָיו אַרְצָה וַיִּשְׁתָּחוּ".

TRANSLATION

We learned in a *beraisa*. The *kohanim* [engaged in the Divine service in the *Beis ha-Mikdash*] and the Levites [who sang the Psalm of the day] on their platforms

---

29 - See *Derech Hashem* 3:1.

30 - See *Nefesh ha-Chaim*, *Sha'ar* 3, Chapters 12 and 13.

31 - Commentary to *Vayikra* 16:8, s.v. וגורל אחד לעזאזל.

32 - See *Vayikra* 16.

and the Israelites at their stands [where they guarded the daily public sacrifices while they were offered][33] — all cease their work and come to hear the reading of the *Megillah*. From this [statement] the school of Rebbi drew support [for their ruling] that the learning of Torah is interrupted and all come to hear the reading of the *Megillah*. For a *kal vachomer*[34] can be drawn from the [cessation of the] Divine service. If the Divine service which is stringent [is interrupted for the reading of the *Megillah*], surely the learning of Torah [is interrupted].

Is the Divine service more stringent than the learning of Torah? Does the verse (*Yehoshua* 5:11-14) not state: *And it was when Yehoshua was in Jericho, and he lifted his eyes and he saw and behold, a man was standing in front of him and a drawn sword was in his hand. And Yehoshua approached ... and he said: No, for I am a minister of God's hosts and I have come now. And Yehoshua fell to the ground and prostrated himself.*

COMMENTARY

The Talmud offers the verse from Yehoshua as proof that the interruption of Torah study must be seen as being more serious than the interruption of the Divine service. During the siege of Yericho, an angel of God appeared to Yehoshua with a drawn sword in his hand. Yehoshua immediately understood from the angel's appearance that he had done something wrong. As the Talmud will point out, the angel's presence was meant as an admonishment to Yehoshua for two shortcomings. When his armies had surrounded the city of Yericho, Yehoshua had ordered the people to stay at their posts and he therefore caused both the sacrifice of the daily afternoon offering and the study of Torah to be interrupted. There had been no reason for the people to have remained at their posts when the time for the sacrifice of the daily offering had come in the late afternoon, for there was no reason to believe that there would be any fighting when darkness came. Similarly, there was no reason to interrupt the public study of Torah by keeping all of the people at their posts, for there would be no battle at night.

---

33 - See *Rashi*, s.v. ישראל במעמדם.

34 - I.e., through use of a *kal va-chomer* analogy, the school of Rebbi was able to establish their ruling that Torah study may be interrupted for the reading of the *Megillah*. For an explanation of the use of *kal va-chomer*, see *A Practical Guide to Torah Leraning*, Aronson Publishers, pgs. 120-123.

It should be noted that the incident with the angel occurred during the siege of Yericho, whereas the verse cited later about Yehoshua dwelling among the people, refers to the siege of the city of Ai. It would seem that the Talmud is combining the two events. After the angel appeared to him in Yericho, Yehoshua accepted his admonishment and therefore avoided making the same mistake when beseiging the second city.

TALMUD

וְהֵיכִי עָבִיד הָכֵי? וְהָאָמַר רַבִּי יְהוֹשֻׁעַ בֶּן לֵוִי: אָסוּר לוֹ לְאָדָם שֶׁיִּתֵּן שָׁלוֹם לַחֲבֵרוֹ בַּלַּיְלָה, חַיְישִׁינָן שֶׁמָּא שֵׁד הוּא? שָׁאנִי הָתָם דְּקָאָמַר לֵיהּ: "כִּי אֲנִי שַׂר צְבָא ה', עַתָּה בָאתִי". וְדִלְמָא מְשַׁקְּרֵי לֵיהּ? גְּמִירֵי - דְּלָא מַפְּקֵי שֵׁם שָׁמַיִם לְבַטָּלָה.

TRANSLATION

How did he [Yehoshua] do this [i.e., prostrate himself in front of a stranger]? Did R. Yehoshua ben Levi not say: One is forbidden to greet another person at night [if he does not recognize him] for fear that he might be an evil spirit.[35] That case [when Yehoshua prostrated himself in front of the stranger] was different, for he told him: *for I am a minister of the hosts of God. Now I have come ...* Perhaps he [i.e., the stranger whom Yehoshua saw] was lying? It is a principle that [evil spirits] do not mention the name of God in vain.

COMMENTARY

The Talmud interrupts Yehoshua's dialogue with the angel to pose a question. How could Yehoshua have prostrated himself when he saw the stranger, given the principle — as enunciated by R. Yehoshua ben Levi — that one should not greet a stranger at night, for fear that the stranger might really be an evil spirit?

The Talmud answers that the angel had identified himself as being a messenger of God. The Talmud then raises another point: Perhaps the stranger was lying when he identified himself as an angel and perhaps he was, in fact, an evil spirit? In that case, Yehoshua should not have spoken to him, let alone prostrated himself!

---

35 - One is surely forbidden to prostrate himself in front of a demon, for doing so is tantamount to worshipping false gods. See the commentary of *Ramban* to *Vayikra* 17:7, s.v. לשעירים.

The Talmud explains that Yehoshua understood that the stranger could not be an evil spirit, for he had mentioned the name of God and it is an inviolate principle that the name of God is not mentioned in vain.

The Talmud now returns to the original theme.

TALMUD

אָמַר לֵיהּ: אֶמֶשׁ בִּטַּלְתֶּם תָּמִיד שֶׁל בֵּין הָעַרְבַּיִם, וְעַכְשָׁיו בִּטַּלְתֶּם תַּלְמוּד תּוֹרָה. אָמַר לֵיהּ: עַל אֵיזֶה מֵהֶם בָּאתָ? אָמַר לֵיהּ: עַתָּה בָאתִי. מִיָּד – "וַיֵּלֶן יְהוֹשֻׁעַ בַּלַּיְלָה הַהוּא בְּתוֹךְ הָעָם". וְכָתוּב אֶחָד אוֹמֵר: "בְּתוֹךְ הָעֵמֶק". אָמַר רַבִּי יוֹחָנָן: מְלַמֵּד שֶׁלָּן בְּתוֹךְ עֲמָקָהּ שֶׁל הֲלָכָה.

TRANSLATION

He [the angel] said: Yesterday you interrupted the daily afternoon sacrifice, and now you have interrupted the study of Torah. He [Yehoshua] asked him: For which have you come [i.e., which is the more serious infraction]? He answered: *I have come now* [i.e., for the interruption of Torah study]. Immediately, [Yehoshua took heed of the angel's implied reprimand, as the verse (*Yehoshua* 8:9) states:] *And Yehoshua dwelled that night amidst the people.* Another verse (ibid. :13) states [however]: *And Yehoshua went that night through the valley* [which would seem to suggest that Yehoshua did not implement that which the angel had been sent to tell him]. R. Yochanan explained [this seeming contradiction]: **[3b]** This teaches us [i.e., the second verse should be understood as meaning] that he spent the night in the depths[36] of the halachah [i.e., in Torah study].

COMMENTARY

The parallel reading in the Talmud is somewhat less clear than the version brought by the *Ein Yaakov*. There, the Talmud quotes the verse as stating that *Yehoshua dwelled that night in the valley* which R. Yochanan interpreted as meaning that "he spent the night in the depths of the halachah." *Tosafos* points out that there is no such verse and explains that the Talmud was combining verses 9 and 13 — a practice that is not unusual.[37] According to the text in the

---

36 - The word עמק in the verse can be explained as if it was written with a *cholam* after the ע and a *segol* under the מ which would change the meaning from valley to depths.

37 - ד"ה וילן יהושע. Interestingly, *Tosafos* writes that verse 9 refers to the battle of Yericho whereas the verse would seem to be clearly referring to the battle of Ai.

Talmud, R. Yochanan's statement should thus not be seen as coming to resolve a contradiction. In the parallel version brought in *Eruvin* (63b), the Talmud cites verse 13 correctly. *Bach*, in his glosses there, corrects the text of the Talmud according to the version brought in the *Ein Yaakov*.

TALMUD

וְאָמַר רַב שְׁמוּאֵל בְּרַבִּי אוּנְיָא: גָּדוֹל תַּלְמוּד תּוֹרָה יוֹתֵר מֵהַקְרָבַת תְּמִידִין, שֶׁנֶּאֱמַר: "עַתָּה בָאתִי"? לָא קַשְׁיָא, הָא – דְּרַבִּים הָא – דְּיָחִיד.

TRANSLATION

And R. Shmuel b'R. Unia said: The learning of Torah is more important than the offering of the daily sacrifice, as the verse states: *Now I have come* [i.e., the angel told Yehoshua that he had been sent to admonish him for what he had done now — interrupting the study of Torah — rather than for what he had done previously — interrupting the offering of the daily sacrifice]. There is no contradiction [between the inference from the episode of the angel and Yehoshua that the interruption of Torah study is more serious and what the school of Rebbi had said previously]. One [i.e., the former] is [referring to] many people [who interrupted their Torah study and that is why it is judged more seriously] and one [the ruling of the school of R. Yehuda] is referring to an individual [who interrupts his study to hear the reading of the *Megillah*].

COMMENTARY

R. Shmuel b'R. Unia's statement — deduced from the fact that the angel had admonished Yehoshua for having interrupted Israel's Torah study to lay siege to Yericho — is brought by the Talmud to contradict the *kal va-chomer* that the school of Rebbi had offered to prove that Torah study is interrupted for the reading of the *Megillah*. The siege of Yericho was no less important than the reading of the *Megillah*. Nevertheless, Yehoshua was admonished by the angel for having interrupted the study of Torah during the siege of Yericho which would suggest that Torah study is paramount. The Talmud answers that Yehoshua's action affected all of Israel and was therefore wrong, whereas the principle enunciated by the school of Rebbi refers specifically to individuals — i.e., situations like those prevalent in his time where only part of the community was engaged in Torah study. In that case, Torah study is interrupted for the *Megillah* reading.

TALMUD

אָמַר רַבִּי יְהוֹשֻׁעַ בֶּן לֵוִי: נָשִׁים חַיָּבוֹת בְּמִקְרָא מְגִלָּה, שֶׁאַף הֵן הָיוּ בְּאוֹתוֹ הַנֵּס.

TRANSLATION

[4a] R. Yehoshua ben Levi said: Women are obligated in the reading of the *Megillah*, for they too were included in the miracle.

COMMENTARY

The reading of the *Megillah* is a mitzvah which is dependent upon a specific time period; thus, women should theoretically not be obligated in its performance.[38] R. Yehoshua ben Levi therefore points out that because they too were saved by the miracle, they are obligated to express their gratitude and recognition by reading the *Megillah*. *Tosafos* adds that women are obligated in the mitzvah of reading the *Megillah* — as well as in the mitzvos of Chanukah — because the miracle itself was brought about through the efforts of a woman — Esther.[39]

TALMUD

וְאָמַר רַבִּי יְהוֹשֻׁעַ בֶּן לֵוִי: חַיָּב אָדָם לִקְרוֹת הַמְּגִלָּה בַּלַּיְלָה, וְלִשְׁנוֹתָהּ בַּיּוֹם, שֶׁנֶּאֱמַר: "אֱלֹהַי, אֶקְרָא יוֹמָם וְלֹא תַעֲנֶה, וְלַיְלָה וְלֹא דוּמִיָּה לִי". סָבוּר מִינָהּ: לְמִיקְרְיָהּ בְּלֵילְיָא, וּלְמִיתְנָא מַתְנִיתִין דִּידָהּ בִּימָמָא. אָמַר לֵיהּ רַבִּי יִרְמְיָה: לְדִידִי מִפָּרְשָׁא לִי מִינֵּיהּ דְּרַבִּי חִיָּא בַּר אַבָּא: כְּגוֹן דְּאָמְרֵי אֱנָשֵׁי: אֶעֱבוֹר פַּרְשָׁתָא דָא וְאִתְנְיַהּ. אִתְּמַר נַמֵּי, אָמַר רַבִּי חֶלְבּוֹ, אָמַר עוּלָּא בִירָאָה: חַיָּב אָדָם לִקְרוֹת הַמְּגִלָּה בַּלַּיְלָה, וְלִשְׁנוֹתָהּ בַּיּוֹם. שֶׁנֶּאֱמַר: "לְמַעַן יְזַמֶּרְךָ כָבוֹד וְלֹא יִדֹּם, ה' אֱלֹהַי, לְעוֹלָם אוֹדֶךָּ".

TRANSLATION

And R. Yehoshua ben Levi said: One is required to read the *Megillah* at night, and repeat it [i.e. read it again] during the day, as the verse (*Tehillim* 22:3) states: *My God, I call [to You] by day and You do not answer, at night and I shall not*

---

38 - See *Kiddushin* 29a.

39 - In the case of Chanukah, woman are also considered to have played a major role — i.e., the assasination of Helifornes by Yehudis.

be silent.[40] They [R. Yehoshua's students] understood [from their teacher's statement] that it should be read at night and its contents studied by day.[41] R. Yirmiyahu said to them: I have an explicit tradition from R. Chiya bar Abba [that when R. Yehoshua's used the term לשנותה, his intention was] as people are wont to say: I will finish this portion and I will repeat it again [i.e., R. Yehoshua intended that it be read twice rather than studied in the morning]. It was also said: R. Chelbo taught in the name of Ula [from the city of] Biriah: One is required to read the *Megillah* at night and repeat [the reading] by day,[42] as the verse (*Tehillim* 30:13) states, *So that I might sing to Your honor and not be silent: God, my Lord, I shall forever express my gratitude to You.*[43]

COMMENTARY

The verse cited by R. Yehoshua ben Levi as support for his ruling can be explained in the following manner. Just as in times of trouble we turn to God both by day and by night to seek His salvation, so too should we praise God at times of thanksgiving both by day and by night through the reading of the *Megillah*.

Rashi explains that the verse cited by Ula can be separated into two distinct obligations: *sing to Your honor* referring to the requirement to read the *Megillah*

---

40 - The Talmud (*Yoma* 22a) notes that this psalm is a prophetic vision referring to the period of Purim — *ayeles ha-shachar* being a symbolic reference to Esther. *Ibn Ezra* (ad loc.) explains the text in the following manner: Though it seems that God has chosen not to answer my prayers — the first phrase of the verse — I nevertheless continue to pray to Him at night.

41 - The Hebrew/Aramaic term לשנותה can be understood either as repeating the reading or as studying the reading.

42 - *Tosafos* points out that the primary mitzvah is the reading by day. It is for this reason that we recite the *berachah* of *Shehecheyanu* both by day and night, even though this *berachah* is usually recited only the first time that a periodic mitzvah is performed and would therefore normally be recited only at night.

43 - *Rashi* (quoting the *Pesikta d'Rav Kahana*) notes that this psalm is a reference to the period of Mordechai and Esther. R. Chelbo's statement that we are required to read the *Megillah* at night and again during the day is based on the last verse, for by reading the *Megillah*, we publicize God's miracles and thus bring everyone to praise Him.

by day, and *not be silent* referring to the reading of the *Megillah* by night.[44]

Maharsha adds that the verse's final phrase — *God, my Lord, I shall forever express my gratitude to You* — can be understood as an allusion to the statement in the Talmud that, unlike the other holidays, the festival of Purim will never cease to be celebrated.

❖ ❖ ❖

The *Mishnah* ruled that cities that had been surrounded by walls at the time when Yehoshua conquered the Land of Israel read the *Megillah* on the fifteenth of Adar rather than on the fourteenth. The Talmud notes that Chizkiyah read the *Megillah* in Tveria on both the fourteenth and the fifteenth because he was not sure whether the city had been surrounded by a wall from the time of Yehoshua. The question is then raised as to how he could have been doubtful since the verse (*Yehoshua* 19:35) states: *and the fortified cities ... Chamas, Rakas and Kinneres* and Rakas is traditionally identified as Tveria. The Talmud now proceeds to establish the basis for the tradition of identifying Rakas as Tveria as well as identifying the other cities mentioned in the verse.

It should be noted that the name Tveria was given to the city by Herod, who rebuilt its ruins and named it after the Roman emperor Tiberius. Nevertheless, the Talmud — as is often the case with words or names taken from other languages — treats the name as if it was Hebrew and explains it as if it was an acronym.[45]

TALMUD

אָמַר רַבִּי יוֹחָנָן: כִּי הֲוֵינָא טַלְיָא, אָמְרִינָא מִילְתָא, וְשָׁאִילְנָא לְסָבַיָּא, וְאִישְׁתַּכַּח כְּוָותִי. "חַמַּת" – זוֹ טְבֶרְיָא. וְלָמָּה נִקְרָא שְׁמָהּ "חַמַּת"? עַל שׁוּם חַמֵּי טְבֶרְיָא. "רַקַּת" – זוֹ צִפּוֹרִי, וְלָמָּה נִקְרָא שְׁמָהּ "רַקַּת"? מִשּׁוּם דְּמִידַּלְיָא כְּרַקְתָּא דְּנַהֲרָא. "כִּנֶּרֶת" – זוֹ גִּינוֹסַר, וְלָמָּה נִקְרָא שְׁמָהּ "כִּנֶּרֶת"? דִּמְתִיקֵי פֵּירָא כְּקָלָא דְּכִינָּרֵי.

TRANSLATION

[5b] R. Yochanan said: When I was young, I made the [following] statement,

---

44 - *Rashi's* exegesis, which deduces the reading of the *Megillah* by day first and then refers to the reading by night would seem to indicate that he, like *Tosafos*, viewed the reading by day as the essence of the mitzvah.

45 - Another example is the name Acheshverosh — see page 85.

and asked the elders [6a] and they agreed with me. Chamas is [another name for] Tveria. Why is it [also called] Chamas? Because of the hot springs of Tveria.[46] Rakas is [another name for] Tzippori. Why was it [also called] Rakas? Because it is elevated [above its surroundings] like the banks of a river.[47] Kinneres is another name for Ginnosar. Why was it [also called] Kinneres? Because its fruits are as sweet as the sound of the violin.

COMMENTARY

Maharsha, quoting the *Aruch,* explains that קלא דכינרי is a fruit which was especially sweet. Thus, Ginnosar was also known as Kinneres because its fruits were as sweet as קלא דכינרי.

TALMUD

אָמַר רָבָא: מִי אִיכָּא לְמָאן דְּאָמַר: "רַקַּת" לָאו טְבֶרְיָא הִיא? וְהָא כִּי שָׁכִיב אֵינָשׁ הָכָא, הָתָם סָפְדֵי לֵיהּ הָכֵי: גָּדוֹל הוּא בְּשֵׁשַׁךְ, וְשֵׁם לוֹ בְּרַקַּת. וְכִי מַסְקֵי אֲרוֹנָא לְהָתָם, סָפְדֵי לֵיהּ הָכֵי: אוֹהֲבֵי שְׂרִידִים יוֹשְׁבֵי רַקַּת, צְאוּ וְקַבְּלוּ הֲרוּגֵי עֵמֶק. כִּי נָח נַפְשֵׁיהּ דְּרַבִּי זֵירָא, פָּתַח עֲלֵיהּ הַהוּא סַפְדָנָא: אֶרֶץ שִׁנְעָר הָרָה וְיָלְדָה. אֶרֶץ צְבִי גִּדְּלָה שַׁעֲשׁוּעֶיהָ, אוֹי נָא לָהּ אָמְרָה רַקַּת, כִּי אָבְדָה כְּלִי חֶמְדָּתָהּ.

TRANSLATION

Rava asked [rhetorically]: Is there anyone who says that Rakas is not Tveria [i.e., how could R. Yochanan have said that Rakas is Tzippori]? When a man dies here [in Bavel], they eulogize him there [in Tveria] in the following manner: He [the deceased] was great in Sheshach[48] [Bavel] and he acquired a [good] name in Rakas [in Tveria]! And when his coffin is taken there [to Tveria for burial], they eulogize him in the following manner: The beloved remnants[49] who dwell in Rakas, come and greet those who were killed in the valley [i.e., in Bavel].

---

46 - The name Chamas being etymologically related to the Hebrew word חם — hot.

47 - Rakas in Aramaic means a river bank.

48 - *Rashi* explains that Sheshach is a euphemism for Bavel based on the system of reversing the letters of the Hebrew alphabet known as א-ת, ב-ש [i.e., א — the first letter — is represented by ת — the last letter, ב is represented by ש and so on]. Thus ש-ש-ך is equivalent to ב-ב-ל.

49 - *Rashi* explains that the reference is to the remnants of Israel who have survived the exile. *Iyun Yaakov* explains that remnants is a reference to the Torah scholars, as in the verse (*Yoel* 3:8): *and to the remants to whom God calls.*

When R. Zeira[50] died, one of those who eulogized him began [his eulogy by saying]: The land of Shin'ar [Bavel] conceived and bore [him], and the land [that is] like the deer[51] raised her [child of] delight.[52] Woe is to her, said Rakas [of herself], for she has lost her beautiful vessel.

COMMENTARY

Maharsha notes that the eulogy said for R. Zeira was significantly different from the two other eulogies quoted in the Talmud. In R. Zeira's case, consolation is offered to both Bavel and *Eretz Yisrael* for their loss, whereas in the first two eulogies, the speakers refer to the person who died. He explains that the Talmud is referring to three different situations: The first eulogy was said for a person who died and was buried in Bavel. The second eulogy was said for a person who died in Bavel and was buried in *Eretz Yisrael*. He is characterized as being one who "was killed in the valley," for he is considered to be a sinner for having preferred to stay in Bavel rather than live in *Eretz Yisrael*.[53]

The third eulogy was said for R. Zeira who went to *Eretz Yisrael* while still alive and died there. This type of person is considered to be righteous, for he merited to both live and die in *Eretz Yisrael*. As a righteous man, we do not mourn for him, for his righteousness lives on. Rather, we mourn our own loss, as the speaker noted in his eulogy.

TALMUD

אֶלָּא אָמַר רַבָּה: "חַמַּת" – זוֹ חַמֵּי גְּרָר. "רַקַּת" – זוֹ טְבֶרְיָא. "כִּנֶּרֶת" – זוֹ גִּנּוֹסַר. וְלָמָּה נִקְרָא שְׁמָהּ "רַקַּת"? שֶׁאֲפִלּוּ רֵיקָנִין שֶׁבָּהּ מְלֵאִין מִצְוֹת כְּרִמּוֹן.

---

50 - *Rashi* explains that R. Zeira was born in Bavel, but moved to *Eretz Yisrael* and died in Tveria. See *Moed Katan* 22b where the Talmud quotes R. Zeira repeating a law that he learned from R. Yochanan who resided in Tveria.

51 - I.e., *Eretz Yisrael* — see *Yirmiyahu* 3:19.

52 - Compare to *Yirmiyahu* 31:19.

53 - In *Kesubos* 111a, the Talmud tells of a man who approached R. Chanina and asked him if he should perform the mitzvah of *yibum* with the wife of his brother who died in Bavel. R. Chanina answered: "Blessed is God for having killed him" — i.e., he deserved to have died for having chosen to stay in Bavel rather than ascend to *Eretz Yisrael*.

רַבִּי יִרְמְיָה אָמַר: "רַקַּת" שְׁמָהּ, וְלָמָּה נִקְרָא שְׁמָהּ "טְבֶרְיָא"? שֶׁיּושֶׁבֶת
בְּטַבּוּרָהּ שֶׁל אֶרֶץ יִשְׂרָאֵל.

רָבָא אָמַר: "רַקַּת" שְׁמָהּ, וְלָמָּה נִקְרָא שְׁמָהּ "טְבֶרְיָא"? שֶׁטּוֹבָה רְאִיָּתָהּ.

אָמַר זְעֵירִי: "קִטְרוֹן" – זוֹ צִפּוֹרִי, וְלָמָּה נִקְרָא שְׁמָהּ "צִפּוֹרִי"? שֶׁיּושֶׁבֶת בְּרֹאשׁ
הָהָר כְּצִפּוֹר.

TRANSLATION

Rather [because of the proof offered] Rabah said: Chamas is Chamei Gerar. Rakas
is Tveria. Kineres is Ginosar. And why was she [also] called Rakas? Because
even those [of her citizens] who are [considered to be] empty, are filled with
mitzvos like a pomegranate [is filled with seeds].

R. Yirmiyah said: Rakas is her name. And why was she [also] called Tveria?
Because she sits in the middle[54] of Eretz Yisrael.

Rava said: Rakas is her name. And why was she [also] called Tveria? Because
her appearance is good.[55]

Zeiri said: Kitron is Tzippori. And why was she [also] called Tzippori? Because
she sits atop the hill like a bird.

COMMENTARY

Rabah's explanation that Tveria was known as Rakas because her empty
citizens are as full of mitzvos as a pomegranate deserves further examination.
The characterization is based on the Talmud's[56] exegesis of the verse in *Shir ha-
Shirim* (4:3): *Your temples are like a slice of pomegranate. Turei Even* points
out that the Talmud there is referring to the people of Israel as a whole — not
only to the citizens of Tveria. He explains that if this characterization is true of
the nation as a whole, it is surely true of Tveria, for the city was the spiritual
center of the nation.

Rashi notes that the characterization of Tveria as being located in the center
of the country should not be taken literally, for Tveria is not in the geographical
center of the country. R. Yirmiyah was referring to Tveria's role as the major
spiritual center after the destruction of the second *Beis ha-Mikdash* — and in that

---

54 - Literally, at the navel.

55 - Rava's explanation is based on interpreting the name Tveria as an acronym of
two words — *tov* [good] and *ri'iyah* [appearance].

56 - ברכות נז.

sense the city can be characterized as being in the center of the country.

TALMUD

וְ"קִטְרוֹן" "צִפּוֹרִי" הִיא?! וְהָא קִטְרוֹן בְּחֶלְקוֹ שֶׁל זְבוּלוּן הָיָה, דִּכְתִיב: "זְבֻלוּן
לֹא הוֹרִישׁ אֶת יוֹשְׁבֵי קִטְרוֹן וְאֶת יוֹשְׁבֵי נַהֲלֹל". וּזְבוּלוּן מִתְרַעֵם עַל מִדּוֹתָיו
הֲוָה, דִּכְתִיב: "זְבֻלוּן עַם חֵרֵף נַפְשׁוֹ לָמוּת", מַה טַּעַם? מִשּׁוּם דְּ"נַפְתָּלִי עַל
מְרוֹמֵי שָׂדֶה". אָמַר זְבוּלוּן לִפְנֵי הַקָּדוֹשׁ בָּרוּךְ הוּא: רִבּוֹנוֹ שֶׁל עוֹלָם, לְאַחַי
נָתַתָּ לָהֶם אֲרָצוֹת, וְלִי נָתַתָּ יַמִּים וּנְהָרוֹת. לְאַחַי נָתַתָּ לָהֶם שָׂדוֹת וּכְרָמִים,
וְלִי נָתַתָּ הָרִים וּגְבָעוֹת. אָמַר לֵיהּ: כֻּלָּן צְרִיכִין לְךָ עַל יְדֵי חִלָּזוֹן, שֶׁנֶּאֱמַר:
"עַמִּים הַר יִקְרָאוּ וְגוֹ' וּשְׂפֻנֵי טְמוּנֵי חוֹל". וְתָנֵי רַב יוֹסֵף: "שְׂפֻנֵי" - זֶה חִלָּזוֹן.
"טְמוּנֵי" - זוֹ טָרִית. "חוֹל" - זוֹ זְכוּכִית לְבָנָה.

TRANSLATION

And is Kitron [the same place as] Tzippori? It is [known] that Kitron was in the part [of the land allotted to the tribe of] Zevulun, as the verse (*Shoftim* 1:11) states: *Zevulun failed to uproot the settlers of Kitron and the settlers of Nahalal.* Moreover, Zevulun complained about his portion [of the land which he was given when the lots were drawn], as the verse (ibid. 5:18) states: *Zevulun is a people who were willing to give up their lives and die.* Why was this so [i.e., what made them willing to sacrifice their lives in the battle against Sisro?] Because [they were jealous of the portion alloted to the tribe of Naftali, as the verse (ibid.) states:] *Naftali is [settled] on the fields of high [i.e., on fertile and valuable land].* Zevulun said to God: Master of the World, to my brother You granted land and to me You granted rivers. God answered: All [of the tribes] have need for [the gifts which are to be found in the portion granted] you [and must come to you] for the *chilazon* [which is found in your portion], as the verse (*Devarim* 33:19) states: *The nations will gather by the mountain, [there they shall offer thanksgiving for] the important things hidden in the sand.* R. Yosef explained [the meaning of this verse]. [The phrase] *the important things* — this refers to the *chilazon.*[57] [The word] *hidden* — this refers to the [fish called] taris.[58] [The phrase] *in the sand* — this refers to crystal [which is made from the sand found in your portion].

---

57 - A sea snail found in the Mediterranean from whose blood a dye was made for use as *techeles* in the *tzitzis* — see *Menachos* 44a.

58 - *Rashi* identifies the fish as tuna.

COMMENTARY

The exegesis of the verse from *Shoftim* bears further explanation, for the simple interpretation would seem to indicate that Devorah was praising Zevulun for their willingness to sacrifice their lives in battle. The Talmud, however, interprets the verse as implied criticism of Zevulun — as if their willingness to sacrifice themselves was based solely on jealousy.

Maharsha explains that the end of the verse which describes Naftali as *settled on the fields of high* does not seem to offer any praise of the tribe. On the literal level, it is no more than a geographical description. However, since Devorah linked her comments about Naftali to those about Zevulun — comments which clearly portray the latter's character traits — the Talmud concludes that there is a contextual connection. The Talmud therefore explains that the first part of the verse, where Zevulun is described as being ready for self-sacrifice, is a result of the second part of the verse; his jealousy of Naftali's fertile portion.

Zevulun's dissatisfaction with his portion bears explanation. As the Talmud will point out, even when God informed them of the special qualities of their portion, they still were jealous of the abundant natural resources that Naftali had. Perhaps Zevulun's complaints were based on the very fact that the gifts which they were granted — a disproportionate share of land *flowing with milk and honey* and the *chilazon* — were "unnatural" resources dependent upon Divine favor. Whereas the tribe of Yissachar — with whom Zevulun shared land and for whom they provided, allowing them to devote their lives to Torah — did not complain about being dependent upon God's gifts for their sustenance, Zevulun, as practical businessmen, would have preferred land which was naturally productive and would thus insure their continued well-being. Whereas Yissachar, by nature, could appreciate the gift of having received a Divinely blessed portion, Zevulun — whose nature was different — could very well have found the necessity to rely upon "unnatural gifts" as a source of consternation which would lead them to complain to God about their lot.

TALMUD

אָמַר לְפָנָיו: רִבּוֹנוֹ שֶׁל עוֹלָם, מִי מוֹדִיעֵנִי אָמַר לֵיהּ: "שָׁם יִזְבְּחוּ זִבְחֵי צֶדֶק". סִימָן זֶה יִהְיֶה לָךְ, שֶׁכָּל הַנּוֹטֵל מִמְּךָ בְּלֹא דָמִים, אֵינוֹ מוֹעִיל בִּפְרַקְמַטְיָא שֶׁלּוֹ כְּלוּם.

וְאִי סַלְקָא דַעְתָּךְ: "קִטְרוֹן" – זוֹ "צִפּוֹרִי", אַמַּאי מִתְרָעֵם עַל מִדּוֹתָיו? וְהָא
הֲוָה צִפּוֹרִי מִלְּתָא דַעֲדִיפָא טוּבָא? וְכִי תֵימָא, דְּלֵית בָּהּ "אֶרֶץ זָבַת חָלָב
וּדְבַשׁ", וְהָאָמַר רֵישׁ לָקִישׁ: לְדִידִי חֲזִי לִי "זָבַת חָלָב וּדְבַשׁ" דְּצִפּוֹרִי, וַהֲוָיָא
שִׁיתְּסַר מִיל עַל שִׁיתְּסַר מִיל. וְכִי תֵימָא: דְּלָא נָפִישׁ דִּידֵיהּ כְּדַאֲחוּהּ, וְהָאָמַר
רַבָּה בַּר בַּר חָנָה, אָמַר רַבִּי יוֹחָנָן: לְדִידִי חֲזִי לִי "זָבַת חָלָב וּדְבַשׁ" דְּכָל אֶרֶץ
יִשְׂרָאֵל, וַהֲוָה כְּמִבֵּי־כּוּבֵי וְעַד אַקְרָא דְּתוּלְבַּנְקֵי, וְהַוְיָא עֶשְׂרִין וְתַרְתֵּי פַרְסֵי
בְּאוּרְכָּא, וּבְפוּתְיָהּ שִׁיתָּא פַרְסֵי?! אֲפִלּוּ הָכִי – שָׂדוֹת וּכְרָמִים עֲדִיפֵי לֵיהּ.
דַּיְקָא נַמֵּי, דִּכְתִיב: "וְנַפְתָּלִי עַל מְרוֹמֵי שָׂדֶה", שְׁמַע מִינָהּ.

TRANSLATION

Zevulun replied: Master of the World, who will acknowledge this [i.e., who will admit that these gifts are mine and will be willing to pay for them]? God replied: [The verse itself indicates that you have no reason to fear that these gifts will be taken from you, for it states:] *there they will offer thanksgiving.* And this shall be a sign for you. Anyone who takes it from you without payment, will be unsuccesful in selling it.[59]

And if you would think that Kitron is Tzippori, why did Zevulun complain about his portion? Tzippori was an especially bountiful portion! If you would want to say that it lacked [the quality of being a portion which] *flows with milk and honey (Shemos 3:8)* — Resh Lakish said: I myself saw that Tzippori was *flowing with milk and honey* and it [the area that was blessed] was sixteen *mil* by sixteen *mil*! Perhaps you might think that his portion was not as blessed as that of his brothers [and this is why Zevulun complained to God] — we see that Rabba bar bar Chana said in the name of R. Yochanan: I myself saw [the portions which were] *flowing with milk and honey* in all of the Land of Israel, and [the area which was so blessed] was like [the distance between] Bei Kuchei and Akra Desolbunki[60] which is twenty-two *parsaos* wide and six *parsaos* long.

Even so [i.e., even though Zevulun's allotment was especially blessed], he preferred fields and vineyards. This can also be seen from the verse which states: *and*

---

59 - *Rashi* (ד״ה אמר לו) explains that God quoted the verse to indicate that just as one cannot use a stolen animal to bring a sacrifice, so too, no one would be able to derive any benefit from the *chilazon* if they failed to pay Zevulun.

60 - Two cities in Bavel.

Naftali is on the fields on high.[61]

COMMENTARY

Maharsha points out that it is difficult to accept that Zevulun was worried that the other tribes might actually steal the *chilazon.* He explains that Zevulun was concerned that even if the *chilazon* was only to be found in his area, it was still no guarantee of prosperity, for the other tribes might decide to use indigo dye and claim that they too had *techeles.*[62]

The Talmudic dialogue would seem to support our previous contention that Zevulun's complaint was based on his fear of being dependent upon Divine favor for his sustenance. We see that God, as it were, reassured Zevulun that the other tribes would require those resources which only he could provide — i.e., that his portion would have commercial qualities which he could take advantage of naturally. Nevertheless, as the Talmud points out, this too was not sufficient to calm Zevulun who continued to be jealous of Naftali's natural riches, for his ability to take advantage of his portion was contingent upon the recognition of the other tribes that the gifts found in his portion were indeed his and could only be exploited if God interceded, as it were, and guaranteed that any of the tribes who tried to cheat him would have no blessing.

TALMUD

אָמַר רַבִּי אַבָּהוּ: "עֶקְרוֹן תֵּעָקֵר" – זוֹ קֵסָרִי בַּת אֱדוֹם, שֶׁיּוֹשֶׁבֶת בֵּין הַחוֹלוֹת, וְהִיא הָיְתָה יָתֵד תְּקוּעָה לְיִשְׂרָאֵל בִּימֵי יְוָנִים, וּכְשֶׁגָּבְרוּ מַלְכֵי בֵּית חַשְׁמוֹנַאי וּלְכָדוּהָ, הָיוּ קוֹרִין אוֹתָהּ: "אֲחִידַת מִגְדַּל שִׁיר".

TRANSLATION

R. Abahu said: *Ekron shall be uprooted* (*Tzefaniah* 2:4) — this [refers to] Caesarea of the Romans which is located on the sand dunes. And she [Caesarea] was a [foreign] stronghold established [within the territory of] Israel from the time of the Greeks. And when the House of Chashmonai overcame and captured

---

61 - I.e., although Zevulun had a disproportionate share of land *flowing with milk and honey*, he was still jealous of Naftali whose allotment was rich in natural resources.

62 - See *Bava Metzia* 61b. *Rosh* (ad loc.) notes that the Talmud there is referring not only to a person who uses indigo dye in his own *tzitzis*, but also to one who sells the dye to others and claims that it is *techeles* from the *chilazon*.

her, they renamed her Achidas Migdal Tzur.[63]

COMMENTARY

Having explained the use of different names for a number of cities in *Eretz Yisrael*, the Talmud now turns to identify a number of other cities established by the Greeks and the Romans.

In his prophecy regarding the future redemption, Zechariah refers to a number of cities that were thorns in the sides of the Jews and are destined to be destroyed. *Maharsha* notes that the *gematria* [numerical value] of the Hebrew word עקר — uprooted — is equal to the *gematria* of קסרי — Caesarea.

The Talmud's identification of Ekron as Caesarea is somewhat difficult to understand, for Ekron is mentioned as one of the city/states of the Phillistines — see *Shmuel* I 5:10 — and thus predates the Greek and Roman conquests of *Eretz Yisrael*. *Tosafos*[64] posits that Ekron might have been conquered from the Phillistines by the Romans who then established it as their administrative center. However, this too is somewhat difficult to understand, for Ekron is listed (*Yehoshua* 15:45) as being in the portion allotted to the tribe of Yehudah, while Caesarea was in the portion allotted to Menashe.[65]

TALMUD

אָמַר רַבִּי יוֹסֵי בַּר חֲנִינָא: מַאי דִּכְתִיב: "וַהֲסִירֹתִי דָמָיו מִפִּיו"? זוֹ בֵית בָּמְיָא שֶׁלָּהֶן. "וְשִׁקֻּצָיו מִבֵּין שִׁנָּיו"? – זוֹ בֵית גַּלְיָא שֶׁלָּהֶן. "וְנִשְׁאַר גַּם הוּא לֵאלֹהֵינוּ"? – אֵלּוּ בָּתֵּי כְנֵסִיּוֹת וּבָתֵּי מִדְרָשׁוֹת שֶׁבֶּאֱדוֹם. "וְהָיָה כְּאַלֻּף בִּיהוּדָה וְעֶקְרוֹן כִּיבוּסִי"? אֵלּוּ טִיאַתְרִיאוֹת וְקַרְקְסִיאוֹת שֶׁלָּהֶן, שֶׁעֲתִידִין שָׂרֵי יְהוּדָה לְלַמֵּד בָּהֶם תּוֹרָה בָּרַבִּים.

TRANSLATION

R. Yosi bar Chanina said: What is the meaning of the verse (*Zechariah* 9:7) that states, *and I shall remove his blood from his mouth*? This refers to their altar

63 - The parallel text in the Talmud refers to Achidas Migdal Shir. Caesarea was first built by the King of Sidon and was known by the Greek name Tower of Straton which in Hebrew would be Migdal Sharshon or Shir.

64 - עקרון תעקר ד״ה.

65 - It is possible that there were two cities known as Ekron, one in the portion of Yehudah and one in the portion of Menashe. There are numerous examples of two cities with the same name recorded in *Yehoshua*; e.g., Chatzor in Yehudah and Chatzor in Naftali.

[upon which they spilled the blood of their sacrifices to idols]. *And his abominations from between his teeth* (ibid.)? This refers to their House of Galia.[66] *And this too shall be left for God* (ibid.)? This refers to the synagogues and study halls of Edom [which will miraculously remain standing when Edom is destroyed]. *And they shall be a place of training for Yehudah and Ekron will be like the Yevusi* (ibid.)?[67] This refers to the theaters and circuses that the leaders of Yehudah are destined to use to teach Torah publicly.

COMMENTARY

Having explained the verse in *Zechariah* as pointing out that Caesarea was destined to be uprooted, the Talmud continues with the same theme and notes that all vestiges of Roman rule in *Eretz Yisrael* are destined to be destroyed, quoting another verse from *Zechariah*. *Maharsha* notes that the concept of the houses of idolatry of Edom being transformed into study halls for Israel is alluded to in the very terminology used to describe Edom/Rome. In Hebrew, the princes of Edom are referred to as אלופים, and the word אלוף can also be interpreted as meaning teaching.[68]

TALMUD

אָמַר רַבִּי יִצְחָק: "לֶשֶׁם" – זוֹ פַּמְיָאס. "עֶקְרוֹן תֵּעָקֵר" – זוֹ קֵסָרִי בַּת אֱדוֹם, שֶׁהִיא הָיְתָה מֶטְרוֹפּוֹלִין שֶׁל מְלָכִים. אִיכָּא דְּאָמְרֵי: דִּמְרַבּוּ בָּהּ מַלְכֵי. וְאִיכָּא דְּאָמְרֵי: דְּמוֹקְמֵי מִינָּה מַלְכֵי.

TRANSLATION

R. Yitzchak said: Leshem is Pamias.[69] *Ekron shall be uprooted* — this refers to Caesarea of the Romans which was a metropolis of kings. Others say: Kings are trained there. Others say: Kings are appointed from there.

COMMENTARY

Rashi explains that the Greek word מטרופולין — *metropolis* — is a com-

---

66 - *Rashi* notes that Galia was one of the chief idols of Edom. *Maharsha* identifies Galia as the place where ceremonies of worship were conducted.

67 - I.e., Jerusalem — see *Shoftim* 19:10.

68 - E.g., ואאלפך חכמה — *and I will teach you wisdom* (*Iyov* 33:33).

69 - I.e., Banias, at the headwaters of the Jordan. The site was named after the Greek god, Pan. The familiar name Banias is a corruption of the name Pamias, a result of the tendency of speakers of Arabic to substitute the letter B for the letter P.

bination form meaning mother city. Caesarea was the center of Roman authority and as such, served as the training center for Roman officials. She was the mother city of the Romans stationed in the Land of Israel in the sense that she shaped the policy and personalities of those who served there.

Maharsha notes that in Rome, rule was not necessarily passed from father to son. The Talmud[70] explains that this is the meaning of the verse (*Ovadiah* 1:2): *I have made you [Edom] the smallest of the nations, you are greatly contemptible* — [for] they do not crown a son as king. Given the "democratic" rules of succession that they used, the Romans found it necessary to establish a training grounds for future kings — a center they established in Caesarea.

TALMUD

"קֵיסָרִי" וְ"יְרוּשָׁלַיִם", אִם יֹאמַר לְךָ אָדָם: שֶׁחָרְבוּ שְׁתֵּיהֶן, אַל תַּאֲמֵן; וְיָשְׁבוּ שְׁתֵּיהֶן, אַל תַּאֲמֵן; חָרְבָה קֵיסָרִי וְיָשְׁבָה יְרוּשָׁלַיִם חָרְבָה יְרוּשָׁלַיִם וְיָשְׁבָה קֵיסָרִי, תַּאֲמֵן. שֶׁנֶּאֱמַר: "אִמָּלְאָה הֶחֳרָבָה". אִי מָלְאָה זוֹ – חָרְבָה זוֹ, אִי מָלְאָה זוֹ – חָרְבָה זוֹ.

רַב נַחְמָן בַּר יִצְחָק אָמַר מֵהָכָא: "וּלְאֹם מִלְאֹם יֶאֱמָץ".

וְאָמַר רַבִּי יִצְחָק: מַאי דִכְתִיב: "יֻחַן רָשָׁע בַּל לָמַד צֶדֶק, בְּאֶרֶץ נְכֹחוֹת יְעַוֵּל, וּבַל יִרְאֶה גֵּאוּת ה'". אָמַר יִצְחָק לִפְנֵי הַקָּדוֹשׁ בָּרוּךְ הוּא: רִבּוֹנוֹ שֶׁל עוֹלָם, יוּחַן עֵשָׂו. אָמַר לֵיהּ: רָשָׁע הוּא. אָמַר לֵיהּ: "בַּל לָמַד צֶדֶק"? אָמַר לֵיהּ: "בְּאֶרֶץ נְכֹחוֹת יְעַוֵּל". אָמַר לֵיהּ: אִם כֵּן, "בַּל יִרְאֶה גֵּאוּת ה'" [וְגוֹ'].

TRANSLATION

Caesarea and Jerusalem: If someone tells you that they are both destroyed, do not believe them. That they are both inhabited [i.e., flourishing], do not believe them. That Caesarea has been destroyed and Jerusalem is inhabited, or that Jerusalem has been destroyed and Caesarea is inhabited, believe them. As the verse (*Yechezkel* 26:2) states: *I shall be filled with that which is destroyed.* If this one is filled [i.e., flourishing], then the other is destroyed, and if this one is filled than the other is destroyed.

R. Nachman bar Yitzchak said: This is the source [of the tradition that Caesarea and Jerusalem cannot flourish simultaneously]. *And one nation shall struggle with the other nation* (*Bereishis* 25:23).

R. Yitzchak also said: What is the meaning of the verse (*Yeshayahu* 26:10) that

---

70 - עבודה זרה י.

states: *Grant grace to the wicked, but he will not learn righteousness. He will act iniquitously in the land of the upright, let him not behold the majesty of God*? Yitzchak said to God: "Master of the World, *grant grace* to Esav." God replied: "He is *wicked*." Yitzchak said: "*He will not learn righteousness* [i.e., is there no one who can defend him]?" God replied: "*He will act iniquitously in the land of the upright* [i.e., he is destined to destroy the *Beis ha-Mikdash* and is thus lacking any source of merit]." Yitzchak said: "If so, *let him not behold the majesty of God.*"

COMMENTARY

Having identified Ekron as Caesarea, the Talmud quotes a statement which emphasizes the radical differences between the two major cities in *Eretz Yisrael* — Jerusalem and Caesarea — and the ongoing struggle between them for domination. The struggle of these two cities is representative of the continuing battle between Esav and Yaakov.

While yet in the womb of their mother Rivkah, Esav and Yaakov — the founding fathers of Edom and Israel — were already engaged in battle. Rivkah felt their struggle and approached Shem, who prophecied that *two nations are in your womb, and two nationalities shall separate from your insides.*[71] In his commentary to the Torah, *Malbim* explains that the word גוי — nations — is used to describe a group united politically, while the term לאום — nationalities — is used to describe a group sharing common beliefs. The struggle between Yaakov/Israel and Esav/Rome is both political and religious in nature and the differences between them are so diametrically opposed that it is impossible for them to flourish at the same time. Whereas Yaakov represents truth and light, Esav represents falsehood and darkness and the two can never coexist.

TALMUD

וְאָמַר רַבִּי יִצְחָק: מַאי דִכְתִיב: "אַל תִּתֵּן ה' מַאֲוַיֵּי רָשָׁע, זְמָמוֹ אַל תָּפֵק, יָרוּמוּ, סֶלָה". אָמַר יַעֲקֹב לִפְנֵי הַקָּדוֹשׁ בָּרוּךְ הוּא: רִבּוֹנוֹ שֶׁל עוֹלָם, אַל תִּתֵּן לְעֵשָׂו תַּאֲוַת לִבּוֹ. "זְמָמוֹ אַל תָּפֵק, יָרוּמוּ, סֶלָה". זוֹ גֶּרְמוּמְיָא שֶׁל אֱדוֹם, שֶׁאִלְמָלֵא הֵן יוֹצְאִין, מַחֲרִיבִין אֶת כָּל הָעוֹלָם כֻּלּוֹ. דְּאָמַר רַבִּי חָמָא בַּר חֲנִינָא: שְׁלֹשׁ מֵאוֹת קַטְרֵי תָאגֵי אִיכָּא בְּגֶרְמוּמְיָא שֶׁל רוֹמִי, וּשְׁלֹשׁ מֵאוֹת

---

71 - See *Bereishis Rabbah* 63.

שְׁשִׁים וַחֲמִשָּׁה מַרְזַבְנֵי אִיכָּא בְּבָבֶל, כָּל יוֹמָא נָפְקֵי הַנֵּי לְאַפֵּי הַנֵּי, וּמִקְטִיל
אוֹ חָד מֵהַנֵּי אוֹ חָד מֵהַנֵּי, וּמִטְרְדֵי לְאוּקְמֵי מַלְכָּא אַחֲרִינָא.

TRANSLATION

And R. Yitzchak said: What is the meaning of the verse (*Tehillim* 140:9) that states: *God, do not grant the desires of the wicked, do not bring his plans to fruition, that they might become exalted.* Yaakov said to God: "Master of the world, do not grant the desires of Esav the wicked." *Do not bring his plans to fruition, that they might become exalted* — this refers to [6b] Garmumya[72] [which is one of the nations] of Edom, for if they were to go out, they would destroy the entire world. As R. Chama bar Chanina said: There are three hundred bearers of crowns [i.e., princes] in Garmumya of Rome and three hundred and sixty-five nobles in Bavel. Every day they face each other [in battle] and one or the other of them is killed and they are busy appointing another king [in place of the one who was killed].

COMMENTARY

Michtav me-Eliyahu[73] points out that every nation possesses a characteristic that serves as the motivational force for its activities. Most nations — and individuals as well — are driven by self-serving desires which are fulfillable. Once those desires are met, those whom they subjugate are no longer in danger.

Esav/Edom, however, is not driven by desire but by pride which is limitless and which can never be totally satisfied. Yaakov/Israel's very existence is a threat to that pride and it is Esav/Edom's hatred for him and all that he represents which is the driving force in his life. Thus, their murderous activities are endlessly dangerous and threatening. It is only because Esav/Edom is constantly beset by internecine fighting that they are unable to realize their desire to totally annihilate the Jews.

---

72 - See *Yoma* 10a. *Gra* changes the text there to read גרמניא — Germany — although he does not do so here. *Maharsha* notes that the Talmud in *Yoma* identifies Garmumya as the son of Yefet whereas here, Garmumya is linked to Edom/Esav — a descendent of Shem. He concludes that the reference is to two different nations with the same name. We can conjecture that *Gra* only changed the text in *Yoma* but not here so as to avoid this problem.

73 - Vol. II, pg. 50, s.v. שרי האומות.

Having quoted R. Yitzchok, the Talmud offers another of his statements, albeit regarding a completely different subject.

TALMUD

וְאָמַר רַבִּי יִצְחָק: אִם יֹאמַר לְךָ אָדָם: יָגַעְתִּי וְלֹא מָצָאתִי, אַל תַּאֲמֵן; מָצָאתִי וְלֹא יָגַעְתִּי, אַל תַּאֲמֵן; יָגַעְתִּי וּמָצָאתִי, תַּאֲמֵן. וְהָנֵי מִילֵי בְּדִבְרֵי תוֹרָה, אֲבָל בְּמַשָּׂא וּמַתָּן - סִיַּעְתָּא דִשְׁמַיָּא הִיא. וּבְדִבְרֵי תוֹרָה, לָא אֲמַרָן, אֶלָּא לְאִיחְדוּדֵי, אֲבָל לְאוּקְמֵי גִירְסָא - סִיַּעְתָּא דִשְׁמַיָּא הִיא.

TRANSLATION

And R. Yitzchok said: If someone tells you I have toiled but I did not find [i.e., I made an effort but did not understand], do not believe [him, for had he truly made an effort, he would have understood]. [And if someone tells you] I found [i.e., I achieved understanding] without effort, do not believe [him, for if he made no effort he surely cannot have reached any level of understanding]. [And if he says] I made an effort and I understand, believe [him]. This applies to words of Torah, but as concerns business, it is [dependent upon] Divine assistance [i.e., the reward one earns is not proportionate to the effort invested, for success in business is dependent upon the extent of the Divine assistance which one merits].[74] And as concerns words of Torah, we only spoke of sharp reasoning [i.e., understanding the Torah]. But as concerns remembering what has been learned, it is [dependent upon] Divine assistance.

COMMENTARY

The Talmud[75] notes that success in Torah study is also dependent upon negating one's ego. The Sages derived this from the verse (*Bamidbar* 21:18) that states: *and from Midbar they travelled to Matanah* — one who makes himself like a *midbar* [a desert; i.e., devoid of self-interest] merits that the Torah is given to him as a *matanah* [a gift].

Ksav Sofer, noting that success in Torah study is dependent both upon the

---

74 - I.e., God decides how much money a person will earn during a given period of time based on the reward due him as well as other factors. Thus, man's efforts alone are not enough to insure that he earn recompense. As regards understanding, however, there is a direct link between the amount of effort invested and the results achieved.

75 - נדרים נח.

effort one invests as well as Divine assistance, comments that it is for this reason that we recite the blessing *nosen ha-Torah* in present tense, rather than using the past tense. As the Talmud[76] records: What should man do so as to acquire [Torah] wisdom? He should request it from He who possesses wisdom.

TALMUD

וְאָמַר רַבִּי יִצְחָק: אִם רָאִיתָ רָשָׁע שֶׁהַשָּׁעָה מְשַׂחֶקֶת לוֹ, אַל תִּתְגָּרֶה בּוֹ, שֶׁנֶּאֱמַר: "אַל תִּתְחַר בַּמְּרֵעִים" וְגוֹ', וְלֹא עוֹד אֶלָּא שֶׁדְּרָכָיו מַצְלִיחִין, שֶׁנֶּאֱמַר: "יָחִילוּ דְרָכָיו בְּכָל עֵת". וְלֹא עוֹד אֶלָּא שֶׁזּוֹכֶה בַּדִּין, שֶׁנֶּאֱמַר: "מָרוֹם מִשְׁפָּטֶיךָ מִנֶּגְדּוֹ". וְלֹא עוֹד אֶלָּא שֶׁרוֹאֶה בְּשׂוֹנְאָיו, שֶׁנֶּאֱמַר: "כָּל צוֹרְרָיו יָפִיחַ בָּהֶם".

TRANSLATION

And R. Yitzchak said: If you see a wicked man who enjoys temporary success, do not incite him, for the verse (*Tehillim* 10:5) states: *Do not anger the wicked.* Moreover, he is also successful in all of his ways, as the verse (ibid.) states: *His ways are always successful.* Moreover, he also is successful [even when the world is ruled by Divine] judgement, as the verse (ibid.) states: *The heights of Your judgement are far from him.*[77] Moreover, he sees his enemies fall, as the verse (ibid.) states: *All his enemies he blows away.*

COMMENTARY

Perhaps the most perplexing question facing man when he tries to understand the way through which God exercises His dominion over this world is the success of those whose actions are obviously evil. Why does God allow evil to exist? How can the wicked be successful if there is a God who judges man and punishes him for his failures?

A cardinal principle of the Jewish view of God establishes that man was created with free will; i.e., God allows man to err and follow his own will — even when that will is diametrically opposed to the will of God. Had man been created without free will, he would be unworthy of receiving reward, for his actions would be predetermined. Moreover, the very reason for Creation was to give man the opportunity to exercise his free will and find true good — God's

---

76 - נדה ע:.
77 - See *Malbim* ad loc.

path — through his own efforts.[78] Hence, man's search is dependent upon evil being attractive, for if were not so, man would have no choice but to be good and the purpose of the Creation would remain unrealized.

At the same time, God judges man for his actions and will ultimately reward him for the good that he has done and punish him for the evil which he has caused. Even the wicked whose life is full of evil may well have done some good and be deserving of some reward. God, a true and faithful judge, does not withold the reward of evil men for the good which they have accomplished in this world. He gives them that which they have earned. However, unlike the righteous whose reward is paid in the World to Come, the reward due the wicked is paid in this world.

R. Yitzchok therefore notes that if one sees the wicked enjoying temporary success, he is not to incite him, nor is he to view that success as evidence of a lack of Divine judgement. The success is a result of his being rewarded by God and is the way which God has chosen to rule His world.

TALMUD

אִינִי?! וְהָאָמַר רַבִּי יוֹחָנָן מִשּׁוּם רַבִּי שִׁמְעוֹן בֶּן יוֹחַי: מֻתָּר לְהִתְגָּרוֹת בָּרְשָׁעִים בָּעוֹלָם הַזֶּה, שֶׁנֶּאֱמַר: "עֹזְבֵי תוֹרָה יְהַלְלוּ רָשָׁע, וְשֹׁמְרֵי תוֹרָה יִתְגָּרוּ בָם", וְתַנְיָא, רַבִּי דּוֹסְתַּאי בַּר מָתוּן אָמַר: מֻתָּר לְהִתְגָּרוֹת בָּרְשָׁעִים בָּעוֹלָם הַזֶּה. וְאִם לָחָשְׁךָ אָדָם לוֹמַר: "אַל תִּתְחַר בַּמְּרֵעִים, וְאַל תְּקַנֵּא בְּעוֹשֵׂי עַוְלָה" – מִי שֶׁלִּבּוֹ נוֹקְפוֹ אוֹמֵר כֵּן. אֶלָּא: "אַל תִּתְחַר בַּמְּרֵעִים" – לִהְיוֹת כַּמְּרֵעִים. "וְאַל תְּקַנֵּא בְּעוֹשֵׂי עַוְלָה" – לִהְיוֹת כְּעוֹשֵׂי עַוְלָה.

וְאוֹמֵר: "אַל יְקַנֵּא לִבְּךָ בַּחַטָּאִים" וְגוֹ'? לָא קַשְׁיָא, הָא – בְּמִילֵּי דִידֵיהּ, הָא – בְּמִילֵּי דִשְׁמַיָּא. וְאִיבָּעֵית אֵימָא: הָא וְהָא – בְּמִילֵּי דִידֵיהּ, וְלָא קַשְׁיָא, הָא – בְּצַדִּיק גָּמוּר, הָא – בְּצַדִּיק שֶׁאֵינוֹ גָמוּר, דְּאָמַר רַב הוּנָא: מַאי דִּכְתִיב: "לָמָּה תַבִּיט בּוֹגְדִים, תַּחֲרִישׁ בְּבַלַּע רָשָׁע צַדִּיק מִמֶּנּוּ". צַדִּיק מִמֶּנּוּ – בּוֹלֵעַ, צַדִּיק גָּמוּר – אֵינוֹ בּוֹלֵעַ. וְאִי בָּעֵית אֵימָא, שָׁעָה מְשַׂחֶקֶת לוֹ שָׁאנֵי.

TRANSLATION

Is this so? Did R. Yochanan not say in the name of R. Shimon ben Yochai: It is permissible to incite the wicked in this world, as the verse (*Mishlei* 28:4) states: *Those who leave the Torah praise evil, and those who observe the Torah incite them.* And we learned in a *beraisa*, R. Dustai bar Masun said: It is

---

78 - See *Derech Hashem*, Chapter II:1.

permissible to incite the wicked in this world. And if someone whispers to you and says: *Do not anger the wicked and be not envious of those who act iniquitously (Tehillim 37:1)* — one who is afraid [of his own sins] says this [i.e., interprets the verse in this manner].[79] Rather, [the meaning of the verse is] *Do not compete with the wicked* and be like the wicked. *And do not be envious of those who act iniquitously* to be like those who act iniquitously.

[But] the verse (ibid. 23:7) states, *Let your heart not be envious of those who sin* [i.e., this verse seems to point out that one should not be envious of the wicked. How then could R. Yitzchok have explained that the Psalmist maintained that one should not be zealous in inciting the wicked at those times when they are succesful]?[80] This is not difficult. This [R. Yitzchok's view that one should not incite the wicked] is referring to his own matters [i.e., the personal affairs of the wicked person] and this [R. Dustai's interpretation of the verse which explains that one should not be jealous of the wicked but should battle them] is referring to the matters of Heaven [i.e., when the wicked man sins]. And you could also say that both are referring to his own [i.e., the wicked person's] matters and it is not difficult. This is referring to a totally righteous person [i.e., the opinion which maintains that one may incite a wicked person] and this is referring to a righteous person who is not perfect [i.e., he should not incite the wicked]. As R. Huna explained: What is the meaning of the verse (*Chavakuk* 1:13) which states: *Why do You look at the traitors, [why] are You silent when the wicked swallows [he who] is more righteous*? If he *is more righteous* then he is swallowed, but if he is a completely righteous person then he is not swallowed. And you could also say that the time when he [the wicked person] is temporarily successful is different [i.e., in normal circumstances, one should incite the wicked. But when the wicked person is enjoying temporary success, then one should not incite him].

---

79 - I.e., he is afraid to act zealously and confront the wicked because of his own sins, fearing that he might be subject to ridicule for having the audacity to confront the wicked when he himself is less than perfect.

80 - Although we do not find that R. Yitzchak explained the word קנא as zealous rather than envious, the Talmud assumes that he would do so to be consistent with his opinion that one should not incite the wicked. Interpreting the word קנא as zealous would be hard to justify based on the verse cited by R. Dustai, for it would seem to clearly be referring to jealousy rather than zeal.

COMMENTARY

R. Dustai, as cited in the *beraisa*, did not accept R. Yitzchok's view, explaining that the verse in *Tehillim* was no proof that one should refrain from castigating the wicked at those times when they enjoy success. Man is duty-bound to speak out against evil, to recognize it and do whatever he can to destroy it. One's fears of being ridiculed or being characterized as a fanatic should not prevent him from doing what he must do.[81]

The Talmud then cites another verse from *Tehillim* which would seem to contradict R. Yitzchok's contention that one should avoid dealing with the wicked at those times when they are enjoying success. The verse seems to support R. Dustai's viewpoint that the Psalmist was only warning people not to be jealous of the wicked and thereby be enticed to follow their path.

The Talmud concludes that both R. Dustai's and R. Yitzchok's views are correct in different situations. One opinion in the Talmud posits that R. Yitzchak was referring to a person who was personally suffering from the actions of an evil person. He should refrain from inciting him, for he is very likely being driven by his own interests rather than trying to destroy evil. On the other hand, if the evil person is acting against Heaven, as it were, R. Yitzchak would agree with R. Dustai that one is dutybound to castigate the evil person and make every effort to foil his actions.

The second opinion in the Talmud posits that one may incite the wicked person even if the evil being done affects one personally. R. Yitzchok, however, maintains that one should only do so if he is completely righteous. If he is himself not completely righteous, he should avoid confronting the wicked person, for it is possible that the latter's success is both payment of the reward due him as well as punishment to expiate the sins of the one who is not completely righteous.

The Talmud now expands on the earlier statement[82] of R. Chama bar Chanina which described Garmumya of Rome as having three hundred bearers of crowns, adding Ula's description of Rome's greatness.

---

81 - See *Biur Halachah* to *Orech Chaim* 1, s.v. ולא יתבייש.
82 - See page 43.

TALMUD

אָמַר עוּלָא: אִיטַלְיָא שֶׁל יָוָן, זֶה כְּרַךְ גָּדוֹל שֶׁל רוֹמִי, וְהָוְיָא שְׁלֹשׁ מֵאוֹת
פַּרְסָה עַל שְׁלֹשׁ מֵאוֹת פַּרְסָה. וְיֵשׁ בָּהּ שְׁלֹשׁ מֵאוֹת שִׁשִּׁים וַחֲמִשָּׁה שְׁוָקִים,
כְּמִנְיָן יְמוֹת הַחַמָּה, וְקָטָן שֶׁבְּכֻלָּם - שֶׁל מוֹכְרֵי עוֹפוֹת, וְהָוְיָא שִׁשָּׁה עָשָׂר מִיל
עַל שִׁשָּׁה עָשָׂר מִיל, וּמֶלֶךְ סוֹעֵד בְּכָל יוֹם בְּאֶחָד מֵהֶן. וְהַדָּר בּוֹ - אַף עַל פִּי
שֶׁאֵינוֹ נוֹלַד בּוֹ, נוֹטֵל פְּרָס מִבֵּית הַמֶּלֶךְ. וְהַנּוֹלַד בּוֹ, אַף עַל פִּי שֶׁאֵינוֹ דָר בּוֹ -
נוֹטֵל פְּרָס מִבֵּית הַמֶּלֶךְ. וּשְׁלֹשֶׁת אֲלָפִים בֵּי-בָנֵי יֵשׁ בּוֹ, וַחֲמֵשׁ מֵאוֹת חַלּוֹנוֹת
מַעֲלִים עָשָׁן חוּץ לַחוֹמָה. צִדּוֹ אַחַת יָם, וְצִדּוֹ אַחַת הָרִים וּגְבָעוֹת. צִדּוֹ אַחַת
מְחִיצָה שֶׁל בַּרְזֶל, וְצִדּוֹ אַחַת חוֹלְסִית וּמְצוּדָה.

TRANSLATION

Ula said: Italia of Greece[83] — this is the major city, Rome. It is three hundred *parsah* by three hundred *parsah* [in area] and it has three hundred sixty-five markets, like the number of days in the solar year. The smallest of them is the market of those who sell fowl, and it is sixteen *mil* by sixteen *mil*. And the king dines in a different one [i.e., market] each day. One who lives there, even though he was not born there, receives food[84] from the king's household. And one who was born there [i.e., in that market] even if he does not live there [when the king comes to dine there] receives food from the king's household. And there are three thousand bath-houses there and five hundred windows which let steam escape outside the walls. One side [of the city] faces the sea and one side faces mountains and hills. One side has an iron wall and one side has soft sand and a fortress.

COMMENTARY

Rashi quotes a Midrash which notes that Rome was founded when King Menashe brought an idol into the *Beis ha-Mikdash* (*Melachim* II 21:7). The Talmud[85] offers two opinions in the matter: Rome was founded when Shlomo built a home for Pharaoh's daughter or when Yeravam ben Nvat established idols at Dan and Beis El.

---

83 - Usually used as a reference to the southern part of Italy which was originally ruled by the Greeks.

84 - See *Rashi*, s.v. פרס.

85 - שבת נו:.

Maharal [86] notes that the numbers quoted in the Talmud are obviously exaggerated; three hundred *parsah* by three hundred *parsah* is equivalent to almost 520,000 square miles! [87] The Talmud often uses numbers symbolically and sometimes will use numbers which are exaggerated to emphasize its point; in this case, the greatness of Rome. The number 365, which the Talmud uses to describe the number of markets in the city, is symbolic of Esav/Rome's belief that God does not involve himself in this world but has left it to follow natural order. [88]

Maharsha writes that the Talmud's exaggerated description of Rome's greatness is meant to serve as a source of consolation to Israel. If God granted Rome such greatness despite the evil which she represents, then He will surely reward Israel with even greater rewards when He chooses to bring her final redemption.

TALMUD

"לְקַיֵּם אֶת אִגֶּרֶת הַפֻּרִים הַזֹּאת הַשֵּׁנִית", אָמַר רַב שְׁמוּאֵל בַּר יְהוּדָה: בִּתְחִלָּה קְבָעוּהָ בְּשׁוּשָׁן, וּלְבַסּוֹף קְבָעוּהָ בְּכָל הָעוֹלָם.

אָמַר רַב שְׁמוּאֵל בַּר יְהוּדָה: שָׁלְחָה לָהֶם אֶסְתֵּר לַחֲכָמִים: קִבְעוּנִי לְדוֹרוֹת. שָׁלְחוּ לָהּ: קִנְאָה אַתְּ מְעוֹרֶרֶת עָלֵינוּ בֵּין הָאֻמּוֹת. שָׁלְחָה לָהֶם: כְּבָר כְּתוּבָה אֲנִי עַל סֵפֶר דִּבְרֵי הַיָּמִים לְמַלְכֵי מָדַי וּפָרַס.

TRANSLATION

[7a] *To fulfill this second Purim letter* (*Esther* 9:29). R. Shmuel bar Yehudah explained: At first they established it [the *Megillah* reading] in Shushan. In the end [after the second Purim letter was sent] they established it all over the world.

R. Shmuel bar Yehuda said: Esther sent [a request] to the Sages [asking that they] establish her [the reading of the *Megillah* as being obligatory] in all generations. They responded: You will stir up hatred[89] [that will be focused] upon us by the nations. She responded: I am already recorded in the Chronicles of the Kings of Media and Persia.

---

86 - נצח ישראל יז.

87 - According to R. Chaim Na'eh, a *parsah* is 2.4 miles. According to *Chazon Ish*, a *parsah* is 2.88 miles.

88 - See רנה של תורה, the Commentary of the *Netziv* to *Shir ha-Shirim*, pg. 23.

89 - Our translation of קנאה as *hatred* is based on the context. *Iyun Yaakov* maintains that the Sages were concerned that if the miracle was publicized, other nations might follow Achashverosh's example hoping to duplicate his success.

COMMENTARY

Maharsha explains that the Talmud is responding to an unasked question. Why was it necessary for Mordechai and Esther to send out two Purim letters? In the wake of the miraculous deliverance from the plot of Haman and Achashverosh to destroy them, Mordechai and Esther saw fit to establish the anniversary of that date as a holiday, marked by the public reading of the *Megillah* as a means of publicizing the miracle.

The Sages, however, were reluctant to accept the *Megillah* reading as binding on all of Israel, for they were concerned that public recounting of the miracle might arouse other nations to hate Israel for flaunting the fall of their enemies.[90] Thus, at first, the reading of the *Megillah* was limited to Shushan, for the people in the capital were fully aware of the miracle that had transpired.

In response to the Sages' decision not to make the reading universally binding, Mordechai and Esther replied with their second Purim letter, noting that the nations were well aware of all that had transpired since the entire series of events had been recorded in the chronicles of Media and Persia. Thus, there was no reason to be concerned that the public reading of the *Megillah* would serve to arouse hatred.

Maharsha notes that the Sages never questioned the propriety of establishing Purim as a Rabbinically obligatory holiday.

TALMUD

רַב, וְרַבִּי חֲנִינָא, וְרַבִּי יוֹחָנָן, וְרַב חֲבִיבָא מַתְנוּ, וּבְכוּלֵיהּ סֵדֶר מוֹעֵד, כָּל כִּי הַאי זוּגָא, חֲלוֹפֵי רַבִּי יוֹחָנָן וּמְעַיֵּיל רַבִּי יוֹנָתָן.

שָׁלְחָה לָהֶם אֶסְתֵּר לַחֲכָמִים: כִּתְבוּנִי לְדוֹרוֹת. שָׁלְחוּ לָהּ: "הֲלֹא כָתַבְתִּי לְךָ שָׁלִישִׁים בְּמוֹעֵצוֹת וָדָעַת". "שָׁלִישִׁים" וְלֹא רְבִיעִים. עַד שֶׁמָּצְאוּ לָהּ מִקְרָא מִן הַתּוֹרָה, שֶׁנֶּאֱמַר: "כְּתֹב זֹאת זִכָּרוֹן בַּסֵּפֶר". "כְּתֹב זֹאת", מַה שֶּׁכָּתוּב כָּאן וּבְמִשְׁנֵה תוֹרָה. "זִכָּרוֹן", מַה שֶּׁכָּתוּב בַּנְּבִיאִים. "בַּסֵּפֶר", מַה שֶּׁכָּתוּב בַּמְּגִלָּה.

TRANSLATION

Rav and R. Chanina and R. Yochanan and R. Chaviva taught [the statement which follows]. And in all of *Seder Moed*, whenever one finds this group [mentioned as having studied together], remove R. Yochanan and substitute R. Yonasan.

---

90 - See *Rashi*, s.v. קנאה.

Esther sent the Sages [this request]: Write me [i.e., establish the *Megillah*] for all times [as part of Scripture].[91] They answered: [The verse (*Mishlei* 22:20) states:] *I have already written it three times in counsel and wisdom* [and the inference from this verse is that a subject is written] three times and not four.[92] [They did not accede to her request] until they found grounds [to again mention the destruction of Amalek] in a verse in the Torah (*Shemos* 17:14) which states: *And you shall write this as a commemoration in the book. And you shall write this* — this refers to what is written here [in *Shemos*] and in *Mishneh Torah* [the Book of *Devarim*]. *As a commemoration* — this refers to what is written in the Prophets. *In the book* — this refers to what is written in the *Megillah.*[93]

COMMENTARY

The Sages referred to as having been the address for Esther's requests were the Members of the Great Assembly.[94] This body of 120 Sages[95] included the last of the Prophets — Chaggai, Zechariah and Malachi — and functioned as the supreme legislative and religious authority when the Jews returned to the Land of Israel after the Babylonian exile. The Assembly began during the period of Ezra and Nechemiah and lasted through the time of Shimon *ha-tzaddik* — a period of some one hundred and fifty years. Among the enactments credited to the Great Assembly are the composition of the *Shemoneh Esrai*[96] and the final composition of a number of the Books of Scripture.[97] It would appear that in this latter role, the Assembly decided which works of prophecy and books

---

91 - I.e., establish *Megillas Esther* as one of the twenty-four books of *Tanach*.

92 - I.e., we can infer from this verse that if a theme is written three times, there is no need to repeat it a fourth time. The major theme of *Megillas Esther* — the destruction of Amalek — is recorded twice in the Torah (*Shemos* 17:14 and *Devarim* 28:17) and once in *Nevi'im* (*Shmuel* I 15:2). Thus, there is no reason to write it a fourth time in *Kesuvim*.

93 - The implication from this last phrase is that the destruction of Amalek should be mentioned in *Kesuvim* as well. Thus, there are grounds for including the Book of *Esther* as one of the Books of Scripture.

94 - See *Maharitz Chayes*, *Mevoh laTalmud*, Chapter 10.

95 - Interestingly, the *Yerushalmi* (*Megillah* 1:5) speaks of eighty-five Sages, among them thirty prophets, who were troubled by Esther's requests.

96 - See page 231.

97 - See *Bava Basra* 15a.

written with Divine inspiration would be included as part of Scripture, and it for this reason that Mordechai and Esther turned to them asking that the *Megillah* be included.

The Talmud notes that the first question which had to be decided in dealing with this request was whether the contents of the *Megillah* were worthy of inclusion. Even if Mordechai and Esther had the status of Prophets, that alone was insufficient reason to include the *Megillah* as part of Scripture. Many works of prophecy and Divinely inspired writings existed which had not been included — e.g., Shlomo's three thousand parables.[98]

Maharsha notes that the Sages were troubled by an even more important problem. Were they to accede to Esther's request, the reading of the *Megillah* and the holiday of Purim would be elevated to a status above those of other Rabbinic enactments.[99] This was clearly forbidden by the dictum that even a Prophet could not enact new laws which had Torah status.[100] It was for this reason that they had to find a source within the Torah which would allow them to grant Esther's request.

Esther argued that the very subject of the *Megillah* — the destruction of Amalek — was included in Scripture already and was thus fit to be included again. The Sages answered that there was a tradition — as seen from the verse in *Mishlei* — that once a subject had been dealt with three times, there was no basis to mention it a fourth time in Scripture. In this case, the ongoing battle with Amalek was already included twice in the Torah and once in the Book of *Shmuel*. Esther thereupon replied that the Torah itself seemed to point to the

---

98 - See page 58.

99 - Esther's earlier request that the Sages make the reading of the *Megillah* obligatory everywhere posed no such problem, for it was clearly a Rabbinic enactment. However, including the work as part of *Tanach* would lend it an importance beyond that of any other Rabbinic enactment, leading people to believe that it had the status of a Torah obligation. This would set a dangerous precedent, for it would open the door to adding to the Torah. If the Rabbis were capable of adding to the Torah, then they were also capable of subtracting from the Torah!

Maharal (Commentary to *Esther* 9:27) points out that Mordechai and Esther intended that Purim have the status of a Torah obligation. It was this intention which made it difficult for the Sages to accede to her request.

100 - See page 1.

necessity of recording the battle with Amalek in each of the three sections of *Tanach*. Since the battle with Amalek had not as yet been dealt with in *Kesuvim*, there were no grounds to exclude the *Megillah* based on its subject matter.

Gra[101] notes that the Sages' insistence on only writing something three times was also based on the fact that the Talmud[102] specifically speaks of the benefit of the three part Torah[103] given to a people made up of three units[104] by the third person[105] on the third day[106] in the third month.[107]

The *Megillah* could only be included in Scripture if it was written with Divine inspiration. The Talmud now sets out to prove that the authors of the work were indeed Divinely inspired.

TALMUD

תַּנְיָא, רַבִּי אֱלִיעֶזֶר אוֹמֵר: מְגִלַּת אֶסְתֵּר בְּרוּחַ הַקֹּדֶשׁ נֶאֶמְרָה, שֶׁנֶּאֱמַר: "וַיֹּאמֶר הָמָן בְּלִבּוֹ". רַבִּי עֲקִיבָא אוֹמֵר: מְגִלַּת אֶסְתֵּר בְּרוּחַ הַקֹּדֶשׁ נֶאֶמְרָה, שֶׁנֶּאֱמַר: "וַתְּהִי אֶסְתֵּר נֹשֵׂאת חֵן בְּעֵינֵי כָּל רֹאֶיהָ". רַבִּי מֵאִיר אוֹמֵר: מְגִלַּת אֶסְתֵּר בְּרוּחַ הַקֹּדֶשׁ נֶאֶמְרָה, שֶׁנֶּאֱמַר: "וַיִּוָּדַע הַדָּבָר לְמָרְדֳּכַי וַיַּגֵּד לְאֶסְתֵּר הַמַּלְכָּה". רַבִּי יוֹסֵי בֶּן דּוּרְמַסְקִית אוֹמֵר: מְגִלַּת אֶסְתֵּר בְּרוּחַ הַקֹּדֶשׁ נֶאֶמְרָה, שֶׁנֶּאֱמַר: "וּבַבִּזָּה לֹא שָׁלְחוּ אֶת יָדָם".

אָמַר שְׁמוּאֵל: אִי הֲוָאִי הָתָם, הֲוָה אָמְרֵי לְהוּ מִילְתָא דְעֲדִיפָא מִדְּכוּלְּהוּ, שֶׁנֶּאֱמַר: "קִיְּמוּ וְקִבְּלוּ הַיְּהוּדִים". קִיְּמוּ לְמַעֲלָה מַה שֶּׁקִּבְּלוּ לְמַטָּה.

אָמַר רָבָא: לְכוּלְּהוּ אִית לְהוּ פִּירְכָא, לְבַר מִדִּשְׁמוּאֵל, דְּלֵית לֵיהּ פִּירְכָא, רַבִּי אֱלִיעֶזֶר, סְבָרָא הוּא; דְּלָא הֲוָה אֱינַשׁ דְּחָשִׁיב לְמַלְכָּא כְּוָותֵיהּ, וְהַאי כִּי קָא מַפִּישׁ טוּבָא וְאָמַר, אַדַּעְתָּא דְנַפְשֵׁיהּ קָאָמַר.

דְּרַבִּי עֲקִיבָא, דִּילְמָא כְּרַבִּי אֶלְעָזָר דְּאָמַר: מְלַמֵּד שֶׁכָּל אֶחָד וְאֶחָד נִדְמְתָה לוֹ כְאֻמָּתוֹ.

וְהָא דְּרַבִּי מֵאִיר, דִּילְמָא כְּרַבִּי חִיָּא בַּר אַבָּא, דַּאֲמַר: בִּגְתָן וָתֶרֶשׁ שְׁנֵי טַרְסִיִּים הָיוּ.

---

101 - Commentary to *Mishlei*.

102 - שבת פח.

103 - I.e., *Torah, Nevii'im* and *Kesuvim*.

104 - *Kohanim,* Levites and Israelites.

105 - I.e., Moshe, who was his mother's third child.

106 - I.e., of separation from their wives — see *Shemos* 19:15.

107 - I.e., Sivan which is the third month when counting from Nisan.

וְהָא דְרַבִּי יוֹסֵי בֶּן דּוּרְמְסָקִית, דְּיִלְמָא פְּרִיסְתְּקֵי שָׁדוּר.

TRANSLATION

We learned in a *beraisa*: R. Eliezer said: *Megillas Esther* was said [i.e., written] with Divine inspiration, for the verse (*Esther* 6:6) states: *and Haman said to himself*.[108] R. Akiva said: *Megillas Esther* was said [i.e., written] with Divine inspiration, for the verse (ibid. 2:15) states: *and Esther found favor in the eyes of those who saw her*.[109] R. Meir said: *Megillas Esther* was said [i.e., written] with Divine inspiration, for the verse (ibid. 2:21) states: *and it became known to Mordechai and he told Esther the Queen*.[110] R. Yosi ben Durmaskis said: *Megillas Esther* was said [i.e., written] with Divine inspiration, for the verse (ibid. 9:16) states: *and they did not take from the spoils*.[111]

Shmuel said: Had I been there I would have told them something better than any of theirs. [The evidence that *Megillas Esther* was written with Divine inspiration can be drawn from] the verse (ibid. 9:27)] which states: *The Jews established and accepted* — [the seemingly redundant terminology is used to indicate that] Heaven *established* that which they [the Jews] had *accepted* below [i.e., on earth].

Rava said: All of them [i.e., the verses offered as proof that *Megillas Esther* was written with Divine inspiration] can be contradicted, except for that of Shmuel which cannot be contradicted. R. Eliezer [who saw the reference to what Haman was thinking as indicating that the *Megillah* had to have been written with Divine inspiration] can be explained logically [i.e., there is no need for Divine inspiration to know what Haman was thinking, for it is logical to assume that he said to himself] that there was no one as important to the king as he was, and all of the requests that he made were for his own benefit.[112]

---

108 - Had *Megillas Esther* not been written with Divine inspiration, how could the author have known what Haman was thinking?

109 - Had *Megillas Esther* not been written with Divine inspiration, how could the author have known what those who saw Esther thought?

110 - Had Mordechai not had Divine inspiration, how could he have understood what Bigsan and Seresh were plotting?

111 - Without Divine inspiration, how could they have known that none of the people had taken from the spoils?

112 - When Achashverosh asked Haman (*Esther* 6:6) *what should be done for a person whom the king desires to honor*, Haman had every reason to believe that Achashverosh intended to reward him.

That of R. Akiva [who saw the verse that states that *Esther found favor in the eyes of all who saw her* as proving that *Megillas Esther* was written with Divine inspiration] can perhaps be explained like R. Elazar who interpreted [the verse as meaning] that each and every one thought she was from their nation.[113]

That of R. Meir [who saw the verse that states: *and it became known to Mordechai and he told Esther the Queen* as proving that *Megillas Esther* was written with Divine inspiration] can perhaps be explained like R. Chiya bar Abba who interpreted [the verse by explaining that] Bigsan and Seresh were both Tarshians [and that is why Mordechai, who was fluent in their language, understood their plot and was able to inform Esther].[114]

That of R. Yosi ben Durmaskis [who saw the verse which states that *and they did not take from the spoils* as proving that *Megillas Esther* was written with Divine inspiration is also questionable for] it is possible that messengers were sent [by Mordechai and Esther ordering the Jews not to take spoils].

COMMENTARY

No work — no matter who the author — would be included in *Tanach* unless it could be established as having been written with Divine inspiration. The Sages therefore sought exegetical proof from the *Megillah* itself, each of them pointing to another verse which showed that the authors must have been guided by Divine inspiration.

The four *tannaim* quoted in the *beraisa* deduce that the *Megillah* was written with Divine inspiration because the author speaks of things which could not have been known to him; he describes events as well as the motivations of others. Shmuel, on the other hand, did not necessarily view these factors as proving that the *Megillah* was Divinely inspired, for as Rava pointed out, each and every proof that they offered had a logical explanation. Shmuel preferred to establish the Divine inspiration of the *Megillah* from the fact that the author

---

113 - Since Esther adamantly refused to reveal her nationality, every nation in the Persian empire claimed her as their own This is what is meant by the verse *and Esther found favor in the eyes of all who saw her.*

114 - I.e., Mordechai, as a member of the *Sanhedrin*, was fluent in seventy languages. Hence, his ability to understand the conversation of Bigsan and Seresh can be explained logically and cannot be taken as an indication that the *Megillah* was written with Divine inspiration.

was given the Divine awareness that what he had written was accepted by Heaven — clear and incontrovertible evidence that his pen must have been Divinely inspired.

TALMUD

דִּשְׁמוּאֵל – וַדַּאי לֵית לֵיהּ פִּירְכָא. אָמַר רָבִינָא: הַיְנוּ דְּאָמְרֵי אֱנָשֵׁי: טָבָא חֲדָא פִּלְפְּלָא חֲרִיפָא מִמַּלְיָא צָנָא דְּקָרֵי.

רַב יוֹסֵף אָמַר מֵהָכָא: "וִימֵי הַפּוּרִים הָאֵלֶּה לֹא יַעַבְרוּ מִתּוֹךְ הַיְּהוּדִים".

וְרַב נַחְמָן בַּר יִצְחָק אָמַר מֵהָכָא: "וְזִכְרָם לֹא יָסוּף מִזַּרְעָם".

TRANSLATION

That of Shmuel surely cannot be contradicted.[115] Ravina added: This is what people say: "Better a single hot pepper than a basket full of pumpkins."[116]

R. Yosef said [that proof that *Megillas* Esther was written with Divine inspiration can be drawn] from here [i.e., from the verse (ibid. 9:28) which states]: *and these days of Purim shall never pass from among the Jews.*

R. Nachman bar Yitzchok said from here (ibid.): *and the commemoration shall never cease from among their descendents.*

COMMENTARY

R. Yosef's exegesis bears examination. Why did he feel it necessary to offer evidence after Shmuel had already done so? We can conjecture that R. Yosef felt that Shmuel's evidence was inconclusive, for it was based on an exegetical interpretation of a verse which could also be explained in another manner. While Shmuel had seen the verse as indicating that the author of the *Megillah* was aware of Heaven's thoughts — clear indication that he must have written with Divine inspiration — the literal meaning of the verse does not unequivocally indicate this. Indeed, *Tosafos*[117] points out that this same verse was exegetically interpreted by the Sages[118] as meaning that the Jews observed that which they

---

115 - I.e., the fact that the author of the *Megillah* wrote that Heaven accepted what the Jews established is unequivocal proof that the *Megillah* was written with Divine inspiration.

116 - I.e., just as a small hot pepper gives more flavor than a basket full of pumpkins, so too the opinion of Shmuel — an *amora* who is considered to be small in comparison to the four *tannaim* quoted earlier — is more "flavorful".

117 - ד"ה לכלולהו.

118 - See *Shabbos* 88a.

had already accepted — i.e., through the miracle of Purim, the Jews re-established their commitment to observe the Torah received at Sinai. R. Yosef therefore saw fit to offer an additional piece of evidence from the text which showed that the author had Divine inspiration, for without this influence, he could not have known that *these days of Purim shall never pass from among the Jews.*

R. Nachman bar Yitzchok then pointed out that R. Yosef's evidence was also inconclusive. *Tosafos*[119] explains that the verse cited by R. Yosef could be interpreted as referring only to the Jews of that generation. The author's statement did not have to be seen as referring to the future and was thus no proof that he was Divinely inspired. *Maharsha* points out that the verse could be interpreted as meaning that the Jews of that generation firmly resolved that the celebration of Purim would never cease.

R. Nachman therefore cited the latter part of the same verse. The declarative statement that *the commemoration shall never cease* could only have been made if the author was Divinely inspired.

TALMUD

תַּנְיָא, רַבִּי שִׁמְעוֹן בֶּן מְנַסְיָא אוֹמֵר: קֹהֶלֶת' אֵינוֹ מְטַמֵּא אֶת הַיָּדַיִם, מִפְּנֵי שֶׁחָכְמָתוֹ שֶׁל שְׁלֹמֹה הִיא. אָמְרוּ לוֹ: וְכִי זוֹ בִּלְבַד אָמַר?! וַהֲלֹא כְּבָר נֶאֱמַר: "וַיְדַבֵּר שְׁלֹשֶׁת אֲלָפִים מָשָׁל". וְאוֹמֵר: "אַל תּוֹסְףְ עַל דְּבָרָיו". מַאי ,וְאוֹמֵר'? וְכִי תֵּימָא: מֵימַר טוּבָא אָמַר, דְּאִי בָּעֵי אִיכְּתוּב וּדְאִי בָּעֵי לָא אִיכְּתוּב, תָּא שְׁמַע: "אַל תּוֹסְףְ עַל דְּבָרָיו".

TRANSLATION

We learned in a *beraisa*: R. Shimon ben Menasya said: [The Book of] *Koheles* does not render the hands ritually impure, for it is the wisdom of Shlomo. They said to him: Is this all that he said?[120] The verse (*Melachim* I 5:12) states: *And he spoke three thousand parables.* [Moreover, Shlomo himself indictated that his works were written with Divine inspiration for] the verse (*Mishlei* 30:6) states: *Do*

---

119 - ד״ה ורב נחמן.

120 - *Rashi* explains this statement as a question. There are many works of wisdom ascribed to Shlomo, as the verse in *Melachim* indicates. Yet *Koheles* was committed to writing, while the parables were *spoken*. This would seem to suggest that it differs from the other works of wisdom in that it was Divinely inspired. How then is it possible to state that it does not render the hands impure?

not add to that which he said. Why [was it necessary to offer proof from that which] it states [in the second verse]?[121] If you would think that he [Shlomo] said many things and [he decided] if they should be written or they should not be written, we see [from the verse which states] *Do not add to that which he said* [that nothing may be added to those things which he wrote, for they are Divinely inspired].[122]

COMMENTARY

The Talmud[123] explains that it was customary to store fruits which had been separated as *terumah* together with Holy works so as to insure that the fruit did not become ritually impure. This practice, however, eventually was seen as being unsatisfactory, for the mice who nibbled at the stored fruit would also destroy the Holy works. The Sages therefore ordained that when something — e.g., *terumah* or a person's hands — come into contact with the Holy works, they become ritually impure. This edict insured that fruits and Holy works would be stored separately.

Having established that *Megillas Esther* was written with Divine inspiration, the Talmud rules that it too must be stored separately from *terumah*. Tangenitally, the Talmud cites the opinion of R. Shimon ben Menassia that the Book of *Koheles* would not render something ritually impure since it was the wisdom of Shlomo and not a Divinely inspired work. The Talmud proceeds to prove that Shlomo himself had indicated that the work was Divinely inspired and thus rendered hands which had touched them ritually impure.

It should be noted that the inclusion of *Koheles* as one of the twenty-four Books of Scripture was the subject of much Talmudic discussion. While here the question revolves around whether the work was written with Divine inspiration, the Talmud elsewhere[124] questions whether the contents were fit for inclusion.

TALMUD

מִשְׁנָה. אֵין בֵּין סְפָרִים לִתְפִלִּין וּמְזוּזוֹת, אֶלָּא שֶׁהַסְּפָרִים נִכְתָּבִים בְּכָל לָשׁוֹן,

---

121 - I.e., in what way is the question strengthened through the citation of the second verse?

122 - See *Rashi*, ד״יה ת״ש אל תוסף.

123 - שבת יד.

124 - שבת ל:.

וּתְפִלִּין וּמְזוּזוֹת אֵין נִכְתָּבִים אֶלָּא אַשּׁוּרִית. רַבָּן שִׁמְעוֹן בֶּן גַּמְלִיאֵל אוֹמֵר:
אַף בַּסְּפָרִים לֹא הִתִּירוּ שֶׁיִּכָּתְבוּ אֶלָּא בְּלָשׁוֹן יְוָנִית.
גְּמָרָא. תַּנְיָא, אָמַר רַבִּי יְהוּדָה: אַף כְּשֶׁהִתִּירוּ רַבּוֹתֵינוּ יְוָנִית, לֹא הִתִּירוּ אֶלָּא
בְּסֵפֶר תּוֹרָה, וּמִשּׁוּם מַעֲשֵׂה דְתַלְמַי הַמֶּלֶךְ.

TRANSLATION

[8b] [MISHNAH] There is no difference between [the laws that apply to the writing
of] Books of Scripture and [those that apply to the writing of] *tefillin* and
mezuzos, except that Books of Scripture may be written in any language, while
tefillin and *mezuzos* may only be written in *Ashuris* [script].[125] R. Shimon ben
Gamliel said: Even Books of Scripture were only permitted [to be written] in
Greek.

[9a] [TALMUD] We learned [in a *beraisa*]. R. Yehudah said: Even when the
Sages permitted Greek, they only permitted its use for writing the Torah and
only [did so] because of the incident of King Talmai.

COMMENTARY

The Talmud[126] exegetically derives that it is forbiden to commit the orally
transmitted Torah to writing. *Rashi* explains that this ban can only be lifted if
there is reason to fear that the oral tradition will be forgotten. *Maharitz*

---

125 - The Talmud (*Sanhedrin* 21b-22a) records a difference of opinion regarding the
use of *Ashuris* script. Mar Zutra maintains that the Torah was originally written in
old Hebrew script which was changed to *Ashuris* by Ezra. Rebbi maintains that the
Torah was originally written in *Ashuris* which was lost through the years and was
reinstated by Ezra. *Ritva* explains that the *luchos* that Moshe brought from Heaven
were written in *Ashuris* while the rest of the Torah was originally written in old
Hebrew.

126 - See *Gittin* 60b. *Rambam*, in the Introduction to the Commentary on the
Mishnah, explains that the written word is far more susceptible to misinterpretation
than an orally transmitted explanation. *Semag* (Introduction) writes that had the
orally transmitted Torah been committed to writing, the nations who also accept the
veracity of Scripture would have corrupted it just as they corrupted the Bible. *Maharal*
(*Tiferes Yisrael* 68) notes, quoting the *Midrash Tanchuma*, that the orally transmitted
Torah was left unwritten to provide means to distinguish the Jews from the other
nations who accepted the Divine origin of Scripture. It is for this reason that the
orally transmitted Torah is seen (Talmud, ad loc.) as being the basis for the special
covenant between God and Israel, for it is its acceptance that distinguishes the Jews
from other nations.

Chayes[127] points out that translations of the Torah fall within the classification of the oral tradition, for by definition they are interpretive and serve as a means of understanding the written Torah. Thus, a written translation of the Torah would generally be forbidden. *Ritva* comments that as a part of the orally transmitted Torah, the Aramaic *Targum* of the Torah was not fully committed to writing — because of the ban — but was passed down orally from generation to generation. As we noted earlier, inference can be drawn from the Talmud that the *Targum* was recited by heart and was not read from a written text. This would also explain why the Targum was forgotten and had to be reestablished by Onkelos.[128]

The *Mishnah* rules that even in those situations when the Torah may be written in a foreign language, this applies only to Scripture but not to *tefillin* and *mezuzos*. Rabban Shimon ben Gamliel further qualifies this, ruling that the ban was only lifted if the language used was Greek. This was then further qualified by the *beraisa* quoting R. Yehudah who maintains that the ban was only lifted as concerns the Torah itself, but not as regards the rest of Scripture.[129]

Chazon Ish[130] writes that since the relaxation of the ban against committing the orally transmitted Torah to writing is considered to be *horo'as sha'ah* — a ruling made because of an extraordinary situation — it can only be done by a *beis din* acting on behalf of all of Israel. Moreover, it is preferable that the translation not follow the form of the written Torah — e.g., it should not be written on parchment or on prepared lines — so that it remains clear that the translation is not the written Torah.

---

127 - See כל ספרי מהרי"ץ חיות, חלק ב', אגרת הבקורת.

128 - See page 19. *Otzar Yisrael* points out that the Aramaic Targum was fully committed to writing at the same time that Rebbi permitted the *Mishnah* to be recorded.

129 - We can conjecture that R. Yehudah did not see the danger of the material being forgotten as sufficient grounds for writing the Torah in a foreign language and therefore added that the Sages had only permitted it to be translated and written in Greek because they were forced to do so by Talmai.

It should be noted that the scholars gathered by Talmai only translated the Torah. Yet, it seems that within the space of but a few years, a Greek translation of *Nevi'im* and *Kesuvim* was also written. Some scholars maintain that this translation was the work of Aquilas.

130 - אורח חיים, סימו ס', ס"ק י.

Turei Even notes that the mitzvah of writing a *sefer Torah* can only be fulfilled by writing it in *lashon ha-kodesh* and *Ashuris* script. In this sense, there is no difference between the Torah and *tefillin* and *mezuzos*. The question dealt with in the Mishnah concerns writing a Torah to be used for study. The anonymous first opinion maintains that such scrolls may be written in any language and any script whereas *tefillin* or *mezuzos* — even if written for study rather than for ritual purposes — may only be written in *lashon ha-kodesh*.

TALMUD

מַאי הִיא? דְּתַנְיָא, מַעֲשֶׂה בְּתַלְמֵי הַמֶּלֶךְ שֶׁכִּנֵּס שִׁבְעִים וּשְׁנַיִם זְקֵנִים, וְהוֹשִׁיבָם בְּשִׁבְעִים וּשְׁנַיִם בָּתִּים, וְלֹא גִּלָּה לָהֶם עַל מַה כִּנְּסָם. וְנִכְנַס אֵצֶל כָּל אֶחָד וְאֶחָד, וְאָמַר לָהֶם: כִּתְבוּ לִי תּוֹרַת מֹשֶׁה רַבְּכֶם! נָתַן הַקָּדוֹשׁ בָּרוּךְ הוּא עֵצָה בְּלֵב כָּל אֶחָד וְאֶחָד, וְהִסְכִּימָה דַעְתָּם לְדַעַת אֶחָד,

TRANSLATION

What was this [i.e., what was the incident of Talmai]? We learned in a *beraisa*: It once happened that King Talmai gathered seventy-two Sages and placed them in seventy-two houses and did not reveal to them why he had assembled them. He went in to each and everyone [separately] and told them: "Write [i.e., translate] the Torah of your master Moshe for me." God granted each of them wisdom and they reached identical conclusions [as to the changes that were to be made].

COMMENTARY

The Talmud[131] records: *The day on which the Torah was translated into Greek was as calamitous for Israel as the day on which they made the golden calf, for it was impossible to translate the Torah adequately.*

In *Megillas Ta'anis*, the Sages described the day in the following manner: On the eighth day of Teves, the Torah was translated into Greek during the reign of King Talmai, and darkness came to the world for three days.

Why was the Greek translation of the Torah considered to be so calamitous? *Da'as Soferim* explains that though the translation was made for Talmai, it soon came into the hands of the Jewish population in Alexandria and from there spread to other communities as well. It was the first work of Judaica published in Greek and as such, hastened the process of the assimilation of Greek culture

---

131 - סופרים א:ז.

— a phenomenon that had disastrous results within but a few decades.

Josephus[132] writes that Talmai was an avid bibliophile and ordered that the Torah be translated into Greek so as to enrich his personal library. A contemporary account of the translation of the Torah into Greek can be found in the Letter of Aristeas, which was translated into Hebrew by R. Ovadiah ben Moshe *min ha-Adumim*. The translation of the seventy-two scholars became widely known as the Septuagint and became the basis for almost every subsequent non-Jewish translation of the Torah.

TALMUD

וְכָתְבוּ לוֹ: "אֱלֹהִים בָּרָא בְּרֵאשִׁית". "אֶעֱשֶׂה אָדָם בְּצֶלֶם וּבִדְמוּת". "וַיְכַל בַּיּוֹם הַשִּׁשִּׁי, וַיִּשְׁבּוֹת בַּיּוֹם הַשְּׁבִיעִי". "זָכָר וּנְקֵבָה בְּרָאוֹ", וְלֹא כָּתְבוּ: "בְּרָאָם". "הָבָה אֵרְדָה וְאִבְלָה שָׁם שְׂפָתָם". "וַתִּצְחַק שָׂרָה בִּקְרוֹבֶיהָ לֵאמֹר". "כִּי בְאַפָּם הָרְגוּ שׁוֹר, וּבִרְצֹנָם עִקְּרוּ אֵבוּס". "וַיִּקַּח מֹשֶׁה אֶת אִשְׁתּוֹ וְאֶת בָּנָיו וַיַּרְכִּבֵם עַל נוֹשֵׂא בְּנֵי אָדָם". "וּמוֹשַׁב בְּנֵי יִשְׂרָאֵל אֲשֶׁר יָשְׁבוּ בְמִצְרַיִם וּבִשְׁאָר אֲרָצוֹת, שְׁלֹשִׁים שָׁנָה וְאַרְבַּע מֵאוֹת שָׁנָה". "וַיִּשְׁלַח אֶת זַאֲטוּטֵי בְּנֵי יִשְׂרָאֵל". "וְאֶל זַאֲטוּטֵי בְּנֵי יִשְׂרָאֵל לֹא שָׁלַח יָדוֹ". "לֹא חֶמֶד אֶחָד מֵהֶם נָשָׂאתִי". "אֲשֶׁר חָלַק ה' אֱלֹקֶיךָ אוֹתָם לְהָאִיר לְכָל הָעַמִּים תַּחַת כָּל הַשָּׁמָיִם". "וַיֵּלֶךְ וַיַּעֲבֹד אֱלֹהִים אֲחֵרִים אֲשֶׁר לֹא צִוִּיתִי לְעָבְדָם". וְכָתְבוּ לוֹ בִּמְקוֹם: "הָאַרְנֶבֶת" – "אֶת צְעִירַת הָרַגְלַיִם". וְלֹא כָּתְבוּ לוֹ: "אֶת הָאַרְנֶבֶת", מִפְּנֵי שֶׁאִשְׁתּוֹ שֶׁל תַּלְמַי הַמֶּלֶךְ, "אַרְנֶבֶת" שְׁמָהּ, כְּדֵי שֶׁלֹּא יֹאמַר: שָׂחֲקוּ בִּי יְהוּדָאֵי, וְכָתְבוּ שֵׁם אִשְׁתִּי בַּתּוֹרָה.

TRANSLATION

And they wrote for him[133]: *And God created in the beginning*[134] — *I shall make man with an image and a form*[135] — *and He finished on the sixth day and*

---

132 - Antiquities, Book XII, Chapter 2.

133 - I.e., they made the following changes when translating.

134 - They changed the word order of *Bereishis* 1:1 so that Talmai would not interpret the verse as indicating that God had been created by a being called *Bereishis*.

135 - The first phrase in *Bereishis* 1:26 was changed from the plural form — *Let us make man* — to the singular form so that Talmai could not claim that the verse proved that there was more than one god who created the world. The second phrase — *in our form and image* — was changed to read *with a form and an image*, for Talmai would be unable to understand how it is possible for man to have been created in God's image yet remain human.

He rested on the seventh day[136] — *He created him male and female* and they did not write *He created them*[137] — *Come, I shall descend and I will confuse their language*[138] — *and Sarah laughed in front of those who were near her [i.e., publicly]*[139] — *for in their anger they killed an ox and willfully they uprooted a trough*[140] — *and Moshe took his wife and sons and transported them on [animals used to] carry people*[141] — *and the settlement of Israel which they dwelled in Egypt and in other lands was four hundred and thirty years*[142] — *and he sent the young men of Israel*[143] — *and to the young men of Israel He did not*

---

136 - The phrase in *Bereishis* 2:2 was changed from *and on the seventh day, God finished the work which He had done* so that the verse could not be seen as indicating that God had worked on the seventh day.

137 - In *Bereishis* 5:1, the word בראם — *He created them* — was changed to the singular so that no inference could be drawn that God had created two men who both had male and female faces.

138 - In *Bereishis* 11:7, the text was translated as if it was written in the singular, rather than the plural, so that no one could draw inference that God was only able to confuse the language of those who had created the Tower of Bavel — and by extension control man's activities on earth — with the assistance of the angels.

139 - In *Bereishis* 18:12, the word בקרבה — *to herself* — was translated as if it said בקרוביה — *to those around her*. In verse 18:13, we find that God asked *why has Sarah laughed* which indicates that God was displeased, as it were, with Sarah's reaction to the news of the impending birth of Yitzchak. Had it been translated as written, those reading the translation might well accuse God of discriminating against Sarah, for in *Bereishis* 17:17, we find that Avraham also laughed when informed of Yitzchak's birth, yet we find no expression of Divine displeasure for his having done so.

140 - The verse in *Bereishis* 49:6 was changed from *they killed a man* to *they killed an ox* so that Talmai could not cite the verse as proving that the forefathers of the Jews were as bloodthirsty and murderous as the forefathers of other nations.

141 - The verse in *Shemos* 4:20 was changed from *and Moshe transported his wife and children on a donkey* so that Talmai would not sarcastically ask: "Did your master Moshe not own a camel or a horse?"

142 - The phrase *and in other lands* was added to *Shemos* 12:40, for a calculation based on the years mentioned in the Torah would indicate that the Jews were only in Egypt for two hundred and ten years.

143 - *Rashi* explains that in place of the word נערי in *Shemos* 24:5, the Sages used the Greek word *za'atutei* which means young men who have a certain amount of importance. Had they left the original, Talmai might have said that Moshe had not sent the most important people to offer sacrifices. For consistency's sake, the Sages also changed verse 24:11 from *atzilei* to *za'atutei*.

send His hand [i.e., strike][144] — **[9b]** *I have taken nothing precious of theirs*[145] — *which the Lord your God has set in place as illumination for all of the nations everywhere*[146] — *and they went and served other gods that I have not commanded that they be served*[147] — and instead of writing *the hare*[148] [they wrote] *the swift of foot* and the reason why they did not write *the hare* was because Talmai's wife's name was [the Greek equivalent of] *hare* and this way [i.e., by changing the phrase] he could not say: "The Jews are mocking me and [therefore] wrote my wife's name in the Torah."

פִּיסְקָא. רַבָּן שִׁמְעוֹן בֶּן גַּמְלִיאֵל אוֹמֵר וכו'. אָמַר רַבִּי אַבָּהוּ, אָמַר רַבִּי יוֹחָנָן: הֲלָכָה כְּרַבָּן שִׁמְעוֹן בֶּן גַּמְלִיאֵל. אָמַר רַבִּי יוֹחָנָן: מַאי טַעֲמָא דְּרַבָּן שִׁמְעוֹן בֶּן גַּמְלִיאֵל? דִּכְתִיב: "יַפְתְּ אֱלֹהִים לְיֶפֶת, וְיִשְׁכֹּן בְּאָהֱלֵי שֵׁם" – דְּבָרָיו שֶׁל יֶפֶת יִהְיוּ בְּאָהֱלֵי שֵׁם. וְאֵימָא: "גֹּמֶר וּמָגוֹג"? אֶלָּא אָמַר רַבִּי חִיָּא בַּר אַבָּא: הַיְינוּ טַעֲמֵיהּ: אָמַר קְרָא: "יַפְתְּ אֱלֹהִים לְיֶפֶת", מִיָּפְיוּתוֹ שֶׁל יֶפֶת יִהְיוּ בְּאָהֱלֵי שֵׁם.

This is the *halachah* [regarding that which the Mishnah quoted] Rabban Shimon ben Gamliel [as having] said. R. Abahu said in the name of R. Yochanan: The *halachah* is like Rabban Shimon ben Gamliel. R. Yochanan said: What is the reason of Rabban Shimon ben Gamliel [that only Greek may be used as a language

---

144 - *Tosafos* notes that the previous verse could have well been changed to read *atzilei — the nobility —* as stated in this second verse from 24:11. However, had the Sages done so, they would have altered the meaning of the first verse. *Maharsha* adds that נערי in ths first verse refers to the first-born who were called to serve even though they were not necessarily the most important. Using אצילי would have totally corrupted the meaning. The Sages therefore chose to use the Greek *za'atutei* which has a dual connotation.

145 - The Sages substituted the word חמד — *something precious —* for the word חמור — donkey — in *Bamidbar* 16:15 so that Talmai could not say that the inference from Moshe's declaration was that he might not have taken a donkey, but he did take other things.

146 - In the verse in *Devarim* 4:16, the Sages added the word להאיר — *to illuminate.* Without this addition, Talmai might have interpreted the verse as indicating that only Jews were forbidden to worship the sun, moon, stars and planets.

147 - The Sages added the word לעבדם — *that they be served —* to the verse in *Devarim* 17:3 so that Talmai not mistakenly interpret the verse *that I have not commanded,* as proof that God did not command the existence of the sun, moon, stars and planets, but that they came into existence either through another power or by themselves.

148 - See the list of non-kosher animals in *Vayikra* 11:6.

for writing the Torah]? The verse (*Bereishis* 9:27) states: *Beauty has been given to Yefes and it shall dwell in the tents of Shem* — i.e. let the words [language] of Yefes be used in the tents of Shem. Why not say [that this verse indicates that the languages of] *Gomer and Magog*[149] [should also be permissible since they too were descendents of Yefes]? Rather, R. Chiya bar Abba explained: This is the reason [why R. Shimon ben Gamliel only permitted the use of Greek]. The verse states: *Beauty has been given to Yefes* — i.e., the most beautiful [language] of Yefes [i.e., Greek] shall be [used] in the tents of Shem.

COMMENTARY

The *Yerushalmi* writes that the Sages searched and found that no language other than Greek was suitable for use in translating, for only in Greek would the translation be exact. *Rambam*[150] writes that the Greek referred to by the Talmud as being the most beautiful of the languages of Yefes is no longer known to us, for it has been corrupted through the years by other dialects.

In his commentary to the Torah,[151] R. Samson Rafael Hirsch expands on the concept of the beauty of Yefes being used within the tents of Shem. He writes that Yefes' role in this world is to use his intellectual and aesthetic gifts to develop the infrastructure which will serve Shem. The aesthetic achievements of Yefes are not destined to be destroyed when Shem becomes predominant. Rather, they will be of use to him as he fulfills his own spiritual role. This is what the Talmud meant when it stated that the circuses and theaters of Rome are destined to be transformed into study halls and synagogues.

TALMUD

"וַיְהִי בִּימֵי אֲחַשְׁוֵרוֹשׁ", אָמַר רַבִּי לֵוִי, וְאִיתֵימָא רַבִּי נָתָן: דָּבָר זֶה מָסוֹרֶת הוּא בְּיָדֵינוּ מֵאַנְשֵׁי כְנֶסֶת הַגְּדוֹלָה, שֶׁכָּל מָקוֹם שֶׁנֶּאֱמַר: "וַיְהִי", אֵינוֹ אֶלָּא לְשׁוֹן צַעַר. "וַיְהִי בִּימֵי אֲחַשְׁוֵרוֹשׁ" - הֲוָה הָמָן. "וַיְהִי בִּימֵי שְׁפֹט הַשֹּׁפְטִים" - הֲוָה רָעָב. "וַיְהִי כִּי הֵחֵל הָאָדָם לָרֹב עַל פְּנֵי הָאֲדָמָה" וְגוֹ' - "וַיַּרְא ה' כִּי רַבָּה רָעַת הָאָדָם". "וַיְהִי בְּנָסְעָם מִקֶּדֶם" וְגוֹ' - "הָבָה נִבְנֶה לָּנוּ עִיר". "וַיְהִי בִּימֵי אַמְרָפֶל מֶלֶךְ שִׁנְעָר" וְגוֹ' - "עָשׂוּ מִלְחָמָה". "וַיְהִי בִּהְיוֹת יְהוֹשֻׁעַ בִּירִיחוֹ" -

---

149 - *Abarbanel*, in his commentary to *Bereishis* 10:2, identifies Gomer and Magog as ancient France and Spain.

150 - הלכות תפילין א:יט.

151 - *Bereishis* 9:27.

"וַיִּשָּׂא עֵינָיו וַיַּרְא וְהִנֵּה אִישׁ עֹמֵד לְנֶגְדּוֹ וְחַרְבּוֹ שְׁלוּפָה בְּיָדוֹ". "וַיְהִי ה' אֶת יְהוֹשֻׁעַ" - "וַיִּמְעֲלוּ בְנֵי יִשְׂרָאֵל מַעַל". "וַיְהִי אִישׁ אֶחָד מִן הָרָמָתַיִם" - "כִּי אֶת חַנָּה אָהֵב וַה' סָגַר רַחְמָהּ" "וַיְהִי כַּאֲשֶׁר זָקֵן שְׁמוּאֵל" - "וְלֹא הָלְכוּ בָנָיו בִּדְרָכָיו". "וַיְהִי דָוִד לְכָל דְּרָכָיו מַשְׂכִּיל, וַה' עִמּוֹ" - "וַיְהִי שָׁאוּל עוֹיֵן אֶת דָּוִד". "וַיְהִי כִּי יָשַׁב הַמֶּלֶךְ בְּבֵיתוֹ" - "רַק אַתָּה לֹא תִבְנֶה הַבַּיִת".

וְהִכְתִיב: "וַיְהִי בַּיּוֹם הַשְּׁמִינִי", וְתָנָא: אוֹתוֹ הַיּוֹם שִׂמְחָה גְדוֹלָה הָיְתָה לִפְנֵי הַקָּדוֹשׁ בָּרוּךְ הוּא כְּיוֹם שֶׁנִּבְרְאוּ בּוֹ שָׁמַיִם וָאָרֶץ, כְּתִיב הָכָא: "וַיְהִי בַּיּוֹם הַשְּׁמִינִי", וּכְתִיב הָתָם: "וַיְהִי עֶרֶב וַיְהִי בֹקֶר יוֹם אֶחָד"? הָא שָׁכִיב נָדָב וַאֲבִיהוּא.

TRANSLATION

[10b] *And it was in the days of Achashverosh* (*Esther* 1:1). R. Levi said, and some say that it was R. Yonasan: This [following explanation] is a tradition which we have from the members of the Great Assembly. Wherever [Scripture] states *and it was*, [the phrase] is an [indication that it was a time of] travail. *And it was in the days of Achashverosh* — there was Haman. *And it was in the days of the reign of the Judges* (*Shoftim* 1:1) — there was famine. *And it was when man began to multiply upon the earth* (*Bereishis* 6:1) — and God saw that man's wickedness was great (ibid. :5). *And it was when they traveled from the east* (ibid. 11:2) — *come let us build a city* (ibid. :4). *And it was in the days of Amrafel, King of Shin'ar* (ibid. 14:1) — *they waged war* (ibid. :2). *And it was when Yehoshua was in Jericho* (*Yehoshua* 5:13) — *and he lifted his eyes and he saw and behold, a man was standing in front of him and a drawn sword was in his hand. And God was with Yehoshua* (ibid. 7:1) — *and the children of Israel transgressed the ban.*[152] *And there was a man from Ramasayim* (*Shmuel* I 1:1) — *and he loved Chanah and God had closed her womb* (ibid. :5). *And it was when Shmuel became old* (ibid. 8:1) — *and his sons did not follow in his path* (ibid. :3). *And it was that David was wise in all of his ways and God was with him* (ibid. 18:14) — *and Shaul was hostile to Dovid* (ibid 18:9). *And it was when the King sat in his palace* (ibid. II 7:1) — [*And God said to Dovid*] *but you will not*

---

152 - I.e., spoils were taken despite the ban that Yehoshua had proclaimed.

build the Sanctuary (Divrei ha-Yamim II 6:9).[153]

But does the verse (*Vayikra* 9:1) not state: *And it was on the eighth day,* and we learned that on that day there was as much rejoicing before God as on the day when heaven and earth were created.[154] The verse states here: *And it was on the eighth day* and there (*Bereishis* 1:5) it states: *and it was evening and it was morning, the first day*? [On the eighth day] Nadav and Avihu died [and thus it was a time of travail].

COMMENTARY

Maharal notes that the Hebrew word ויהי can be used in either past, present or future, whereas והיה can only be used in the past or future. He explains that the former form was chosen whenever the author sought to express an ongoing circumstance — i.e., when the past affects both the present and the future. In this case, because it was in the days of Achashverosh — a time when the Divine presence was hidden — it was a period of travail for Israel. Had the author used the והיה form, it would refer to events that had occurred and no longer had affect or had yet to occur.

The Talmud quotes R. Levi as saying that this interpretation was a tradition handed down from the members of the Great Assembly. It should be noted that the Talmud records that the *Megillah* was committed to writing by the members of the Great Assembly — i.e., because of the tradition that they had as to the deeper meaning of the term ויהי, they chose that term rather than using והיה. The other verses cited are cited as proof that ויהי has this connotation.

TALMUD

וְהָכְתִיב: "וַיְהִי בִשְׁמוֹנִים שָׁנָה וְאַרְבַּע מֵאוֹת שָׁנָה לְצֵאת בְּנֵי יִשְׂרָאֵל"? וְהָכְתִיב: "וַיְהִי כַּאֲשֶׁר רָאָה יַעֲקֹב אֶת רָחֵל בַּת לָבָן אֲחִי אִמּוֹ"? וְהָכְתִיב: "וַיְהִי עֶרֶב וַיְהִי בֹקֶר יוֹם אֶחָד"? וְהָאִיכָּא "שֵׁנִי"? וְהָאִיכָּא "שְׁלִישִׁי"? וְהָאִיכָּא "וַיְהִי" טוּבָא?

---

153 - Although the second verse is from *Divrei ha-Yamim*, it is the reply that David received through the prophet Nasan to his stated desire to build the *Beis ha-Mikdash* as brought in the verse in *Shmuel* II.

154 - I.e., how can you say that the phrase *and it was* in the verse in *Vayikra* points to a time of travail when the Sages deduced that the day when the Tabernacle was consecrated was as joyous as the day when the heavens and earth were created. The Talmud goes on to explain the source for this derivation, noting that the term *day* was used in both instances.

אֶלָּא אָמַר רַב אַשִׁי: כָּל "וַיְהִי", אִיכָּא הָכֵי וְאִיכָּא הָכֵי; כָּל "וַיְהִי בִימֵי", וַדַּאי לְשׁוֹן צַעַר הוּא, וַהֲווּ חֲמִשָּׁה: "וַיְהִי בִימֵי אֲחַשְׁוֵרוֹשׁ". "וַיְהִי בִימֵי שְׁפֹט הַשֹּׁפְטִים". "וַיְהִי בִימֵי אַמְרָפֶל". "וַיְהִי בִימֵי אָחָז". "וַיְהִי בִימֵי יְהוֹיָקִים".

TRANSLATION

But the verse (*Melachim* I 6:1) states: *And it was in the four hundredth and eightieth year from when Israel left Egypt*? But the verse (*Bersishis* 29:10) states: *And it was when Yaakov saw Rachel the daughter of Lavan [who was] his mother's brother*? But the verse (*Bereishis* 1:5) states: *And it was evening and it was morning, the first day*? And [the same is true of] the second [day]? And [the same is true of] the third [day]? And there are many [other places where the phrase] *and it was* [is used]?[155]

R. Ashi therefore explained: Each time the phrase *and it was* is used, it can be explained either way [i.e., it can allude to travail or may not allude to travail]. But every [time the phrase] *and it was in the days of* [is used], it is definitely a phrase [used to indicate] travail. And there are five [such instances]: *And it was in the days of Achashverosh, And it was in the days of the reign of the Judges, And it was in the days of Amrafel, And it was in the days of Achaz* (*Yeshayahu* 7:1), *And it was in the days of Yehoyakim* (*Yirmiyahu* 1:3).

COMMENTARY

Maharsha explains that the Talmud reasons that the phrase ויהי בימי — *and it was in the days* — should be interpreted as indicating that it was a time of travail because the word ויהי in this case is superfluous. The term בימי already sets the narrative into past tense. Hence, if the author saw fit to add ויהי, he must have done so to add additional meaning — i.e., that it was a time of travail.

The *Targum* to the first verse of Esther details the travail that occurred in each of the first four verses quoted, but does not explain what transpired during the days of Yehoyakim. The Talmud[156] records that in that period, Yehoyakim took the Book of *Eichah* that Yirmiyahu had written concerning the impending destruction, and cast it into the fire.

---

155 - In all of the examples offered, the term ויהי is used, yet we find no indication that these were times of travail.

156 - מועד קטן כא. See also *Yalkut Shimoni* to *Yirmiyahu* 324.

TALMUD

אָמַר רַבִּי לֵוִי: דָּבָר זֶה מָסוֹרֶת הוּא בְּיָדֵינוּ מֵאֲבוֹתֵינוּ: אָמוֹץ וַאֲמַצְיָה, אַחִי
הֲווּ. מַאי קָא מַשְׁמַע לָן? כִּי הָא דְּאָמַר רַבִּי שְׁמוּאֵל בַּר נַחְמָנִי, אָמַר רַבִּי
יוֹנָתָן: כָּל כַּלָּה שֶׁהִיא צְנוּעָה בְּבֵית חָמִיהָ, זוֹכָה וְיוֹצְאִין מִמֶּנָּה מְלָכִים
וּנְבִיאִים. מְנָא לָן? מִתָּמָר, דִּכְתִיב: "וַיִּרְאֶהָ יְהוּדָה וַיַּחְשְׁבֶהָ לְזוֹנָה, כִּי כִסְּתָה
פָנֶיהָ". מִשּׁוּם דְּכִסְּתָה פָנֶיהָ, וַיַּחְשְׁבֶהָ לְזוֹנָה?! אֶלָּא מִשּׁוּם שֶׁכִּסְּתָה פָנֶיהָ בְּבֵית
חָמִיהָ, וְלֹא הֲוָה יָדַע לָהּ, לְפִיכָךְ יָצְאוּ מִמֶּנָּה מְלָכִים וּנְבִיאִים. מְלָכִים -
מִדָּוִד. וּנְבִיאִים - מֵאָמוֹץ, דְּאָמַר רַבִּי לֵוִי: מָסוֹרֶת בְּיָדֵינוּ מֵאֲבוֹתֵינוּ, אָמוֹץ
וַאֲמַצְיָה אַחִי הֲווּ, וּכְתִיב: "חֲזוֹן יְשַׁעְיָהוּ בֶּן אָמוֹץ אֲשֶׁר חָזָה".

TRANSLATION

R. Levi said: It is a tradition that we have from our forefathers that Amotz and Amatziah were brothers. What does this teach us [i.e., what importance is there in knowing that they were brothers]? Like that which R. Shmuel bar Nachmani taught in the name of R. Yonasan. Every bride who acts modestly in her father-in-law's home merits that kings and prophets will be descended from her. From where do we derive this? From Tamar, for the verse (*Bereishis* 38:15) states: *And Yehudah saw her and thought her to be a prostitute, for she covered her face.* Because she covered her face he thought her to be a prostitute?![157] Rather, because she covered her face when she was in her father-in-law's home, he did not recognize her. As a consequence [i.e., as a reward for her modesty], kings and prophets were descended from her. Kings — from David; Prophets — from Amotz. For R. Levi said: It is a tradition which we have from our forefathers that Amotz and Amatziah were brothers, and the verse (*Yeshayahu* 1:1) states: *The vision of Yeshayahu, the son of Amotz.*[158]

---

157 - I.e., the verse must be interpreted in the following manner. When Yehudah saw Tamar sitting at the side of the road, he thought her to be a prostitute. He failed to recognize her for she had always covered her face in his home. See *Rashi* to *Bereishis* 38:15 and *Maharsha* to *Sotah* 10b.

158 - Had we not had a tradition that Amotz and Amatziah were brothers, we would not see that both kings — Amatziah — and prophets — Amotz — were descended from Tamar as a reward for her modesty in her father-in-law's home.

In the Talmud, the text ends at this point. In the text brought in *Ein Yaakov*, the author adds in parantheses, *and every place where a prophet is also mentioned in conjunction with his father [e.g., Yeshayahu, the son of Amotz], we learned that the father was also a prophet.* See page and *Vayikra Rabbah* 6.

COMMENTARY

There were kings descended from Tamar who were also prophets — e.g., Dovid and Shlomo. Why does the Talmud use Amotz and Amatziah as the example of Tamar's reward. We might suggest that the Talmud held that her reward can be seen as being greater since her descendents included both kings and prophets rather than kings who were themselves prophets. Note that the Talmud refers to Amotz as a prophet based on the tradition that when the name of the father of a known prophet is written, the father was also a prophet.

TALMUD

וְאָמַר רַבִּי לֵוִי: דָּבָר זֶה מָסוֹרֶת בְּיָדֵינוּ מֵאֲבוֹתֵינוּ, מְקוֹם אָרוֹן אֵינוֹ מִן הַמִּדָּה. תַּנְיָא נַמִי הָכֵי: אָרוֹן שֶׁעָשָׂה מֹשֶׁה, יֵשׁ לוֹ עֶשֶׂר אַמּוֹת לְכָל רוּחַ, וּכְתִיב: "וְלִפְנֵי הַדְּבִיר עֶשְׂרִים אַמָּה אֹרֶךְ". כְּתִיב: "כְּנַף הַכְּרוּב הָאֶחָד עֶשֶׂר אַמּוֹת, וּכְנַף הַכְּרוּב הָאֶחָד עֶשֶׂר אַמּוֹת". אָרוֹן גּוּפֵיהּ הֵיכָא הֲוָה קָאֵי? אֶלָּא לָאו שְׁמַע מִינָהּ בְּנֵס הָיָה עוֹמֵד.

TRANSLATION

And R. Levi said: This is a tradition handed down from our ancestors. The space of the *aron* [in the *Beis ha-Mikdash*] is not [counted] in the measurement [for the *aron* miraculously took up no space]. We learned this also in a *beraisa*: The *aron* that Moshe built had ten *amos* of [empty] space on every side. And the verse (*Melachim* I 6:20) states: *and [the space] inside the partition [which separated the kodesh ha-kodashim from the kodesh] was twenty amos long.* And the verse[159] teaches us that the wings of one cherub were ten *amos* and the wings of the other cherub were ten *amos*. Where then was there room for the *aron* itself [if the wings of the cherubs took up the entire twenty *amos* of space inside the *kodesh ha-kodoshim*]? From this we can see that it stood through a miracle.

COMMENTARY

Maharsha[160] points out that even in the material world different elements

---

159 - The Talmud uses the term וכתיב — *and it is written* — which usually signifies the quotation of a verse. The citation brought, however, is not found in *Tanach*, but is the net result of that which the verse states in *Melachim* I 6:24. While it is not unusual for the Talmud to slightly alter the text of a verse, it is rare for the Talmud to use the term כתיב when a verse does not exist.

160 - Commentary to *Bava Basra* 99b. See also *Maharal*, Preface II to *Gevuros Hashem*.

can utilize the same space without infringing upon each other. For example, sound and light exist simultaneously even though they are both physical elements because they occupy different planes within the same space. It is on this basis that we can begin to understand how the spiritual and secular can exist simultaneously and even share the same place without infringing upon each other. The presence of one does not necessarily preclude the presence of the other. The *aron* was spirtual in nature and as such, did not preclude the space in the *kodesh ha-kedoshim* being used for a physical entity as well.[161]

TALMUD

רַבִּי יוֹנָתָן פָּתַח לָהּ פִּתְחָא לְהַאי פַּרְשְׁתָא מֵהָכָא: "וְקַמְתִּי עֲלֵיהֶם נְאֻם ה' צְבָאוֹת, וְהִכְרַתִּי לְבָבֶל שֵׁם וּשְׁאָר וְנִין וָנֶכֶד נְאֻם ה'". "שֵׁם" – זֶה הַכְּתָב. "וּשְׁאָר" – זֶה הַלָּשׁוֹן. "וְנִין" – זֶה מַלְכוּת. "וָנֶכֶד" – זֶה וַשְׁתִּי.

TRANSLATION

R. Yonasan opened his lectures on this subject [i.e., on *Megillas Esther*] with the following verse (*Yeshayahu* 14:22): *And I shall rise up aganst them, said God. And I shall cut off from Bavel [her] name and remnant and [her] great-grandchildren and grandchildren.* [The word] *name* refers to her script; [the word] *remnant* refers to her language;[162] *and her great-grandchildren* refers to the kingdom; *and her grandchildren* refers to Vashti.[163]

COMMENTARY

It was often the practice of the Sages to preface their lectures on *aggadah* with the citation of a verse from a different source which shed light on the subject to be discussed. These opening comments were referred to as a *pischa* —

---

161 - It would seem necessary to add that the miracle that R. Levi spoke of was the fact that the *aron* appeared to have a purely physical nature, and as such, it could not have been inside the *kodesh ha-kedoshim* without having taken up physical space. Miraculously, its spiritual essence permitted it to do so.

162 - *Maharsha* notes that the Hebrew שאר is usually a reference to a relative (e.g., in ויקרא כא:ב). It is exegetically explained in this instance to refer to language since common forms of expression are what draw people close together.

163 - Vashti was Nevuchadnezer's great-granddaughter, yet the prophecy refers to a grandchild! The answer would seem to be that the fulfillment of Yeshayahu's curse regarding the destruction of the Babylonian empire was first seen with the death of Belshetzar — Vashti's grandfather.

the Aramaic form of the Hebrew *psicha* — opening.[164] The Sages quoted by the Talmud each sought to show how verses from other works could easily be interpreted as being relevant to what transpired on Purim.

In Biblical times, Bavel was one of the greatest city/states and was a dominant force in world affairs in that it sat on the crossroads of Europe, Asia and Africa. One might have expected Bavel to remain a major force forever based on her accomplishments under Nevuchadnezer. However, because of her inherent wickedness, she was cursed by Yeshayahu, who prophesied that she would soon be destroyed and no remnant of her glory would remain. Many kings sought to rebuild the city after she was destroyed but to no avail. Alexander the Great sought to establish the capital of his empire on the site of ancient Bavel, and even sent workmen to begin construction. But he died before the task was accomplished and the curse placed on the site remained.

Tosafos explains that in the days of Nevuchadnezer, the kings spoke Babylonian which differed from Aramaic — the language of the nations in the area. This language disappeared in fulfillment of Yeshayahu's curse.

The miracle of Purim was a fulfillment of the prophetic vision of Yeshayahu, for all saw that the mighty Babylonian empire — and the empires who had succeeded her — were powerless in the face of the Divine will.

TALMUD

רַבִּי שְׁמוּאֵל בַּר נַחְמָנִי פָּתַח לָהּ פִּתְחָא לְהַאי פָּרְשְׁתָא מֵהָכָא: "תַּחַת הַנַּעֲצוּץ יַעֲלֶה בְרוֹשׁ, וְתַחַת" וְגוֹ'. "תַּחַת הַנַּעֲצוּץ" – זֶה הָמָן הָרָשָׁע, שֶׁעֲשָׂה עַצְמוֹ עֲבוֹדָה זָרָה, דִּכְתִיב "וּבְכֹל הַנַּעֲצוּצִים וּבְכֹל הַנַּהֲלוֹלִים". יַעֲלֶה בְרוֹשׁ" – זֶה מָרְדְּכַי הַצַּדִּיק שֶׁנִּקְרָא "רֹאשׁ לַבְּשָׂמִים", שֶׁנֶּאֱמַר: "וְאַתָּה קַח לְךָ בְּשָׂמִים רֹאשׁ, מָר דְּרוֹר", וּמְתַרְגְּמִינָן: מֵירָא דַכְיָא.

"וְתַחַת הַסִּרְפַּד", תַּחַת וַשְׁתִּי הָרָשָׁעָה בַּת בְּנוֹ שֶׁל נְבוּכַדְנֶאצַר הָרָשָׁע שֶׁשָּׂרַף רְפִידַת בֵּית ה', דִּכְתִיב בֵּיהּ: "רְפִידָתוֹ זָהָב". "יַעֲלֶה הֲדַס" – זוֹ אֶסְתֵּר הַצַּדֶּקֶת שֶׁנִּקְרֵאת "הֲדַסָּה", שֶׁנֶּאֱמַר: "וַיְהִי אֹמֵן אֶת הֲדַסָּה".

"וְהָיָה לַה' לְשֵׁם" – זוֹ מִקְרָא מְגִלָּה. "לְאוֹת עוֹלָם לֹא יִכָּרֵת", – אֵלּוּ יְמֵי פוּרִים.

---

164 - See for example the introductory comments on *Eichah Rabbah* which are referred to as the *psichta l'Eichah*.

TRANSLATION

R. Shmuel bar Nachmani opened his lectures on this subject [i.e., on *Megillas Esther*] with the following verse (*Yeshayahu* 55:13): *In place of the thorn a cypress shall rise, and in place of the brier a myrtle shall rise. In place of the thorn* — the [thorn is an] allusion to Haman the wicked who made himself into a false god, as the verse (ibid. 7:19) states: *and upon all the thorns and upon all the brambles.*[165] *a cypress shall rise* — the [cypress is an] allusion to Mordechai the righteous who is called the finest of the aromatic scents,[166] for the verse (*Shemos* 30:23) states: *And you shall take for yourself the finest of scents, mor dror* which the Targum translates as *maira dachya.*

And in place of the brier — the [brier is an] allusion to Vashti the wicked, the daughter of the son of Nevuchadnezer who burned the mats of the House of God, regarding which the verse (*Shir ha-Shirim* 3:10) states: *Its mats were of gold.*[167] *a myrtle shall rise* — the [myrtle is an] allusion to Esther the righteous who was also called Hadassah, as the verse (*Esther* 2:7) states: *and he raised Hadassah.*[168]

And it shall be a commemoration for God — this refers to the reading of the *Megillah. An eternal sign which shall not cease* — this refers to the days of Purim.

COMMENTARY

The verse quoted by R. Shmuel bar Nachmani is Yeshayahu's prophetic vision of the nature of Israel's redemption when they repent their sins. The Prophet speaks of a time when the wicked will disappear like thorns and briers,

---

165 - I.e., from the verse in *Yeshayahu* 7, we see that *thorns* are used as an allusion to false gods.

166 - The Talmud's exegesis is based on the similarity in sound between the word ברוש — myrtle — and בראש — the finest. It is then reinforced by the similarity between the name Mordechai and the *Targum's* translation of *mor dror* as *maira dachya.*

167 - Again, the Talmud's exegesis is based upon the similarity of sounds of words. The Hebrew סרפד — *brier* — is similar to an acronym of the words שרף רפד — *burned the mats.* The Talmud then deduces from the verse in *Shir ha-Shirim* that רפד — *mats* — is an allusion to the *Beis ha-Mikdash.*

168 - In this case the Talmud's exegesis is based on the similarity between הדס — *myrtle* — and הדסה — Esther's Hebrew name.

replaced by the righteous who will stand in their place. R. Shmuel bar Nachmani related this theme to Purim noting that Haman and Vashti, the most powerful wicked people who influenced Achashverosh's every move, were destroyed and replaced by Mordechai and Esther.

Rav Gedaliah Schorr zt"l once explained that the word תחת in Yeshayahu's prophecy can be understood in its literal sense — *under*. Even at the darkest moments of Israel's exiles, the seeds of her redemption are waiting to sprout forth. They are literally underneath the manifestations of evil that cause Israel harm. Once the evil is removed, through Israel's repentance and return to God, the seeds blossom and flower.

Maharal notes that the incense offered in the *Beis ha-Mikdash* had the ability to stop plagues, for it symbolized the dominance of the spiritual over the physical. Even after the destruction of the *Beis ha-Mikdash*, the recitation of the Torah portion that describes the incense can do so, as the *Zohar* to *parashas Vayera* records R. Acha as having done. Thus, Mordechai — whose very name is reminiscent of the incense — was able to destroy Haman, whose powers of evil were purely physical.[169]

TALMUD

רַבִּי יְהוֹשֻׁעַ בֶּן לֵוִי פָּתַח לָהּ פִּתְחָא לְהַאי פַּרְשָׁתָא מֵהָכָא: "וְהָיָה כַּאֲשֶׁר שָׂשׂ ה' עֲלֵיכֶם לְהֵטִיב אֶתְכֶם, וְגוֹ' כֵּן יָשִׂישׂ" וְגוֹ'. וּמִי חָדֵי קוּדְשָׁא בְּרִיךְ הוּא בְּמַפַּלְתָּן שֶׁל רְשָׁעִים?! וְהָכְתִיב: "בְּצֵאת לִפְנֵי הֶחָלוּץ, וְאֹמְרִים הוֹדוּ לַה' כִּי לְעוֹלָם חַסְדּוֹ". וְאָמַר רַבִּי יוֹחָנָן: מִפְּנֵי מָה לֹא נֶאֱמַר: "כִּי טוֹב", בְּהוֹדָאָה זוֹ? לְפִי שֶׁאֵין הַקָּדוֹשׁ בָּרוּךְ הוּא שָׂמֵחַ בְּמַפַּלְתָּן שֶׁל רְשָׁעִים. וְאָמַר רַבִּי יוֹחָנָן: מַאי דִּכְתִיב: "וְלֹא קָרַב זֶה אֶל זֶה כָּל הַלָּיְלָה", בְּאוֹתָהּ שָׁעָה בִּקְשׁוּ מַלְאֲכֵי הַשָּׁרֵת לוֹמַר שִׁירָה לִפְנֵי הַקָּדוֹשׁ בָּרוּךְ הוּא, אָמַר הַקָּדוֹשׁ בָּרוּךְ הוּא: מַעֲשֵׂה יָדַי טוֹבְעִין בַּיָּם וְאַתֶּם אוֹמְרִים שִׁירָה לְפָנַי?! אָמַר רַבִּי אֶלְעָזָר: הוּא אֵינוֹ שָׂשׂ, אֲבָל אֲחֵרִים מֵשִׂישׂ. דַּיְקָא נָמִי, דִּכְתִיב: "כֵּן יָשִׂישׂ", וְלֹא כְּתִיב: "יָשׂוּשׂ", שְׁמַע מִינָהּ.

TRANSLATION

R. Yehoshua ben Levi opened his lectures on this subject [i.e., on Megillas

169 - See Introduction to *Ohr Chadash*. *Maharal* notes that the physical power of evil in this world is caused by the influence of Mars and points out that the numerical value of the Hebrew name המן is 95, equivalent to the numerical value of מאדים — *Mars*. See also note 428.

Esther] with the following verse (*Devarim* 28:63): *And it shall be that just as God rejoiced to provide you with good ... so too will He bring rejoicing [when you are destroyed].* Does God rejoice when the wicked[170] are punished? Does the verse (*Divrei ha-Yamim* II 20:21) not state: *As they went out before the soldiers, saying: Praise God for His grace endures forever.* And R. Yochanan explained: Why did they not say for He is good[171] in this praise? Because God does not rejoice when the wicked are punished.[172] And R. Yochanan added: What is [the meaning of the] verse (*Shemos* 14:20): *And they did not come near one another for the entire night?* At that time, the ministering angels sought to sing praise before God. God told them: The work of My hands is drowning in the sea and you sing praises before Me! R. Elazar explained: God does not rejoice [when the wicked fall], but He brings rejoicing to others.[173] This can also be seen [from the grammatical structure of the verse] which states *so too will He bring rejoicing* rather than *so too will He rejoice.* From this it can be seen.

COMMENTARY

Maharsha[174] explains that the verse in *Divrei ha-Yamim* omits the word טוב — *good* — because the term can only be used when God's original will is fulfilled. The verse (*Yechezkel* 18:32) states: *For I do not desire the death of the wicked, but that he return from his ways and live.* God's original will is that the wicked return rather than be destroyed. Thus, the necesity, as it were, to destroy Amon and Moav, the subjects of the verse, can not be categorized as being good, for God would have preferred that they abandon their evil ways. *Maharsha* adds that it is for this reason that in the verses in *Bereishis* describing Creation, each day of the Creation has the phrase *and God saw that it was good* as a suffix — i.e., the Torah characterizes the day's activities as being *good* because His

---

170 - A euphemism for Israel.

171 - I.e., the refrain *praise God, for His grace endures forever* usually includes the words *for He is good* — see *Tehillim* 106:1, 107:1, 118:1.

172 - The verse is referring to the praises sung before the armies went out to battle with Amon and Moav. If God does not rejoice when war is waged against Israel's enemies, He surely does not rejoice when Israel is defeated.

173 - R. Elazar's statement is brought as an answer to the question which R. Yehoshua had posed.

174 - Commentary to *Sanhedrin* 39b. Note that in the parallel text quoted there, the answer is offered by R. Yosi bar Chanina.

original will had been fulfilled.[175]

TALMUD

רַבִּי אַבָּא בַּר כַּהֲנָא פָּתַח לָהּ פִּתְחָא לְהַאי פַּרְשָׁתָא מֵהָכָא: "כִּי לְאָדָם שֶׁטּוֹב לְפָנָיו נָתַן חָכְמָה וְדַעַת" וְגוֹ'. "כִּי לְאָדָם שֶׁטּוֹב לְפָנָיו", זֶה מָרְדְּכַי הַצַּדִּיק. "וְלַחוֹטֶא נָתַן עִנְיָן לֶאֱסֹף וְלִכְנוֹס", זֶה הָמָן הָרָשָׁע. "לָתֵת לְטוֹב לִפְנֵי הָאֱלֹהִים", זֶה מָרְדְּכַי וְאֶסְתֵּר, דִּכְתִיב בֵּיהּ: "וַתָּשֶׂם אֶסְתֵּר אֶת מָרְדְּכַי עַל בֵּית הָמָן".

TRANSLATION

R. Abba bar Kahana opened his lectures on this subject [i.e., on *Megillas Esther*] with the following verse (*Koheles* 2:26): *For to the man who is good before Him, He gave knowledge and wisdom ... to the man who is good before Him* — this refers to Mordechai the righteous. [The verse continues] *And to the sinner He gave reason to gather and assemble* — this refers to Haman the wicked. [The verse continues] *So that it be given to he who is good before God* — this refers to Mordechai and Esther of whom the verse (*Esther* 8:2) states: *And Esther placed Mordechai in charge of Haman's household.*[176]

COMMENTARY

Chovas ha-Levavos[177] explains that wealth and success are given to the wicked to guard temporarily until there arises a righteous person whose actions make him worthy of receiving them. In this case, all of Haman's successes and treasures were only given to him so that he might pass them on to Mordechai.

TALMUD

רַבָּה בַּר עוֹפְרָן פָּתַח לָהּ פִּתְחָא לְהַאי פַּרְשָׁתָא מֵהָכָא: "וְשַׂמְתִּי כִסְאִי בְּעֵילָם, וְהַאֲבַדְתִּי מִשָּׁם מֶלֶךְ וְשָׂרִים, נְאֻם ה'". "מֶלֶךְ" – זוֹ וַשְׁתִּי. "וְשָׂרִים" – זֶה הָמָן וַעֲשֶׂרֶת בָּנָיו.

רַב דִּימִי בַּר יִצְחָק פָּתַח לָהּ פִּתְחָא לְהַאי פַּרְשָׁתָא מֵהָכָא: "כִּי עֲבָדִים אֲנַחְנוּ, וּבְעַבְדֻתֵנוּ לֹא עֲזָבָנוּ אֱלֹהֵינוּ, וַיַּט עָלֵינוּ חֶסֶד לִפְנֵי מַלְכֵי פָרָס". אֵימָתַי בִּימֵי מָרְדְּכַי.

---

175 - In *Rinah shel Torah* — his commentary to *Shir ha-Shirim* — *Netziv* explains how God's original will is altered, as it were, by man's actions. See his explanation to *Shir ha-Shirim* 5:2 and 5:13.

176 - I.e., God allowed Haman to accrue wealth so that it could eventually be transferred to Mordechai and Esther when Haman fell.

177 - Beginning of שער הבטחון.

רֵישׁ לָקִישׁ פָּתַח לָהּ פִּתְחָא לְהַאי פַּרְשָׁתָא מֵהָכָא: "אֲרִי נֹהֵם וְדֹב שׁוֹקֵק,
מוֹשֵׁל רָשָׁע עַל עַם דָּל". "אֲרִי נֹהֵם" – זֶה נְבוּכַדְנֶאצַר הָרָשָׁע, דִּכְתִיב בֵּיהּ:
"עָלָה אַרְיֵה מִסֻּבְּכוֹ". "וְדֹב שׁוֹקֵק" – זֶה אֲחַשְׁוֵרוֹשׁ, דִּכְתִיב בֵּיהּ, בְּמַלְכוּת
פָּרַס: "וַאֲרוּ חֵיוָה אָחֳרִי תִנְיָנָה דָּמְיָה לְדֹב", וְתָנֵי רַב יוֹסֵף: אֵלּוּ פַּרְסִיִּים
שֶׁאוֹכְלִין וְשׁוֹתִין כְּדֹב, וּמְסֻרְבָּלִין בָּשָׂר כְּדֹב, וּמְגַדְּלִין שֵׂעָר כְּדֹב, וְאֵין לָהֶם
מְנוּחָה כְּדֹב. "מוֹשֵׁל רָשָׁע" – זֶה הָמָן. "עַל עַם דָּל" – אֵלּוּ יִשְׂרָאֵל שֶׁהֵם דַּלִּים
מִן הַמִּצְוֹת.

רַבִּי יוֹחָנָן פָּתַח לָהּ פִּתְחָא לְהַאי פַּרְשָׁתָא מֵהָכָא: "זָכַר חַסְדּוֹ וֶאֱמוּנָתוֹ לְבֵית
יִשְׂרָאֵל, רָאוּ כָל אַפְסֵי אָרֶץ אֵת יְשׁוּעַת אֱלֹהֵינוּ", אֵימָתַי "רָאוּ כָל אַפְסֵי"
וְגוֹ'? זֶה בִּימֵי מָרְדְּכַי וְאֶסְתֵּר.

רַבִּי חֲנִינָא בַּר פָּפָּא פָּתַח לָהּ פִּתְחָא לְהַאי פַּרְשָׁתָא מֵהָכָא: "הִרְכַּבְתָּ אֱנוֹשׁ
לְרֹאשֵׁנוּ, בָּאנוּ בָאֵשׁ וּבַמַּיִם, וַתּוֹצִיאֵנוּ לָרְוָיָה". "בָּאנוּ בָאֵשׁ" – בִּימֵי
נְבוּכַדְנֶצַּר הָרָשָׁע. "וּבַמַּיִם" – בִּימֵי פַרְעֹה. "וַתּוֹצִיאֵנוּ לָרְוָיָה" – בִּימֵי הָמָן.

TRANSLATION

Rabba bar Efron opened his lectures on this subject [i.e., on *Megillas Esther*]
with the following verse (*Yirmiyahu* 49:38): *And I shall place My throne in
Eilam,*[178] *and I shall destroy there a king and officers. A King* — this refers to
Vashti. *And officers* — this refers to Haman and his ten sons.

R. Dimi bar Yitzchak opened his lectures on this subject [i.e., on *Megillas
Esther*] with the following verse (*Ezra* 9:10): **[11a]** *For we are slaves, but in our
servitude we have not been abandoned by our God, and He has spread grace upon
us before the kings of Persia.* When [did this transpire]? In the days of
Mordechai.

R. Chanina bar Pappa opened his lectures on this subject [i.e., on *Megillas
Esther*] with the following verse (*Tehillim* 66:12): *You placed men to rule us,
we have come through fire and water and You have delivered us to abundance.
We have come through fire* — during the days of Nevuchadnezer the wicked.[179]
And water — during the days of Pharaoh. *And You have delivered us to
abundance* — in the days of Haman.

R. Yochanan opened his lectures on this subject [i.e., on *Megillas Esther*] with
the following verse (*Tehilllim* 98:3): *His grace and His faith were shown to the*

---

178 - Shushan was located in the province of Eilam — see *Doniel* 8:2.

179 - Who cast Chanaya, Mishael and Azaryah into the furnace.

House of Israel, all who dwell in the corners of the earth saw the salvation [brought us by] our God. When did *all who dwell in the corners of the earth see*? In the days of Mordechai and Esther.

Resh Lakish opened his lectures on this subject [i.e., on *Megillas Esther*] with the following verse (*Mishlei* 28:15): *The lion roars and the bear stirs and the wicked rule over the poor. The lion roars* — this [refers to] Nevuchadnezer the wicked of whom the verse (*Yirmiyahu* 4:7) states: *The lion has risen from his lair. And the bear stirs* — this [refers to] Achashverosh, for the verse (*Doniel* 7:5) states regarding the kingdom of Persia: *And another second animal came which was like a bear.* And R. Yosef taught: These [i.e., the bear referred to] are the Persians who eat and drink like bears, who are fat like bears, who are covered with hair like bears and who are restless like bears. *The wicked rule* — this [refers to] Haman. *Over the poor* — this [refers to] Israel who were poor in mitzvos.[180]

TALMUD

רַבִּי אֶלְעָזָר פָּתַח לָהּ פִּתְחָא לְהַאי פַּרְשְׁתָא מֵהָכָא: "בַּעֲצַלְתַּיִם יִמַּךְ הַמְּקָרֶה" וְגוֹ'. בִּשְׁבִיל עַצְלוּת שֶׁהָיָה בָּהֶם בְּיִשְׂרָאֵל שֶׁלֹּא עָסְקוּ בַּתּוֹרָה נַעֲשָׂה "שׂוֹנְאוֹ שֶׁל מָקוֹם" – מָךְ, וְאֵין "מָךְ" אֶלָּא עָנִי, שֶׁנֶּאֱמַר: "וְאִם מָךְ הוּא מֵעֶרְכֶּךָ". וְאֵין "מְקָרֶה" אֶלָּא הַקָּדוֹשׁ בָּרוּךְ הוּא, שֶׁנֶּאֱמַר: "הַמְקָרֶה בַמַּיִם עֲלִיּוֹתָיו".

רַב נַחְמָן בַּר יִצְחָק פָּתַח לָהּ פִּתְחָא לְהַאי פַּרְשְׁתָא מֵהָכָא: "שִׁיר הַמַּעֲלוֹת לְדָוִד, לוּלֵי ה' שֶׁהָיָה לָנוּ וְגוֹ', בְּקוּם עָלֵינוּ אָדָם". "אָדָם" וְלֹא מֶלֶךְ.

רָבָא פָּתַח לָהּ פִּתְחָא לְהַאי פַּרְשְׁתָא מֵהָכָא: "בִּרְבוֹת צַדִּיקִים יִשְׂמַח הָעָם, וּבִמְשֹׁל רָשָׁע יֵאָנַח עָם". "בִּרְבוֹת צַדִּיקִים", זֶה מָרְדְּכַי וְאֶסְתֵּר. "יִשְׂמַח הָעָם", כְּדִכְתִיב: "לַיְּהוּדִים הָיְתָה אוֹרָה וְשִׂמְחָה וְשָׂשֹׂן וִיקָר". "וּבִמְשֹׁל רָשָׁע יֵאָנַח עָם", זֶה הָמָן, וְכֵן הוּא אוֹמֵר: "וְהַמֶּלֶךְ וְהָמָן יָשְׁבוּ לִשְׁתּוֹת, וְהָעִיר שׁוּשָׁן נָבוֹכָה".

TRANSLATION

R. Elazar opened his lectures on this subject [i.e., on *Megillas Esther*] with the following verse (*Koheles* 10:18): *Through turpitude the covering shall be weakened.* Because of the turpitude that was apparent in Israel, in that they did

---

180 - Amalek's ability to harm Israel is intrinsically linked to those times when Israel is lax — and thus poor — in the observance of mitzvos. See *Tanna D'vei Eliyahu* 23.

not occupy themselves with the Torah, it was as if the enemy of God[181] became weak. The [word] *weak* refers to poverty, as the verse (*Vayikra* 27:8) states: *And if he is poorer than the evaluation.* The [word] *covering* refers to God, as the verse (*Tehillim* 104:3) states: *[He] who covers His heavens with water.*

R. Nachman bar Yitzchak opened his lectures on this subject [i.e., on *Megillas Esther*] with the following verse (*Tehillim* 124:1): *A song of ascents of Dovid. Were it not for God who we had when a man stood up against us.* When a man stood up against us — a *man* and not a king.

Rava opened his lectures on this subject [i.e., on *Megillas Esther*] with the following verse (*Mishlei* 29:2): *When the righteous are many the people shall rejoice and when the wicked reign the people will sigh.* When the righteous are many — this [refers to] Mordechai and Esther. *The people will rejoice* as the verse (*Esther* 8:16) states: *And the Jews had light, happiness, rejoicing and prestige. And when the wicked reign the people shall sigh* — this [refers to] Haman, as the verse (ibid. 3:15) states: *And the king and Haman sat down to dine and the city of Shushan was saddened.*

COMMENTARY

R. Nachman bar Yitzchak's opening remarks point out that the danger posed by a common man is often greater than that posed by a king. The latter's stature — and his ability to govern — is based primarily upon the loyalty of his subjects. Thus, it is against his own best interests for a king to destroy his own people or those whom he seeks to make subservient. A common man, on the other hand, is under no such restraint and will do all that he can to destroy anyone who stands in his way as he strives to achieve power. This was the case with Haman — and is true of anti-Semites throughout history.

Ralbag and *Malbim*, in their commentaries to the verse (*Mishlei* 21:1) that states: *The hearts of kings are in God's hands*, point out that kings are instru-

---

181 - The phrase שונאו של מקום — enemy of God — is used here as a euphemism for God. The Sages refrained from describing God as being weakened because of Israel's laxity, for such a characterization would be inappropriate. *Rashi* explains that because of Israel's turpitude it was as if God was unable to save them. Figuratively, the ability of the *Shechinah* to intervene on behalf of Israel is dependent upon Israel's Torah study. Thus, the verse (*Tehillim* 68:35) states: *Give strength to God*; i.e., by studying Torah, Israel figuratively provides God with the strength to save them. See *Nefesh ha-Chaim, Sha'ar* IV, Chapter 12 and *Ramchal, Derech Eitz Chaim.*

ments that God utilizes to achieve His will in this world. In this sense, all of their decisions are completely in God's hands, for they only act and issue decrees so as to bring about the realization of God's will. Kings, as opposed to common men who seek to influence history or destroy the Jewish people, act without free will, for it is through them that God brings forth the Divine plan for mankind. Thus, we see that Pharaoh's heart was hardened and he was unable to make his own decisions, for his position called upon him to serve as an instrument of God's will.[182]

Maharal adds that when Israel is placed at the mercy of a common man and are thus seemingly dependent upon that person's exercise of his own free will, they are in greater danger than they would be were their enemy a king or ruler. This was the point that Dovid *ha-Melech* was raising when he said: *Were it not for God who we had when a man stood up against us*; i.e., had God not intervened at that time, we would have been doomed, for Haman's attempt to annihilate Israel was his own initiative rather than God using him as a tool.

TALMUD

רַב מַתְנָא אָמַר מֵהָכָא: "כִּי מִי גוֹי גָּדוֹל אֲשֶׁר לוֹ אֱלֹהִים קְרֹבִים אֵלָיו, כַּה' אֱלֹהֵינוּ בְּכָל קָרְאֵנוּ אֵלָיו".

רַב אַשִׁי אָמַר מֵהָכָא: אוֹ הֲנִסָּה אֱלֹהִים לָבוֹא" וְגו'.

TRANSLATION

R. Masna said [i.e., began his lectures] from this [verse (*Devarim* 4:7)]: *For who is a great nation who has a God who is close to them like God our Lord to whom we can always call.*

R. Ashi said [i.e., began his lectures] from this [verse (ibid. :34)]: *Or did He attempt to come and take out a nation from amidst [another] nation.*

COMMENTARY

Maharsha notes that Haman told Achashverosh that he no longer need fear that God would be displeased, as it were, if the king decreed that the Jews be annihilated, for God no longer was close to them and would not intervene on

---

182 - See *Melachim* II 18:25 where Ravshekah — Sancheriv's general — taunts Chizkiyahu by declaring that his king's desire to conquer Jerusalem was a result of God's will. See also *Rambam, Hilchos Teshuvah* 6:3 regarding the question as to how Pharaoh was culpable if he had acted as an instrument of God's will.

their behalf. Haman's plot was a specific denial of the applicability of the verses cited by R. Masna and R. Ashi which refer to the redemption from Egypt, but teach us that God has promised that He will always remain close to Israel and will intervene on their behalf. In the end, Haman and his allies were subjected to the same kind of treatment that they had planned for the Jews — complete eradication. This parallels the punishment that the Egyptians suffered, for they too were subjected to the precise treatment that they had sought to inflict upon the Jews — drowning in the sea in retribution for their plan to cast the sons of the Jews into the river.

TALMUD

"וַיְהִי בִּימֵי אֲחַשְׁוֵרוֹשׁ". אָמַר רַב: "וַי" וְ"הִי", נִתְקַיֵּם מַה שֶּׁכָּתוּב בַּתּוֹרָה: "וְהִתְמַכַּרְתֶּם שָׁם לְאֹיְבֶיךָ לַעֲבָדִים וְלִשְׁפָחוֹת וְאֵין קֹנֶה".

וּשְׁמוּאֵל אָמַר: "לֹא מְאַסְתִּים וְלֹא גְעַלְתִּים לְכַלֹּתָם". "לֹא מְאַסְתִּים" – בִּימֵי יְוָנִים. "וְלֹא גְעַלְתִּים" – בִּימֵי נְבוּכַדְנֶצַּר. "לְכַלֹּתָם" – בִּימֵי הָמָן. "לְהָפֵר בְּרִיתִי אִתָּם" – בִּימֵי פַרְסִיִּים. "כִּי אֲנִי ה' אֱלֹהֵיהֶם" – לִימוֹת גּוֹג וּמָגוֹג.

בְּמַתְנִיתָא תָּנָא: "לֹא מְאַסְתִּים" – בִּימֵי כַשְׂדִּים, שֶׁהֶעֱמַדְתִּי לָהֶם דָּנִיֵּאל, חֲנַנְיָה, מִישָׁאֵל וַעֲזַרְיָה. "וְלֹא גְעַלְתִּים" – בִּימֵי הָמָן, שֶׁהֶעֱמַדְתִּי לָהֶם מָרְדְּכַי וְאֶסְתֵּר. "לְכַלֹּתָם" – בִּימֵי יְוָנִים, שֶׁהֶעֱמַדְתִּי לָהֶם שִׁמְעוֹן הַצַּדִּיק, וּמַתִּתְיָה בֶּן יוֹחָנָן כֹּהֵן גָּדוֹל, וְחַשְׁמוֹנָאִי וּבָנָיו. "לְהָפֵר בְּרִיתִי אִתָּם" – בִּימֵי פַרְסִיִּים, שֶׁהֶעֱמַדְתִּי לָהֶם שֶׁל בֵּית רַבִּי וְחַכְמֵי דוֹרוֹת. "כִּי אֲנִי ה' אֱלֹהֵיהֶם" – לֶעָתִיד לָבוֹא, דְּאֵין כָּל אֻמָּה וְלָשׁוֹן שׁוֹלֶטֶת בָּהֶם.

TRANSLATION

And it was in the days of Achashverosh (Esther 1:1) — Rav said: [the word וַיְהִי can be explained as a combination of] woe and oh,[183] fulfilling that which the Torah (*Devarim* 28:69) states: *And you will be sold there to your enemies as slaves and maidservants and no one will purchase.*

Shmuel taught [in his opening remarks on the *Megillah*]: [The verse (*Vayikra* 26:44) states:) *And I did not despise them or abhor them so as to destroy them [and break My covenant with them, for I am the Lord their God]. I did not despise them* — during the period of the Greeks; *or abhor them* — during the

183 - I.e., the word וַיְהִי can be separated into two words וַי and הִי, both of which are expressions of anguish. The travail which the Jews experienced during the days of Achashverosh was exceedingly great, for it was then that the verse cited found fulfillment.

days of Nevuchadnezer;[184] *to destroy them* — during the days of Haman; *and break My covenant with them* — during the period of the Persians; *for I am the Lord their God* — [and My rule over them will become obvious] during the days of Gog and Magog.

In the *beraisa* it was taught: *I did not despise them* — during the period of the Chaldeans, [and this can be seen by virtue of the fact that] I provided Doniel, Chananyah, Mishael and Azaryah [to guide them]; *or abhor them* — during the days of Haman, for I provided Mordechai and Esther [to guide them]; *to destroy them* — during the period of the Greeks, for I provided Shimon the Righteous, Matisyahu the son of Yochanan *Kohen Gadol* and the Chashmonai and his sons [to guide them]; *and break My covenant with them* — during the period of the Persians,[185] for I provided them with the household of Rebbi and the Sages of each generation; *for I am the Lord their God* — [and My rule over them will become clear] in the Days to Come, when no nation or language[186] will have influence upon them.

COMMENTARY

It would seem that Rav's comment is a preface to his lecture rather than

---

184 - In some editions of the Talmud, the text states *in the days of Vespasian*. It would appear that the name Nevuchadnezer which appears in the text of *Ein Yaakov* and in the Vilna edition was substituted by the Christian censors of the Talmud.

185 - In some editions of the Talmud, the text reads *in the days of the Romans* which chronologically would be more appropriate. The reference to the House of Rebbi — which provided spiritual and political leadership for the Jews in both Israel and Bavel in the period after the destruction of the second *Beis ha-Mikdash* — would also be more understandable, for there were many Jewish leaders who were not members of the House of Rebbi during the period when the Land of Israel was under Persian domination. Our text would seem to reflect a substitution made by the censors of the Talmud. It is possible, however, that the reference to Persians in our text is to the Zoroastrian sects that flourished in Persia and caused the Jews of Bavel much trouble during the period after the destruction of the second *Beis ha-Mikdash*. See *Tosafos* (*Shabbos* 11a), s.v. ולא תחת חבר. The reference to the House of Rebbi, if our conjecture is true, would be to the House of the Exilarch, for the Exilarchs of Bavel were all descendents of the Davidic line as was Rebbi.

186 - Although we have translated לשון as *language*, it would seem that the Talmud uses the word in the sense of ideas — i.e., in the Days to Come, Israel will no longer be influenced by the ideas and thoughts of other nations, but will be totally loyal to God.

exegesis on the *Megillah* itself. He pointed out that the Torah's prophecy regarding what would happen if the Jews failed to live according to the Torah was fulfilled in the days of Achashverosh. The Jews might have thought that they could save themselves by becoming servants to other nations, but the Torah told them that none would be interested in purchasing them. This parallels Esther's plea (6:4) to Achashverosh that *had we been sold as slaves and maidservants I would be silent*.

Shmuel drew his prefatory remarks from the same Torah portion as Rav, but chose the verse after the series of admonishments in which God promised Israel that He would be with them throughout the various exiles. Note that Shmuel's explanation of the verse does not follow the chronological order of events, for he begins with the Greeks, goes back to Nevuchadnezer and then goes forward to Haman.

The *beraisa* brought by the Talmud offers a different interpretation to the verse and does not quote Shmuel as being the source. This latter interpretation follows the chronological order of events.

TALMUD

רַבִּי לֵוִי פָּתַח לָהּ פִּתְחָא לְהַאי פַּרְשְׁתָא מֵהָכָא: "וְאִם לֹא תוֹרִישׁוּ אֶת יוֹשְׁבֵי הָאָרֶץ".

רַבִּי חִיָּא אָמַר מֵהָכָא: "וְהָיָה כַּאֲשֶׁר דִּמִּיתִי לַעֲשׂוֹת לָהֶם, אֶעֱשֶׂה לָכֶם".

TRANSLATION

R. Levi opened his lectures on this subject [i.e., on *Megillas Esther*] with the following verse (*Bemidbar* 33:55): *And if you shall not inherit the residents of the land*.

R. Chiya said [i.e., began his lecture] from this [verse [ibid. :56)]: *And it shall be that as I thought to do to them I shall do to you*.

COMMENTARY

As a preface to his lecture on the *Megillah*, R. Levi opened with the verse in which the Torah explains the reason for the calamities that occur in Israel's national destiny. The enemies sent to cause Israel travail are instruments of the Divine will and their ability to cause harm is a result of Israel's failure to live up to its national role. When the children of Israel first entered the Land and set out to establish their rule, they were commanded to rid the land of its original inhabitants, for were they to allow them to stay — even in a subservient role — they would remain as thorns in the side of the national body and would eventually corrupt the Jewish state. Regrettably, Israel was lax in fulfilling the command to drive all of the nations from the land, and from the very beginning of its existence, experienced the troubles which the Torah had spoken of. The events of Purim also had their roots in Israel's failure to fully separate themselves from the nations with whom they lived. Shaul — Israel's first king — had been commanded to completely eradicate Amalek but failed to do so, allowing Agag — Haman's direct ancestor — to live out of a misguided sense of mercy.

Maharal points out that the evil that man causes himself is far greater than that caused by external factors. The nations would have been unable to harm Israel had she not provided them with the means to do so by failing to fulfill her Divine mission. It is to this that the prophet addressed himself when he said (*Yeshayahu* 49:17): *For those who destroy you and ruin you will stem from you.*

TALMUD

"וַיְהִי בִּימֵי אֲחַשְׁוֵרוֹשׁ", אָמַר רַבִּי לֵוִי: אָחִיו שֶׁל רֹאשׁ, וּבֶן גִּילוֹ שֶׁל רֹאשׁ. אָחִיו שֶׁל רֹאשׁ – אָחִיו שֶׁל נְבוּכַדְנֶאצַּר הָרָשָׁע שֶׁנִּקְרָא "רֹאשׁ", שֶׁנֶּאֱמַר: "אַנְתְּ הוּא רֵאשָׁה דִּי דַהֲבָא". וּבֶן גִּילוֹ שֶׁל רֹאשׁ; נְבוּכַדְנֶאצַּר הָרַג, וְהוּא בִּקֵּשׁ לַהֲרֹג. נְבוּכַדְנֶאצַּר הֶחֱרִיב, וְהוּא בִּקֵּשׁ לְהַחֲרִיב. וְכֵן הוּא אוֹמֵר: "וּבְמַלְכוּת אֲחַשְׁוֵרוֹשׁ בִּתְחִלַּת מַלְכוּתוֹ כָּתְבוּ שִׂטְנָה עַל יֹשְׁבֵי יְהוּדָה וִירוּשָׁלָיִם".

TRANSLATION

And it was in the days of Achashverosh (*Esther* 1:1). R. Levi expounded: [The name] Achashverosh [can be interpreted as] the brother of the one who stood at the head[187] and [also] as the one who shared the traits of the one who stood at the head. The one who stood at the head — this [refers to] Nevuchadnezer the wicked who was called the head, as the verse (*Doniel* 2:38) states: *And you are the head of gold [on the idol that I saw in my dream].* And the one who shared the traits of the one who stood at the head — Nevuchadnezer murdered and he

---

187 - The Talmud's exegesis is based on interpreting the name Achashverosh as a Hebrew acronym made up of the words אחיו של ראש. Note that even though the name is not Hebrew, the Talmud still interprets the name as if it were.

[Achashverosh] sought to murder. Nevuchadnezer destroyed and he sought to destroy, as the verse (*Ezra 4:6*) states: *And during the reign of Achashverosh, in the beginning of his reign, they wrote slander about the residents of Yehudah and Jerusalem*.[188]

COMMENTARY

Having quoted various introductory comments of the Sages, the Talmud now proceeds to expound on the verses of the *Megillah* itself. Throughout the literature of the Talmud and Midrash, we find numerous examples of this type of linguistic exposition to *aggadah* that is quite similar in structure to the parallel halachic derivations through which the Talmud is able to find support and/or the basis for Torah law. Unlike halachic derivation — which in many instances can only be used if there is a tradition supporting either the *halachah* derived or the source used[189] — aggadic exposition, in that it is homiletical in purpose, has no such constraints.

R. Levi points out that the very name Achashverosh indicates that he shared the traits of his predecessor on the throne of Bavel, Nevuchadnezer.

Maharal adds that the authors of the *Megillah*, in omitting the title king before Achashverosh's name, sought to teach us that not only was this his surname, but it also characterized him; i.e., he was a brother in deed to the one who had stood at the head of the kingdom before him.

TALMUD

וּשְׁמוּאֵל אָמַר: שֶׁהֻשְׁחֲרוּ פְּנֵיהֶם שֶׁל יִשְׂרָאֵל בְּיָמָיו כְּשׁוּלֵי קְדֵרָה.

רַבִּי יוֹחָנָן אָמַר: שֶׁכָּל הַזוֹכְרוֹ, אוֹמֵר: אַח לְרֹאשׁוֹ.

רַבִּי חֲנִינָא אָמַר: שֶׁהַכֹּל נַעֲשׂוּ בְּיָמָיו רָשִׁים, שֶׁנֶּאֱמַר: "וַיָּשֶׂם הַמֶּלֶךְ אֲחַשְׁוֵרוֹשׁ מַס עַל הָאָרֶץ".

TRANSLATION

Shmuel said: [The name Achashverosh alludes to the fact that] in his time, the

---

188 - The verse does not detail what slander was written. The Talmud therefore maintains that the slander was no more than an excuse to provide Achashverosh with a justification to destroy Jerusalem again, for no proof was offered that the residents of Jerusalem and Yehudah were guilty of any crime against the king.

189 - For specific examples, see *A Practical Guide to Torah Learning*, Aronson Publishers, N.J., 1995, pgs. 117-140.

faces of Israel became charred[190] like the the bottom of a pot.

R. Yochanan said: [The name Achashverosh is an acronyym which indicates that] everyone who remembers him says, "Woe to my head."[191]

R. Chanina said: [The name Achashverosh indicates that] in his time all became poor,[192] as the verse (Esther 10:1) states: And King Achashverosh levied taxes on all the lands.

COMMENTARY

Maharsha explains that R. Yochanan's exegesis can be understood in two ways. The people sighed because of the troubles they experienced during his reign and their lament can also be understood as denigrating Achashverosh who they viewed as a commoner that circumstance had brought to power. Maharal adds that R. Chanina commented that when people looked back at Achashverosh's rule, what they remembered was the heavy burden of taxation that he imposed.

TALMUD

"הוּא אֲחַשְׁוֵרוֹשׁ", הוּא בְּרִשְׁעוֹ מִתְּחִלָּתוֹ וְעַד סוֹפוֹ. "הוּא עֵשָׂו אֲבִי אֱדוֹם", הוּא בְּרִשְׁעוֹ מִתְּחִלָּתוֹ וְעַד סוֹפוֹ. "הוּא הַמֶּלֶךְ אָחָז", הוּא בְּרִשְׁעוֹ מִתְּחִלָּתוֹ וְעַד סוֹפוֹ. וְכֵן: "הוּא דָתָן וַאֲבִירָם". "אַבְרָהָם הוּא אַבְרָם", הוּא בְּצִדְקָתוֹ מִתְּחִלָּתוֹ וְעַד סוֹפוֹ. "הוּא מֹשֶׁה וְאַהֲרֹן", הֵן בְּצִדְקָתָן מִתְּחִלָּתָן וְעַד סוֹפָן. "דָּוִד הוּא הַקָּטָן", הוּא בְּקַטְנוּתוֹ מִתְּחִלָּתוֹ וְעַד סוֹפוֹ, וּכְשֵׁם שֶׁבְּקַטְנוּתוֹ הִקְטִין אֶת עַצְמוֹ אֵצֶל מִי שֶׁגָּדוֹל מִמֶּנּוּ בַּתּוֹרָה, כָּךְ בְּמַלְכוּתוֹ הִקְטִין אֶת עַצְמוֹ אֵצֶל מִי שֶׁגָּדוֹל מִמֶּנּוּ בְּחָכְמָה.

TRANSLATION

He is [the] Achashverosh (Esther 1:1) — he remained wicked from beginning to end. [Similarly] He is [the] Esav, the father of Edom (Bereishis 36:43) — he remained wicked from beginning to end. He is [the] King Achaz (Divrei ha-Yamim II 28:22) — he remained wicked from beginning to end. Similarly, They

---

190 - Maharal explains that Shmuel interpreted the name Achashverosh as being a combination of the Hebrew words שחור — black or charred — and אש — fire.

191 - R. Yochanan's explained that the name Achashverosh could be seen as an acronym made up of the words אח ראש.

192 - R. Chanina's exegesis is based on the similarity in sound between the name Achashverosh and the Hebrew word רש — poor.

were [the] Dasan and Aviram (Bamidbar 26:9).[193] Avraham is [the] Avram (Divrei ha-Yamim I 1:27)— he remained righteous from beginning to end. They are [the] Moshe and Aharon (Shemos 6:27) — they were righteous from beginning to end. Dovid, he is [the] youngest (Shmuel I 17:14)— he was modest [literally, smallest] from beginning to end, for just as he humbled himself when he was young before those who were greater than he in Torah [learning], so too when he reigned, he humbled himself before he who was greater than he in wisdom.[194]

COMMENTARY

Wherever Scripture prefaces a name with the word he, the intent is to indicate that the description that follows is the essence of the person and that the trait described was true of the person throughout his life. As noted in the verses cited, this is true in both the positive and negative senses. Thus, Esav remained wicked throughout his life, while Avraham remained righteous throughout his life, for in both cases this was the essence of their being. Maharal adds that though Achashverosh did order that Haman be put to death and though he elevated Mordechai to a position of great influence in his court, these actions should not be seen as indicating that he had a change of heart and abandoned his evil ways. Rather, both of these actions were done to serve his own interests.

TALMUD

"הַמֶּלֶךְ", אָמַר רַב: שֶׁמָּלַךְ מֵעַצְמוֹ. אָמְרֵי לָהּ לְשֶׁבַח, וְאָמְרֵי לָהּ לִגְנַאי. לְשֶׁבַח – דְּלָא הֲוָה אֱינַשׁ דְּחָשִׁיב לְמַלְכָּא כְּוָותֵיהּ. לִגְנַאי – דְּלָא הֲוָה חֲזִי לְמַלְכוּתָא, וִיהַב מָמוֹנָא יְתֵירָא וְקָם.

TRANSLATION

Who reigned (Esther 1:1) — Rav said: He reigned on his own. Some say this complimentarily and some say this derogatorily. Complimentarily — for there was no one as important as he to reign. Derogatorily — that he was not fit to reign, but gave a lot of money and rose [to power].

---

193 - They were wicked while young men in Egypt (see Shemos 2:13), they were wicked in the beginning of the stay in the wilderness — for it was Dasan and Aviram who had saved a portion of the manna for the next day in violation of the Divine order not to do so — and they were wicked until the end of the stay in the wilderness when they joined with Korach in his rebellion against Moshe's leadership.

194 - See Berachos 4a.

COMMENTARY

Maharsha explains that Rav's exegesis is based on the word המלך in present tense rather than שמלך in past tense which would be the logical term given that the *Megillah* begins with the words ויהי בימי — *and it was in the days*.

As the Talmud will go on to explain, Achashverosh was not of royal stock. Indeed, as Vashti later pointed out, he was a minor official in the Babylonian court who took advantage of a vacuum in leadership and seized control of the empire after the death of Darius.

Maharal comments that Achashverosh's banquets and celebrations, as well as his willingness to seek advice from a variety of advisers who did not necessarily have his best interests at heart, indicate that he was engaged in a constant struggle to earn the support and fealty of his subjects. This is further supported by his search for a queen to replace Vashti, for we see that he was willing to accept candidates from all parts of the empire — behavior that would be unsuitable for one of royal lineage.

TALMUD

"מֵהֹדּוּ וְעַד כּוּשׁ", רַב וּשְׁמוּאֵל, חַד אָמַר: הֹדּוּ בִּתְחִלַּת הָעוֹלָם, וְכוּשׁ בְּסוֹף הָעוֹלָם. וְחַד אָמַר: הֹדּוּ וְכוּשׁ גַּבֵּי הֲדָדֵי הֲווֹ קַיְימֵי, כְּשֵׁם שֶׁמָּלַךְ עַל הֹדּוּ וְכוּשׁ, כָּךְ מָלַךְ בְּכָל הָעוֹלָם כֻּלּוֹ. כַּיּוֹצֵא בַּדָּבָר אַתָּה אוֹמֵר: "כִּי הוּא רֹדֶה בְּכָל עֵבֶר הַנָּהָר מִתִּפְסַח וְעַד עַזָּה", רַב וּשְׁמוּאֵל, חַד אָמַר: תִּפְסַח בְּסוֹף הָעוֹלָם, וְעַזָּה בְּסוֹף הָעוֹלָם. וְחַד אָמַר: תִּפְסַח וְעַזָּה בַּהֲדֵי הֲדָדֵי הֲווֹ קַיְימֵי, אֶלָּא כְּשֵׁם שֶׁמָּלַךְ עַל תִּפְסַח וְעַזָּה, כָּךְ מָלַךְ בְּכָל הָעוֹלָם כֻּלּוֹ.

TRANSLATION

From Hodu unto Kush (ibid.) — Rav and Shmuel [interpreted this phrase differently]. One said: Hodu was on one side of the world and Kush was on the other side of the world. And the other one said: Hodu and Kush were adjacent to each other [and the verse uses them as an example]. Just as he reigned over Hodu and Kush, so too did he reign over the rest of the world.[195] A similar usage is found [in the verse (*Melachim* I 5:4) which states:] *And he [Shlomo] held power over all [the lands] on the other side of the river, from Tifsach unto Azza.* Rav and Shmuel [interpreted this phrase differently]. One said: Tifsach was on one

---

195 - I.e., his sovereignty was as strong in the far reaches of his kingdom as it was in countries that were adjacent to each other.

side of the world and Azza was on the other side of the world. And the other one said: Tifsach and Azza were adjacent to each other [and the verse uses them as an example]. Just as he reigned over Tifsach and Azza, so too did he reign over the rest of the world.

COMMENTARY

Maharal notes that the difference of opinion between Rav and Shmuel bears examination, for it is quite uncommon to find *tannaim* and *amoraim* arguing about facts that can be determined. He therefore writes that Hodu and Kush were indeed adjacent countries, but since the world is round, they could be seen as being next to each other if one travelled in one direction or as far apart as possible if one went in the other direction. R. Yaakov Emden writes that Kush was an Arab state near India and should not be confused with Ethiopia.

We might conjecture that the reference is to Kashmir which is located on the northern tip of the Indian peninsula. Alternatively, the reference might be to present day Afghanistan — which borders Persia to the east — and has a mountain range which is still referred to as Hindu-Kush.

TALMUD

"שֶׁבַע וְעֶשְׂרִים וּמֵאָה מְדִינָה", אָמַר רַב חִסְדָּא: בַּתְּחִלָּה מָלַךְ עַל שֶׁבַע, וּלְבַסּוֹף מָלַךְ עַל עֶשְׂרִים, וּלְבַסּוֹף מָלַךְ עַל מֵאָה. אֶלָּא מֵעַתָּה דִּכְתִיב: "וּשְׁנֵי חַיֵּי עַמְרָם שֶׁבַע וּשְׁלֹשִׁים וּמְאַת שָׁנָה", מַאי דָּרְשַׁתְּ בֵּיהּ? שַׁאֲנֵי הָכָא דִּקְרָא יְתֵירָא הוּא, מִכְּדֵי כְּתִיב: "מֵהֹדּוּ וְעַד כּוּשׁ", "שֶׁבַע וְעֶשְׂרִים וּמֵאָה מְדִינָה" לָמָּה לִי? שְׁמַע מִינָהּ לִדְרָשָׁה.

TRANSLATION

Seven and twenty and a hundred states (*Esther* 1:1) — R. Chisda explained: At first he ruled over seven, and then he ruled over twenty and in the end he ruled over a hundred. But now [if you maintain that the order of the numbers has exegetical significance], the verse (*Shemos* 6:20) that states: *And the years of Amram were seven, and thirty and a hundred years* — how do you interpret this?[196] This case [i.e., the number of states over which Achashverosh ruled] is

---

196 - The Talmud's question is rhetorical, for it was known that there was no exegetical or homiletical interpretation based on the form in which Amram's age was recorded. It therefore follows that there is no principle that when years are recorded in this manner they point to an interpretation.

different, for the verse is superfluous. The verse (*Esther* 1:1) states: *from Hodu unto Kush*. Why do we need [the added information that he ruled over] *seven and twenty and a hundred states*? It was added so as to be interpreted.

COMMENTARY

Numbers are normally recorded in descending order — e.g., *And the life of Sarah was one hundred and twenty and seven years (Bereishis* 23:1). The fact that the author of the *Megillah* recorded the number of states over which Achashverosh was sovereign in ascending order would thus suggest that he was alluding to an additional point. The Talmud notes, however, that the years of Amram's life are also recorded in ascending order and no exegesis is offered. The Talmud answers that in that case, the number is not superfluous, whereas in our case it is superfluous since we already know that Achashverosh ruled the entire world.

TALMUD

תָּנוּ רַבָּנָן: שְׁלֹשָׁה מְלָכִים הֵם שֶׁמָּלְכוּ בַּכִּפָּה, וְאֵלּוּ הֵן: אַחְאָב בֶּן עָמְרִי,
וּנְבוּכַדְנֶאצַּר, וַאֲחַשְׁוֵרוֹשׁ. אַחְאָב בֶּן עָמְרִי – דְּקָאָמַר לֵיהּ עוֹבַדְיָהוּ לְאֵלִיָּהוּ:
"חַי ה' אֱלֹהֶיךָ, אִם יֶשׁ גּוֹי וּמַמְלָכָה אֲשֶׁר לֹא שָׁלַח אֲדֹנִי שָׁם לְבַקֶּשְׁךָ, וְאָמְרוּ
אָיִן, וְהִשְׁבִּיעַ אֶת הַמַּמְלָכָה וְאֶת הַגּוֹי" וְגוֹ'. וְאִי לָאו דַּהֲוָה מָלִיךְ עֲלַיְיהוּ,
הֵיכִי מָצֵי לְאַשְׁבּוּעִינְהוּ?
וּנְבוּכַדְנֶאצַּר – דִּכְתִיב בֵּיהּ: "וְהָיָה הַגּוֹי וְחַמַּמְלָכָה אֲשֶׁר לֹא יַעַבְדוּ אֹתוֹ, אֶת
נְבוּכַדְנֶאצַּר מֶלֶךְ בָּבֶל".
אֲחַשְׁוֵרוֹשׁ – הָא דְאָמְרָן.

TRANSLATION

The Sages taught: Three kings ruled over all of the world and they are: Achav the son of Omri, Nevuchadnezer and Achashverosh. [How do we know this to be true about] Achav the son of Omri? For Ovadyah said to Eliyahu (*Melachim* I 18:10): *By God, if there is a nation or a kingdom to which my master has not sent [messengers] to search for you. And they said that you were not there, and he made the nations and kingdoms swear, for he could not find you.* Had he not ruled over them, how could he have made them swear?
[Regarding] Nevuchadnezer, the verse (*Yirmiyahu* 27:8) states: *And it shall be that the nation or kingdom who shall not serve him, Nevuchadnezer, King of Bavel.*

[Regarding] Achashverosh, as we said [i.e., the proof is from the verse previously cited].

COMMENTARY

Scripture (*Melachim* I 16:30) records that *Achav the son of Omri did evil in the eyes of God, more so than all who had preceded him* and (ibid. :33) *and Achav did more to enrage God, the Lord of Israel, more than all the kings of Isreal who preceded him.* Yet, despite his wickedness, God granted him sovereignty over the entire world! The Talmud[197] notes that he was generous with his wealth and supported Torah Sages. Had it not been for his murder of Navos, he would have been forgiven his sins.[198]

TALMUD

וְתוּ לֵיכָּא?! וְהָא אִיכָּא "שְׁלֹמֹה"? שְׁלֹמֹה לָא סָלִיק מַלְכוּתֵיהּ. הָא נִיחָא לְמָאן דְּאָמַר: מֶלֶךְ וְהֶדְיוֹט. אֶלָּא לְמָאן דְּאָמַר: מֶלֶךְ וְהֶדְיוֹט וְמֶלֶךְ, מַאי אִיכָּא לְמֵימָר? שָׁאנֵי שְׁלֹמֹה, דְּמִילְתָא אַחֲרִיתִי הֲוָה בֵיהּ – שֶׁמָּלַךְ עַל הָעֶלְיוֹנִים וְעַל הַתַּחְתּוֹנִים, שֶׁנֶּאֱמַר: "וַיֵּשֶׁב שְׁלֹמֹה עַל כִּסֵּא ה'" וְגו'.

TRANSLATION

[11b] And are there no others? There is Shlomo [who also ruled over the entire world]? Shlomo did not reign until the end. This [answer] is sufficient according to the one who says that he was a king and then became a commoner.[199] But according to the one who says that he was a king, [then became a] commoner and [then regained his throne and once again became] king — what can you say [i.e., why is he not included as one of the kings who ruled over the entire world]? Shlomo had a different quality [and can thus not be included with the other kings] for he ruled over [both] the supernal and the lower [worlds], as the verse (*Melachim* I 2:18) states: *And Shlomo sat on the throne of God.*

COMMENTARY

Regarding Shlomo, the verse (*Melachim* I 5:1) states: *And Shlomo ruled over all the kingdoms.* However, the character of Shlomo's sovereignty was different than that of the other kings whom the Talmud mentions, for Shlomo's powers extended to the supernal world as well and he can therefore not be counted

---

197 - .סנהדרין קב:

198 - See also *Pirkei d'Rebbi Eliezer*, 43.

199 - See *Gittin* 68b.

together with Achav, Nevuchadnezer and Achashverosh whose sovereignty extended only to the physical realm.

Rashba, quoted by the author of *Ein Yaakov*, writes that the ability to impose one's will on another is sovereignty. Clearly, only God is sovereign in the supernal world, as the verse (*Tehillim* 115:16) states: *the heavens are the heavens of God and the earth was given to mankind.* However, since Shlomo understood the order of the heavens and the means through which the supernal world acts, he was able to utilize this knowledge for his own needs and can thus be said to have been sovereign in the higher world as well.

Rashba adds that an alternative explanation can also be offered. Achav, Nevuchadnezer and Achashverosh ruled the entire world through force, whereas Shlomo — who was entirely a man of peace and was thus deemed worthy of building the *Beis ha-Mikdash* — exerted his influence over mankind by virtue of his unparalleled wisdom. Thus, because Shlomo was a ruler in the supernal world — i.e., because he had been granted his extraordinary wisdom — he also ruled in the lower physical world.

Eitz Yosef points out that Shlomo did not actually rule over all of the countries of the world, for we see that the verses refer to the kings of Egypt and Tyre as well as the Queen of Sheva. Rather, Shlomo was considered to have ruled over the entire world because his kingdom was so solidly based, that no other king or nation posed any threat to him. On this basis, we can also understand how Achav can be considered to have ruled over the entire world, for the Talmud only offered circumstantial support from the fact that Ovadiah told Eliyahu that Achav had made the nations swear that they were not hiding the prophet. However, if we understand the concept of being sovereign over the entire world in the sense of enjoying a position of strength whereby one has no fears of any external enemies, and indeed they fear the king instead, Achav's ability to force his will upon others can be seen as a form of sovereignty.

TALMUD

וְהָאִיכָּא סַנְחֵרִיב, דִּכְתִיב בֵּיהּ: "מִי בְּכָל אֱלֹהֵי הָאֲרָצוֹת אֲשֶׁר הִצִּילוּ אֶת אַרְצָם מִיָּדִי"? הָא הֲוָיָא יְרוּשָׁלַיִם דְּלָא כָּבִישׁ לָהּ.

וְהָא אִיכָּא דָּרְיָוֶשׁ, דִּכְתִיב: "דָּרְיָוֶשׁ מַלְכָּא כְּתַב לְכָל עַמְמַיָּא וְגוֹ' שְׁלָמְכוֹן יִשְׂגֵּא"? הֲוָיָא שְׁבַע דְּלָא מְלַךְ עֲלַיְיהוּ, דִּכְתִיב: "שְׁפַר קֳדָם דָּרְיָוֶשׁ וַהֲקֵים עַל מַלְכוּתָא לַאֲחַשְׁדַּרְפְּנַיָּא מְאָה וְעֶשְׂרִין".

וְהָא אִיכָּא כּוֹרֶשׁ, דִּכְתִיב בֵּיהּ: "כֹּה אָמַר כּוֹרֶשׁ מֶלֶךְ פָּרַס, כָּל מַמְלְכוֹת הָאָרֶץ נָתַן לִי ה'" וְגוֹ'? הָתָם אִשְׁתַּבּוּחֵי הוּא דְּקָא מִשְׁתַּבַּח בְּנַפְשֵׁיהּ.

TRANSLATION

And there is Sancheriv, regarding whom the verse (*Melachim* II 19:38) states: *Who among the gods of all the lands has saved their country from me.* There was Jerusalem which he did not capture [thus, he did not rule all the countries of the world].

And there is Daryavesh, regarding whom the verse (*Doniel* 6:26) states: *Daryavesh the King wrote to all the nations ... peaceful greetings.* There were seven [nations] over whom he did not rule, as the verse (ibid. :2) states: *It found favor before Daryavesh and he appointed governors over the one hundred and twenty [states in his kingdom].*

And there is Koresh, of whom the verse (*Divrei ha-Yamim* II 36:23) states: *Thus says Koresh, King of Persia. All of the nations of the land have been given to me by God.* There, he was praising himself [for he did not actually reign over all of the nations].

COMMENTARY

Maharsha points out that the Talmud does not answer that Sancheriv, like Koresh later, was praising himself when he said: *who among the gods of all of the lands has saved their country from me.* Since he was addressing the people of Jerusalem who were well aware of the fact that he had not yet conquered the city, his statement would have been ridiculed had he meant to brag about his accomplishments. Rather, it must be understood literally as a threat; i.e., just as I have conquered all of the nations of the world, so too will I capture Jerusalem. However, since he failed to do so, he cannot be included among those kings who exercised worldwide dominion.

It is interesting to note that the capture of Jerusalem was always viewed as being *prima facie* evidence of world dominion.[200] Thus, we find that Alexander the Great interrupted his campaign against the Parthians and headed south to add Jerusalem to his crown — even though the city at that time was surely one of the least important in the area and was far from the main road to the Far East.

---

200 - Compare to *Yalkut Shimoni* to *Yehoshua* 7: *Any kingdom or government that did not exercise dominion over a part of Eretz Yisrael was considered worthless.*

This is further supported by later history where we find that incredible sums were raised and spent during the Middle Ages to send vast armies of Crusaders to Jerusalem to rescue her from the Moslem infidels, even though the city at the time was a tiny backwater without economic or political significance.

TALMUD

"בַּיָּמִים הָהֵם כְּשֶׁבֶת הַמֶּלֶךְ" וּכְתִיב בַּתְרֵיהּ: "בִּשְׁנַת שָׁלוֹשׁ לְמָלְכוֹ". אָמַר רָבָא: מַאי "כְּשֶׁבֶת". לְאַחַר שֶׁנִּתְיַשְּׁבָה דַעְתּוֹ. אָמַר: בֵּלְשַׁאצַּר מָנָה וְטָעָה, אֲנָא מָנִינָא וְלָא טָעֵינָא. מַאי הִיא? דִּכְתִיב: "כֹּה אָמַר ה', כִּי לְפִי מְלֹאת לְבָבֶל שִׁבְעִים שָׁנָה אֶפְקֹד אֶתְכֶם" וְגוֹ'. וּכְתִיב: "לִמְלֹאות לְחָרְבוֹת יְרוּשָׁלַיִם שִׁבְעִים שָׁנָה". חָשִׁיב אַרְבָּעִים וְחָמֵשׁ שְׁנִין דִּנְבוּכַדְנֶאצַּר, וְעֶשְׂרִים וְשָׁלֹשׁ דֶּאֱוִיל מְרוֹדַךְ, וְתַרְתֵּי דִידֵיהּ, הֲווֹ שִׁבְעִים. אַפִּיק מָאנֵי דְּבֵי מַקְדְּשָׁא וְאִשְׁתַּמֵּשׁ בְּהוֹן.

TRANSLATION

In those days, as the king sat (Esther 1:2). The verse continues: *in the third year of his reign.* Rava explained: What is the meaning of *as he sat*? After he became calm. He [Achashverosh] said [to himself]: "Balshetzar calculated and erred. I calculated and did not err." To what does this [calculation] refer? The verse *(Yirmiyahu 29:10)* states: *Thus says God. For when seventy years have been filled in Bavel, I shall redeem you.* And [another] verse states: *When seventy years have been filled from the destruction of Jerusalem.* [Balshetzar] calculated forty-five years of [the reign of] Nevuchadnezer, twenty-three years of Evel Merodach and two years of his own [reign, bringing the total to] seventy years. He took out the vessels [that had been taken as spoils from the] *Beis ha-Mikdash* and used them.

COMMENTARY

Balshetzer died on the very night that he celebrated his calculation that Yirmiyahu's prophecy would no longer be fulfilled. Achashverosh followed his example and also arranged a festive celebration when his calculations showed that the prophecy was to remain unfulfilled. Why were idol-worshipping gentile kings so concerned with the vision of a Prophet in whom they did not believe?

It would seem that the story of Pharaoh's Egypt and Israel's miraculous deliverance was still fresh in the minds of the Babylonian rulers. While they may not have worshipped the true God themselves, they knew and recognized that He was all powerful, and should He so desire, could instantaneously bring their empire to ruin. However, they also believed that He had become angry with Israel, the instrument for the expression of His will on earth, and was therefore content to allow the world to follow an order without His intervention. Thus, when Yirmiyahu prophesied that the exile — the expression of God's anger with Israel — was only to last for seventy years, the Babylonian kings lived in fear, for they understood that their hegemony was temporary. If that prophecy was to remain unfulfilled, on the other hand, it was an indication that God's anger with His people had not subsided and He was still content to allow others to rule the world as they saw fit. Thus, when Balshetzar — and later Achashverosh — calculated that the seventy years had passed, their joy was boundless, for they believed that God was no longer a threat to them.

TALMUD

וּמְנָא לָן דִּנְבוּכַדְנָאצַר – אַרְבָּעִים וְחָמֵשׁ שְׁנִין מָלַדְּי דְּאָמַר מַר: גָּלוּ בְשִׁבְעָה, גָּלוּ בִשְׁמוֹנֶה. גָּלוּ בִשְׁמוֹנֶה עֶשְׂרֵה, גָּלוּ בִתְשַׁע עֶשְׂרֵה.

גָּלוּ בְשִׁבְעָה לְכִבּוּשׁ יְהוֹיָקִים – גָּלוּת יְהוֹיָכִין, שֶׁהִיא שְׁנַת שְׁמוֹנֶה לִנְבוּכַדְנָאצַר. גָּלוּ בִשְׁמוֹנֶה עֶשְׂרֵה לְכִבּוּשׁ יְהוֹיָקִים – גָּלוּת צִדְקִיָּהוּ, שֶׁהִיא שְׁנַת תְּשַׁע עֶשְׂרֵה לְמַלְכוּת נְבוּכַדְנָאצַר. דְּאָמַר מַר: שָׁנָה רִאשׁוֹנָה – כִּבֵּשׁ נִינְוֵה. שָׁנָה שְׁנִיָּה – כִּבֵּשׁ יְהוֹיָקִים מֶלֶךְ יְהוּדָה. וּכְתִיב: "וַיְהִי בִשְׁלֹשִׁים וָשֶׁבַע שָׁנָה לְגָלוּת יְהוֹיָכִין מֶלֶךְ יְהוּדָה, בִּשְׁנֵים עָשָׂר חֹדֶשׁ בְּעֶשְׂרִים וְשִׁבְעָה לַחֹדֶשׁ, נָשָׂא אֱוִיל מְרֹדַךְ מֶלֶךְ בָּבֶל, בִּשְׁנַת מָלְכוֹ, אֶת רֹאשׁ יְהוֹיָכִין מֶלֶךְ יְהוּדָה, מִבֵּית כֶּלֶא". תַּמְנֵי, וּתְלָתִין וָשֶׁבַע, הֲרֵי אַרְבָּעִים וְחָמֵשׁ שְׁנִין דִּנְבוּכַדְנָאצַר,

TRANSLATION

And how do we know that Nevuchadnezer reigned for forty-five years? A Sage said: They were exiled in the seventh year, in the eighth year, in the eighteenth year and in the nineteenth year.

They were exiled in the seventh year after the conquest of Yehoyakim — the exile of Yehoyachin — which was the eighth year of the reign of Nevuchadnezer. And they were exiled in the eighteenth year of the conquest of Yehoyakim — the exile of Tzdkiyahu — which was in the nineteenth year of the reign of Nevuchadnezer. As a Sage said: In the first year [of his reign, Nevuchadnezer] conquered Nineveh. In the second year, he conquered Yehoyakim, king of Yehudah. And the verse (*Melachim* II 25:27) states: *And in the thirty-*

seventh year of the exile of Yehoyachin, king of Yehudah, on the twenty-seventh day of the twelfth month, Evel Merodach king of Bavel, in the first year of his reign, released Yehoyachin king of Yehudah from prison. Eight and thirty-seven equals the forty-five years of Nevuchadnezer.[201]

TALMUD

וְעֶשְׂרִים וְשָׁלֹש דֶאֱוִיל מְרוֹדַךְ – גְּמָרָא. וְתַרְתֵּי דִידֵיהּ הָא שִׁבְעִים. אֲמַר: תּוּ לָא אִיפְּרְקֵי, אַפִּיק וְאַיְיתֵי מָאנֵי דְבֵי מַקְדְּשָׁא וְאִשְׁתַּמֵּש בְּהוֹן. וְהַיְינוּ דְקָאֲמַר לֵיהּ דָּנִיֵּאל לְבֵלְשַׁאצַּר: "וְעַל מָרֵא שְׁמַיָּא הִתְרוֹמַמְתָּ, וּלְמָאנַיָּא דִי בַיְתֵהּ הַיְתִיו קֳדָמָךְ". וּכְתִיב: "בֵּהּ בְּלֵילְיָא קְטִיל בֵּלְאשַׁצַּר מַלְכָּא כַשְׂדָּאָה". וּכְתִיב: אֲמַר: אִיהוּ מָנָה וּטְעָה, אֲנָא מָנִינָא וְלָא טָעֵינָא. מִי כְּתִיב: "לְמַלְכוּת בָּבֶל"? "לְבָבֶל" כְּתִיב! מַאי "לְבָבֶל"? "לְגָלוּת בָּבֶל". כַּמָּה בְּצִירָן? תַּמְנֵי, חָשֵׁיב וְעַיֵּל תַּמְנֵי חִילוּפַיְיהוּ, חֲדָא דְבֵלְשַׁאצַּר, וְחָמֵשׁ דְּדָרְיָוֶשׁ וְדִכוֹרֶשׁ, וְתַרְתֵּי דִידֵיהּ, הָא שִׁבְעִין. כֵּיוָן דַּחֲזָא דְמָלוּ שִׁבְעִין, וְלָא אִיפְּרוּק, אֲמַר: הַשְׁתָּא וַדַּאי תּוּ לָא מִפְּרְקֵי. אַפִּיק וְאַיְיתֵי מָנַיָא דְבֵי מִקְדְּשָׁא, וְאִשְׁתַּמֵּש בְּהוֹן. אָתָא שָׂטָן וְרִקֵּד בֵּינֵיהֶם, וְהָרַג אֶת וַשְׁתִּי.

COMMENTARY

The twenty-three [years] of Evel Merodach are a tradition. Add his [Balshetzar's] two years [as king] and the total is seventy. [Balshetzar] said [to himself]: "They will no longer be redeemed [since seventy years have passed]. I will take out the vessels of the *Beis ha-Mikdash* and use them." And it was [in response] to this that Doniel said to Balshetzar (*Doniel 5:23*): *Before the Master of Heaven you have been haughty and the vessels of His house have been brought before you.* And the verse (ibid.) states: *And that very night, Balshetzar, king of the Chaldeans, was killed.* And the verse (ibid. 6:1) states: *And Daryavesh the Mede succeeded to the throne when he was sixty-two.*

He [Achashverosh] said [to himself]: "He [Balshetzar] calculated [the seventy years] and erred. I will make the calculation and will not err. The verse does not say *to the kingdom of Bavel*! It states *to Bavel* — i.e., to the exile of Bavel."

201 - I.e., since we know that Yehoyachin was exiled in the eighth year of Nevuchadnezer's reign, we can calculate that he reigned as king for a total of forty-five years, since the verse states that Yehoyachin was released from prison when Evel Merodach became king, thirty-seven years after he had been taken captive by Nevuchadnezer.

How many [years] were missing [from the seventy years of the prophecy]? Eight
[years]. He [Achashverosh] calculated and found eight additional years: One [year
during which] Balshetzar [reigned]; five [years] of Daryavesh and Koresh and two
of his own, for a total of seventy. When he saw that seventy years had passed
and they [the Jews] had not been redeemed, he said: "Now they will surely no
longer be redeemed." He went and brought the vessels from the *Beis ha-Mikdash*
and used them. Satan then came and danced between them and killed Vashti.

COMMENTARY

When Balshetzar celebrated the end of the threat of Yirmiyahu's prophecy by
using the vessels from the *Beis ha-Mikdash*, he paid for his transgression with
his life that very night. Yet when Achashverosh did the very same thing, he was
not punished directly or immediately! *Maharal* explains that Belshetzar was more
culpable than Achashverosh, for he had set a precedent. Although Achashverosh
should have understood what happened and should have therefore been even more
reluctant to use the holy vessels, we can understand that Achashverosh could
very well have interpreted Belshetzar's demise as being the result of natural
causes — the intrigues of his palace guard who supported the rebellion of
Koresh and Daryavesh — rather than Divine anger.

TALMUD

וְהָא שַׁפִּיר חָשִׁיב? אִיהוּ נַמִי מִיטְעָא טָעָה, דַּהֲוָה לֵיהּ לְמִימְנֵי מֵחָרְבוֹת
יְרוּשָׁלַיִם. סוֹף סוֹף כַּמָּה בְּצִירָן? חָד סְרֵי, אִיהוּ כַּמָּה מָלַדּ? אַרְבֵּיסָר.
וּבְאַרְבֵּיסָר דִּילֵיהּ אִיבָּעֵי לֵיהּ לְאִיבְּנוּיֵי מַקְדְּשָׁא? אַלָּמָה כְּתִיב: "בֵּאדַיִן בְּטֵלַת
עֲבִידַת בֵּית אֱלָהָא דִּי בִירוּשְׁלֶם", (וַהֲוָת בָּטְלָא עַד שְׁנַת תַּרְתֵּין לְמַלְכוּת
דָּרְיָוֶשׁ מֶלֶדּ פָּרָס)?
אָמַר רָבָא: שָׁנִים מְקֻטָּעוֹת הָווּ. תַּנְיָא נַמִי הָכֵי: עוֹד שָׁנָה אַחֶרֶת לְבָבֶל, וְעָמַד
דָּרְיָוֶשׁ וְהִשְׁלִימָהּ.

TRANSLATION

But did he [Acheshverosh] not calculate correctly? He too erred, for he should
have counted from the destruction of Jerusalem. In any event, how many [years]
were missing [from his count]? Eleven [years]. How many years did he reign?
Fourteen. [According to the calculation then] in the fourteenth year of his reign
the *Beis ha-Mikdash* should have already been built [since the seventy years

prophecied by Yirmiyahu had already passed]. Why then does the verse (*Ezra* 4:24) state: *And with this the work on the House of God in Jerusalem ceased* [from the time of Koresh I until the second year of the reign of Daryevesh II]?[202]

Rava explained: Some of the years [of the reign of these kings] were not complete. **[12a]** We learned similarly [in a *beraisa*]: There was still one year of Bavel [i.e., of the seventy years which Yirmiyahu had prophecied that the exile would last] and Daryevesh [II] completed it.

COMMENTARY

Balshetzar's calculation of the seventy years of exile began from the year 3318 when Nevuchadnezer had ascended the throne. Thus, he determined that in the year 3389 there were no longer grounds to fear that the prophecy would be fulfilled. Achashverosh made his calculation beginning from the year 3327, when Nevuchadnezer took King Yechonyah of Yehudah captive. The true calculation should be made from the year 3338, the year when the *Beis ha-Mikdash* was destroyed. Thus, the seventy years of exile ended in 3408 when Darius II permitted the resumption of the construction of the *Beis ha-Mikdash* that had begun in 3392 under Koresh.

TALMUD

אָמַר רָבָא: וְאַף דָּנִיֵּאל בְּהַהוּא מִנְיָנָא מָנָה וְטָעָה, דִּכְתִיב: "בִּשְׁנַת אַחַת
לְמָלְכוֹ, אֲנִי דָּנִיֵּאל בִּינֹתִי בַּסְּפָרִים, מִסְפַּר הַשָּׁנִים אֲשֶׁר הָיָה דְבַר ה' אֶל
יִרְמְיָה הַנָּבִיא, לְמַלֹּאות לְחָרְבוֹת יְרוּשָׁלַיִם שִׁבְעִים שָׁנָה". מִדְּקָאָמַר: "אֲנִי
דָּנִיֵּאל בִּינֹתִי בַּסְּפָרִים", מִכְּלָל דְּאִיהוּ נַמֵי טָעָה.

TRANSLATION

Rava taught: Even Doniel counted [the seventy years] and erred in his calculation. The verse (*Doniel* 9:2) states: *In the first year of his* [Daryevesh I]

---

202 - *Rashi* (ד"ה באדין) notes that Daryevesh II was also known as Koresh and Artachashta. He resumed construction of the second *Beis ha-Mikdash*, which had begun under Koresh I — Achashverosh's predecessor on the Persian throne. The seventy years prophesied by Yirmiyahu are thus calculated from the destruction of Jerusalem until the rebuilding by Daryevesh II. Given the years that Nevuchadnezer, Evel Merodach, Balshetzer, Daryevesh I, Koresh I and Achashverosh ruled before Daryevesh II, it would seem that more than seventy years had elapsed.

reign, I, Doniel, examined the figures[203] *[to calculate] the number of years that had passed from when God spoke to the Prophet Yirmiyahu, when the seventy years of the destruction of Jerusalem would be complete.* Since the verse states *I, Doniel, examined the figures*, this implies that he too erred.

COMMENTARY

While a prophet — in this case Doniel — can see a vision that informs him of what will happen in the future, he is not necessarily privy to the timing of that event or of the full import of his message.

Rambam[204] writes: *All of these things [calculations of the redemption] and those that are similar to them are beyond man's comprehension and will not be known until they occur, for they are hidden from the Prophets and even the Sages have no tradition regarding them [i.e., their meaning].*

TALMUD

מִכָּל מָקוֹם קָשׁוּ קְרָאֵי אַהֲדָדֵי, כְּתִיב: "לְפִי מְלֹאת לְבָבֶל שִׁבְעִים שָׁנָה". וּכְתִיב: "לְחָרְבוֹת יְרוּשָׁלַיִם"? אָמַר רָבָא: לִפְקִידָה בְּעָלְמָא, וְהַיְינוּ דִכְתִיב: "כֹּה אָמַר כּוֹרֶשׁ מֶלֶךְ פָּרַס, כָּל מַמְלְכוֹת הָאָרֶץ נָתַן לִי ה' אֱלֹהֵי הַשָּׁמַיִם, וְהוּא פָקַד עָלַי לִבְנוֹת לוֹ בַיִת בִּירוּשָׁלָיִם".

TRANSLATION

In any event, the verses contradict each other! The verse (*Yirmiyahu* 29:10) states: *When seventy years have been filled in Bavel* and the other verse (*Doniel* 9:2) states: *When the seventy years of the destruction of Jerusalem [would be complete]*? Rava explained: [the reference in the verse in *Yirmiyahu* is to] a partial redemption, as the verse (*Ezra* 1:2) states: *Thus said Koresh, king of Persia. All of the nations of the land have been given to me by God, the Lord of the Heavens, and He commanded me to build a home for Him in Jerusalem.*

COMMENTARY

Koresh ascended to the throne in 3389, when Balshetzar died and control of the Babylonian empire passed into the hands of the Medes and Persians. One of his first acts was to allow Ezra and Nechemiah to take the Jews back to the Land of Israel and begin construction of the *Beis ha-Mikdash*. Although this was brought to a stop due to the intervention of Israel's enemies, as the Talmud will

---

203 - See *Rashi*, ד״ה בינתי בספרים.
204 - *Hilchos Melachim* 12:2.

go on to explain, it can surely be seen as a partial redemption. This took place seventy years after King Yehoyachin of Yehudah had been taken into captivity.

The term פקידה — *command* — is often used in connection with redemption — on both the national and personal level. Thus we find it used in terms of the redemption from Egypt as well as in the concept of God ordering the wombs of barren women to give birth.[205] R. Tzadok *ha-Kohen* of Lublin explains that פקידה refers to the concept of God reviewing, as it were, the state of the world so as to determine if it is following a path that is consistent with the intent of Creation, or if mankind has degenerated to an extent that calls for Him to intervene so as to return them to the proper path.[206]

In this same sense, we can understand the Divine command to Koresh. God, as it were, had examined the state of His people and determined that the time was suitable for a change in their status — i.e., the Babylonian exile could be ended at this point and they could be permitted to return to their land. The seventy years of exile could be counted from the captivity of Yehoyachin rather than from the destruction of the *Beis ha-Mikdash*.

TALMUD

דָּרַשׁ רַב נַחְמָן בַּר רַב חִסְדָּא: מַאי דִּכְתִיב: "כֹּה אָמַר ה' לִמְשִׁיחוֹ לְכוֹרֶשׁ". וְכִי כּוֹרֶשׁ מָשִׁיחַ הָיָה?! אֶלָּא אָמַר הַקָּדוֹשׁ בָּרוּךְ הוּא לַמָּשִׁיחַ: קוֹבֵל אֲנִי עָלֶיךָ עַל כּוֹרֶשׁ, אֲנִי אָמַרְתִּי: הוּא יִבְנֶה בֵיתִי, וִיקַבֵּץ גָּלִיּוֹתִי, וְהוּא אָמַר: "מִי בָכֶם מִכָּל עַמּוֹ, ה' אֱלֹהָיו עִמּוֹ וְיָעַל".

TRANSLATION

R. Nachman bar R. Chisda taught: What is the meaning of the verse (*Yeshayahu* 45:1) [that states:] *Thus said God to His messiah, Koresh*? Was Koresh messiah? Rather, God said to the messiah: I complain to you about Koresh. I said: He will build My home and gather My exile, and He [Koresh] said (*Divrei ha-Yamim* II 36:23): *Those among you of His people whom God is with shall go up [and rebuild the Beis ha-Mikdash].*

COMMENTARY

Rashi points out that the cantillation supports R. Nachman bar Chisda's

---

205 - E.g., *Bereishis* 21:1.

206 - R. Tzadok's interpretation would seem to suggest that God changes His plans, as it were, to react to man's actions. See also *Rinah Shel Torah*, The Commentary of the *Netziv* to *Shir ha-Shirim*, 5:1 where the author develops a similar idea.

explanation, for the note under the word *meshicho* — His messiah — is a *zarka* which serves to separate the word from the following word Koresh, indicating that God was speaking to the messiah about Koresh.

Koresh had the opportunity to fulfill a historical role, for it was a time of Divine favor and had he so chosen, he could have brought about the construction of the second *Beis ha-Mikdash* by ordering the Jews to return to the Land of Israel. However, he chose to make their return voluntary and in doing so brought God, as it were, disappointment.

In his commentary to *Shir ha-Shirim, Netziv* explains that the Jews were reluctant to return with Ezra and Nechemiah, despite the Divine opportunity granted them through Koresh, because they feared that they would once again fall into the trap of worshipping false gods and would again incur Divine wrath. They therefore preferred to remain in exile in Bavel where there was less temptation to stray from the path of God.

TALMUD

כְּתִיב: "חֵיל פָּרַס וּמָדַי הַפַּרְתְּמִים". וּכְתִיב: "לְמַלְכֵי מָדַי וּפָרַס". אָמַר רָבָא: אִתְנוּיֵי אִתְּנוּ בַּהֲדֵי הֲדָדֵי: אִי מְנַיְיכוּ מַלְכֵי, מִינָן אֲפַרְכֵי. וְאִי מִינָן מַלְכֵי, מְנַיְיכוּ אֲפַרְכֵי.

TRANSLATION

The verse (*Esther* 1:3) states: *The officers of Persia and Media, the officials*, [whereas] another verse (ibid. 10:2) states: *[... are recorded in the chronicles] of the kings of Media and Persia*? [The verses are contradictary, for the former seems to establish that the Medes were no more than officials, whereas the latter verse would seem to imply that they also served as rulers of the empire.] Rava explained: They [the Persians and the Medes] reached an agreement with each other. If the kings are [appointed] from you [i.e., from one of the two nations], then the local officials will be [appointed] from [among] us. And if the kings are [appointed] from us, then the local officials will be [appointed] from [among] you.

COMMENTARY

Gra points out that throughout the *Megillah*, the Persian are referred to before the Medes. It is only in the last verse that the Medes are mentioned first. However, the first ruler of this joint kingdom was Daryavesh — a Mede! He answers that all of the verses of the *Megillah* are contemporary accounts written in the time of Achashverosh who was a Persian. Thus, it was natural to mention the Persians first. The last verse, however, refers to the chronicles of the joint kingdom — chronicles that begin from Daryavesh the Mede. That verse therefore refers to the Medes first.

TALMUD

"בְּהַרְאֹתוֹ אֶת עֹשֶׁר כְּבוֹד מַלְכוּתוֹ, וְאֶת יְקָר תִּפְאֶרֶת" וְגוֹ'. אָמַר רַבִּי יוֹסֵי בְּרַבִּי חֲנִינָא: מְלַמֵּד שֶׁלָּבַשׁ בִּגְדֵי כְהֻנָּה. כְּתִיב הָכָא: "וְאֶת יְקָר תִּפְאֶרֶת גְדוּלָתוֹ". וּכְתִיב הָתָם: "לְכָבוֹד וּלְתִפְאָרֶת".

"יָמִים רַבִּים שְׁמוֹנִים וּמְאַת יוֹם". וּכְתִיב: "וּבִמְלוֹאת הַיָּמִים הָאֵלֶּה" וְגוֹ'. רַב וּשְׁמוּאֵל, חַד אָמַר: מֶלֶךְ פִּקֵּחַ הָיָה. וְחַד אָמַר: מֶלֶךְ טִפֵּשׁ הָיָה. לְמַאן דְּאָמַר: פִּקֵּחַ הָיָה, שַׁפִּיר עָבִיד דְּקָרִיב רְחִיקֵי בְּרֵישָׁא, דִּבְנֵי מָאתֵיהּ כָּל אֵימַת דְּבָעֵי לְהוּ מִקְרַב לְהוּ. וּמַאן דְּאָמַר: טִפֵּשׁ הָיָה, בְּנֵי מָאתֵיהּ אִיבְּעֵי בְּרֵישָׁא לִקְרוּבֵי – דְּאִי מָרְדוּ בֵּיהּ הַנָּךְ, קָיְימֵי הַנֵּי וְהָווּ בַּהֲדֵיהּ.

שָׁאֲלוּ תַּלְמִידָיו אֶת רַבִּי שִׁמְעוֹן בַּר יוֹחַאי: מִפְּנֵי מָה נִתְחַיְּבוּ שׂוֹנְאֵיהֶם שֶׁל יִשְׂרָאֵל שֶׁבְּאוֹתוֹ הַדּוֹר כְּלָיָה? אָמַר לָהֶם: אִמְרוּ לִי אַתֶּם. אָמְרוּ לוֹ: מִפְּנֵי שֶׁנֶּהֱנוּ מִסְּעוּדָתוֹ שֶׁל אוֹתוֹ רָשָׁע. אָמַר לָהֶם: אִם כֵּן שֶׁל שׁוּשָׁן יֵהָרֵגוּ, שֶׁל כָּל הָעוֹלָם כֻּלּוֹ לֹא יֵהָרֵגוּ? אָמְרוּ לוֹ: אֱמוֹר לָנוּ אָתָּה. אָמַר לָהֶם: מִפְּנֵי שֶׁהִשְׁתַּחֲווּ לַצֶּלֶם. אָמְרוּ לוֹ: וְכִי מַשּׂוֹא פָנִים יֵשׁ בַּדָּבָר?! אָמַר לָהֶם: הֵם לֹא עָשׂוּ אֶלָּא לְפָנִים, אַף הַקָּדוֹשׁ בָּרוּךְ הוּא לֹא עָשָׂה עִמָּהֶם אֶלָּא לְפָנִים, וְהַיְינוּ דִּכְתִיב: "כִּי לֹא עִנָּה מִלִּבּוֹ, וַיַּגֶּה בְּנֵי אִישׁ".

TRANSLATION

[The verse (*Esther* 1:4) states:] *When he flaunted the wealth of the honor of his kingdom and the expense of the splendor [of his greatness]*. R. Yosi b'R. Chanina explained: This teaches us that he [Achashverosh] wore the garments of the *kohen gadol*. The verse here states *and the splendor of the greatness* and there (*Shemos* 28:40) [regarding the special garments of the *kohen gadol*] the verse states: *[and you shall make holy garments for your brother Aharon] for honor and splendor*.

[The verse (*Esther* 1:5) states:] *for many days — one hundred and eighty days*, and it states (ibid.) *and when these days were finished [the king made a celebration for all of the people in the capital Shushan, from great to insignificant, a party lasting seven days]*. Rav and Shmuel [differed as to what can be inferred from Achashverosh's actions]. One said: [This indicates that] he was a clever king. And one said: [This indicates that] he was a foolish king. According to the one who says that he was a clever king, he [Achashverosh] acted correctly, for he first won the allegiance of those who lived far away [from the capital by making a celebration for them], for the residents of his area could be drawn close to him whenever he chose to do so. And according to the one who said that he was a foolish king; he should have first won the allegiance of the residents of his area, for if those [the people who lived far away] would rebel against him, these [the residents of his area] would remain loyal and support him.

R. Shimon ben Gamliel's students asked him: Why were the enemies of Israel[207] in that generation deserving of annihilation? He answered them: You tell me! They replied: Because they enjoyed the feast of that wicked person [Achashverosh]. He said to them: If so [i.e., if the reason is as you explained], then only those in Shushan should be killed and those in the rest of the world should not be killed [since they did not participate in Achashverosh's feast]? They then said to him: You tell us [why they were deserving of death]. He answered: Because they bowed down to the idol [which Nevuchadnezer established in Bavel].[208] They asked him: Is there favoritism here [i.e., if they were guilty of idolatry, why were they saved and not killed]? He replied: They only acted on the surface [i.e., they only prostrated themselves to Nevuchadnezer's idol because they were forced to do so]. As a consequence [i.e., because they never truly accepted the idol], God only threatened them on the surface [i.e., the threat against them was external and could thus be averted through their repentance]. This is what the verse (*Eichah* 3:23) states: *Since he did not afflict willingly, his pain is from man.*

COMMENTARY

The verse cited from *Eichah* is offered as support for Rabban Gamliel's contention that God does not ordain irrevocable punishment if man sins because of extenuating circumstances. While the Jews were dutybound to refuse to bow down to Nevuchadnezer's idol — as did Chananiah, Mishael and Azaryah who were cast into the furnace as a result — their failure to do so is understandable under the circumstances. *Maharsha* explains that in these situations, God allows their enemies to gain the upper hand and threaten them with extinction.

---

207 - The Talmud often uses this phrase as a euphemism for the Jews themselves.
208 - See *Doniel* 3:1.

Realizing then that their only hope is to place their trust in God, they repent and all of their sins are thus forgiven.[209]

TALMUD

"בַּחֲצַר גִּנַּת בִּיתַן הַמֶּלֶךְ". רַב וּשְׁמוּאֵל, חַד אָמַר: הָרָאוּי לְחָצֵר - לְחָצֵר, הָרָאוּי לַגִּנָּה - לַגִּנָּה, הָרָאוּי לַבִּיתָן - לַבִּיתָן. וְחַד אָמַר: הוֹשִׁיבָן בֶּחָצֵר - וְלֹא הֶחֱזִיקָתָן, בַּגִּנָּה - וְלֹא הֶחֱזִיקָתָן, עַד שֶׁהִכְנִיסָם לַבִּיתָן וְהֶחֱזִיקָתָן. בְּמָתְנִיתָא תָּנָא: הוֹשִׁיבָן בֶּחָצֵר וּפָתַח לָהֶם שְׁנֵי פְּתָחִים, אֶחָד לַגִּנָּה וְאֶחָד לַבִּיתָן.

TRANSLATION

[The verse (*Esther* 1:5) states:] *In the courtyard of the garden of the king's orchard.* Rav and Shmuel [differed as to how this should be explained]. One said: Those who were worthy of [being seated in] the courtyard, were in the courtyard. Those who were worthy of [being seated in] the garden, were in the garden. Those who were worthy of [being seated in] the orchard, were in the orchard. And the other said: He [first] seated them in the courtyard, but it was not large enough. [He then seated some of the guests] in the garden, but it was not large enough. Finally, he placed them in the orchard and it was large enough.

In a *beraisa* we learned. He seated them in the courtyard and made two openings for them — one to the garden and one to the orchard.

COMMENTARY

It would seem that the dispute here between Rav and Shmuel is an extension of their earlier dispute as to whether Achashverosh was clever or foolish. According to the opinion that he was clever, his use of the garden, courtyard and orchard was planned so that he could separate his guests according to their stature — those who were most important would be seated in the orchard, those less important in the courtyard and the least important guests in the garden. According to the opinion that he was foolish, the use of the garden, courtyard and orchard reveals that Achashverosh's celebration was marked by poor preparation and the guests were seated throughout the palace grounds.

TALMUD

"חוּר כַּרְפַּס וּתְכֵלֶת". מַאי "חוּר"? רַב וּשְׁמוּאֵל, חַד אָמַר: חוֹרֵי חוֹרֵי. וְחַד אָמַר: מֵילַת לְבָנָה הִצִּיעַ לָהֶם.

---

209 - See *Sanhedrin* 97b and *Rambam, Hilchos Teshuvah* 7:8.

"כַּרְפַּס", אָמַר רַבִּי יוֹסֵי בַּר חֲנִינָא: כָּרִים שֶׁל פַּסִים.

"מִטּוֹת זָהָב וָכֶסֶף", תַּנְיָא, אָמַר רַבִּי יְהוּדָה: הָרָאוּי לַכֶּסֶף - לַכֶּסֶף. הָרָאוּי
לַזָּהָב - לַזָּהָב. אָמַר לוֹ רַבִּי נְחֶמְיָה: אִם כֵּן, קִנְאָה אַתָּה מַטִּיל בַּסְעָדָה? אֶלָּא
- הֵן שֶׁל כֶּסֶף וְרַגְלֵיהֶם שֶׁל זָהָב.

"רִצְפַת בַּהַט וָשֵׁשׁ", מַאי "בַּהַט"? אָמַר רַבִּי אַסִּי: אֲבָנִים שֶׁמִּתְחוֹטְטוֹת עַל
בַּעֲלֵיהֶן. וְכֵן הוּא אוֹמֵר: "כִּי אַבְנֵי נֵזֶר מִתְנוֹסְסוֹת עַל אַדְמָתוֹ".

"וְדַר וְסֹחָרֶת", רַב אָמַר: דָּאֲרֵי דָאֲרֵי. וּשְׁמוּאֵל אָמַר: אֶבֶן טוֹבָה יֵשׁ בִּכְרַכֵּי
הַיָּם וְדָרָה שְׁמָהּ, הוֹשִׁיבָהּ בְּאֶמְצַע סְעוּדָה וּמְאִירָה לָהֶם כַּצָּהֳרַיִם. דְּבֵי רַבִּי
יִשְׁמָעֵאל תָּנָא: שֶׁקָּרָא דְרוֹר לְכָל בַּעֲלֵי סְחוֹרָה.

TRANSLATION

[The verse (*Esther* 1:6) states:] *There were curtains of white, fine cotton and blue, held with cords of fine linen and purple.* What is *chur*?[210] Rav and Shmuel [differed as to how this should be explained]. One said: They were lace. And the other said: He made them translucent.[211]

[What is meant by] *karpas*? R. Yosi bar Chanina explained: Pillows with stripes.[212]

[The verse (*Esther* 1:6) states:] *Beds of gold and silver.* We learned in a *beraisa*, R. Yehudah said: The ones who were worthy of silver were given silver and those who were worthy of gold were given gold. R. Nechemyah said to him: If so [i.e., if this is the interpretation] this would have caused jealousy at the feast.[213] Rather, they [the beds] were of silver and their legs were made of gold.

[The verse (*Esther* 1:6) states:] *A pavement of precious stones and marble.* What is *bahat*? R. Asi explained: Stones which a person has to search for. As the verse (*Zecharyah* 9:16) states: *Like precious stones uplifted from the ground.*

[The verse (*Esther* 1:6) states:] *And dar and sochares.* Rav explained: [The word *dar*

210 - The Talmud's question is based on the use of the word חור for curtains rather than the more common וילון. The Talmud responds that the word was used because it also describes the design of the curtains.

211 - The first interpretation is based on interpreting the word חור as having holes. The second interpretation is based on interpreting the word as pale white. See *Rashi*, מילת לבנה ד"ה and ד"ה חורי חורי.

212 - I.e., the word כרפס is interpreted as an acronym of the words כרים של פסים — *striped pillows.*

213 - I.e., if Achashverosh displayed favoritism by giving some of his guests gold beds, he would have fostered jealousy which would be antithetical to that which he was trying to accomplish — winning popular support for himself as king.

means] they were arranged in rows. Shmuel explained: There is a stone in the depths of the sea called *dara*.[214] He placed it in the middle of the banquet [hall] and it gave light[215] like the afternoon. The school of R. Yishmael expounded: [The inference from the use of the phrase *dar* and *sochares* is that] he [Acheshverosh] granted freedom[216] to all of the businessmen.

TALMUD

"וְהַשְׁקוֹת בִּכְלֵי זָהָב וְכֵלִים מִכֵּלִים שׁוֹנִים", "מְשׁוּנִים" מִבָּעֵי לֵיהּ! אָמַר רָבָא: יָצְתָה בַּת־קוֹל וְאָמְרָה לָהֶם: רִאשׁוֹנִים כָּלוּ מִפְּנֵי כֵלִים, וְאַתֶּם שׁוֹנִים וְשׁוֹתִים בָּהֶם?!

"וְיֵין מַלְכוּת רָב", אָמַר רַב: מְלַמֵּד שֶׁכָּל אֶחָד וְאֶחָד הִשְׁקָהוּ יַיִן שֶׁהוּא גָּדוֹל מִמֶּנּוּ בְּשָׁנִים.

"וְהַשְׁתִיָּה כַדָּת", אָמַר רַב חָנָן מִשּׁוּם רַבִּי מֵאִיר: כְּדָת שֶׁל תּוֹרָה, מַה דָּת שֶׁל תּוֹרָה – אֲכִילָה מְרֻבָּה מִשְׁתִיָּה, אַף סְעֻדָּתוֹ שֶׁל אוֹתוֹ רָשָׁע – אֲכִילָה מְרֻבָּה מִשְׁתִיָּה.

TRANSLATION

[The verse (*Esther* 1:7) states:] *And he poured from golden pitchers into similar vessels.* It should say *different*?[217] Rava explained: A Heavenly voice went out and declared to them: The first ones were destroyed because of [the use of] vessels and you repeat [their transgression] and drink from them!?

---

214 - Steinsaltz identifies the term as coming from the Arabic *dura — a pearl*.

215 - *Rashi* writes that Shmuel's explanation is based on the similarity between the word *sochares* and the Aramaic *sihara* which means light. R. Akiva Eiger points out that later (13a, s.v. אסתהר) *Rashi* quotes the *Targum* which renders *sihara* as moon. Perhaps the word *sihara* is related to *zohar — shining —* and can thus be used either for moon or for another source of light. See *Metzudas David* to *Yechezkel* 5:2, s.v. כמראה זהר.

216 - I.e., he freed them from the obligation to pay taxes so that they would not claim that they had financed the banquet. Unlike Rav and Shmuel who interpret the phrase *dar* and *sochares* as describing the lavishness of the banquet consistent with the previous phrases, the school of R. Yishmael offer a homiletical interpretation based on the similarity between the phrase *dar* and *sochares* and the Hebrew *dror — freedom —* and *sochares — sechorah — commerce*.

217 - I.e., the Hebrew שונים can be interpreted as repeated. Had the author intended to inform us that each person was served in a different type of vessel, the term משונים would be more appropriate. Rava therefore explained that the author chose the term to indicate that Belshetzar's transgression of using the vessels looted from the *Beis ha-Mikdash* was repeated at the banquet prepared by Acheshverosh.

[The verse (*Esther* 1:7) states:] *And much royal wine.* Rav explained: This teaches us that each and everyone was poured wine older than he in years.[218]

[The verse (*Esther* 1:8) states:] *And the drinking was as ordained.* R. Chanan explained in the name of R. Meir: As the Torah ordains [that there be] more food than drink, so too was it with the banquet of that wicked man — more food than drink.

COMMENTARY

Maharsha comments that Achashverosh may have thought that Balshetzar was punished because the people at his celebration became intoxicated while using the vessels from the *Beis ha-Mikdash*. Achashverosh was therefore careful to serve more food than wine so that the people would not become drunk and thus the use of the holy vessels would not be considered to have degraded them.

TALMUD

"אֵין אֹנֵס", אָמַר רַבִּי אֶלְעָזָר: מְלַמֵּד שֶׁכָּל אֶחָד וְאֶחָד הִשְׁקָהוּ יַיִן שֶׁל מְדִינָתוֹ.

"כִּי כֵן יִסַּד הַמֶּלֶךְ עַל כָּל רַב בֵּיתוֹ, לַעֲשׂוֹת כִּרְצוֹן אִישׁ וָאִישׁ", אָמַר רָבָא: לַעֲשׂוֹת כִּרְצוֹן מָרְדְּכַי וְהָמָן. מָרְדְּכַי, דִּכְתִיב: "אִישׁ יְהוּדִי הָיָה". הָמָן, דִּכְתִיב: "אִישׁ צַר וְאוֹיֵב".

TRANSLATION

[The verse (*Esther* 1:8) states:] *There was no force.* R. Elazar explained: This teaches us that each and everyone was given wine from his country of origin [and was thus not forced to drink wine that he was unfamiliar with].

[The verse (*Esther* 1:8) states:] *For thus had the king established to all of the servants of his home, [ordering them] to fulfill the wishes of every man.* Rava explained: [The phrase *to fulfill the desire of every man* means] to fulfill the desires of Mordechai and Haman. [As regards] Mordechai, the verse states: *There was a Jewish man.* [As regards] Haman, the verse states: *A man who causes trouble and who is an enemy.*

---

218 - It would seem that Rav was reluctant to literally interpret the word רב as copious, for it is self-evident that much wine would be served at a royal banquet. Moreover, the quantity of wine served would not necessarily testify to the royal nature of the feast. Instead, he explained that רב is to be understood as older (as used, for example, in *Bereishis* 25:23), indicating that Achashverosh served the finest wines from the royal storehouses.

COMMENTARY

Riaf comments that both Mordechai and Haman were interested that the Jews not become intoxicated, but for diametrically opposite reasons. Mordechai was afraid that the Jews who participated in the king's celebration might become drunk and act like their gentile neighbors. Haman wanted them to remain sober so that they could be judged culpable by God for having participated in the festivities.

TALMUD

"גַּם וַשְׁתִּי הַמַּלְכָּה עָשְׂתָה מִשְׁתֵּה נָשִׁים בֵּית הַמַּלְכוּת", "בֵּית הַנָּשִׁים" מִיבָּעֵי
לֵיהּ! אָמַר רָבָא: מְלַמֵּד שֶׁשְּׁנֵיהֶם לִדְבַר עֲבֵירָה נִתְכַּוְּנוּ, הַיְינוּ דְאָמְרֵי אֱנָשֵׁי:
אִיהוּ - בֵּי-קָרֵי, וְאִתְּתֵיהּ - בֵּי-בּוּצִינֵי.

TRANSLATION

[The verse (*Esther* 1:9) states:] *Vashti the queen also made a banquet, for the women in the royal house* . It should say *in the house of the women* [rather than *in the royal house*]? Rava explained: This teaches us that both of them intended to sin.[219] As people are wont to say: He uses pumpkins and his wife **[12b]** uses squash.

COMMENTARY

The Talmud[220] quotes R. Yochanan as teaching that if a man is unfaithful to his wife, his wife will be unfaithful to him and ends with the same parable. *Rashi* explains that just as pumpkins and squash are of the same family of vegetables, whatever a man does, he can expect his wife to do the same. In this case, just as Achashverosh acted without restraint and allowed his celebration to degenerate into a public display of liscentiousness, so too did Vashti act when she held her celebration in the palace rather than in her own quarters. *Eitz Yosef*, quoting *Tosafos Shantz*, explains that while a man uses pumpkin leaves which are large to figuratively hide his infidelity, a woman uses squash·leaves, which are small, to hide hers, for if she is drawn to act immorally, she is even more brazen than her husband.

---

219 - I.e., Vashti had no sense of propriety and was perfectly willing to show off her beauty to all of the assembled guests. She therefore held her celebration on the palace grounds rather than in her own private palace — the house of the women.

220 - סוטה י..

TALMUD

"בַּיּוֹם הַשְּׁבִיעִי כְּטוֹב לֵב הַמֶּלֶךְ בַּיָּיִן", אַטוּ עַד יוֹם הַשְּׁבִיעִי לָא טָב לִבֵּיהּ
בְּיָיִן?! אָמַר רָבָא: יוֹם הַשְּׁבִיעִי – שַׁבָּת הָיָה, שֶׁיִּשְׂרָאֵל אוֹכְלִין וְשׁוֹתִין,
מַתְחִילִין בְּדִבְרֵי תוֹרָה וּבְדִבְרֵי תוּשְׁבָּחוֹת. אֲבָל גּוֹיִם (עוֹבְדֵי כּוֹכָבִים)
שֶׁאוֹכְלִין וְשׁוֹתִין, אֵין מַתְחִילִין אֶלָּא בְּדִבְרֵי תִפְלוּת. וְכֵן בִּסְעוּדָתוֹ שֶׁל אוֹתוֹ
רָשָׁע. הַלָּלוּ אוֹמְרִים: מָדִיּוֹת נָאוֹת, וְהַלָּלוּ אוֹמְרִים: פַּרְסִיּוֹת נָאוֹת. אָמַר לָהֶם
אֲחַשְׁוֵרוֹשׁ: כְּלִי שֶׁאֲנִי מִשְׁתַּמֵּשׁ בּוֹ, אֵינוֹ לֹא מָדִי וְלֹא פַּרְסִי, אֶלָּא כַּשְׂדִּי.
רְצוֹנְכֶם לִרְאוֹתָהּ? אָמְרוּ לֵיהּ: אִין, וּבִלְבַד שֶׁתְּהֵא עֲרֻמָּה. שֶׁבְּמִדָּה שֶׁאָדָם
מוֹדֵד, בָּהּ מוֹדְדִין לוֹ, מְלַמֵּד שֶׁהָיְתָה וַשְׁתִּי הָרְשָׁעָה מְבִיאָה אֶת בְּנוֹת יִשְׂרָאֵל
וּמַפְשִׁיטָתָן עֲרֻמּוֹת, וְהָיְתָה עוֹשָׂה בָּהֶן מְלָאכָה בְּשַׁבָּת, וְהַיְינוּ דִכְתִיב: "זָכַר
אֶת וַשְׁתִּי וְאֵת אֲשֶׁר עָשָׂתָה, וְאֵת אֲשֶׁר נִגְזַר עָלֶיהָ", כַּאֲשֶׁר עָשְׂתָה – כֵּן נִגְזַר
עָלֶיהָ.

TRANSLATION

[The verse (*Esther* 1:10) states:] *On the seventh day, when the king was in a good
mood because of the wine.* And until the seventh day did the wine not put him
into a good mood!? Rava explained: *The seventh day* — it was Shabbos. [On
this day] when Israel eats and drinks, they speak words of Torah and praises [of
God]. But the gentiles, when they eat and drink, [they] even begin with
vulgarity. And so it was with the banquet of that wicked man. Some of them
[those present] contended: The women of Media are the prettiest. And some
contended: The women of Persia are the prettiest. Achashverosh told them: The
vessel [i.e., Vashti] which I use is neither Median or Persian, but is a Casdean.
Would you like to see her? They responded: Yes, but only if she is naked. [And
why was Vashti punished in this manner?] In the manner in which man sins, so is
he punished [i.e., the form of punishment is similar to the crime for which the
person is punished]. This [the form of punishment that Vashti was subjected to]
teaches us that Vashti the wicked would bring Jewish girls, strip them naked and
make them work on Shabbos.[221] And this is what the verse says: *H e
remembered Vashti, and what she had done and what had been ordered upon her
— as she did, so was ordered upon her.

---

221 - I.e., the fact that Vashti was forced to appear naked on the seventh day of the
banquet shows us that she herself was guilty of the same type of crime.

COMMENTARY

While the literal meaning of the word ערומה is naked, it is somewhat difficult to understand how Achashverosh could have lost all vestiges of royal propriety and ordered that his queen appear without clothes. Surely one of his advisers would have quietly approached him and told him that he was degrading himself publicly! Moreover, even though we have already seen that Achashverosh intended to sin — i.e., that he was not adverse to immoral behavior — the Talmud later points out that he did have a sense of modesty.[222] How then can we understand his agreement that Vashti appear naked?

We might conjecture that Achashverosh's guests contended that Vashti's beauty was no more than a result of her dressing in royal clothing and benefitting from the cosmetic treatments of the palace beauticians. "Dress her like a commoner and her beauty will disappear," they may well have said. Achashverosh accepted their challenge and this is what he ordered Vashti to do. Vashti's reaction — she stressed her royal lineage and Achashverosh's lack thereof — is thus most understandable.

The Talmud[223] records that R. Yochanan used to refer to his clothing as מכבדי — that which brings me honor. When a respected person has his fine clothing taken away from him and is forced to dress like everyone else, he is stripped of his honor and is naked in a sense. Support for this can also be drawn from Scripture (*Yeshayahu* 3:20) where the verse states: *as My servant Yeshayahu went, naked and barefoot for three years.* The Talmud[224] explains that the Prophet wore torn clothing.[225]

TALMUD

"וְתְּמָאֵן הַמַּלְכָּה וַשְׁתִּי", מִכְּדִי, פְּרִיצְתָּא הַוְיָא, דְּאָמַר מַר: שְׁנֵיהֶם לִדְבַר עֲבֵירָה נִתְכַּוְּנוּ, אַמַּאי לָא אֶתָאי? אָמַר רַבִּי יוֹסֵי בַּר חֲנִינָא: מְלַמֵּד שֶׁפָּרְחָה בָה צָרַעַת. בְּמַתְנִיתָא תָּנָא: בָּא גַבְרִיאֵל וְעָשָׂה לָהּ זָנָב.

TRANSLATION

[The verse (*Esther* 1:12) states:] *And Vashti the queen refused.* Was she not wanton, as the teacher explained that both of them [Achashverosh and Vashti]

---

222 - See page 131.
223 - שבת קיג.
224 - Ibid. 114a.
225 - See also *Bava Kama* 86b.

intended to sin? Why did she refuse to come?[226] R. Yosi bar Chanina explained: This teaches us that she became afflicted with *tzara'as*. In the *beraisa* we learned: Gavriel came and made her a tail.

TALMUD

"וַיִּקְצֹף הַמֶּלֶךְ מְאֹד" אַמַאי דְּלָקָה בֵּיה כּוּלֵי הַאי? אָמַר רָבָא: שָׁלְחָה לֵיהּ: אַהוּרְיָירֵיהּ דְּאַבָּא! אַבָּא לָקֳבֵל אַלְפָּא חַמְרָא שָׁתֵי וְלָא רָוֵי, וְהַאי גַּבְרָא אִשְׁתְּטֵי לֵיהּ מֵחַמְרָא?! מִיָּד – "וַחֲמָתוֹ בָּעֲרָה בוֹ".

TRANSLATION

[The verse (*Esther* 1:12) states:] *And the king became very angry [and his anger burned within him].* Why did he become so angry? Rava explained: She [Vashti] sent him [a message]: Stablemaster of my father. My father could drink against a thousand men and not get drunk. And this man [you, Achashverosh] becomes intoxicated after [a small amount of] wine! Immediately, *and his anger burned within him.*[227]

COMMENTARY

Gra explains that Achashverosh was infuriated for two reasons: because of Vashti's refusal to appear as ordered and because of her insulting answer as reported by the chamberlains. The verse therefore stresses that Achashverosh *became very angry* — anger which he could show, for he could inform his guests that Vashti refused to appear; *and his anger burned within him* — anger that he could not show, for he could not tell his guests what Vashti had said.

TALMUD

"וַיֹּאמֶר הַמֶּלֶךְ לַחֲכָמִים יֹדְעֵי הָעִתִּים", מָאן "חֲכָמִים"? – רַבָּנָן. "יוֹדְעֵי הָעִתִּים", שֶׁיּוֹדְעִים לְעַבֵּר שָׁנִים וְלִקְבּוֹעַ חֳדָשִׁים.

TRANSLATION

[The verse (*Esther* 1:13) states:] *And the king said to his wise men, those who knew astronomy.* Who were his *wise men*? The [Jewish] Sages. *Who knew*

---

226 - The Talmud had earlier noted that Vashti was no less immoral than was Achashverosh and would not have been averse to appearing before the guests at the banquet without clothing. Her refusal to appear then must have stemmed from some other reason. The Talmud explains either that she was afflicted with *tzara'as* or suddenly grew a tail and this is why she refused the royal summons.

227 - I.e., Achashverosh's fury was a result of Vashti's insulting remarks which emphasized the difference between her royal heritage and his common background.

astronomy? Who know how to calculate the leap years and establish the appearance of the months.[228]

COMMENTARY

Maharal explains that Achashverosh chose to consult with the Jewish Sages rather than with his regular advisers because they were well versed in astronomy and could thus determine the most auspicious time to punish Vashti.

We might add that Achashverosh could well have preferred to consult with the Jewish Sages rather than with his regular counsellors, for they had the least reason to serve their own interests. While other nations could well see benefit in replacing Vashti with a queen from their own daughters as a means of increasing their influence within the royal court, the Jewish Sages would be most reluctant to do so.

In his commentary to *Megillas Esther*, *Yosef Lekach* notes that Achashverosh was forced to consult with advisers to determine Vashti's punishment, for the laws of Persia did not permit him to judge her himself.

TALMUD

"כְּדָת מַה לַּעֲשׂוֹת", אָמַר לְהוּ: דַּיְינוּהָ נִיהֲלָהּ. אָמְרֵי: הֵיכִי נַעֲבִיד? נֵימָא דְּלִיקְטְלָהּ, לְמָחָר מְפַכַּח לֵיהּ חַמְרָא, וְדָכִיר לָהּ, וּבָעֵי לָהּ מִינָן. נֵימָא לֵיהּ: לִשְׁבְּקָהּ הַשְׁתָּא, לֵימָא: לָא אִיכְפַּת לְהוּ בְּזִילוּתָא דִּילֵיהּ וּמַלְכוּתֵיהּ. אָמְרוּ לוֹ: מִיּוֹם שֶׁחָרַב בֵּית הַמִּקְדָּשׁ וְגָלִינוּ מֵאַרְצֵנוּ, נִטְלָה עֵצָה מִמֶּנּוּ, וְאֵין אָנוּ יוֹדְעִין לָדוּן דִּינֵי נְפָשׁוֹת. אֶלָּא זִיל לְגַבֵּי עַמּוֹן וּמוֹאָב, דְּיָתְבֵי אַדּוּכְתַּיְיהוּ כְּחַמְרָא דְּיָתִיב עַל דּוּרְדְּיֵהּ וְטַעֲמָא אָמְרוּ לֵיהּ, דִּכְתִיב: "שַׁאֲנַן מוֹאָב מִנְּעוּרָיו, וְשֹׁקֵט הוּא אֶל שְׁמָרָיו, וְלֹא הוּרַק מִכְּלִי אֶל כֶּלִי, וּבַגּוֹלָה לֹא הָלָךְ, עַל כֵּן עָמַד טַעְמוֹ בּוֹ וְרֵיחוֹ לֹא נָמָר".

TRANSLATION

[The verse (*Esther* 1:15) states:] *To determine what should be done. He* [Achashverosh] said to them: Judge her! They said [to themselves]. How shall we act? If we tell him to execute her, tomorrow he will become sober and will remember her and will demand retribution for her [death] from us [for he will accuse us of having caused her death]. If we tell him to let her be, he will say: You

---

228 - According to the Talmud's explanation of the verse, the phrase *wise men who knew astronomy* is to be understood as a reference to the members of the *Sanhedrin* who, among their other duties, were responsible for calculating the calendar.

are not concerned with the affront shown him and his kingdom. They [therefore] told him: From the time since the *Beis ha-Mikdash* was destroyed and we were exiled from our land, sagacity has been taken from us and we do not know how to judge capital crimes. Go to Ammon and Moav [and consult with them],[229] for they sit in their places like wine whose yeast has settled. And their advice was good, for the verse (*Yirmiyahu* 48:11) states: *Moav is tranquil since its youth, and it is [like wine which is] quiet upon its yeast. It has not been transferred from vessel to vessel and did not go into exile. Therefore its taste has been preserved and its bouquet has not faded.*

COMMENTARY

The dilemma of the Sages was obvious, for no matter what answer they offered, they stood a chance of arousing Achashverosh's anger. They therefore explained that if he was approaching them because of their expertise in judging cases as members of the *Sanhedrin* — a court that had capital experience — he should know that the court's ability to adjudicate capital cases was contingent upon all seventy-one members sitting in the Chamber of Hewn Stones in the courtyard of the *Beis ha-Mikdash*. The courts of twenty-three members that sat in each major city were never empowered to judge capital cases.

Note that they told Achashverosh to consult with Ammon and Moav and did not suggest that he confer with his own advisers or judge her according to local law. It would seem that they understood that Persian law did not provide a precedent for judging Vashti — otherwise, there would have been no reason for the king to seek outside counsel.

Yosef Lekach — in his commentary to the *Megillah* — notes that according to local custom, Achashverosh was not allowed to judge cases independently and

---

229 - *Rabbenu Tam* (תוסי ד"ה זיל לגבי עמון ומואב) changes the text to read Moav alone, for he points out that after Sancheriv's armies came to the area, many of the people became intermingled and could no longer be identified by national origin. He offers proof that Ammon was one of the nations whose national identity became confused by virtue of the fact that the Sages of the Talmud permitted men to marry proselytes from Ammon — even though they are prohibited by Torah law — because there was no means of being sure that people who claimed to be Ammonites were indeed descendents of that nation. This was not true of proselytes from Moav and Egypt who remained prohibited. Support for *Tosafos'* textual emendation can be drawn from the fact that the Talmud quotes a verse that refers to Moav alone.

was also not allowed to appoint judges to adjudicate cases in which he had a personal interest. He therefore had no choice but to consult with others and turned first to the former members of the *Sanhedrin*.

Maharsha conjectures that some of the advisers mentioned in the verse may have been from Ammon and Moav and the Sages therefore directed him to the wise men of those nations. It is also possible that the Sages suggested that he turn to Ammon and Moav since these nations are also descendents of Shem and therefore share the innate wisdom that characterizes his progeny.

TALMUD

מִיָּד – "וְהַקָּרֹב אֵלָיו כַּרְשְׁנָא, שֵׁתָר, אַדְמָתָא, תַּרְשִׁישׁ, מֶרֶס, מַרְסְנָא, מְמוּכָן". אָמַר רַבִּי לֵוִי: פָּסוּק זֶה כֻּלּוֹ עַל שֵׁם קָרְבָּנוֹת נֶאֱמַר; "כַּרְשְׁנָא" – אָמְרוּ מַלְאֲכֵי הַשָּׁרֵת לִפְנֵי הַקָּדוֹשׁ בָּרוּךְ הוּא: רִבּוֹנוֹ שֶׁל עוֹלָם! כְּלוּם הִקְרִיבוּ לְפָנֶיךָ גּוֹיִם (עוֹבְדֵי כּוֹכָבִים). כָּרִים בְּנֵי שָׁנָה, כְּדֶרֶךְ שֶׁהִקְרִיבוּ יִשְׂרָאֵל לְפָנֶיךָ?! "שֵׁתָר" – כְּלוּם הִקְרִיבוּ לְפָנֶיךָ שְׁתֵּי תוֹרִים?! "אַדְמָתָא" – כְּלוּם בָּנוּ לְפָנֶיךָ מִזְבֵּחַ שֶׁל אֲדָמָה, כְּדִכְתִיב: "מִזְבַּח אֲדָמָה תַּעֲשֶׂה לִי"?! "תַּרְשִׁישׁ" – כְּלוּם שִׁמְּשׁוּ לְפָנֶיךָ בְּבִגְדֵי כְהֻנָּה, דִּכְתִיב בְּהוּ: "תַּרְשִׁישׁ וְשֹׁהַם וְיָשְׁפֵה"?! "מֶרֶס" – כְּלוּם מֵרְסוּ לְפָנֶיךָ בְּדָם?! "מַרְסְנָא" – כְּלוּם מֵרְסוּ לְפָנֶיךָ בִּמְנָחוֹת?! "מְמוּכָן" – כְּלוּם הֵכִינוּ לְפָנֶיךָ שֻׁלְחָן שֶׁל לֶחֶם הַפָּנִים?! מִיָּד:

TRANSLATION

Immediately[230] [the verse (*Esther* 1:14) continues:] *And those close to him [Achashverosh] were Carshana, Shesar, Admasa, Tarshish, Meres, Masana and Memuchan.* R. Levi explained: This entire verse is [homiletically interpretable as] referring to the sacrificial service. *Carshana* — the ministering angels said to the Holy One, blessed is He: Master of the world. Did the gentiles ever offer year old sheep[231] before You as Israel has done? *Shesar* — did they ever offer two fowl[232] before You? *Admasa* — did they ever build an earthen[233] altar for

---

230 - I.e., because the Sages declined to offer Achashverosh specific advice, he turned to his own advisers and solicited their opinion as to what should be done to Vashti.

231 - The exegesis is based on interpreting the name כרשנה as an acronym for כר שנה — *year old sheep* — which were offered as sacrifices.

232 - The exegesis is based on interpreting the name שתר as an acronym for שתי תר— *two fowl* — which were offered as sacrifices.

233 - The exegesis is based on interpreting the name אדמתא as related to the Hebrew אדמה — *earth* — from which the altar used for the sacrificial services was made.

You, as the verse (*Shemos* 20:21) states: *And you shall make Me an earthen altar?*[234] *Tarshish* — did they ever serve You with the vestments[235] of the *kohanim*, concerning which the verse (ibid. 28:20) states: *Tarshish, shoham and yoshpeh*. *Meres* — Did they dilute[236] the blood before You. *Marsana* — did they mix[237] the grain offerings before You. *Memuchan* — did they ever prepare[238] the table with the *lechem ha-panim* before You?

COMMENTARY

The Talmud's homiletical explanation of the names of Achashverosh's advisers bears further examination. The *Midrash*[239] explains that whenever the author of the *Megillah* refers to the king without adding Achashverosh, the reference is to God as well as to Achashverosh. Based on this premise, the verse needs explanation, for are there advisers who can be described as *close to Him*? The Talmud therefore explains that the verse can be interpreted as a symbolic dialogue between the celestial angels and God. The former came to defend Isreal at a time when they were most susceptible to Divine judgement for having participated in Achashverosh's feast. They said to God: "Is there another people who offer You sacrifices and thus show their fealty and devotion to You? Is there another nation who is as careful to fulfill Your will?" It is as if the angels were calling upon God to take advantage of Achashverosh's anger with Vashti

---

234 - In his commentary to *parashas Yisro*, R. Samson Rafael Hirsch points out that the Torah ordains that the altar used for sacrifices must be made of earth and could not be made of stone. He explains that the Jewish concept of offering a sacrifice calls for elevating the physical world — the earth — to the supernal level rather than bringing the supernal world down to earth.

235 - The exegesis is based on interpreting the name תרשיש as referring to the stone of the same name which was one of the twelve precious stones emplaced on the breastplate worn by the *kohen gadol*.

236 - The exegesis is based on interpreting the name מרס as related to the Hebrew מרס — *stir*. The blood sprinkled on the altar as part of the sacrificial service was stirred to prevent it from clotting.

237 - See the previous note for the basis for the exegesis. The grain offerings were mixed with oil.

238 - The exegesis is based on the similarity between the name ממוכן and the Hebrew מן המוכן. The *lechem ha-panim* was always present on the table in the Sanctuary and was thus always מוכן — *prepared*.

239 - See *Esther Rabbah* 3.

— who was the prime enemy of the Jews[240] — so as to save Israel. The angels pointed out that though Israel might have sinned by participating in the feast arranged by Achashverosh, the nation still possessed the merit of the Divine service which only she carried out.

Note that the verse begins with the phrase, *and those close to Him.* The word קרבן — *sacrifice* — comes from the root קרב — *to come close* — for this is the purpose of the sacrifices. They serve to draw man close to God, in contrast to the gentile concept of sacrifices as fulfilling a need of God's, as it were. The angels thus defended Israel by reminding God, as it were, that only Israel was *close to Him* and they were therefore worthy of being saved despite their having transgressed.

TALMUD

"וַיֹּאמֶר מְמוּכָן", תָּנָא: "מְמוּכָן" זֶה הָמָן, וְלָמָּה נִקְרָא שְׁמוֹ "מְמוּכָן"? שֶׁמּוּכָן לְפוּרְעָנוּת. אָמַר רַבִּי כַּהֲנָא: מִכָּאן שֶׁהֶדְיוֹט קוֹפֵץ בָּרֹאשׁ.

TRANSLATION

Immediately,[241] *and Memuchan said* (ibid.). We learned in a *beraisa*: Memuchan is [another name for] Haman. And why was he [also] called Memuchan? Because he was ready to punish [others]. R. Kahana explained: From this we see that a simple person pushes ahead.

COMMENTARY

Memuchan's/Haman's advice was clever, for he convinced Achashverosh that there was a means of punishing Vashti without sacrificing his power base. As a commoner who had usurped power, Achashverosh was constantly searching for a way to insure that his reign would be strengthened. He was reluctant to kill

---

240 - The *Midrash* (*Esther Rabbah*) notes that it was Vashti who had convinced Achashverosh not to allow the Jews to continue to rebuild the *Beis ha-Mikdash*.

241 - I.e., when Achashverosh consulted with his advisers as to what should be done to Vashti. The Talmud notes that Haman was always willing to punish others; hence he is referred to here as Memuchan, from the Hebrew מוכן — *ready*. This is another example of the Sages' practice of expounding on foreign names or words as if they were Hebrew. R. Kahana adds that Memuchan is the last of the advisers listed in the verse, indicating that he was the least important. Nevertheless, he did not wait until it was his turn to offer his opinion and showed no deference to the other advisers. R. Kahana explained that this type of impulsive behavior is symptomatic of simple people.

Vashti, for her royal lineage provided him with the prestige and legitimacy that he lacked. Haman pointed out to Achashverosh that were he to spare Vashti, he would become the laughingstock of the entire country, for there were numerous witnesses to Vashti's refusal to appear before him and the story would undoubtedly be spread by the king's enemies who would be only too happy to embarrass him. Achashverosh, Haman suggested, had no option but to kill her and show that he was worthy of reigning in his own right and did not need Vashti's pedigree.

Yosef Lekach points out that Haman had another suggestion as well. Until this point, Achashverosh was powerless to judge Vashti himself, for Persian law did not allow the king to adjudicate cases. Haman therefore suggested that Achashverosh change the law and take over these juridicial powers as well, using Vashti's case as a precedent to show the advisers how critical it was that the king be allowed to judge cases since others might be reluctant to judge the queen, fearing that doing so might be considered as a slight to the king. Once juridicial powers were exclusively the king's, Haman argued, Achashverosh would no longer have to fear that his background might continue to be an issue.

TALMUD

"לִהְיוֹת כָּל אִישׁ שֹׂרֵר בְּבֵיתוֹ" אָמַר רָבָא: אִלְמָלֵא אִגְּרוֹת רִאשׁוֹנוֹת, לֹא נִשְׁתַּיֵּר מִשֹּׂנְאֵיהֶם שֶׁל יִשְׂרָאֵל שָׂרִיד וּפָלִיט. אָמְרִי: מַאי הַאי דְּשַׁדַּר לָן: "לִהְיוֹת כָּל אִישׁ שׁוֹרֵר בְּבֵיתוֹ"? פְּשִׁיטָא, דַּאֲפִלּוּ קָרְחָא בְּבֵיתֵיהּ, פַּרְדַּשְׁכָּא לִיהֱוֵי.

TRANSLATION

[The verse (*Esther* 1:22) states:] *So that every man might be dominant in his home.* Rava explained: Were it not for the first letters [that Achashverosh sent out before the letters calling for the destruction of the Jews] not a remnant of Israel's enemies[242] would be left. They [the people] said: What is the meaning of this that he [Achashverosh] has sent us that each man should be dominant in his home? This is obvious, for even one worthy of contempt is a prince in his own home.

COMMENTARY

The Talmud notes that Achashverosh's letter had an effect that was totally

242 - A euphemism for the Jews themselves.

unexpected, for in writing something that was totally obvious — *so that every man might be dominant in his own home* — he showed that his written directions to the people need not be taken very seriously. The ground was miraculously laid and his later letter, that called for the extermination of the Jews, was also treated with less than total respect, for people suspected that he was a fickle king.

Iyun Yaakov explains that Rava was troubled by the question as to why the author of the *Megillah* felt it necessary to tell us the contents of the letter that Achashverosh wrote when this first letter seemed to have no bearing on the miraculous deliverance of the Jews. He therefore explained that this letter too had an effect as we have seen.

TALMUD

"וַיַּפְקֵד הַמֶּלֶךְ פְּקִידִים", אָמַר רָבָא: מַאי דִּכְתִיב: "כָּל עָרוּם יַעֲשֶׂה בְדָעַת, וּכְסִיל יִפְרֹשׂ אִוֶּלֶת". "כָּל עָרוּם יַעֲשֶׂה בְדָעַת", זֶה דָוִד מֶלֶךְ יִשְׂרָאֵל, דִּכְתִיב בֵּיהּ: "וַיֹּאמְרוּ לוֹ עֲבָדָיו, יְבַקְשׁוּ לַאדֹנִי הַמֶּלֶךְ נַעֲרָה בְתוּלָה", וְכָל מָאן דַּהֲנָה לֵיהּ בְּרַתָּא, אַיְיתָהּ נִהֲלֵיהּ. "וּכְסִיל יִפְרֹשׂ אִוֶּלֶת" זֶה אֲחַשְׁוֵרוֹשׁ, דִּכְתִיב בֵּיהּ: "וַיַּפְקֵד הַמֶּלֶךְ פְּקִידִים", דְּמָאן דַּהֲנָה לֵיהּ בְּרַתָּא, אַטַמְרָהּ מִינֵּיהּ.

TRANSLATION

[The verse (*Esther* 2:3) states:] *The king appointed messengers.* Rava said: What is the meaning of the verse (*Mishlei* 13:16): *Every act of deceit is done with forethought, but the fool's acts spreads inequity. Every act of deceit is done with forethought* — this refers to Dovid *ha-Melech*, regarding whom the verse states (*Melachim* I 1:2): *and his servants said to him, a young maiden should be sought for our master the king.* Everyone who had a daughter brought her forward. *And the fool spreads inequity* — this refers to Achashverosh, regarding whom the verse (*Esther* 2:3) states: *The king appointed messengers.* Every man who had a daughter hid her from him.

COMMENTARY

Rava notes that in both cases — David and Achashverosh — young girls were sought for the king, but in the case of David, all were prepared to cooperate whereas in the case of Achashverosh, all sought to prevent their daughters from being taken.

This serves to emphasize the difference between the two kings, for in David's case every one sought to be the one whose daughter would be chosen to serve the king, for they knew that doing so would bring them honor. In the case of Achashverosh, however, they feared that their daughters would be cast away as soon as the king changed his mind and they were therefore reluctant to have their daughters taken. Thus, even though the fool — Achashverosh — acted in the same way as did the wise man — David, the results were very different. [243]

TALMUD

"אִישׁ יְהוּדִי הָיָה בְּשׁוּשַׁן הַבִּירָה, וּשְׁמוֹ מָרְדֳּכַי" וְגוֹ'. מַה קָאָמַר? אִי לְיַחוּסֵיהּ קָא אָתָא, לְיַחְסֵיהּ וְלֵיזִיל עַד בִּנְיָמִין, מַאי שְׁנָא הַנֵי תְלָתָא, וְתוּ לָא? תָּנָא, כֻּלָּן עַל שְׁמוֹ נִקְרְאוּ: "בֶּן יָאִיר" – בֶּן שֶׁהֵאִיר עֵינֵיהֶם שֶׁל יִשְׂרָאֵל בִּתְפִלָּתוֹ. "בֶּן שִׁמְעִי" – בֶּן שֶׁשָּׁמַע אֵל תְּפִלָּתוֹ. "בֶּן קִישׁ" – שֶׁהִקִּישׁ עַל דַּלְתֵי רַחֲמִים וּפָתְחוּ לוֹ.

TRANSLATION

[The verse (*Esther* 2:5) states:] *There was a Jew in Shushan the capital, and his name was Mordechai [the son of Yair, the son of Shimi, the son of Kish, a man of Binyamin].* What is the verse saying? If the purpose is to show us his genealogy, let it list all the [generations] back to Binyamin. Why are these three different [in that they are mentioned] and others are not? We learned in a *beraisa*: All of them [mentioned] are referred to because they are his names.[244] *The son of Yair* — the son who brought light to the eyes of Israel through his prayers. *The son of Shimi* — the son whose prayers God heard. *The son of Kish* — the son who knocked at the gates of mercy and they were opened for him.[245]

COMMENTARY

Names in *Tanach* are more than appellations; they also serve to describe the character of the person referred to. Thus, if the author of the *Megillah* saw fit to list certain ancestors of Mordechai while skipping others, it is because the

243 - See *Targum Yonasan* (ad loc.). According to his translation, the verse would be best tranlated into English in the following manner — *Every act of deceit is undertaken with planning, but in the fool's case it turns out to reveal his stupidity.*
244 - I.e., the three names listed are references to Mordechai as well as to his ancestors.
245 - I.e., Yair from the Hebrew להאיר — *to illuminate*; Shimi from the Hebrew לשמוע — *to hear*, Kish from the Hebrew להקיש — *to knock*.

names of these ancestors describe aspects of Mordechai's character and are therefore applicable to him as well.[246]

Rav Dessler[247] explains that this is the essence of the concept of זכות אבות — the worthiness of the forefathers — which serves as a source of merit for their descendents. Our ancestors have implanted within us certain character traits that serve as a source of merit for us because they find expression in our actions.

TALMUD

קָרֵי לֵיהּ "יְהוּדִי", וְקָרֵי לֵיהּ "יְמִינִי"?! קָרֵי לֵיהּ "יְהוּדִי", אַלְמָא מִיהוּדָה קָאָתֵי. וְקָרֵי לֵיהּ "יְמִינִי", אַלְמָא מִבִּנְיָמִין קָאָתֵי? אָמַר רַב נַחְמָן: מָרְדְּכַי - מֻכְתָּר בְּנִימוּסוֹ הָיָה. רַבָּה בַּר רַב הוּנָא, וְרַבָּה בַּר בַּר חָנָה מִשְּׁמֵיהּ דְּרַבִּי יְהוֹשֻׁעַ בֶּן לֵוִי אָמְרוּ: אָבִיו מִבִּנְיָמִין, וְאִמּוֹ מִיהוּדָה. וְרַבָּנָן אָמְרֵי: מִשְׁפָּחוֹת מִתְגָּרוֹת זוֹ בָּזוֹ, מִשְׁפַּחַת יְהוּדָה אוֹמֶרֶת: אֲנָא גְרַמִית דְּמִתְיַלִּיד מָרְדְּכַי, דְּלָא קַטְלֵיהּ דָּוִד לְשִׁמְעִי בֶן גֵּרָא. וּמִשְׁפַּחַת בִּנְיָמִין אוֹמֶרֶת: מִינִי קָאָתֵי. רָבָא אָמַר: כְּנֶסֶת יִשְׂרָאֵל הִיא דְּקָאָמְרָה, לְהַד גִּיסָא וּלְהַד גִּיסָא: רְאוּ מֶה עָשָׂה לִי יְהוּדִי, וּמַה שִּׁלֵּם לִי יְמִינִי.

TRANSLATION

The verse refers to him [Mordechai] as *Yehudi* and it refers to him as *Yemini*. By calling him *Yehudi* we can infer that he was from the tribe of Yehudah. By calling him *Yemini* we can assume that he was from the tribe of Binyamin. [How can we resolve this apparent contradiction?][248] R. Nachman explained: Mordechai was crowned with good names.[249] Raba bar R. Huna and Raba bar bar Chana explained in the name of R. Yehoshua ben Levi: His father was from the tribe of Binyamin and his mother from the tribe of Yehudah. The Sages

---

246 - See *Shmuel* I 25:25 where Avigail, in speaking about her husband Naval, tells David — כשמו כן הוא — *he is like his name*. See also *Malbim* to *Bereishis* 2:19 and R. Tzadok *ha-Kohen* of Lublin in *Or Zarua la-Tzadik*.

247 - See מכתב מאליהו, חלק א, pg. 14.

248 - The name Yehudi, had it been used alone, would have been interpreted as Jew, for after the destruction of the *Beis ha-Mikdash*, the nation was no longer referred to according to their tribal affiliations but became known as יהודים since the majority of the people came from that tribe. However, since the verse refers to Mordechai as being both איש יהודי and איש ימיני, we can conclude that the author of the *Megillah* was referring to his tribal background.

249 - I.e., the names *Yehudi* and *Yemini* were used to show the respect that people had for Mordechai and should not be understood as indicating his tribal affiliation.

explained: The families used to argue with each other [as to who was responsible for Mordechai's birth].[250] The families of the tribe of Yehudah would say: We caused Mordechai to be born, for Dovid did not kill Shimi ben Geira.[251] And the families of the tribe of Binyamin said: He came from us [for his parents were from the tribe of Binyamin]. Rava explained: The congregation of Israel referred to him as such [i.e., as being from both Yehudah and from Binyamin] and [they] saw both [Yehudah and Binyamin as being responsible for the travail of the people in the time of Mordechai and Haman]. [They said:] See what the *Yehudi* has done to us and how the *Yemini* has paid us.

TALMUD

מֶה עָשָׂה לִי יְהוּדִי – דְּלָא קַטְלֵיהּ דָּוִד לְשִׁמְעִי בֶּן גֵּרָא, שֶׁאִלְמָלֵא הָיָה שִׁמְעִי בֶּן גֵּרָא, וְקַטְלֵיהּ דָּוִד, לָא הֲוָה מִתְיַלֵּיד מָרְדְּכַי, דְּמַקְנֵי בֵּיהּ הָמָן, וְגָרַם לֵיהּ צַעֲרָא לְיִשְׂרָאֵל. וּמַה שִׁלֵּם לִי יְמִינִי – דְּלָא קַטְלֵיהּ שָׁאוּל לַאֲגָג, שֶׁאִלְמָלֵא הָיָה אֲגָג, וְקַטְלֵיהּ שָׁאוּל, לָא הֲוָה מִתְיַלֵּיד הָמָן, וְגָרַם לֵיהּ צַעֲרָא לְיִשְׂרָאֵל. וְרַבִּי יוֹחָנָן אָמַר: לְעוֹלָם מִבִּנְיָמִין קָאָתֵי, וְאַמַּאי קָרֵי לֵיהּ "יְהוּדִי"? עַל שֵׁם שֶׁכָּפַר בַּעֲבוֹדָה זָרָה, שֶׁכָּל הַכּוֹפֵר בַּעֲבוֹדָה זָרָה נִקְרָא "יְהוּדִי", שֶׁנֶּאֱמַר: "אִיתַי גֻּבְרִין יְהוּדָאִין דִּי מַנִּיתָ יָתְהוֹן" וְגוֹ'.

TRANSLATION

What did the *Yehudi* do to us [i.e., in what way is the tribe of Yehudah responsible for our current troubles]? **[13a]** Because Dovid [who was from the tribe of Yehudah] did not kill Shimi ben Geira. Had Shimi ben Geira been killed by Dovid, Mordechai — whom Haman was jealous of and therefore caused Israel travail — would not have been born. [To what were they referring when they said] how did the *Yemini* pay us? [They were referring to the fact that] Shaul did not kill Agag. Had Agag been killed by Shaul, Haman would not have been born and would not have caused Israel trouble.

R. Yochanan said: The truth is that Mordechai was from the tribe of Binyamin. Why was he referred to as *Yehudi* [which would lead us to infer that he was from the

---

250 - The Sages did not accept R. Yehoshua ben Levi's explanation, for the fact that his mother was from Yehudah would not be sufficient grounds to identify him as a member of that tribe.

251 - Shimi, Mordechai's ancestor, was deserving of death for having cursed Dovid. However, Dovid spared him and as a result, Mordechai was born. See *Shmuel* II 19:24.

tribe of Yehudah]? Because he denied [the authenticity of] idol worship, for one who denies idol worship is referred to as Yehudi, as the verse (*Doniel* 3:12) states: *Yehudi men came.*

COMMENTARY

Maharal explains that the name Yehudi, which was used to describe the Jews who refused to bow down to the idol that Nevuchadnezer had constructed in Bavel, was used to describe them as being followers of the God whose name is י-ה-ו-ה and is not necessarily related to them being descendents of the tribe of Yehudah. He adds that the name can also be seen as being related to the word יחידי — unique or alone — for they worshipped one God alone. *Chidushei ha-Rim* adds that the name יהודי became a synonym for Israel for not only does the name signify their relationship to the tribe of Yehudah, it also describes the nation's trait of הודאה — praising and thanking God for their existence.

Having offered one source that explains the name Yehudi as being a reference to one who denies the authenticity of idolatry, the Talmud now offers another example from Bisyah, the daughter of Pharaoh.

TALMUD

כִּדְרַבִּי שִׁמְעוֹן בֶּן פָּזִי, דְּאָמַר רַבִּי שִׁמְעוֹן בֶּן פָּזִי: דְּכִי הֲוָה פָּתַח אַבָּא פָּזִי בְּדִבְרֵי הַיָּמִים, אָמַר: כָּל דְּבָרֶיךָ אֶחָד הֵם, וְאָנוּ יוֹדְעִין לְדוֹרְשָׁן. "וְאִשְׁתּוֹ הַיְהֻדִיָּה יָלְדָה אֶת יֶרֶד אֲבִי גְדוֹר, וְאֶת חֶבֶר אֲבִי שׂוֹכוֹ, וְאֶת יְקוּתִיאֵל אֲבִי זָנוֹחַ, וְאֵלֶּה בְּנֵי בִתְיָה בַת פַּרְעֹה אֲשֶׁר לָקַח מָרֶד". וְלָמָּה נִקְרָא שְׁמָהּ "יְהֻדִיָּה"? עַל שֶׁכָּפְרָה בַּעֲבוֹדָה זָרָה, דִּכְתִיב: "וַתֵּרֶד בַּת פַּרְעֹה לִרְחֹץ עַל הַיְאֹר". וְאָמַר רַבִּי יוֹחָנָן: שֶׁיָּרְדָה לִרְחֹץ מִגִּלּוּלֵי בֵּית אָבִיהָ.

TRANSLATION

[And that which R. Yochanan taught is] like R. Shimon ben Pazi, for R. Shimon ben Pazi said: When my father Pazi would begin to expound upon *Divrei ha-Yamim*, he would say: All that you [i.e., Ezra who authored *Divrei ha-Yamim*] have said refers to one [i.e., all of the many names recorded refer to a single person].[252] [The verse (*Divrei ha-Yamim* I 4:15-18) states:] *And his wife, the Yehudiyah, bore Yered the father of Gedor, and Chever the father of Socho, and Yekusiel the father of Zanoach, and these are the children of Bisyah, the daughter of Pharaoh, who was taken as a wife by Mared.* Why was she called *Yehudiyah*?

---

252 - The translation is based on Rashi, s.v. כל דבריך אחת הן.

Because she denied [the authenticity of] idol worship, as the verse (*Shemos* 2:5) states: *And she went down to bathe in the river.* R. Yochanan explained: She went down to cleanse herself of the filth of her father's home.

TALMUD

"יָלְדָה"?! וְהָא רְבוּיֵי רְבִיתֵיהּ! אֶלָּא לוֹמַר לְךָ: שֶׁכָּל הַמְגַדֵּל יָתוֹם וִיתוֹמָה
בְּתוֹךְ בֵּיתוֹ, מַעֲלֶה עָלָיו הַכָּתוּב כְּאִלּוּ יְלָדוֹ.
"יֶרֶד" – זֶה מֹשֶׁה, וְלָמָּה נִקְרָא שְׁמוֹ "יֶרֶד"? שֶׁיָּרַד לָהֶם לְיִשְׂרָאֵל מָן בְּיָמָיו.
"גְּדוֹר" – שֶׁגָּדַר פִּרְצוֹתֵיהֶן שֶׁל יִשְׂרָאֵל. "חֶבֶר" – שֶׁחִבֵּר אֶת יִשְׂרָאֵל לַאֲבִיהֶם
שֶׁבַּשָּׁמַיִם. "שׂוֹכוֹ" – שֶׁנַּעֲשָׂה לָהֶם לְיִשְׂרָאֵל כְּסֻכָּה. "יְקוּתִיאֵל" – שֶׁקִּוּוּ יִשְׂרָאֵל
לָאֵל בְּיָמָיו. "זָנוֹחַ" – שֶׁהִזְנִיחַ עֲוֹנוֹתֵיהֶם שֶׁל יִשְׂרָאֵל. "אֲבִי", "אֲבִי", "אֲבִי" –
אָב בְּחָכְמָה, אָב בַּתּוֹרָה, אָב בַּנְּבִיאוּת.

TRANSLATION

[The verse states] *She bore him*? She raised him! [I.e., she was not Moshe's[253] biological mother. Why then does the verse refer to Bisyah as being his mother?] This comes to teach you that one who raises an orphan within his home is considered by the verse as if he had borne him.[254]

Yered is Moshe. Why was he called *Yered*? For in his days, manna descended for Israel. [Why was Moshe called] *Gedor*? Because he fenced in the openings of Israel.[255] [Why was Moshe called] *Chever*? Because he joined Israel to their father in heaven. [Why was Moshe called] *Socho*? Because he was like a

---

253 - The Talmud explains that all of the names recorded in the verse as being the sons of Bisyah are references to Moshe.

254 - Paranthetically, we might add that this can serve as an explanation to a question raised by many of the commentators. *Rashi* to *Shemos* 1:22 explains that the Egyptians ordered all male children drowned because their astrologers had seen that a child was destined to be born who would save Israel. However, the astrologers did not know if this savior would be Jewish or Egyptian. and the order was therefore expanded to include Egyptian sons as well. This is puzzling, for how is it possible that this crucial bit of information was not seen in the stars. However, based on the Talmud's dictum that one who raises an orphan is considered to have borne him, we can surmise that the Egyptian astrologers knew that the child would be born Jewish, but if he was raised by an Egyptian, he would be identified as such.

255 - The commentaries note that the reference is to the fact that Moshe taught Israel good manners — a prerequisite to their acceptance of the Torah. See, for example, *Yoma* 75b where the Talmud notes that Moshe taught Israel to eat meat at night so that they not appear like roosters at the scrap heap, searching for food.

protective covering for Israel. [Why was Moshe called] *Yekusiel*? For in his day Israel placed their trust in God.[256] [Why was Moshe called] *Zanoach*? For he caused the sins of Israel to be forgotten.[257] [Why does the verse repeat the phrase] *the father of* three times? He was their father in wisdom, their father in Torah and their father in prophecy.

TALMUD

"וְאֵלֶּה בְּנֵי בִתְיָה בַת פַּרְעֹה אֲשֶׁר לָקַח מָרֶד", וְכִי "מָרֶד" שְׁמוֹ?! וַהֲלֹא "כָּלֵב" שְׁמוֹ?! אָמַר הַקָּדוֹשׁ בָּרוּךְ הוּא: יָבֹא כָּלֵב שֶׁמָּרַד בַּעֲצַת מְרַגְּלִים, וְיִשָּׂא בִתְיָה בַת פַּרְעֹה שֶׁמָּרְדָה בְּגִלּוּלֵי בֵית אָבִיהָ.

"אֲשֶׁר הָגְלָה מִירוּשָׁלַיִם", אָמַר רָבָא: שֶׁגָּלָה מֵעַצְמוֹ.

TRANSLATION

And these are the children of Bisyah, the daughter of Pharaoh, who was taken as a wife by Mared. Was his name *Mared*? His name was Calev! The Holy One, blessed is He, said: Let Calev — who rebelled[258] against the advice of the spies — come and marry Bisyah, the daughter of Pharaoh, who rebelled against the filth of her father's home.

[The verse (*Esther* 2:6) states:] *Who was exiled from Jerusalem.* Rava explained: He exiled himself.[259]

COMMENTARY

According to the verse, Mordechai left Jerusalem with the exiles who accompanied Yehoyachin, eleven years before the destruction of the *Beis ha-Mikdash*. This exile — referred to as the exile of the חרש ומסגר[260] — included the members of the *sanhedrin* as well as most of the religious

---

256 - The exegesis is based on interpreting the name Yekusiel as an acronym — יקוה א-ל — *placing hope in God*. Maharsha explains that the specific reference is to the manna which was provided on a daily basis and could not be stored for use on the following day. This taught the people that they had to place their trust in God.

257 - Zanoach from the Hebrew להזניח — *to abandon*.

258 - The name מרד is etymologically similar to the word מרד — *to rebel*.

259 - Rava's exegesis is based on the fact that the verse states *who was exiled from Jerusalem with the exile that was exiled with Yechoniah, king of Yehudah.* The use of this repetitive form — rather than the simpler form *who was among those who were exiled from Jerusalem* — is explained as inferring that Mordechai exiled himself, unlike the rest of the populace who were forced into exile.

260 - See *Melachim* II 24.

leadership of the people. Nevuchadnezer took them to Bavel as a means of further subjugating the dying nation of Yehudah, which now became no more than a vassal state with a puppet king — Tzidkiyahu — appointed by the Babylonian emperor. Among those who remained behind was the Prophet Yirmiyahu.

Based on the tradition that the *Sanhedrin* was exiled at this point, it would seem that Mordechai — who is later counted as a member of that body — had not yet been appointed, for otherwise, his exile could not be seen as being voluntary. *Yalkut Shimoni* records that Mordechai returned to Jerusalem and was again exiled after the destruction of the *Beis ha-Mikdash*. He returned once again as one of the Persian governors of the city when Koresh gave his permission to rebuild the *Beis ha-Mikdash* and then went back to Persia when the permission was rescinded and construction stopped.[261]

Riaf writes that Mordechai voluntarily chose to accompany the *Sanhedrin* into exile because he wanted to continue his studies, something that was impossible to accomplish in Jerusalem in the period before the destruction of the *Beis ha-Mikdash*. *Tiferes Shlomo*, in his commentary to the *Megillah*, explains that Mordechai voluntarily exiled himself to Bavel to create the religious infrastructure for the exiles who were soon to follow.[262]

TALMUD

"וַיְהִי אוֹמֵן אֶת הֲדַסָּה הִיא אֶסְתֵּר", קָרֵי לָהּ "אֶסְתֵּר", וְקָרֵי לָהּ "הֲדַסָּה"?! תַּנְיָא, רַבִּי מֵאִיר אוֹמֵר: "אֶסְתֵּר" שְׁמָהּ, וְלָמָּה נִקְרָא שְׁמָהּ "הֲדַסָּה"? עַל שֵׁם הַצַּדִּיקִים שֶׁנִּקְרְאוּ הֲדַסִּים, וְכֵן הוּא אוֹמֵר: "וְהוּא עֹמֵד בֵּין הַהֲדַסִּים אֲשֶׁר בַּמְּצֻלָה". רַבִּי יְהוּדָה אוֹמֵר: "הֲדַסָּה" שְׁמָהּ, וְלָמָּה נִקְרָא שְׁמָהּ "אֶסְתֵּר"? מִפְּנֵי שֶׁהָיְתָה מַסְתֶּרֶת אֶת דְּבָרֶיהָ. וְכֵן הַכָּתוּב אוֹמֵר: "אֵין אֶסְתֵּר מַגֶּדֶת מוֹלַדְתָּהּ וְאֶת עַמָּהּ". רַבִּי נְחֶמְיָה אוֹמֵר: "הֲדַסָּה" שְׁמָהּ, וְלָמָּה נִקְרָא שְׁמָהּ "אֶסְתֵּר"? שֶׁגּוֹיִם הָיוּ קוֹרִין אוֹתָהּ עַל שֵׁם "אִסְתַּהַר". בֶּן עַזַּאי אוֹמֵר: "אֶסְתֵּר" שְׁמָהּ, וְלָמָּה נִקְרָא שְׁמָהּ "הֲדַסָּה"? מִפְּנֵי שֶׁהָיְתָה בֵּינוֹנִית – לֹא אֲרֻכָּה וְלֹא קְצָרָה, אֶלָּא בֵּינוֹנִית כַּהֲדַס. רַבִּי יְהוֹשֻׁעַ בֶּן קָרְחָה, אוֹמֵר: אֶסְתֵּר יְרַקְרֹקֶת הָיְתָה, וְחוּט שֶׁל חֶסֶד מָשׁוּךְ עָלֶיהָ.

---

261 - See also *Targum Sheni* to *Esther* 2:6.
262 - Similarly, *Midrash Tanchuma* writes that Yaakov sent Yehudah down to Goshen first so that he might establish the religious infrastructure for the children of Israel. See *Rashi* to *Bereishis* 46:28, ד״ה להורות לפניו.

TRANSLATION

[The verse (*Esther* 2:7) states:] *And he raised Hadassah, she is [also known as]* *Esther*. She is referred to as *Esther* and she is also referred to as *Hadassah*? [Which was her real name?] We learned in a *beraisa*: R. Meir taught: Her name was *Esther*. Why was she referred to as *Hadassah*? After the righteous who are referred to as *hadassim*, as the verse (*Zecharyah* 1:8) states: *And he stood among the hadassim in the shadow*.[263] R. Yehuda taught: Her name was *Hadassah*. And why was she referred to as *Esther*? Because she hid her intents,[264] as the verse (*Esther* 2:19) states: *Esther would not reveal her nation nor the place of her birth*. R. Nechemyah taught: Her name was *Hadassah*. And why was she referred to as *Esther*? Because the nations called her by the name *Istahar* [as a reference to her great beauty].[265] Ben Azai taught: Her name was *Esther*. And why was she referred to as *Hadassah*? Because she was [of] average [height] — neither tall nor short but average like a willow branch. R. Yehoshua ben Korcha taught: Esther was green[266] [and was thus not pretty] but a thread of grace was cast over her.[267]

COMMENTARY

Obviously, she was referred to by both names, for she and Mordechai wrote the Megillah. The question debated is which of these names was her true appelation and which was added as a description of her. R. Meir's explains that her real name was Esther and the name Hadassah was added as a means of portraying her righteousness — i.e., she was referred to by an additional name because the Sages sought a means of expressing their esteem for her character. The name Hadassah was chosen because it is an appelation suitable for the righteous, as the verse quoted indicates. R. Meir's explanation would seem to be most logical, for she is only referred to as Hadassah in the beginning of the *Megillah* — when she is first introduced, so to speak — whereas, in all other

263 - *Malbim* (ad. loc) explains that the prophet is referring to Alexander the Great, who came to Jerusalem mounted on a horse but dismounted when he saw Shimon *ha-tzaddik* — the *hadas* in Zecharyah's prophecy.

264 - I.e., Esther related to the Hebrew הסתר — *hidden*.

265 - *Rashi* explains that *Istahar* is from the Aramaic *sihara* meaning *moon*. *Targum Sheni* to Esther relates the name to the Greek *estaira* — *Venus*.

266 - I.e., her skin had a greenish tint which made her appear to be ill. See *Maharsha* ad loc.

267 - See *Rashi*, s.v. ירקרקת היתה.

verses she is referred to as Esther.

R. Yehudah maintained that her real name was Hadassah and she was only referred to as Esther because the Sages sought to emphasize her ability to keep her background secret; an ability that played a major role in the miraculous sequence of events. According to R. Yehudah's opinion, we would have to conjecture that the name Esther is used throughout the *Megillah* — rather than her real name Hadassah — because her discretion and fealty to Mordechai who insisted that she not reveal her background until the very last moment — is what led to her success.

R. Nechemyah and Ben Azzai both explained the name Esther as referring to her physical traits. R. Nechemyah maintained that the nations used a name with which they were familiar as a means of expressing their appreciation for her beauty and thus, this name — Esther — is used throughout the *Megillah* which refers to her to in her role as queen of the mightiest power on earth.

Ben Azzai, on the other hand, held that her name was Esther and that is the name which is used to describe her. The Sages, however, referred to her as Hadassah to point out that even though she was only average in her beauty, she was still chosen as queen, despite having to compete with candidates from every nation. This too can be seen as an indication of God's intervention.

R. Yehoshua ben Korcha's exposition is somewhat hard to understand, for the verse (2:7) specifically describes Esther as being *beautiful and of pleasing appearance*. *Gra* explains that Esther was indeed naturally beautiful, but when she was chosen to be Achashverosh's queen, a sickly pallor came upon her. However, it was God's plan that Esther serve as the instrument of His salvation by serving in the king's court, and He placed a thread of grace upon her which made her beautiful once again.

TALMUD

"כִּי אֵין לָהּ אָב וָאֵם", "וּבְמוֹת אָבִיהָ וְאִמָּהּ", לָמָּה לִי? אָמַר רַב אַחָא: עִבְּרַתָּה – מֵת אָבִיהָ, יְלָדַתָּה – מֵתָה אִמָּהּ.

"לְקָחָהּ מָרְדֳּכַי לוֹ לְבַת" תָּנָא מִשּׁוּם רַבִּי מֵאִיר: אַל תִּקְרֵי "לְבַת", אֶלָּא "לְבַיִת", וְכֵן הוּא אוֹמֵר: "וְלָרָשׁ אֵין כֹּל, כִּי אִם כִּבְשָׂה אַחַת קְטַנָּה אֲשֶׁר קָנָה. וַיְחַיֶּהָ, וַתִּגְדַּל עִמּוֹ וְעִם בָּנָיו יַחְדָּו; מִפִּתּוֹ תֹאכַל וּמִכֹּסוֹ תִשְׁתֶּה וּבְחֵיקוֹ תִשְׁכָּב, וַתְּהִי לוֹ כְּבַת". מִשּׁוּם דְּ"מִפִּתּוֹ תֹאכַל", "וַתְּהִי לוֹ כְּבַת"?! אֶלָּא "כְּבַיִת", הָכָא נָמֵי "לְבַיִת".

"וְאֶת שֶׁבַע הַנְּעָרוֹת הָרְאוּיוֹת לָתֶת לָהּ". אָמַר רָבָא: מְלַמֵּד שֶׁהָיְתָה מוֹנָה בָּהֶן
שִׁבְעַת יְמֵי שַׁבָּת.

TRANSLATION

[The verse (*Esther* 2:7) states:] *For she had no mother or father.* Why does the verse tell us (ibid.): *And when her father and mother died* [i.e., since we have already been informed that she had neither mother nor father, the second phrase would seem to be superfluous]. R. Acha explained: When she [Esther's mother] was pregnant, her father died. When she gave birth to her, her mother died.

[The verse (*Esther* 2:7) states:] *And Mordechai adopted her as a daughter.* We learned in the name of R. Meir: Do not read [the verse] as if it says *daughter*, rather [read it as if it] says *home* [i.e., that Mordechai took Esther as a wife]. Similarly,[268] the verse (*Shmuel* II 12:3) states: *and the pooor man had nothing, only a small goat which he had purchased. And he saved her and raised her together with him and his children. She ate from his bread, she drank from his cup and she slept in his arms and she was like a daughter to him.* Because she ate from his bread was she *like a daughter*!? Rather, [do not read the word as *daughter* but as] *a home* [i.e., wife]. Here too [in the case of Esther, read the word as if it was written] *as a home* [i.e., wife].

[The verse (*Esther* 2:9) states:] *And the seven maidens who she was worthy of being given.* Rava explained: This teaches us that she used them to count the days of the week.

COMMENTARY

The *Midrash* relates that Esther, as per Mordechai's instructions, was extraordinarily careful never to allow anyone to even assume that she was Jewish. She therefore took her maidservants and used them as a type of personal calendar, a different one of them serving her each day of the week. The servant who attended her on Shabbos, when she refrained from performing any type of forbidden activity, assumed that Esther acted this way every day of the week. Those who served her on weekdays never knew that she refrained from work on Shabbos for they served her on a specific day. *Maharsha* adds that in fulfillment

---

268 - I.e., the verse also uses the word בת as a shortened form of בית — *home* – referring to a wife. Compare to *Gittin* 52b where R. Nachman is quoted as saying: *I never referred to my wife as my wife but [rather I referred to her] as my home.*

of the dictum that the days of the week should be counted as leading towards Shabbos,[269] Esther gave each maidservant a name that reminded her of the day of the week by referring to something that had been created on that day.

TALMUD

"וַיְשַׁנֶּהָ וְאֶת נַעֲרוֹתֶיהָ לְטוֹב", אָמַר רַב: שֶׁהֶאֱכִילָהּ מַאֲכַל יְהוּדִי. וּשְׁמוּאֵל אָמַר: שֶׁהֶאֱכִילָהּ קְדָלֵי דַחֲזִירֵי. וְרַבִּי יוֹחָנָן אָמַר: שֶׁהֶאֱכִילָהּ זֵרְעוֹנִים. וְכֵן הַכָּתוּב אוֹמֵר: "וַיְהִי הַמֶּלְצַר נוֹשֵׂא אֶת פַּת־בָּגָם וְיֵין מִשְׁתֵּיהֶם, וְנֹתֵן לָהֶם זֵרְעוֹנִים".

TRANSLATION

[The verse (*Esther* 2:9) states:] *And he changed her and her servants for good.* Rav explained: He gave her Jewish [i.e., kosher] food. Shmuel explained: He gave her fatty pork. R. Yochanan explained: He gave her grains, as the verse (*Doniel* 1:16) states: *And the waiter carried [home] the royal bread and the wine [set out for] their feast and gave them grains.*

COMMENTARY

The disagreement between Rav and Shmuel revolves around the correct interpretation of the word *good.* Rav maintained that Hagai, the king's chamberlain, was impressed with Esther and therefore sought to do something that she would consider good. Not knowing which nation she came from — for Esther had not revealed this to anyone — he had no means of knowing what kind of food to prepare for her. He therefore served her kosher food, for that would be something that anyone could eat. Shmuel agreed that Hagai wanted to be especially nice to Esther. However, because he was unaware of her background and thus did not know what kind of food she liked, he brought her food that he considered good — fatty pork!

Paranthetically, there is an interesting disagreement here between *Rashi* and *Tosafos*. *Rashi* maintains that Esther, having no choice, ate the pork while *Tosafos* maintains that she did not.

R. Yochanan on the other hand maintained that Esther knew that she would have a problem with the food served in the royal palace. She therefore told Hagai that she was a vegetarian and asked for grains and nuts. *Rashi* points out that there was a precedent to provide this type of diet in the royal court, as the verse

---

269 - See *Ramban* to *Shemos* 20:8.

referring to Daniel, Chananiah, Mishael and Azariah records.

TALMUD

"שִׁשָׁה חֳדָשִׁים בְּשֶׁמֶן הַמֹּר", מַאי "שֶׁמֶן הַמֹּר"? רַבִּי חִיָּא בַּר אַבָּא אָמַר:
סְטַכְתְּ. רַב הוּנָא אָמַר: שֶׁמֶן זַיִת שֶׁלֹּא הֵבִיא שְׁלִישׁ. תַּנְיָא, רַבִּי יְהוּדָה אוֹמֵר:
אַנְפִּיקִינוֹן – שֶׁמֶן זַיִת שֶׁלֹּא הֵבִיא שְׁלִישׁ, וְלָמָּה סָכִין אוֹתוֹ? שֶׁמַּשִּׁיר אֶת
הַשֵּׂעָר וּמְעַדֵּן אֶת הַבָּשָׂר.

"בָּעֶרֶב הִיא בָאָה, וּבַבֹּקֶר הִיא שָׁבָה", אָמַר רַבִּי יוֹחָנָן: מִגְּנוּתוֹ שֶׁל אוֹתוֹ
רָשָׁע, לָמַדְנוּ שִׁבְחוֹ, שֶׁלֹּא שִׁמֵּשׁ מִטָּתוֹ בַּיּוֹם אֶלָּא בַּלַּיְלָה.

"וַתְּהִי אֶסְתֵּר נֹשֵׂאת חֵן בְּעֵינֵי כָל רֹאֶיהָ", אָמַר רַבִּי אֶלְעָזָר: מְלַמֵּד שֶׁלְּכָל
אֶחָד וְאֶחָד מֵרוֹאֶיהָ נִדְמְתָה לוֹ מֵאֻמָּתוֹ.

TRANSLATION

[The verse (*Esther* 2:12) states:] *Six months with the oil of myrrh.* What is oil of myrrh? R. Chiya bar Abba explained: [Oil derived from] *setacht.*[270] R. Huna explained: Oil [squeezed] from olives which are not yet ripe.[271] We learned in a *beraisa*: R. Yehudah taught: [What is] *anpikinon*? Oil [squeezed] from olives which are not yet ripe. Why is it used for anointing? Because it removes the [body] hairs and softens the skin.

[The verse (*Esther* 2:12) states:] *In the evening she would come and in the morning she would return.* R. Yochanan taught: From the disparaging[272] [remarks about] this wicked man [i.e., Achashverosh] one learns his praise. [The verse indicates] that he only engaged in coitus at night but not in the morning.

[The verse (*Esther* 2:15) states:] *And Esther found favor in the eyes of all who saw her.* R. Elazar taught: This teaches us that each and every one who saw her imagined that she came from their nation.

TALMUD

"וַתִּלָּקַח אֶסְתֵּר וְגו', הוּא חֹדֶשׁ טֵבֵת", אָמַר רַב חִסְדָּא: יֶרַח שֶׁהַגּוּף נֶהֱנֶה מִן
הַגּוּף.

---

270 - The commentaries are divided as to the identity of this oil. *Rambam* (הלכות כלי המקדש א:ג) identifies it as an oil derived from an animal. *Ra'avad* and *Ramban* maintain that it is of vegetable origin, derived either from a plant or bush.

271 - Literally, which have not yet grown a third.

272 - The fact that the verse refers to Achashverosh's conjugal relations at all is disparaging, yet it indicates that he had a modicum of modesty.

"וַיֶּאֱהַב הַמֶּלֶךְ אֶת אֶסְתֵּר מִכָּל הַנָּשִׁים, וַתִּשָּׂא חֵן וָחֶסֶד לְפָנָיו מִכָּל
הַבְּתוּלוֹת", אָמַר רַב בִּקֵּשׁ לִטְעֹם טַעַם בְּתוּלָה – טָעֵם. טַעַם בְּעוּלָה –
טָעֵם.

"וַיַּעַשׂ הַמֶּלֶךְ מִשְׁתֶּה גָדוֹל", עָבַד מִשְׁתְּיָא וְלָא גַלְיָא לֵיהּ; דָּלֵי כְּרַגָּא וְלָא גַּלְיָא
לֵיהּ; שְׁדַר פַּרְדַּשְׁנֵי וְלָא גַלְיָא לֵיהּ.

"וּבְהִקָּבֵץ בְּתוּלוֹת שֵׁנִית" וְגוֹ', אֲזַל, שְׁקַל עֵצָה מִמָּרְדְּכַי, אָמַר לוֹ: אֵין אִשָּׁה
מִתְקַנֵּית אֶלָּא בְּיֶרֶךְ חֲבֶרְתָּהּ, וַאֲפִלּוּ הָכִי לָא גַלְיָא לֵיהּ, דִּכְתִיב: "אֵין אֶסְתֵּר
מַגֶּדֶת מוֹלַדְתָּהּ וְאֶת עַמָּהּ".

TRANSLATION

[The verse (*Esther* 2:16) states:] *And Esther was taken ... [in the tenth month]
which is the month of Teves.* [Why does the verse state that it was Teves after it
had already stated in the tenth month?] R. Chisda explained: In the month when
the body derives pleasure from the body. [273]

[The verse (*Esther* 2:17) states:] *And the king loved Esther more than any of the
women and she found greater favor in his eyes than any of the virgins.* [Why
does the verse first refer to women and then refer to virgins?] Rav explained: He
[Achashverosh] wanted to experience virgins and wanted to experience non-
virgins.

[The verse (*Esther* 2:18) states:] *And the king made a great feast.* He made a feast
[in her honor] and she would not reveal [her origin] to him. He lowered taxes [in
her honor] and she would not reveal [her origin] to him. He sent gifts [to the
people in her honor] and she would not reveal [her origin] to him.

[The verse (*Esther* 2:19) states:] *And when the virgins were gathered a second
time.* He [Achashverosh] went and sought advice from Mordechai [as to how he
could bring Esther to reveal her origin]. He [Mordechai] told him: A woman is
only jealous of her friend's beauty.[274] And even so, she did not reveal [her
origin] to him, as the verse (ibid.) states: *Esther would not reveal her country of
origin or her people.*

---

273 - *Rashi* (ד"ה שהגוף) explains that this too was a result of God's intervention, for
the selection take place during the winter months when the cold air insures that
people have maximum pleasure from their bodies.

274 - I.e., the idea of assembling the virgins again, ostensibly to continue the
search for a new queen, was a ruse suggested by Mordechai to arouse Esther's jealousy
and lead her to reveal her origin to Achashverosh.

COMMENTARY

We might conjecture that Mordechai's advice to Achashverosh served a number of purposes. On one hand, it was a means of forcing Esther to reveal her origin as Achashverosh sought. On the other hand, if Achashverosh found a more suitable queen in the second round of selection, Esther would be able to return to Mordechai and would no longer be forced to subject herself to the king. And if Esther continued to refuse to reveal her secret, the Divine plan that had brought her to the Persian court could proceed, as it were, unhindered.

This would also explain how Mordechai — who was the one who had told Esther not to reveal her origin — could also offer Achashverosh advice as to how he could cause Esther to reveal her secret. Mordechai was insistent that the truth be witheld from Achashverosh, for reasons that the Talmud will later outline.[275] Nevertheless, when Achashverosh approached him for advice, he could not ignore the king's request. He therefore offered advice which made sense to Achashverosh, explaining that by making Esther jealous, he would force her hand. At the same time, he continued to urge Esther not to reveal her secret.

TALMUD

אָמַר רַבִּי אֶלְעָזָר: מַאי דִּכְתִיב: "לֹא יִגְרַע מִצַּדִּיק עֵינָיו", בִּשְׂכַר צְנִיעוּת שֶׁהָיְתָה בְּרָחֵל, זָכְתָה וְיָצָא מִמֶּנָּה שָׁאוּל. וּבִשְׂכַר צְנִיעוּת שֶׁהָיָה בְּשָׁאוּל, זָכָה וְיָצָאת מִמֶּנּוּ אֶסְתֵּר. וּמַאי צְנִיעוּתָא דְּהַוְיָא בְּרָחֵל? דִּכְתִיב: "וַיַּגֵּד יַעֲקֹב לְרָחֵל כִּי אֲחִי אָבִיהָ הוּא", וְכִי "אֲחִי אָבִיהָ הוּא"?! וַהֲלֹא בֶן אֲחוֹת אָבִיהָ הוּא?! אֶלָּא אָמַר לָהּ: מִנַסְּבַתְּ לִי? אָמְרָה לֵיהּ: אִין, מִינְסִיבְנָא לָךְ, אֶלָּא - אַבָּא רַמַּאי הוּא, וְלָא מָצִית לְמֵיקַם בֵּיהּ. אָמַר לָהּ: אִי רַמַּאי הוּא, אֲחוּהּ אֲנָא בְּרַמָּאוּתָא. אָמְרָה לֵיהּ: וּמִי שָׁרֵי לְצַדִּיקֵי לְסַגּוּיֵי בְּרַמָּיוּתָא? אָמַר לָהּ: אִין, דִּכְתִיב: "עִם נָבָר תִּתְבָּרָר, וְעִם עִקֵּשׁ תִּתְפַּתָּל".

TRANSLATION

R. Elazar taught: What is the meaning of the verse (*Iyov* 36:6): [13b] *His eyes will not be witheld from the righteous*? As reward for the modesty of Rachel, she merited that Shaul would descend from her. And in the merit of the modesty of Shaul, he merited and Esther was descended from him. What was the modesty of Rachel? The verse (*Bereishis* 29:12) states: *And Yaakov told Rachel that he was her father's brother.* Was he her father's brother? He was the son of her

---

275 - See note 410.

father's sister! Rather, he asked her: Will you marry me? She replied: Yes, I will marry you, but my father is a swindler and you will be unable to best him. He replied: If he is a swindler, then I am his brother [i.e., his equal] in swindling. She told him: Is a righteous person permitted to engage in swindling? He replied: Yes, as the verse (*Tehillim* 18:26-27) states: *With an honest man deal straightly and with a scoundrel deal crooked.*

TALMUD

אָמַר לָהּ: וּמַאי רַמָּאוּתֵיהּ? אָמְרָה לֵיהּ: אִית לִי אֲחָתָא דְקַשִׁישָׁא מִינָאי, וְלָא מַנְסִיב לִי מִקַּמַּהּ. מָסַר לָהּ סִימָנִים לְרָחֵל. כִּי מָטָא לֵילְיָא, אָמְרָה רָחֵל: הַשְׁתָּא מִכְסְפָא אֲחָתָאי. מִיָּד – אוֹתָן סִימָנִין שֶׁנָּתַן יַעֲקֹב לְרָחֵל, מְסָרָתַן רָחֵל לְלֵאָה. וְהַיְינוּ דִכְתִיב: "וַיְהִי בַבֹּקֶר וְהִנֵּה הִיא לֵאָה", מִכְּלָל דְּעַד הַשְׁתָּא לָאו לֵאָה הִיא?! אֶלָּא מִתּוֹךְ סִמָּנִין שֶׁמָּסַר יַעֲקֹב לְרָחֵל, וְרָחֵל מְסָרָתַן לְלֵאָה, לָא הֲוָה יָדַע עַד הַשְׁתָּא. לְפִיכָךְ זָכְתָה וְיָצָא מִמֶּנָּה שָׁאוּל.

וּמַאי צְנִיעוּתֵיהּ דְּשָׁאוּל? דִּכְתִיב: "וַיֹּאמֶר שָׁאוּל אֶל דּוֹדוֹ: הַגֵּד הִגִּיד לָנוּ כִּי נִמְצְאוּ הָאֲתֹנוֹת, וְאֶת דְּבַר הַמְּלוּכָה לֹא הִגִּיד לוֹ, אֲשֶׁר אָמַר שְׁמוּאֵל", לְפִיכָךְ זָכָה וְיָצָאת מִמֶּנּוּ אֶסְתֵּר.

TRANSLATION

He said to her: In what way is he a scoundrel? She replied: I have an older sister and [my father] will not marry me [to someone] before her [and my father will undoubtedly seek some means to substitue her for me]. He [Yaakov] gave Rachel signs [so that she could identify herself to him]. When night came, Rachel said [to herself]: Now [that Leah has been substituted for me] my sister will be embarrassed [for she will be unable to provide Yaakov with the signs which he gave me to identify myself]. Immediately, those signs which Yaakov gave to Rachel, Rachel gave to Leah. This is what the verse (*Bereishis* 29:25) states: *And it was morning and behold it was Leah.* And until now [i.e., before the morning] it was not Leah? Rather, because of the signs that Yaakov had given Rachel, and which Rachel had given Leah, he did not realize [that Leah had been substituted] until now [i.e., until the morning when he saw her]. Hence, she [Rachel] merited that Shaul was descended from her.

And what was Shaul's modesty? The verse (*Shmuel* I 10:16) states: *And Shaul told his uncle, he told us that the donkeys were found. But he did not tell him about the appointment as king which Shmuel had said to him.* Hence, he merited and Esther was descended from him.

TALMUD

וְאָמַר רַבִּי אֶלְעָזָר כְּשֶׁהַקָּדוֹשׁ בָּרוּךְ הוּא פּוֹסֵק לוֹ גְדֻלָּה לְאָדָם, פּוֹסֵק לוֹ,
וּלְבָנָיו, וְלִבְנֵי בָנָיו עַד סוֹף כָּל הַדּוֹרוֹת, שֶׁנֶּאֱמַר: "וַיֹּשִׁיבֵם לָנֶצַח וַיִּגְבָּהוּ" וְאִם
הֵגִיס דַּעְתּוֹ, הַקָּדוֹשׁ בָּרוּךְ הוּא מַשְׁפִּילוֹ, שֶׁנֶּאֱמַר: "וְאִם אֲסוּרִים בַּזִּקִּים
יִלָּכְדוּן בְּחַבְלֵי עֹנִי".

TRANSLATION

And R. Elazar taught: When the Holy One, blessed is He, decrees greatness for a person, He decrees it for the person, for his children and for his grandchildren throughout the generations. As the verse (*Iyov* 36:7-8) states: *And He settles them for eternity and he is raised.*[276] And if he becomes haughty, the Holy One, blessed is He, lowers him, as the verse states: *and if they are imprisoned in chains, trapped by ropes of poverty.*

COMMENTARY

Maharsha points out that the Talmud could have offered other evidence of Shaul's modesty — e.g., the fact that he went into a cave to relieve himself so that others would not see him doing so.[277] He explains that the Talmud chose the example of Shaul's keeping the fact that he had been anointed as king secret because that transpired before he was chosen to rule.

Maharal adds that modesty is a prerequisite for sovereignty. He explains[278] that modesty is an indication of one's ability to subjugate his desires for the benefit of others — either by foregoing honor or by being self-effacing. As such, this trait is most necessary in a Jewish king, for the kings of Israel are first and foremost public servants. Because Shaul possessed this modesty — inherited as it was from his forebearer Rachel — he was worthy of being appointed king. Moreover, this modesty was genetically passed on to Shaul's descendent Esther and it was this trait that made her be worthy of serving as queen in the Persian court and as the instrument through which Israel's survival was manifested.

---

276 - The basis for R. Elazar's exegesis would seem to be the switch from the plural in the first phrase to the singular in the second phrase; i.e., *He settles them* — the children and grandchildren — when *he is raised.*

277 - See *Shmuel* I 24:4.

278 - See נתיבות עולם—נתיב הצניעות.

TALMUD

"וְאֶת מַאֲמַר מָרְדֳּכַי אֶסְתֵּר עֹשָׂה", אָמַר רַבִּי יִרְמְיָה: מְלַמֵּד שֶׁהָיְתָה מַרְאָה דַּם נִדָּה לַחֲכָמִים.

"כַּאֲשֶׁר הָיְתָה בְאָמְנָה אִתּוֹ", אָמַר רָבָא בַּר לִימָא: מְלַמֵּד שֶׁהָיְתָה עוֹמֶדֶת מֵחֵיקוֹ שֶׁל אֲחַשְׁוֵרוֹשׁ וְטוֹבֶלֶת, וְיוֹשֶׁבֶת בְּחֵיקוֹ שֶׁל מָרְדֳּכַי.

TRANSLATION

[The verse (*Esther* 2:19) states:] *And Esther did that which Mordechai said.* R. Yirmiyah explained: This indicates that she would show her menstrual spots to the Sages.

[The verse (*Esther* 2:19) states:] *As it was when she was being raised with him.* Rava bar Lima explained: This indicates that she would leave the embrace of Achashverosh, immerse herself and sit in the embrace of Mordechai.

COMMENTARY

The exegesis from these verses bears further examination, for why did the Talmud find it necessary to explain that Esther's continued fealty to Mordechai was evidenced by the fact that she showed her menstrual spots to the Sages to determine whether she was ritually pure or impure. *Riaf* explains that the Talmud based itself on the seeming superfluousness of this verse, for the *Megillah* had already informed us that Esther followed Mordechai's instructions. Moreover, the additional phrase in this verse — *as it was when she was raised by him* — would also seem to be superfluous if the *Megillah* meant to inform us that she followed Mordechai's instuctions regarding keeping her background secret. He therefore establishes that the fealty spoken of in this verse refers to Esther's concern that she be able to return to Mordechai's embrace — i.e., to continue their marital relations whenever possible — which called upon her to keep the laws of family purity. She therefore consulted with the Sages so that she would know whether or not she had the status of a menstruant when she returned to Mordechai.

The relationship between Mordechai and Esther is the subject of much discussion in the Talmud and its commentaries. As we have already seen, there is an opinion that they were husband and wife when she was first taken to the king.[279] The Talmud[280] explains that Esther remained permitted to Mordechai even after she was taken as queen by Achashverosh because she had been forced to live with him and her relationship with the king could thus be seen as rape which would not render her forbidden to her husband. This position is consistent with Esther's later lament[281] to Mordechai that by voluntarily presenting herself to the king — so as to thwart Haman's plan — she would no longer have the status of being a forced particpant in her relations with Achashverosh and would thus become forbidden to Mordechai.

TALMUD

"בַּיָּמִים הָהֵם וּמָרְדֳּכַי יוֹשֵׁב בְּשַׁעַר הַמֶּלֶךְ, קָצַף בִּגְתָן וָתֶרֶשׁ" אָמַר רַבִּי חִיָּא בַּר אַבָּא, אָמַר רַבִּי יוֹחָנָן: הִקְצִיף הַקָּדוֹשׁ בָּרוּךְ הוּא אֲדוֹנִים עַל עֲבָדִים, לַעֲשׂוֹת רְצוֹן צַדִּיק. וַעֲבָדִים עַל אֲדוֹנֵיהֶם, לַעֲשׂוֹת נֵס לַצַּדִּיק. אֲדוֹנִים עַל עֲבָדִים, דִּכְתִיב: "פַּרְעֹה קָצַף עַל עֲבָדָיו". לַעֲשׂוֹת רְצוֹן צַדִּיק, וּמַנּוּ? יוֹסֵף, דִּכְתִיב: "וְשָׁם אִתָּנוּ נַעַר עִבְרִי" וְגוֹ'. עֲבָדִים עַל אֲדוֹנֵיהֶם, דִּכְתִיב: "קָצַף בִּגְתָן וָתֶרֶשׁ, שְׁנֵי סָרִיסֵי הַמֶּלֶךְ מִשֹּׁמְרֵי הַסַּף". לַעֲשׂוֹת נֵס לַצַּדִּיק, וּמַנּוּ? מָרְדֳּכַי, דִּכְתִיב: "וַיִּוָּדַע הַדָּבָר לְמָרְדֳּכַי".

אָמַר רַבִּי יוֹחָנָן: בִּגְתָן וָתֶרֶשׁ - טַרְסִיִּים הָווּ, וְהָיוּ מְסַפְּרִים לְשׁוֹן טוּרְסִי, וְאוֹמְרִים זֶה לָזֶה: מִיּוֹם שֶׁבָּאת זוֹ, לֹא רָאִינוּ שֵׁנָה בְּעֵינֵינוּ. בֹּא וְנַטִּיל אֶרֶס שֶׁל סַם מִיתָה בְּסֵפֶל שֶׁל מַיִם, כְּדֵי שֶׁיָּמוּת. וְהֵם לֹא יָדְעוּ שֶׁמָּרְדֳּכַי מִיּוֹשְׁבֵי לִשְׁכַּת הַגָּזִית הָיָה, וְהָיָה יוֹדֵעַ שִׁבְעִים לְשׁוֹנוֹת. אָמַר לוֹ: וַהֲלֹא אֵין מִשְׁמַרְתִּי וּמִשְׁמַרְתְּךָ שָׁוָה? אָמַר לוֹ: אֲנִי אֶשְׁמֹר מִשְׁמַרְתִּי וּמִשְׁמַרְתֶּךָ. וְהַיְינוּ דִּכְתִיב: "וַיְבֻקַּשׁ הַדָּבָר וַיִּמָּצֵא", שֶׁלֹּא נִמְצָא בְמִשְׁמַרְתּוֹ.

TRANSLATION

[The verse (*Esther* 2:19) states:] *At that time Mordechai was sitting at the entrance to to the king's palace, Bigsan and Seresh became angry* ... R. Chiya bar Abba taught in the name of R. Yochanan: The Holy One, blessed is He, [previously] caused a master to become angry with the servants to fulfill the will of the righteous and [in this case caused] the servants [to become angry] with their master so as to perform a miracle for the righteous. [Where do we see that God made] the master [angry] with the servants? The verse (*Bereishis* 41:10) states: *Pharaoh was angry with his servants.* To fulfill the will of the righteous — to

---

279 - See page 129.
280 - See *Sanhedrin* 74b and *Tosafos* (ד"ה והא אסתר בפרהסיא).
281 - See page 177.

whom does this refer? To Yosef, as the verse (ibid.) states: *And with us there was a Hebrew lad.* [Where do we see that God made] the servants [become angry] with their master? The verse (*Esther* 2:20) states: *Bigsan and Seresh became angry.* To perform a miracle for the righteous — to whom does this refer? To Mordechai, as the verse (ibid.) states: *And it became known to Mordechai.*

R. Yochanan taught: Bigsan and Seresh were Tarsi'im and conversed in Tarsis, telling each other: "From the day that she [Esther] came [to become queen] we have had no sleep.[282] Let us place a death potion into a cup of water so that he [Achashverosh] will die." They did not realize that Mordechai was one who sat in the Chamber of Hewn Stone[283] and understood seventy languages. One said: "But my watch and your watch are not simultaneous [and how can we both be absent so as to bring the plot to fruition]?" The other answered: "I will take your watch and my watch [and while I am substituting for you, you can place the potion into the cup]. And this is what is meant by the verse (ibid.) which states: *And they investigated the matter and it was found* — he was not found on his watch [i.e., they discovered that one of the two was missing and this led them to uncover the entire plot].

COMMENTARY

Rashi explains that Bigsan and Seresh had different jobs in the royal palace. Thus, when one of them substituted for the other, it aroused the suspicions of the palace officials and when they investigated the matter, they uncovered the plot to kill Achashverosh. *Maharasha* questions *Rashi's* explanation, pointing out that the Talmud's quote would not seem to suggest that they had different jobs. Moreover, the *Megillah* refers to both of them as being in charge of the palace gate.

Maharsha explains that one said to the other that since they did not serve on the watch at the same time, were he to be absent so as to bring the poison into the royal kitchens, his absence from the gate would be immediately noticed. His

282 - *Rashi* explains that Achashverosh spent an unusual amount of his time with Esther. Bigsan and Seresh, who were in charge of the gates to the palace as well as to preparing the king's bath, were thus kept busy because the king visited the queen — who resided in a separate palace — so often.

283 - I.e., was a member of the Great *Sanhedrin* whose deliberations were held in the Chamber of Hewn Stone on the Temple Mount. One of the prerequisites for membership in the *Sanhedrin* was fluency in seventy languages — see *Sanhedrin* 17a.

co-plotter replied that he would substitute for him and it was this unexplained switching that led to the investigation that eventually uncovered the plot.

Riaf defends Rashi's explanation, noting that if the plot was discovered because they found one substituting for the other at the palace gate, the Talmud would have said that rather than saying that the one who was supposed to be on duty was absent.

We might conjecture that *Rashi* preferred not to explain that one took the second person's watch, for that might not be so unusual as to lead to an investigation. However, if one of them suddenly assumed the position of the other, that would be quite unusual and might lead to an investigation.

TALMUD

"אַחַר הַדְּבָרִים הָאֵלֶּה גִּדַּל הַמֶּלֶךְ אֲחַשְׁוֵרוֹשׁ", וְ("אַחַר" מַאי)? אָמַר רָבָא: אַחַר שֶׁבָּרָא הַקָּדוֹשׁ בָּרוּךְ הוּא, וְהִקְדִּים רְפוּאָה לְמַכָּה. דְּאָמַר רַבִּי שִׁמְעוֹן בֶּן לָקִישׁ: אֵין הַקָּדוֹשׁ בָּרוּךְ הוּא מַכֶּה אֶת יִשְׂרָאֵל, אֶלָּא אִם כֵּן מַקְדִּים וּבוֹרֵא לָהֶם רְפוּאָה בַּתְּחִלָּה, שֶׁנֶּאֱמַר: "כְּרָפְאִי לְיִשְׂרָאֵל", וְאַחַר־כָּךְ - "וְנִגְלָה עֲוֹן אֶפְרַיִם". אֲבָל הַגּוֹיִם, אֵינָן כֵּן, אֶלָּא מַכֶּה אוֹתָן, וְאַחַר כָּךְ רוֹפֵא אוֹתָן, שֶׁנֶּאֱמַר: "וְנָגַף ה' אֶת מִצְרַיִם נָגֹף וְרָפוֹא". בַּתְּחִלָּה - "נָגֹף", וְאַחַר כָּךְ - "רָפוֹא".

TRANSLATION

[The verse (*Esther* 3:1) states:] *After these events, Achashverosh the king promoted [Haman].* After which [events]? Rava explained: After the Holy One, blessed is He, first created a remedy for the affliction.[284] As R. Shimon ben Lakish explained: The Holy One, blessed is He, does not afflict Israel until He first creates a remedy, as the verse (*Hoshea* 7:1) states: *As I cure Israel* and then *the sin of Efraim is revealed.* But this is not true of the gentiles; rather He [first] strikes them and then He heals them, as the verse (*Yeshayahu* 19:22) states: *And God afflicted Egypt, affliction and healing* — first *affliction* and then *healing.*

COMMENTARY

The Talmud's teaching seems to suggest a double standard in the manner in which God punishes those who sin — a point that deserves further elaboration.

---

284 - I.e., Achashverosh promoted Haman to a more important position after God had prepared an antidote — the plot of Bigsan and Seresh which Mordechai overheard. Thus, the threat that Haman's new office would pose to the Jews was tempered by the information that had already been placed in Mordechai's possession.

Malbim, in his commentary to *Bereishis*,[285] points out that God's punishment for man's sins cannot be compared to the punishment that a mortal judge metes out. The latter's motivations are based on society's perceived need to exact retribution as well as to protect itself from the danger that the sinner poses to the continued well-being of the community. These factors play no role in God's plans, for man can not affect God in any way and He thus has no reason to protect Himself nor does retribution have any meaning to Him. Rather, God's punishment is a means of changing man's behavior and that is its intent. In this sense, God punishes man on his behalf, for the punishment is rehabilitation — both in the sense that it leads man to avoid sin in the future as well as in the sense that it provides him with atonement.

While human courts might consider rehabilitation as a byproduct of the judicial process, it is never more than a byproduct and is never the prime consideration when sentencing one who has violated the social order. In God's eyes, however, the purpose of punishment is to rehabilitate man so that he not sin again. In extreme cases, even capital punishment has this purpose, for it is given so that other's might see and hear.

The prerequisite, however, for this type of punishment is the ability to perceive that punishment is from God and that He punishes me for my benefit. This ability is part and parcel of the genetic makeup of the Jews. Indeed, it is this perception that made them worthy of being selected as the recepients of the Torah and their role as a people who could evidence God's dominion in the material world. Hence, they are worthy of having the antidote created before the punishment. Moreover, the creation of the antidote serves the purpose of enabling them to reinforce their perception that God punishes man for his benefit, for they are capable of recognizing that He acts on their behalf. The nations, who have historically conditioned themselves to deny this perception of God's dominion in the material world are unworthy of this consideration and would not benefit from it, for they are intellectually incapable of recognizing God's providence.

---

285 - See commentary to *Bereishis* 3:17 and 8:21 where *Malbim* notes that Divine punishment is preceded by the phrase בעבור האדם — *on man's behalf* — rather than בגלל האדם — *because of man.*

TALMUD

"וַיִּבֶז בְּעֵינָיו לִשְׁלֹחַ יָד בְּמָרְדֳּכַי לְבַדּוֹ". אָמַר רָבָא: בִּתְחִלָּה – "בְּמָרְדֳּכַי
לְבַדּוֹ", וְאַחַר כָּךְ – "בְּעַם מָרְדֳּכַי", מָאן נִינְהוּ? רַבָּנָן. וּלְבַסּוֹף – "לְהַשְׁמִיד
וְלַהֲרֹג וּלְאַבֵּד אֶת כָּל הַיְּהוּדִים".

"הִפִּיל פּוּר הוּא הַגּוֹרָל", תָּנָא, כֵּיוָן שֶׁנָּפַל פּוּר בְּחֹדֶשׁ אֲדָר, שָׂמַח שִׂמְחָה
גְדוֹלָה, אָמַר: נָפַל לִי פּוּר בַּיֶּרַח שֶׁמֵּת בּוֹ מֹשֶׁה רַבָּן. וְהוּא לָא יָדַע שֶׁבְּשִׁבְעָה
בַּאֲדָר מֵת מֹשֶׁה רַבֵּינוּ, וּבְשִׁבְעָה בַּאֲדָר נוֹלַד מֹשֶׁה רַבֵּינוּ.

TRANSLATION

[The verse (*Esther* 3:6) states:] *And it was contemptible in his [Haman's] eyes to strike Mordechai alone.* Rava explained: At first [Haman wanted to strike] Mordechai alone, but then [Haman decided to strike] *Mordechai's people.* To whom does this refer? To the Sages. At the end [Haman decided] *to destroy, kill and eradicate all of the Jews.*[286]

[The verse (*Esther* 3:7) states:] *He [Haman] cast a pur, that is a lot.* We learned [in a *beraisa*]: When the *pur* fell in the month of Adar, he [Haman] was overjoyed. He [said to himself]: "The lot fell for me in the month in which Moshe their teacher died." He did not know that Moshe, our teacher, had died on the seventh of Adar and that on the seventh of Adar, Moshe, our teacher, was born.

COMMENTARY

In the parallel version cited in the *Midrash*, the Sages taught that Haman cast his *pur* month by month, but in every month he found — or was told by his advisers — that the month was not auspicious. Thus, Nisan was not considered to be a fitting month to attack Israel, for in that month Israel celebrated Pesach and thus had great merit. Iyar was considered unfit because of the merit of Pesach Sheni and the manna which began falling on the fifteenth of that month. Sivan was considered unfit because it was the month when Israel received the

---

286 - Rava explains why Haman's hatred for Mordechai brought him to the point where he decided to kill all of the Jews. At first, Haman thought that Mordechai's unwillingness to bow down to him stemmed from Mordechai's personal animosity toward Haman. He soon realized that Mordechai's refusal was based on the fact that Mordechai was the leading Sage of the generation, as the verse states: *for he [Haman] was told of Mordechai's people.* When Haman learned that Mordechai's behavior was based on idealogical grounds, Haman decided to kill all of the Jews, as the verse states: *and Haman sought to destroy all of the Jews within Achashverosh's kingdom.*

Torah. Tamuz and Av both begged God that they not be chosen as the month when Haman's plot was to be brought to fruition, pleading that there were enough catastrophes in those months.[287] Elul was considered unfit, for in that month Nechemyah completed the reconstruction of the walls of Jerusalem. Tishrei was deemed unfit because of the merit of the shofar and the fast of Yom Kippur. Cheshvan was deemed unfit because it was the month in which Sarah died. Kislev was considered unfit because of Chanukah while Teves was deemed unfit because on the twenty-third of that month all of Israel joined together to uproot the evil caused by the incident of the idol of Michah and the concubine at Givah.[288] When the month of Adar came up and Haman found no source of merit, he was overjoyed and ascribed its suitability to the fact that Moshe died on the seventh of the month.

Menos ha-Levi, in his commentary to the *Megillah*, questions why Adar was seen as being more suitable than Cheshvan, for in the latter month Sarah died. *Iyun Yaakov* raises the same question and answers that Sarah is considered to have died without sin, whereas Haman knew that Moshe had died because he had sinned. Thus, Sarah's death could not be seen as making the month an auspicious time to attack Israel whereas Moshe's death would seem to do so.

However, if Haman's astrological assumptions were correct, what difference does it make that Moshe was also born on the same day of the month on which he died? *Rashi* quotes a statement of the Sages[289] that God decided, as it were, to bring about Moshe's death on the day that he was born so that the former would serve as atonement for the latter.

It would appear from the Midrash's description that the casting of the *pur* was a means of determining the suitability of each month rather than a means of choosing the month. Haman started the process from the month of Nisan, for it was then that he decided to annihilate the Jews. *Malbim*, in his commentary to the *Megillah*, points out that his choice of Adar was a sign of Divine intervention, for it gave the Jews the maximum amount of time to repent and thus bring about their salvation.

---

287 - See *Ta'anis* 26a.
288 - See *Shoftim* 18-21.
289 - See *Kidushin* 38a.

TALMUD

"וַיֹּאמֶר הָמָן לַמֶּלֶךְ אֲחַשְׁוֵרוֹשׁ: יֶשְׁנוֹ עַם אֶחָד", אָמַר רָבָא: לֵיכָּא דְיָדַע לִישָׁנָא בִישָׁא כְּהָמָן. אָמַר לוֹ: תָּא וְאִיגְרֵי בְּהוּ. אָמַר לוֹ: מִתְיָרֵא אֲנִי, שֶׁכָּל הַמִּתְגָּרֶה בְּהוֹן, אֱלֹהֵיהֶם עוֹשֶׂה עִמּוֹ דִין. אָמַר לֵיהּ: יָשְׁנוּ מִן הַמִּצְוֹת. אָמַר לֵיהּ: אִית רַבָּנָן בְּגַוַּויְיהוּ דְמִבָּעוּ עֲלַיְיהוּ רַחֲמֵי. אָמַר לֵיהּ: ,עַם אֶחָד הֵן'. וְשֶׁמָּא תֹּאמַר: אֶעֱשֶׂה קָרְחָה בַּמַּלְכוּת? "מְפֻזָּר וּמְפֹרָד", מְפֻזָּרִים הֵם בֵּין הָעַמִּים. וְשֶׁמָּא תֹּאמַר: אִיכָּא מִינַיְיהוּ פֵּירֵי? "וּמְפֹרָד", כְּפִרְדָּה זוֹ שֶׁאֵינָהּ עוֹשָׂה פֵרוֹת. וְשֶׁמָּא תֹּאמַר: דְּאִיכָּא חֲדָא מְדִינָתָא מִינַיְיהוּ? (אוֹ אִסְקַרְתָּא חֲדָא), תַּלְמוּד לוֹמַר: "בְּכֹל מְדִינוֹת מַלְכוּתֶךָ".

TRANSLATION

[The verse (*Esther* 3:8) states:] *And Haman said to King Achashverosh: There is one nation.* Rava taught: There is no one who could slander like Haman.[290] He told him [Achashverosh]: "Come let us enter into conflict with them." He [Achashverosh] replied: "I am afraid, for all who enter into conflict with them, their God executes judgement against them [i.e., against those who seek to enter into conflict with the Jews]." He [Haman] said: "They are lax[291] in [their observance of the] mitzvos [and God will therefore not come to their assistance]." He [Achashverosh] answered: "There are Sages among them who will seek mercy for them." He [Haman] replied: "They are one people [i.e., the Sages are also lax in observing the mitzvos and can thus not seek mercy for them].[292] Perhaps you fear [that destroying them] will create a deficiency in your kingdom; *they are spread out and separate* (ibid.). They are spread throughout your kingdom [and their destruction will not cause any distinguishable loss in the population of your provinces]. And if you think that they are productive [and by permitting their destruction you will suffer monetary loss] — *they are separate* — like a mule

---

290 - Haman's statement to Achashverosh as recorded in the *Megillah* would seem to be needlessly long, for he could have simply stated that he meant the Jews. The descriptions that he offered — *one nation, spread and separated among the nations* — indicates that he was replying to Achashverosh's questions and assuaging the king's fears.

291 - The literal translation is asleep. The statement is based on the similarity between the Hebrew ישנו with a *segol* under the י meaning *there is* and ישנו with a *kamatz* under the י meaning *asleep*. *Maharsha* explains that Haman accused the Jews of having changed the Torah; ישנו related to שינו — *changed*.

292 - See *Maharsha*.

which does not have offspring.[293] And if you think that there is one province which is theirs (or a city which is theirs) — it [the *Megillah* quoting Haman] tells us: *in all the provinces of your kingdom* [i.e., the Jews have no autonomous regions of their own and destroying them will thus not leave your kingdom deficient in any way].

TALMUD

"וְדָתֵיהֶם שֹׁנוֹת מִכָּל עָם", דְּלָא אָכְלֵי בַּהֲדָן, וְלָא שָׁתוּ בַּהֲדָן, וְלָא נָסְבֵי מִינָן, וְלָא מִינְסְבֵי לָן מִנַּיְיהוּ. "וְאֶת דָּתֵי הַמֶּלֶךְ אֵינָם עֹשִׂים" – דְּמַפְּקֵי לֵיהּ לְכוּלָּא שַׁתָּא בְּ"שְׁהָ"י פְּהָ"י". (וְלֹא יהבי כרגא למלכא. ואכלו ושתו ורוו, ונפקי ויתבי בשוקא, ומבזו ליה למלכא). "וְלַמֶּלֶךְ אֵין שֹׁוֶה לְהַנִּיחָם", דְּאָכְלֵי וְשָׁתוּ וּמְבַזּוּ לֵיהּ לְמַלְכָּא. (דבר אחר): שֶׁאֲפִלּוּ נָפַל זְבוּב בְּכוֹסוֹ שֶׁל אֶחָד מֵהֶם, זוֹרְקוֹ וְשׁוֹתֵהוּ. וְאִם אֲדוֹנִי הַמֶּלֶךְ נוֹגֵעַ בְּכוֹסוֹ שֶׁל אֶחָד מֵהֶם, חוֹבְטוֹ בַּקַּרְקַע וְאֵינוֹ שׁוֹתֵהוּ.

TRANSLATION

And their religion is different from that of all nations — i.e., they do not share food with us, nor do they drink with us, nor do they marry our daughters nor marry their daughters to us. *And they do not fulfill the king's edicts* — they excuse themselves [from work] at all times by saying: 'Today is Shabbos or today is Pesach', and they pay no taxes to the king. *And there is no purpose for the king to leave them* — for they eat and drink and mock the king. (Alternatively,) even if a fly would fall into the cup from which one of them was drinking, he would remove it and drink the contents of the cup. But if my master, the king, were to touch a cup of one of them, they would spill the contents onto the ground and not drink it."

COMMENTARY

The Talmud notes that Haman's slander was most efficacious, for he was diabolically clever, masquerading his real motivation — his hatred for Mordechai — behind a facade of half-truths designed to convince Achashverosh that it was in the king's best interests to allow the Jews to be killed. Before Haman approached the king, Achashverosh had no reason to destroy the Jews, for they represented no threat to his hegemony. But by the time that Haman finished,

---

293 - The statement is based on the similarity between the Hebrew words מפרד — *separated* — and פרדה — *mule*.

Achashverosh was a virulent anti-Semite and full partner in Haman's plot. Haman approached Achashverosh, willing to make an incredible contribution[294] to the palace treasury for the right to kill the Jews. But when he left, Achashverosh was prepared to allow him to act without having to make any payment.

Maharsha points out that Haman emphasized the observance of Shabbos and Pesach as indicating that the Jews were not willing to assimilate themselves into Persian society. The observance of Shabbos indicates that the Jews saw themselves as divorced from a lifestyle that was totally committed to financial success, for they were willing to forego any and all economic advantage in order to observe Shabbos. This could be seen as evidence that they did not place the needs of the king and his country above their own and thus, they could be seen as being disloyal subjects. Similarly, their continued observance of Pesach — the symbol of their freedom and their establishment as an independent nation — even while they were in an exile that was benign, proved that they were not to considered as loyal subjects of the king. Moreover, the very concept of Pesach — the end of bondage — was seditious in a state that depended upon forced labor.[295]

TALMUD

"אִם עַל הַמֶּלֶךְ טוֹב, יִכָּתֵב לְאַבְּדָם, וַעֲשֶׂרֶת אֲלָפִים כִּכַּר כֶּסֶף" וְגוֹ', אָמַר רֵישׁ לָקִישׁ: גָּלוּי וְיָדוּעַ לִפְנֵי מִי שֶׁאָמַר וְהָיָה הָעוֹלָם, שֶׁעָתִיד הָמָן הָרָשָׁע לִשְׁקֹל שְׁקָלִים עַל יִשְׂרָאֵל, לְפִיכָךְ הִקְדִּים שִׁקְלֵיהֶם לְשִׁקְלֵי הָמָן. וְהַיְינוּ דִתְנַן: בְּאֶחָד בַּאֲדָר מַשְׁמִיעִין עַל הַשְּׁקָלִים וְעַל הַכִּלְאַיִם.

"וַיֹּאמֶר הַמֶּלֶךְ לְהָמָן: הַכֶּסֶף נָתוּן לָךְ, וְהָעָם לַעֲשׂוֹת בּוֹ כַּטּוֹב בְּעֵינֶיךָ". אָמַר רַבִּי אַבָּא: מָשָׁל דַּאֲחַשְׁוֵרוֹשׁ וְהָמָן, לְמָה הַדָּבָר דּוֹמֶה? לִשְׁנֵי בְּנֵי אָדָם, אֶחָד יֵשׁ לוֹ תֵּל בְּשָׂדֵהוּ, וְאֶחָד יֵשׁ לוֹ חָרִיץ בְּתוֹךְ שָׂדֵהוּ. אָמַר בַּעַל הַתֵּל מִי יִתֶּן לִי חָרִיץ זֶה בְּדָמִים? וּבַעַל חָרִיץ אוֹמֵר: מִי יִתֶּן לִי תֵּל זֶה בְּדָמִים? לְיָמִים נִזְדַּוְּגוּ שְׁנֵיהֶם. אָמַר לוֹ בַּעַל הֶחָרִיץ לְבַעַל הַתֵּל: מְכוֹר לִי תִּלָּךְ. אָמַר לוֹ: הֵילָאי, טוֹל אוֹתוֹ בְּחִנָּם.

---

294 - Haman offered Achashverosh ten thousand *kikar* of silver which is equivalent to approximately 750 tons!

295 - It is interesting to note that historically, Jews have always been in the forefront of the battle for a day of rest and worker's rights — e.g., Marx and Gompers.

TRANSLATION

[The verse (*Esther* 3:9) states:] *If it pleases the king, let it be written that they be destroyed and I will give ten thousand kikar of silver.* Resh Lakish explained: It was obvious and known to He who spoke and the world came to be that Haman would offer *shekalim* to [kill] the Jews. God therefore [ordained] that their [i.e., Israel's] *shekalim* precede the *shekalim* of Haman. And this is what we learned [in a *Mishnah* (*Shekalim* 1:1)]: On the first of Adar announcements are made regarding the *shekalim* and [the prohibition of] crossbreeding.

[The verse (*Esther* 3:11) states:] *And the king said to Haman, the money is given to you, and the nation [i.e., the Jews] to do as pleases you.* R. Aba taught: **[14a]** To what can the agreement between Achashverosh and Haman be compared? To two men, one of whom had a pile of earth in his field and the other had a ditch in his field. The one who had the pile of earth would say: "Who would give me a ditch for money [so that I might dispose of my earth]?" And the one who had the ditch would say: "Who would give me a pile of earth for money [so that I might fill in the ditch]?" The day came when they met one another. The owner of the ditch told the owner of the pile of earth: "Sell me your pile of earth." He replied: "Take it for free!"

TALMUD

"וַיָּסַר הַמֶּלֶךְ אֶת טַבַּעְתּוֹ", אָמַר רַבִּי אַבָּא בַּר כַּהֲנָא: גְּדוֹלָה הֲסָרַת הַטַּבַּעַת, יוֹתֵר מֵאַרְבָּעִים וּשְׁמוֹנָה נְבִיאִים וְשֶׁבַע נְבִיאוֹת שֶׁנִּתְנַבְּאוּ לָהֶם לְיִשְׂרָאֵל, שֶׁאַרְבָּעִים וּשְׁמוֹנָה נְבִיאִים וְשֶׁבַע נְבִיאוֹת שֶׁנִּתְנַבְּאוּ לָהֶם לְיִשְׂרָאֵל, לֹא הֶחֱזִירוּם לְמוּטָב, וְאִלּוּ הֲסָרַת טַבַּעַת הֶחֱזִירָתַן לְמוּטָב.

TRANSLATION

[The verse (*Esther* 3:10) states:] *And the king removed his ring.* R. Aba bar Kahana taught: [The influence of] the removal of the ring was greater [in its effect on the Jews] than the forty-eight prophets and seven prophetesses who prophesied for Israel. The forty-eight prophets and seven prophetesses who prophesied for Israel did not bring them back to good, whereas the removal of the ring brought them back to good.

COMMENTARY

One can imagine the shock that must have rippled through the Jewish community when they learned that the king had given a commoner — albeit a palace official — free reign to do as he pleased. While people might remain skeptical in the face of the remonstrations of a prophet, they could not be apathetic when the king — whom they assumed would never agree to allow them to be attacked if only for economic reasons — suddenly joined forces with an enemy who, as a scion of Amalek, would never show them mercy. Indeed, the effect that the removal of the ring — the symbol of authority — had upon the people was far greater and more immediate than the remonstrations of any of the prophets and prophetesses.

Having made mention that there were forty-eight prophets and prophetesses who served Israel, the Talmud interrupts its exegesis of the verses of the *Megillah* to discuss the issue of prophecy in general and the nature of the prophetic vision of the prophetesses.

TALMUD

תָּנוּ רַבָּנָן: אַרְבָּעִים וּשְׁמוֹנָה נְבִיאִים וְשֶׁבַע נְבִיאוֹת שֶׁנִּתְנַבְּאוּ לָהֶם לְיִשְׂרָאֵל, לֹא פָּחֲתוּ וְלֹא הוֹתִירוּ עַל מַה שֶׁכָּתוּב בַּתּוֹרָה, חוּץ מִמִּקְרָא מְגִלָּה. מַאי דְּרוּשׁ? אָמַר רַבִּי חִיָּא בַר אַבִּין, אָמַר רַבִּי יְהוֹשֻׁעַ בֶּן קָרְחָה: וּמַה מֵעַבְדוּת לְחֵרוּת, אוֹמְרִים שִׁירָה, מִמָּוֶת לְחַיִּים, עַל אַחַת כַּמָּה וְכַמָּה! אִי הָכִי, הַלֵּילָא נַמִי נֵימָא? לְפִי שֶׁאֵין אוֹמְרִים הַלֵּל עַל הַנִּסִּים שֶׁבְּחוּצָה לָאָרֶץ.

TRANSLATION

The Sages taught: Forty-eight prophets and seven prophetesses prophesied for Israel and they neither detracted nor added to that which is written in the Torah except for the [obligation to] read the *Megillah*.[296] What was their source?[297] R. Chiya bar Avin said in the name of R. Yehoshua ben Karcha: If praise [i.e.,

---

296 - It should be noted that the ability to enact binding legislation is a function of the Sages and not of the Prophets. Indeed, Prophets are forbidden to enact legislation based upon prophecy alone. *Maharitz Chayes* writes that Eliyahu was only able to temporarily suspend the prohibition of offering sacrifices outside the *Beis ha-Mikdash* (see *Melachim* I 18) because of his status as a Sage. Similarly, Shlomo's enactments of *netilas yadayim* and *eruvin* were based on his juridicial authority rather than being prophetical. The Talmud's reference here to prophets must therefore be understood to be a reference to the Members of the Great Assembly, among whom were many prophets. It was they who enacted the reading of the *Megillah* — using their juridicial rather than their prophetic authority.

297 - On what basis did they enact the reading of the *Megillah* since it is not an obligation that is written in the Torah?

the Song of the Sea] was sung when servitude was replaced by freedom, when death is replaced by life one should surely [sing praise]! If so, *Hallel* should also be recited? [*Hallel* is not recited] because we do not recite *Hallel* on miracles that occurred outside the Land of Israel.

COMMENTARY

The Talmud previously[298] discussed the reason why the Book of Esther was included in Scripture, finding a veiled reference within the Torah itself that alluded to Esther and Mordechai. We should note that nowhere do we find an opinion maintaining that the reading of the *Megillah* is a Torah obligation. However, the singular status that the *Megillah* enjoys — a status that is beyond that of any other enactment or ordinance including Chanukah — clearly indicates that the Sages based their decision on a reason that transcends the ability of the Sages to enact legislation that is binding upon all of Israel — an ability given them by the Torah.[299]

Rashi asks why the Talmud does not question the basis for the enactment of the lighting of the Chanukah lights. He answers that this took place after the end of the period of prophecy. This would seem to suggest that *Rashi* differentiates between the status of an enactment that took place while the prophets were still active — i.e., the *Megillah* reading — and a later enactment — i.e., Chanukah.

Maharsha clarifies that *Megillah* — and Chanukah — are mitzvos rather than enactments or ordinances. As such, they differ from other examples of Rabbinic legislation — e.g., the enactments of Shlomo's court of *eruvin* and *netilas yadayim* — for their purpose is not to create a protective fence around the Torah but to introduce new legislation. Hence, even though the Sages never intended that these mitzvos be obligatory as Torah law, their enactment is still a departure from accepted practice and must be justified.

Rashi compares the reading of the *Megillah* to the recital of the Song of the Sea — i.e., they are both considered to be songs of praise. Thus, the Talmud's question here would be: On what basis did the Sages see fit to elevate the *Megillah* to the status of the Song of the Sea? However, the comparison is

---

298 - See page 52.
299 - See *Devarim* 17:10-11 and *Sefer ha-Chinuch*, precept 496.

extremely difficult to support, for the recital of the Song of the Sea is a custom rather than an obligation.[300] We might conjecture that *Rashi's* intent was to suggest that the Sages who decided to ordain the reading of the *Megillah* must have done so because they felt that the miracle of Purim demanded an expression of thanksgiving equivalent in scope to the Song of the Sea. This decision had to be based upon either a precedent or a logical derivation in order to be supportable.

Anaf Yosef maintains that the comparison is not to the Song of the Sea, but rather to the recital of *Hallel* on the first day of Pesach which, according to an opinion in the Talmud,[301] was instituted by the prophets among Israel.

R. Samson Rafael Hirsch[302] explains that *shira* — song — is an individualistic expression of the heart's vision, whereas *hallel* — thanksgiving — is a set means of offering praise. Thus, the former enjoys a status that is greater than the latter.[303]

TALMUD

וַהֲרֵי יְצִיאַת מִצְרַיִם, דְּנִסִּים שֶׁבְּחוּצָה לָאָרֶץ, וְקָאָמְרִינַן שִׁירָה? כִּדְתַנְיָא: עַד שֶׁלֹּא נִכְנְסוּ יִשְׂרָאֵל לָאָרֶץ, הֻכְשְׁרוּ כָּל הָאֲרָצוֹת לוֹמַר שִׁירָה. מִשֶּׁנִּכְנְסוּ יִשְׂרָאֵל לָאָרֶץ, לֹא הֻכְשְׁרוּ כָּל הָאֲרָצוֹת לוֹמַר שִׁירָה. רַב נַחְמָן אָמַר: קְרִיאָתָהּ זוֹ הִיא הַלֵּילָא.

רָבָא אָמַר: בִּשְׁלָמָא הָתָם: "הַלְלוּ עַבְדֵי ה'" – וְלֹא עַבְדֵי פַּרְעֹה, הָכָא נֵימָא: "הַלְלוּ עַבְדֵי ה'", וְלֹא עַבְדֵי אֲחַשְׁוֵרוֹשׁ?! אַכַּתִּי עַבְדֵי אֲחַשְׁוֵרוֹשׁ אֲנָן.

בֵּין לְרָבָא וּבֵין לְרַב נַחְמָן קַשְׁיָא הָא תַּנְיָא: מִשֶּׁנִּכְנְסוּ יִשְׂרָאֵל לָאָרֶץ, לֹא הֻכְשְׁרוּ שְׁאָר אֲרָצוֹת לוֹמַר שִׁירָה. כֵּיוָן שֶׁגָּלוּ, חָזְרוּ לְהֶכְשֵׁירָן הָרִאשׁוֹן.

TRANSLATION

But [can a precedent not be drawn from] the exodus from Egypt, [whose attendant] miracles occurred outside the Land of Israel and we do recite songs of praise! [The answer is] as we learned in a *beraisa*: Until they entered the Land of Israel, all lands were fit for the singing of praise. Once they entered the Land of Israel, not all of the lands were fit for singing songs of praise. R. Nachman said: Its

---

300 - See *Rambam, Hilchos Tefillah* 17:13.

301 - See *Pesachim* 117a.

302 - See Commentary to *Bereishis* 9:20-21.

303 - See also *Shem Mishmuel* to *Shemos*, page 217, and *Malbim* in *ha-Karmel*, s.v. *Hallel*.

[i.e., the *Megillah's*] recital is its [the miracles of Purim's] praise.[304]

Rava taught: There[305] it is appropriate [to sing] *Praise [be sung] by the servants of God*, for they were no longer servants of Pharoah. But here, could we say *Praise [be sung] by the servants of God* [which implies that] we are not the servants of Achashverosh? We are still enslaved by Achashverosh![306]

Both according to Rava and according to R. Nachman,[307] the *beraisa* that we learned is problematic. [The *beraisa* says:] Until they entered the Land of Israel, all lands were fit for the singing of praise.[308] [The answer is that] once they were exiled, they [i.e., other lands] became worthy as at first.

COMMENTARY

Having digressed from its exegesis of the verses of the *Megillah* to discuss the basis for the enactment of the reading of the *Megillah*, the Talmud now addresses the issue of prophecy in general.

TALMUD

וְתוּ לֵיכָּא? וְהָכְתִיב: "וַיְהִי אִישׁ אֶחָד מִן הָרָמָתַיִם צוֹפִים", אֶחָד מִמָּאתַיִם צוֹפִים שֶׁנִּתְנַבְּאוּ לָהֶם לְיִשְׂרָאֵל! אִין, אִתְנַבּוּיֵי טוּבָא אִתְנַבּוּ, כִּדְתַנְיָא: הַרְבֵּה נְבִיאִים נִתְנַבְּאוּ לָהֶם לְיִשְׂרָאֵל כִּפְלַיִם כְּיוֹצְאֵי מִצְרַיִם, אֶלָּא נְבוּאָה שֶׁנִּצְרְכָה לְדוֹרוֹת נִכְתְּבָה, שֶׁלֹּא הָצְרְכָה לְדוֹרוֹת לֹא נִכְתְּבָה.

TRANSLATION

Are there no more [than forty-eight prophets and seven prophetesses]? The verse (*Shmuel* I 1:1) states: *And there was one man from Ramasayim Tzofim* [which is interpreted to mean that he — Elkanah — was] one of two thousand seers who

---

304 - I.e., since it was ordained that the *Megillah* be read, it was unnecessary to ordain that *Hallel* be recited as well.

305 - I.e., when the Jews left Egypt, it was appropriate that they offer praise.

306 - I.e., in the aftermath of the Purim miracle, the Jews remained under Achashverosh's dominion. Thus, they could not say *Hallel*, for they were not servants of God alone.

307 - I.e., the previously cited opinion that *Hallel* is unnecessary.

308 - I.e., the *beraisa* rules specifically that *Hallel* is not recited on miracles that occurred outside the Land of Israel in the period after Israel entered the Land. Why then did Rava and R. Nachman find it necessary to offer other reasons for not reciting *Hallel* on Purim?

prophesied for Israel?[309] Yes! There were many prophets who prophesied, as we learned in a *beraisa*: Many prophets prophesied for Israel — twice as many as [the number of people] who left Egypt. However, those prophecies that were applicable for [all] generations were recorded. Those that were not necessary for [all] generations were not recorded.[310]

COMMENTARY

The translation of נביא as prophet is somewhat misleading, for the English term has a connotation of predicting the future which is but one facet of the mission of a נביא. The primary role of the prophet in Jewish traditon is to serve as an instrument for transmitting God's message to man. Thus, the ability to predict the future through Divine inspiration or vision would not be sufficient grounds to count that person as a נביא if that vision of the future has no application for generations other than the one in which the prophet lived.

TALMUD

רַבִּי שְׁמוּאֵל בַּר נַחֲמָנִי אָמַר: אָדָם הַבָּא מִשְׁתֵּי רָמוֹת שֶׁצוֹפוֹת וְרוֹאוֹת זוֹ אֶת זוֹ.

רַבִּי חָנָן אָמַר: אִישׁ אֶחָד הַבָּא מִבְּנֵי אָדָם שֶׁעוֹמְדִים בְּרוּמוֹ שֶׁל עוֹלָם, וּמָאן נִינְהוּ? בְּנֵי קֹרַח, דִּכְתִיב: "וּבְנֵי קֹרַח לֹא מֵתוּ", תָּנָא מִשּׁוּם רַבֵּינוּ מָקוֹם נִתְבַּצֵּר לָהֶם בְּגֵיהִנָּם וְעָמְדוּ עָלָיו.

TRANSLATION

R. Shmuel bar Nachmani taught: [The verse cited can be interpreted literally.] The man who came from two *Ramos* which faced and overlooked each other.

R. Chanan taught: [The verse can be explained as referring to] one man who is

---

309 - In his commentary to *Shmuel, Malbim* explains that the Talmud based its assumption that Elkanah — Shmuel's father — was a prophet on the fact that he is recorded as having come from Ramasayim Tzofim. The word Tzofim is interpreted as meaning *heights of the prophets*, for if it was only the name of the city, it would have been called Tzufim.

310 - Thus, the forty-eight prophets and seven prophetesses to whom the Talmud refers, are those whose prophecies had application throughout the generations. Their prophecies are recorded in *Tanach*. Thus, Elkanah might well have been a Prophet, but since his prophecy did not have application in subsequent generations, he is not counted as one of the forty-eight prophets.

descended from among two men[311] who stood at the heights of the world.[312] And who are they? The children of Korach, as the verse (*Bamidbar* 26:11) states: *And the sons of Korach did not die.* It was taught in a *beraisa* in the name of our master: A place rose up in *gehinnom* and they stood upon it.

COMMENTARY

R. Shmuel bar Nachmani explained that the term *Tzofim* need not be taken as an allusion that Elkanah was a prophet,[313] for the term can be explained as a description of the city rather than the person. R. Chanan taught that *Tzofim* is indeed a reference to Elkanah but need not be taken as an indication that he was a prophet. Rather, he is referred to as coming from *Ramasayim Tzofim* because he was a descendent of the sons of Korach. The appelation is appropriate since they stood at the heights of the world and were blessed with Divine vision in that they wrote psalms which David incorporated into *Tehillim*.

Rashba explains that the sons of Korach are considered to have stood at the heights of the world vis-à-vis those surrounding them. Whereas all of the other members of Korach's group were swallowed alive and descended to *gehinnom*, Korach's sons repented and were therefore placed on an elevated plateau at the entrance to *gehinnom*.

The Talmud does not identify the forty-eight prophets although it does delineate the seven prophetesses. *Rashi*, quoting *Seder Olam*, lists forty-six

---

311 - The text of the *Ein Yaakov* records two men whereas the parallel text in the Talmud omits the word two. The latter would seem to be more appropriate since Elkanah was a descendent of only one of Korach's sons — Evyasaf. *Malbim* (in his commentary to *Divrei ha-Yamim* I 6:7-13) offers a novel interpretation to support *Ein Yaakov's* citation of Elkanah's being a descendent of two men. He notes that one of Elkanah's antecedents — also called Elkanah — is recorded as being the son of both Machas and Amasa. He explains that Amasa died without children and his brother Machas took his widow as a wife in fulfillment of the mitzvah of *yibum*. As the child of a *yibum* relationship, Elkanah was referred to as the son of both his biological father as well as of his father's deceased brother.

312 - R. Chanan's exegesis is based on translating the word רמה as *heights*. The sons of Korach, in that they did not share the fate of the other members of their father's plot, are considered to be on an elevated level.

313 - Compare to page 15 where the Talmud used the term צופים as a description for the prophets.

names in his commentary and states that he was unaware of the identity of two prophets. *Yad Yosef* identifies the the two as Oded and Chanani ha-Ro'eh. *Turei Even*, quoted in *Ahavas Eisan*, identifies them as Eliyahu ben Berachel and Elazar, the son of Aharon. The inclusion of the former is difficult to support, for there is a difference of opinion in the *Yerushalmi*; one *tanna* maintaining that Eliyahu ben Berachel is another name for Bil'am while another *tanna* maintains that it is another name for Yitzchak.

TALMUD

שֶׁבַע נְבִיאוֹת נִתְנַבְּאוּ לָהֶם לְיִשְׂרָאֵל, מָאן נִינְהוּ? שָׂרָה, מִרְיָם, דְּבוֹרָה, חַנָּה, אֲבִיגַיִל, חֻלְדָּה, אֶסְתֵּר.

TRANSLATION

Seven prophetesses prophesied on behalf of Israel. Who are they? Sarah, Miriam, Devorah, Chanah, Avigail, Chuldah and Esther.

COMMENTARY

Interestingly, the Talmud does not ask find it necessary to identify the forty-eight prophets. We might conjecture that the prophets are easily identifiable, whereas the prophetesses — aside from Miriam, Devorah and Chuldah who are specifically referred to as such in Scripture — are less obvious. In general, the qualifications that are a prerequisite for prophecy[314] make it exceedingly difficult for a woman to be granted these powers — especially in terms of acting as the instrument to transmit the Divine will to the people, which as we have seen, is the primary purpose of prophecy. *Tosafos*[315] offers an opinion that the rarity of woman leaders in Israel does not stem from an inherent inability on their part, but rather on the reluctance of the people to accept them as leaders.

TALMUD

שָׂרָה, דִּכְתִיב: "אֲבִי מִלְכָּה וַאֲבִי יִסְכָּה", וְאָמַר רַבִּי יִצְחָק: "יִסְכָּה" זוֹ שָׂרָה, וְלָמָּה נִקְרָא שְׁמָהּ: "יִסְכָּה"? שֶׁסָּכְתָה בְּרוּחַ הַקֹּדֶשׁ. דִּכְתִיב: "כֹּל אֲשֶׁר תֹּאמַר אֵלֶיךָ שָׂרָה שְׁמַע בְּקֹלָהּ". דָּבָר אַחֵר: "יִסְכָּה", שֶׁהַכֹּל סוֹכִין בְּיָפְיָהּ.

TRANSLATION

[Where do we see that] Sarah [prophesied]? The verse (*Bereishis* 11:29) states: *the*

---

314 - See *Rambam, Hilchos Yesodei ha-Torah* 7:1.
315 - See *Bava Kama* 15a, s.v. אשר.

father of Milka and the father of Yiska. R. Yitzchak explained: *Yiska* is [another name for] Sarah. Why was she called Yiska? For she foresaw[316] with the spirit of holiness, as the verse (ibid. 21:12) states: *all that Sarah says to you, listen to her speech.* Alternatively, [why was she called] Yiska? Because all saw her beauty.

COMMENTARY

The alternative explanation of the name Yiska does not mean to suggest that Sarah was not a prophetess. Rather, it points out that it is unlikely that her father Haran would have chosen the name because she was destined to become a prophetess. Hence, the name Yiska must have been given her for some other reason. According to the first opinion, however, it is possible to explain that God gave Haran the inspiration to give her the name Yiska for reasons that he was unaware of. *Ein Yaakov*[317] notes that we find a similar exposition regarding the name Ruth which God inspired Eglon to name his daughter even though he was unaware of its appropriateness.

TALMUD

"מִרְיָם" – דִּכְתִיב: "וַתִּקַּח מִרְיָם הַנְּבִיאָה אֲחוֹת אַהֲרֹן" וְגוֹ'. "אֲחוֹת אַהֲרֹן",
וְלֹא "אֲחוֹת מֹשֶׁה"?! אָמַר רַב נַחְמָן, אָמַר רַב: שֶׁהָיְתָה מִתְנַבְּאָה כְּשֶׁהִיא
אֲחוֹת אַהֲרֹן, וְאוֹמֶרֶת: עֲתִידָה אִמִּי שֶׁתֵּלֵד בֵּן שֶׁמּוֹשִׁיעַ אֶת יִשְׂרָאֵל. כֵּיוָן
שֶׁנּוֹלַד נִתְמַלֵּא כָּל הַבַּיִת כֻּלּוֹ אוֹרָה. עָמַד אָבִיהָ וּנְשָׁקָהּ עַל רֹאשָׁהּ, אָמַר לָהּ:
בִּתִּי, נִתְקַיְּמָה נְבוּאָתֵךְ. וְכֵיוָן שֶׁהִטִּילוּהוּ בַיְאוֹר, עָמַד אָבִיהָ וּטְפָחָהּ עַל
רֹאשָׁהּ וְאָמַר לָהּ: בִּתִּי הֵיכָן נְבוּאָתֵךְ? וְהַיְינוּ דִּכְתִיב: "וַתֵּתַצַּב אֲחֹתוֹ מֵרָחֹק
לְדֵעָה מַה יֵּעָשֶׂה לוֹ", מַה יְהֵא בְּסוֹף נְבִיאוּתָהּ.

TRANSLATION

[Where do we see that] Miriam [prophesied]? The verse (*Shemos* 15:20) states: *and Miriam the prophetess, the sister of Aharon, took* … [Why is she referred to as] the sister of Aharon and not as the sister of Moshe? R. Nachman explained in the name of Rav: She prophesied when she was the sister of Aharon [alone —

---

316 - R. Yitzchak explains that Sarah was given the name Yiska because of her ability to foresee the future; the name Yiska being drawn from the Aramaic *sacha* — see *Targum* to *Melachim* I 18:42. The reference from the verse is to Sarah's insistence that Avraham drive Yishmael out of his house so that he might not influence Yitzchak, an insistence that had its root in Sarah's ability to foresee the future.

317 - See his note to *Berachos* 7b.

i.e., before Moshe's birth]. She said: "My mother is destined to give birth to a son who shall rescue Israel." When he was born, the entire house became filled with light. Her father stood and kissed her head and said to her: "My daughter, your prophecy has been fulfilled." And when they cast him into the river, her father stood and tapped her head and said: "My daughter, what will become of your prophecy?" This is why the verse (ibid. 2:4) states: *and his sister stood from afar to find out what they would do to him* — i.e., to see what would become of her prophecy.

COMMENTARY

Miriam, as a prophetess, could surely not have doubted that her prophecy would be fulfilled, for as *Sefer ha-Chinuch* points out,[318] knowledge imparted through prophecy is accepted by the prophet without the least doubt. Why then did Miriam stand at the riverbank *to find out what they would do to him*?

Note that the Hebrew text of the verse cited states that she stood לדעה rather than לדעת. The latter would imply that she wanted to see whether or not her prophecy would be fulfilled while the former, a most unusual form, suggests that she wanted to see the means through which her prophecy would be fulfilled — i.e., she was curious, or sought the knowledge (דעה), as to how it would be brought to fruition when it seemed that her brother was being abandoned.

TALMUD

דְּבוֹרָה, דִּכְתִיב: "וּדְבוֹרָה אִשָּׁה נְבִיאָה, אֵשֶׁת לַפִּידוֹת". (אָמַר רַבִּי יִצְחָק): מְלַמֵּד שֶׁהָיְתָה עוֹשָׂה פְּתִילוֹת לַמִּשְׁכָּן. "וְהִיא יוֹשֶׁבֶת תַּחַת תֹּמֶר", מַאי שְׁנָא "תַּחַת תֹּמֶר"? אָמַר רַבִּי שִׁמְעוֹן בֶּן אֲבִישָׁלוֹם: מִשּׁוּם יִחוּד. דָּבָר אַחֵר: מַה תָּמָר זֶה, אֵין לוֹ אֶלָּא לֵב אֶחָד, אַף יִשְׂרָאֵל שֶׁבְּאוֹתוֹ הַדּוֹר לֹא הָיָה לָהֶם אֶלָּא לֵב אֶחָד לַאֲבִיהֶם שֶׁבַּשָּׁמַיִם.

TRANSLATION

[Where do we see that] Devorah [prophesied]? The verse (*Shoftim* 4:4) states: *Devorah, the woman prophetess,*[319] *the wife of Lapidos.* [And why does the verse mention that she was *the wife of Lapidos*?] This teaches us that she made wicks for the Tabernacle. *And she sat under the palm [tree]* (ibid.). In what way is a palm

---

318 - מצוה תקט״ז.

319 - The literal translation of אשה נביאה is *woman prophetess* which is redundant in both Hebrew and English. We might conjecture that Devorah's greatness as a woman led the verse to use both terms to describe her.

tree different [that she chose to sit specifically under it]? R. Shimon ben Avishalom explained: [She did so] because [she did not want to violate the laws] of being alone [with a man].[320] Alternatively, just like the palm has but a single heart [i.e., a trunk that grows straight up without separating into branches] so too did Israel in that generation have but a single heart for their Father in Heaven.

COMMENTARY

The Talmud seems to find the Scriptural reference to Devorah as a prophetess to be sufficient grounds to identify her as such without seeking to identify a prophetic vision of hers. This stands in contrast to Miriam, who is also referred to as a prophetess, yet the Talmud finds it necessary to describe a prophetic vision of hers. We might conjecture that Devorah's additional role as Judge of the people was sufficient grounds to establish her as a prophetess, for had she not been blessed with Divine vision, she would never have been accepted as the Judge by the people.[321]

Devorah as judge and leader of the Jews was surely better known than her husband. Why then would the verse describe her as being Lapidos' wife? The Talmud infers that the term wife of Lapidos should be interpreted as teaching us something entirely unrelated to her husband's name. Lapidos — from the Hebrew לפיד — *torch* — is consequently interpreted to mean that she made wicks for use in the Tabernacle.[322] According to *Yalkut Shimoni*, Devorah was married to Barak. The *Midrash* concludes by quoting the verse: *The wisdom of women builds her home* (*Mishlei* 14:1). Devorah's wisdom in finding a way for her husband to associate with the better elements of society built him as a person and might be why she is described as a *woman* as well as a *prophetess*.

320 - The Talmud's exegesis here is based on the apparent superfluousness of the phrase. It therefore explains that as the Judge of Israel, many people came to Devorah for advice and counsel. Rather than meet with them in her home in private, she would meet with them outside so that there not be even a remote possibility of violating the law of a married woman being alone with a man. *Rashi* adds that she chose a palm tree because it gives no shade and her meetings were thus even more public. The alternative explanation offers a homiletical means of understanding the phrase.

321 - See *Tosafos, Nidah* 50a, s.v. כל הכשר.

322 - *Tanna d'Vei Eliyahu* (9) records that Devorah made wicks for the Tabernacle so as to provide her husband, who was not especially learned, with an opportunity to associate with those who occupied themselves with the Divine service.

TALMUD

חַנָּה, דִּכְתִיב: "וַתִּתְפַּלֵּל חַנָּה וַתֹּאמַר: עָלַץ לִבִּי בַּה', רָמָה קַרְנִי". "רָמָה
קַרְנִי", וְלֹא "רָמָה פַּכִּי"? דָּוִד וּשְׁלֹמֹה שֶׁנִּמְשְׁחוּ בְקֶרֶן, נִמְשְׁכָה מַלְכוּתָן.
"אֵין קָדוֹשׁ כַּה', כִּי אֵין בִּלְתֶּךָ, וְאֵין צוּר כֵּאלֹהֵינוּ", אָמַר רַבִּי יְהוּדָה בֶּן
מְנַשְׁיָא: אַל תִּקְרֵי: "בִּלְתֶּךָ", אֶלָּא: "בְּלוֹתֶיךָ", בּוֹא וּרְאֵה, שֶׁלֹּא כְמִדַּת הַקָּדוֹשׁ
בָּרוּךְ הוּא, מִדַּת בָּשָׂר וָדָם; מִדַּת בָּשָׂר וָדָם – מַעֲשֵׂה יָדָיו מְבַלִּין אוֹתוֹ, אֲבָל
הַקָּדוֹשׁ בָּרוּךְ הוּא מְבַלֶּה אֶת מַעֲשָׂיו.
"וְאֵין צוּר כֵּאלֹהֵינוּ", אַל תִּקְרֵי "אֵין צוּר", אֶלָּא "אֵין צַיָּר"; מִנְהָגוֹ שֶׁל
עוֹלָם, אָדָם צָר צוּרָה בְּכֹתֶל, וְאֵין יָכוֹל לְהָטִיל בָּהּ רוּחַ וּנְשָׁמָה, קְרָבַיִם, וּבְנֵי
מֵעַיִם. אֲבָל הַקָּדוֹשׁ בָּרוּךְ הוּא, צָר צוּרָה בְּתוֹךְ צוּרָה, וּמַטִּיל בָּהּ רוּחַ
וּנְשָׁמָה, קְרָבַיִם, וּבְנֵי מֵעַיִם.

TRANSLATION

[Where do we see that] Chanah [prophesied]? [The verse (*Shmuel* I 2:1) states:] *And Chanah prayed and said: My heart is happy with God, my horn has been uplifted.* [What was Chanah alluding to when she said] *my horn has been uplifted* and not *my vessel has been uplifted*? [She was alluding to] Dovid and Shlomo, who were anointed with a horn [of oil], [and] were kings whose rule continued [i.e., sovereignty remained in their families].[323]

There is none as holy as God, for there is none other than Him and there is no rock like our Lord (ibid. :2). R. Yehudah ben Menashya explained: Do not read [the verse as stating] *other than Him*, but rather [as if it says] *for He does not wear out.* Come and see that the trait of the Holy One, blessed is He, is unlike the trait of a mortal. The trait of a mortal is that the work of his hands outlasts him. But the Holy One, blessed is He, outlasts the work of His hands.[324]

And there is no rock like our Lord — Do not read [the verse as stating] *there is no rock*, but rather [as if it says] *there is no artisan.* According to nature, when man makes a carving in a wall, he cannot imbue it with spirit, soul or with

---

323 - The Talmud (14a) continues: But Shaul and Yeihu, who were anointed with a vessel [of oil], were kings whose rule did not continue.

324 - *Maharal*, in the introduction to *Netzach Yisrael*, explains that were God to withdraw His providence for even a moment, natural order would immediately end. Thus, God does not allow the work of His hands to outlast Him — i.e., He does not remove His presence from the world and allow it to exist based on what He has already done.

organs of life. But the Holy One, blessed is He, creates an image [i.e., a child] within an image [i.e., in the mother's womb] and imbues it with spirit, soul and organs of life.

COMMENTARY

Chanah's words — recited when she returned to Beis El after the birth of Shmuel — were not only a prayer of thanksgiving, but also contained a prophetic message wherein she described the lasting sovereignty of those who would be anointed with a horn of oil. Additionally, her prayer included descriptions of the manner in which God's providence is evidenced. As such, it has application to all generations and is therefore considered to be prophecy and was included in the Book of *Shmuel*.

TALMUD

אֲבִיגַיִל, דִּכְתִיב: "וְהָיָה הִיא רֹכֶבֶת עַל הַחֲמוֹר, וְיֹרֶדֶת בְּסֵתֶר הָהָר", "בְּסֵתֶר הָהָר"?! "מִן הָהָר", מִיבָּעֵי לֵיהּ! אָמַר רַבָּה בַּר שְׁמוּאֵל: מְלַמֵּד שֶׁבָּאָה עַל עִסְקֵי הַדָּם הַבָּא מִן הַסְּתָרִים. מְלַמֵּד שֶׁנָּטְלָה דָם בְּחֵיקָהּ, וְהֶרְאֲתָה לוֹ. אָמַר לָהּ: וְכִי רוֹאִין דָּם בַּלַּיְלָה?! אָמְרָה לֵיהּ: וְכִי דָנִין דִּינֵי נְפָשׁוֹת בַּלַּיְלָה?! אָמַר לָהּ: מוֹרֵד בַּמַּלְכוּת הוּא, דְּלָא הֲוָה צָרִיךְ לְמִדְיָינֵיהּ. אָמְרָה לֵיהּ: עֲדַיִן שָׁאוּל קַיָּם הוּא, וְלֹא יָצָא טִבְעֲךָ בָּעוֹלָם. אָמַר לָהּ: "וּבָרוּךְ טַעְמֵךְ, וּבְרוּכָה אָתְּ, אֲשֶׁר כְּלִתִנִי הַיּוֹם הַזֶּה מִבּוֹא בְדָמִים". תְּרֵי דָמִים.

TRANSLATION

[Where do we see that] Avigail [prophesied]? [The verse (*Shmuel* I 25:20) states:] *And she was riding on the donkey and descended through the hidden part of the mountain.* [Why does the verse state] *through the hidden part of the mountain*? It should say [that she descended] *from the mountain*? Raba bar Shmuel explained: This[325] teaches us that she came concerning blood that comes from the hidden parts [of the body]. It teaches us that she took blood with her and showed it to him [so that David would rule whether the blood was menstrual or not]. He said to her: "Is blood examined at night?" She replied: "Does one judge capital cases at night?" He answered: **[14b]** "He [Naval, Avigail's husband, who David had

---

325 - Though the phrase can be understood as referring to a valley between two peaks [see *Metzudas David* ad loc.], the information is superfluous and the terminology must have been used to allude to something else.

sentenced to death] is a rebel against the king and need not be judged!"[326] She said: "Shaul is still alive and your name is not yet known."[327] He said: *Blessed is your reasoning and blessed are you for you have prevented me today from coming to [spill] blood* (ibid. :33). [The verse uses the plural form for blood indicating that there were] two bloods [in question — the blood that she asked about and the blood that would have been shed wrongly had Naval been killed].

COMMENTARY

After Shmuel secretly anointed David as king, Shaul attempted to kill him and David was forced to flee. He hid in the hills along with six hundred of his supporters and met the shepherds of Naval ha-Karmeli. David and his coterie protected Naval's shepherds and asked that they be provided with food in return for their services. David sent ten of his men to Naval while he was celebrating the festival of shearing his sheep, assuming that Naval would be both grateful and generous, but Naval rudely refused their request. David and his men understood Naval's answer as a sign of his unwillingness to recognize David's sovereignty and sentenced him to death. Naval's shepherds understood that David would be angered by their employer's answer and told Avigail — whom Scripture refers to as a wise woman — whereupon she decided to intercede on her husband's behalf.

The Talmud explains the seemingly superfluous phrase that Avigail came *from the hidden part of the mountain* as an allusion to the fact that Avigail did not approach David directly and ask him to spare her husband. Rather, she cleverly asked him a halachic question whose obvious answer would give her the opportunity to chide David for having judged her husband. The wisdom that Avigail showed in the entire incident is evidence that she possessed the sagacity that is the prerequisite for her prophecy which the Talmud proceeds to detail.

---

326 - The regular rules of judgement which preclude trying capital offences at night are suspended in cases of rebelling against the king. See *Sanhedrin* 32a; *Rambam, Hilchos Melachim* 3:8.

327 - I.e., though you have already been anointed as king, you have not yet assumed rule since Shaul is still alive. Since the principle is that two kings cannot rule simultaneously (*Chullin* 60b). Naval cannot be judged for having rebelled against a king — a capital offence — for having refused your request.

TALMUD

אָמְרָה לוֹ: "וְלֹא תִהְיֶה זֹאת לְךָ לְפוּקָה וּלְמִכְשׁוֹל". "זֹאת" – מִכְּלַל דְּאִיכָּא
אַחֲרִיתִי, וּמַאי נִיהוּ? מַעֲשֵׂה דְּבַת שֶׁבַע. וּמַסְקָנָא הֲכִי הֲוָה.
"וְהָיְתָה נֶפֶשׁ אֲדֹנִי צְרוּרָה בִּצְרוֹר הַחַיִּים, אֵת ה' אֱלֹהֶיךָ", כִּי הֲוַת מִיפְטְרָה
מִנֵּיהּ, קָאָמְרָה לֵיהּ: "וְהֵיטִב ה' לַאדֹנִי, וְזָכַרְתָּ אֶת אֲמָתֶךָ", אָמַר רַב נַחְמָן:
הַיְינוּ דְּאָמְרֵי אֱנָשֵׁי: אִיתְּתָא, בַּהֲדֵי שׁוּתָא – פִּילְכָא. אִי נַמִי: שָׁפִיל וְאָזִיל בַּר-
אַוְזָא, וְעֵינוֹהִי מְטַיְיפִין.

TRANSLATION

She revealed her thigh[328] and David followed her light [was filled with lust] for a
distance of three *parsaos* and said to her: "Listen to me [i.e., give yourself over to
me]." She said to him: *Let this not be for you as a stumbling block and an*
obstacle (ibid. :31). [Avigail's use of the word] *this* indicates that there was another
[time that David did stumble]. What was it [i.e., when did this occur]? The incident
of Bas Sheva. And in the end, this is what happened.[329]

[Avigail blessed David and said:] *And may the soul of my master be bound up*
with the living (ibid. :29). When she was leaving, she said to him: And when
God shall be good to my master, remember your maideservant (ibid. :31). R.
Nachman explained: This is what people say: "Women! While they talk they
knit!"[330] Alternatively, "The goose walks with his head down but sees far
away."

---

328 - *Tosafos* (ד"ה שגלתה שוקה) questions how it is possible that Avigail could act so
brazenly. *Iyun Yaakov* points out that she might have done so to insure that she had
David's full attention, for her major concerns were to save her husband's life and
prevent David from shedding blood.

Maharsha explains that this dialogue is an alternative means of understanding what
David meant when he told her that she was blessed for having saved him from two
cases of bloodshed. David was praising her for having saved him from killing Naval
and for having prevented him from cohabiting with her which would have made him
subject to death since she was a married woman.

Gra removes the entire incident from the text.

329 - In that case, David's actions led to the death of Uriah. We thus see that
Avigail's statement *let this not be for you as a stumbling block and an obstacle* was
prophecy, for she foresaw that David would someday stumble and cause the death of a
man.

330 - *Rashi* (ד"ה בהדי שותא) explains the parable. Though Avigail was ostensibly
thanking David for saving Naval, she was alluding to the fact that she would become
David's wife after Naval died. This is another indication of her prophetic vision.

TALMUD

חֻלְדָּה, דִּכְתִיב: "וַיֵּלֶךְ חִלְקִיָּהוּ הַכֹּהֵן, וַאֲחִיקָם, וְעַכְבּוֹר, וְשָׁפָן וַעֲשָׂיָה, אֶל
חֻלְדָּה הַנְּבִיאָה אֵשֶׁת שַׁלֻּם בֶּן תִּקְוָה". וּבְמָקוֹם דְּקָאֵי יִרְמְיָה, הֵיכִי מִתְנַבְּאָה
אִיהִי? אָמְרֵי בֵּי רַב מִשְּׁמֵיהּ דְּרַב: חֻלְדָּה – קְרוֹבַת יִרְמְיָה הָיְתָה, וְלָא אַקְפִּיד
עֲלָהּ.

TRANSLATION

[Where do we see that] Chuldah [prophesied]? [The verse (*Melachim* II 25:20) states:] *And Chilkiyahu the kohen, Achikam, Achbor, Shafan and Asayah went to Chuldah the prophetess, wife of Shalum ben Tikva.* But if Yirmiyahu was still alive, how could she prophesy?[331] It was taught in the school of Rav in the name of Rav: Chuldah was a relative of Yirmiyahu's and he therefore did not mind that she [prophesied].

COMMENTARY

Yoshiyahu served as king of Yehudah following the reigns of Achaz, Menashe and Amon who were all wicked. During the period of their rule, they prevented the people from studying Torah and went so far as to burn the Torah scrolls. One Torah scroll survived their efforts and was found in a tunnel under the *Beis ha-Mikdash.* According to tradition, this scroll was the one that had been written by Moshe before his death.

Torah scrolls are usually rolled from beginning to end, but when Chilkiyahu the *kohen* found this scroll, it was rolled towards the end. When he unrolled it, the Torah opened to the verse from the portion of remonstration in the Book of Devarim that states (28:36): *God shall take you and the king who you shall place upon you to a nation who you do not know.* Chilkiyahu advised Shafan — the king's scribe — of his discovery and the latter informed Yoshiyahu. The king was shaken by the discovery and immediately dispatched a delegation to determine its meaning. The delegation went to Chuldah who prophetically explained the significance of the discovery.

Maharsha comments that Yoshiyahu was afraid that the discovery was an

---

331 - Any prophet alive at the time of Yirmiyahu would have to be considered his disciple. A disciple may not render a legal decision in front of his master, and by extension, a student prophet may not prophecy in his master's presence. However, if Yirmiyahu did not mind, it would be permitted. See *Rambam, Talmud Torah* 8:2.

ominous sign which Yirmiyahu might interpret prophetically as an indication of the imminent doom of his kingdom. He therefore preferred to consult with Chuldah, for even if this was the meaning of what had happened, she would surely pray for mercy on the people's behalf.

TALMUD

וְיֹאשִׁיָהוּ גּוּפֵיהּ הֵיכִי שָׁבִיק יִרְמְיָה, וְקָא מְשַׁדַּר לָהּ לְחֻלְדָּה? אָמַר רַבִּי שִׁילָא: מִפְּנֵי שֶׁהַנָּשִׁים רַחֲמָנִיּוֹת הֵן. רַבִּי יוֹחָנָן אָמַר: יִרְמְיָה הוּא דְּלָא הֲוָה תַּמָּן, שֶׁהָלַךְ לְהַחֲזִיר עֲשֶׂרֶת הַשְּׁבָטִים. וּמִנָּלָן דְּאַהַדוּר? דִּכְתִיב: "כִּי הַמּוֹכֵר אֶל הַמִּמְכָּר לֹא יָשׁוּב", אֶפְשָׁר דְּיוֹבֵל בָּטֵל הוּא, וְנָבִיא מִתְנַבֵּא עָלָיו שֶׁיִּבָּטֵל?! אֶלָּא מְלַמֵּד שֶׁהֶחֱזִירָן יִרְמְיָה, וְיֹאשִׁיָה בֶן אָמוֹן מָלַךְ עֲלֵיהֶם.

TRANSLATION

How did Yoshiyahu leave Yirmiyahu and send messengers to Chuldah? R. Shila answered: Because women are merciful.[332] R. Yochanan answered: Yirmiyahu was not there [in Jerusalem at the time] for he had gone to bring the ten tribes [that Sancheriv led into exile] back. And how do we know that he brought them? The verse (*Yechezkel* 7:13) states: *For the seller shall not return to his goods* [they will not be returned to him because *yovel* will no longer be observed]. Is it possible that the *yovel* had [already] ceased [to be observed] and the Prophet prophesied that it was destined to cease? Rather, this teaches us that Yirmiyahu brought them back and Yoshiyahu ben Amon ruled over them.[333]

TALMUD

דִּכְתִיב: "וַיֹּאמֶר מָה הַצִּיּוּן הַלָּז אֲשֶׁר אֲנִי רֹאֶה? וַיֹּאמְרוּ אֵלָיו אַנְשֵׁי הָעִיר:

---

332 - By right, Yoshiyahu should have consulted with Yirmiyahu, for he was the major prophet. Why then did he ask Chuldah to explain the significance of the discovery of the Book of *Devarim*? R. Shila answered that the king preferred to consult with Chuldah because women are more merciful.

333 - *Yovel* was only observed when all of Israel resided in the Land of Israel (see *Rambam*, *Hilchos Shemitah ve-Yovel* 10:8). *Rashi* (*Sanhedrin* 110b) writes that if there are representatives of all of the tribes residing in Israel, then the land is considered to be in a state wherein all of Israel resides in the Land of Israel and *yovel* can be reinstituted. Thus, if Yirmiyahu had not brought the ten tribes back, the *yovel* would have ceased to be observed even before Yechezkel prophesied that it would cease and his prophecy would be meaningless. The Talmud therefore establishes that Yirmiyahu must have brought them back and they were exiled again— causing the *yovel* to cease — as per Yechezkel's prophecy.

הַקֶּבֶר אִישׁ־הָאֱלֹהִים אֲשֶׁר בָּא מִיהוּדָה, וַיִּקְרָא אֶת הַדְּבָרִים הָאֵלֶּה אֲשֶׁר
עָשִׂיתָ עַל הַמִּזְבֵּחַ בֵּית אֵל". וְכִי מַה־טִּיבוֹ שֶׁל יֹאשִׁיָּה עַל הַמִּזְבֵּחַ בְּבֵית אֵל?
אֶלָּא מְלַמֵּד שֶׁיִּרְמְיָה הֶחֱזִירָן, וְיֹאשִׁיָּהוּ מָלַךְ עֲלֵיהֶם. רַב נַחְמָן אָמַר: מֵהָכָא:
"גַּם יְהוּדָה שָׁת קָצִיר לָךְ, בְּשׁוּבִי שְׁבוּת עַמִּי".

TRANSLATION

[Where do we see that Yoshiyahu ruled over the ten tribes?] The verse (*Melachim* II
23:17) states: *And he said: What is that sign that I see? And the people of the
town answered: It is the grave of the man of God who came from Yehudah and
he read these things that you did on the altar in Beis El.* What was Yoshiyahu
doing at the altar at Beis El? This teaches us that Yirmiyau brought them [the
ten tribes] back and Yoshiyahu ruled over them. R. Nachman said: [Proof that
Yirmiyahu brought them back can be drawn] from here. *And Yehudah will also be
an officer for you when I shall return the remnant of my people* (*Hoshea* 6:11).

COMMENTARY

The discovery of the Torah scroll reinforced Yoshiyahu's determination to
abandon the ways of his predecessors. He gathered the nation at the *Beis ha-
Mikdash* and read the Torah publicly. He then called for a reaffirmation of the
nation's covenant with God and ordered that all of the implements and vessels
that had been used in the service of idolatry be destroyed along with the false
gods that the people had worshipped. Finally, he went to Beis El and destroyed
the altar that Yeravam ben Nevat had constructed. While there, he found a
gravestone and asked the people who was buried there. They told him that it was
the grave of the Prophet Ido, who had died some three hundred years earlier after
having prophesied to Yeravam that a descendent of David was destined to destroy
the altar that he had constructed.

Malbim[334] explains that when Yirmiyahu saw that Yoshiyahu had brought
the people to repent and had set out to destroy all of the idols and false gods that
they worshipped, he determined that the time was ripe to bring the ten tribes
back from the exile of Sancheriv. He adds that had the people not continued to
discretely worship their false gods, Yoshiyahu would have been worthy of
becoming *mashiach*.[335]

---

334 - See his commentary to *Melachim* II 23:25.
335 - See *Rambam, Hilchos Melachim* 11:1.

TALMUD

אֶסְתֵּר, דִּכְתִיב: "וַיְהִי בַּיּוֹם הַשְּׁלִישִׁי וַתִּלְבַּשׁ אֶסְתֵּר מַלְכוּת". "מַלְכוּת"?! "בִּגְדֵי מַלְכוּת" מִיבָּעֵי לֵיהּ! מְלַמֵּד שֶׁלְּבָשַׁתָּה רוּחַ הַקֹּדֶשׁ; כְּתִיב הָכָא: "וַתִּלְבַּשׁ אֶסְתֵּר מַלְכוּת", וּכְתִיב הָתָם: "וְרוּחַ לָבְשָׁה אֶת עֲמָשַׂי".

TRANSLATION

[Where do we see that] Esther [prophesied]? The verse (*Esther* 5:1) states: *And it was on the third day and Esther clothed herself in royalty.* [Why does the verse say] *royalty*? It should say *in royal clothing.* This teaches us that she clothed herself in the spirit of holiness. [How do we know this?] Here the verse states: *and she clothed herself* and elsewhere the verse (*Divrei ha-Yamim* I 12:19) states: *and the spirit was clothed upon Amasai* [and we thus see that *clothed* can be used as a means of describing the assumption of the spirit of holiness — i.e., prophecy].

COMMENTARY

R.Tzadok *ha-Kohen* of Lublin[336] notes that the Talmud's deduction that the use of the term *royalty* rather than *royal clothing* indicates that Esther prophesied is similar to the explanation of the *Midrash* that whenever the word king appears in the *Megillah* without mentioning Achashverosh, the reference is also to God. The name of God does not appear in the *Megillah* because the events transpired at a time of *hester panim* — when God's countenance was hidden. The author used the term *king* as a means of making a veiled reference to God. Hence, the *Megillah's* references to prophecy, which are also manifestations of the Divine presence, are also veiled.

The use of the word *clothed* for prophecy is also found in *Yeshayahu* (57:16) where the verse states: *For the spirit before me clothed me. Rambam*[337] writes: *When the spirit of holiness/prophecy comes upon a prophet, his soul becomes like an angel and he becomes another person and understands that he is no longer what he was before but that he has ascended to a higher plateau.* Thus, the verse (*Shmuel* I 10:6) states regarding Shaul: *And the spirit of God shall come upon you and you shall prophesy and become another person.* This transformation is what the verse describes as being *clothed* in a different manner — in Esther's case as being *clothed in royalty.*

---

336 - מחשבת חרוץ, pg. 91.

337 - See א:ז הלכות יסודי התורה.

TALMUD

וַאֲמַר רַב נַחְמָן: לָא יָאָה יוֹהֲרָא לִנְשֵׁי. תַּרְתֵּי נְבִיאָתֵי הוּא דַהַוְיָאן יְהִירָאִין, וְסַנְיָין שְׁמַיְיהוּ. חֲדָא – שְׁמָה "זְבוּרְתָּא". וַחֲדָא – שְׁמָה "כַּרְכּוּשְׁתָּא". בִּזְבוּרְתָּא כְּתִיב בָּהּ: "וַתִּשְׁלַח וַתִּקְרָא לְבָרָק בֶּן אֲבִינֹעַם", וְאִלּוּ אִיהִי לָא אַזְלָא לְגַבֵּיהּ. בְּכַרְכּוּשְׁתָּא כְּתִיב בָּהּ: "אִמְרוּ לָאִישׁ אֲשֶׁר שָׁלַח אֶתְכֶם אֵלַי", וְלָא קָאֲמְרָה לְהוּ: "אִמְרוּ לַמֶּלֶךְ".

אָמַר רַב נַחְמָן: חֻלְדָּה הַנְּבִיאָה, מִבְּנֵי בָנָיו שֶׁל יְהוֹשֻׁעַ הָיָתָה, כְּתִיב הָכָא: "בֶּן חַרְחַס", וּכְתִיב הָתָם: "וַיִּקְבְּרוּ אוֹתוֹ בִּגְבוּל נַחֲלָתוֹ בְּתִמְנַת חֶרֶס".

TRANSLATION

R. Nachman taught: Haughtiness is unbecoming to women. [How do we see this?] There were two prophetesses who acted haughtily and [in both cases] their names have degraded [associations].[338] One's name was Devorah [which means bee] and the other was Chuldah [which means rat]. Regarding Devorah the verse (*Shoftim* 4:6) states: *And she sent and called for Barak ben Avinoam* but she did not go to him. Regarding Chuldah the verse (*Melachim* II 22:15) states: *Tell the man who sent you* and she did not say *tell the king*.

R. Nachman [also] taught: Chuldah was a descendant of Yehoshua bin Nun. [How do we know this?] The verse here (ibid. :14) states: *[Chuldah the prophetess, the wife of Shalum ben Tikva] ben Charchas* and there (*Shoftim* 2:9) the verse states: *and they buried him [Yehoshua] on the boundary of his portion, in Timnas Cheres.*[339]

COMMENTARY

R. Nachman's criticism of Devorah and Chuldah bears further examination, for as prophetesses their behavior would seem to be defensible — especially in

---

338 - See page 154 where we mentioned that the name given to a person might well relate to later events. In this case, both Devorah and Chuldah might have been given their names — which have disparaging connotations — because they were destined to eventually act in an inappropriate manner.

339 - The Talmud bases itself on the similarity between the names Charchas and Timnas Cheres. *Maharsha* notes that Charchas was Shalum's grandfather and thus not necessarily a relative of Chuldah's. What proof then is there that she was a descendent of Yehoshua? He answers that since Scripture mentions her husband's genealogy, we can assume that both were descendents of the same family.

the case of Devorah. *Michtav me-Eliyahu*[340] writes that Scripture, as well as the Sages, subjected the behavior of the leaders of each generation to scrutiny, for their positions call upon them to serve as role models. Behavior that might be appropriate — or at least understandable — in a person of lesser stature can well be seen as unsuitable when the person occupies a position of leadership. Moreover, if a leader fails to take advantage of a situation to impart a moral lesson or establish a pattern of behavior, he is also subjected to criticism. Thus, both Devorah and Chuldah, who had opportunities to reinforce the inherent traits of self-effacement and modesty that are the hallmarks of Jewish women, are criticized by R. Nachman.[341]

TALMUD

אִיתִיבֵיהּ רַב עֵינָא סָבָא לְרַב נַחְמָן, שְׁמוֹנָה נְבִיאִים וְהֵם כֹּהֲנִים, יָצְאוּ מֵרָחָב הַזּוֹנָה, וְאֵלּוּ הֵן: נֵרִיָּה, בָּרוּדְ, שְׂרָיָה, וּמַחְסֵיָה, יִרְמִיָה, חִלְקִיָּה, חֲנַמְאֵל, וְשַׁלֵּם. רַבִּי יְהוּדָה אוֹמֵר: אַף חֻלְדָּה הַנְּבִיאָה מִבְּנֵי בָנֶיהָ שֶׁל רָחָב הַזּוֹנָה הָיְתָה, כְּתִיב הָכָא: "בֶּן תִּקְוָה", וּכְתִיב הָתָם: "אֶת תִּקְוַת חוּט הַשָּׁנִי הַזֶּה". אָמַר לֵיהּ: עֵינָא סָבָא, וְאָמְרֵי לָהּ: פְּתִיָא אוּכְמָא, מִינִי וּמִינָךְ תִּסְתַּיֵּם שְׁמַעֲתָּתָא, דְּאִיגַיְירָא וְנָסְבָהּ יְהוֹשֻׁעַ. וּמִי הֲווֹ לֵיהּ בָּנֵי לִיהוֹשֻׁעַ? וְהָכְתִיב: "נוּן בְּנוֹ, יְהוֹשֻׁעַ בְּנוֹ"? בָּנֵי, לָא הֲווֹ לֵיהּ, אֲבָל בְּנָתָא הֲווֹ לֵיהּ.

TRANSLATION

R. Aina Sava asked R. Nachman, and some say that [it was] R. Avira Sava who asked R. Nachman: [We have a tradition that] eight prophets who were *kohanim* were descendents of Rachav the prostitute and they are: Neriah, Baruch, Serayah, Machsayah, Yirmiyah, Chilkiyah, Chanamel and Shalum.[342] R. Yehudah said:

---

340 - Vol. I, pg. 161.

341 - This would seem to be the opinion of *Iyun Yaakov* as well, for he notes that the Talmud (*Berachos* 10a) records that the Prophet Yeshayahu insisted that King Chizkiyahu come to him. In that case Yeshayahu held that it was important that the political leader of the generation — Chizkiyahu — show that he too was subservient to the religious leader of the generation — the Prophet. In this case, however, it was more important that Devorah reinforce the sense of modesty among women.

342 - *Rashi* does not include Chilkiyah, Chanamel and Shalum as prophets — even though Scripture quotes a prophecy of Chanamel. Perhaps, he held that their prophecies did not have application to other generations and they are therefore not to be included among the forty-eight prophets.

Chuldah the prophetess was also a descendent of Rachav the prostitute. [How do we know this?] The verse here (op. cit) states: *Ben Tikva* and the verse there (*Yehoshua* 2:18) states: *this cord*[343] *of scarlet thread*. He answered: Aina Sava! And some say that he said: Charred vessel![344] From you [i.e., based on your tradition that Chuldah's husband — and by extension Chuldah herself — was a descendent of Rachav] and from me [who has a tradition that they were descendents of Yehoshua] the [following] teaching can be quoted.[345] She [Rachav] converted and married Yehoshua [and thus Chuldah could be descended from both Yehoshua and Rachav].

Did Yehoshua have sons [and therefore descendents]? The verse (*Divrei ha-Yamim* I 7:28) states: *his son Nun and his son Yehoshua* [and no further children are listed from which we can infer that Yehoshua had no children]? He had no sons but he had daughters.

COMMENTARY

When the Jews were about to cross the Jordan and begin the conquest of the Land of Israel, Yehoshua dispatched two spies. Their entry into Jericho did not go unnoticed and they were hidden by Rachav. She asked that they spare her and her family when they came to beseige the city. They swore that they would do so and told her to gather her immediate family into her home and hang a red thread from the window. According to tradition, she converted after the Jews conquered the city and married Yehoshua.

Tosafos raises an interesting question. How could Yehoshua have married Rachav when the Talmud[346] rules that one is forbidden to marry men or women from the seven nations that inhabited the Land of Canaan? He answers that

---

343 - The Talmud bases itself on the similarity between the name Tikva and the Hebrew term for cord — *tikva* — that the verse uses. Again, though Tikva was the name of Chuldah's father-in-law, the Talmud would seem to assume that she and her husband were descendents of the same family.

344 - A term of endearment.

345 - Our translation of תסתיים שמעתתא is based on *Rashi* (עבודה זרה טז:, ד"ה תסתיים שמעתתא).

346 - See *Yevamos* 76a. *Rambam* (הלכות איסורי ביאה יב:כב) rules that the Torah prohibition of marrying men or women from the seven nations does not apply to converts. *Ramban* and *Sefer ha-Chinuch* agree with *Tosafos* that the prohibition applies to converts from these nations as well.

Rachav must have been from another nation and only lived in Jericho. *Iyun Yaakov* answers that the prohibition of marrying women from the Canaanite nations is based on the *halachah* that all of these people were to be killed. Since Rachav was to be spared, the prohibition of marrying her did not apply.

TALMUD

בִּשְׁלָמָא אִינְהוּ מִפָּרְשֵׁי, אֲבָל אֲבָהָתַיְיהוּ מְנָא לָן? כִּדְעוּלָא, דְּאָמַר עוּלָא: כָּל מָקוֹם שֶׁשְּׁמוֹ וְשֵׁם אָבִיו בִּנְבִיאוּת – בְּיָדוּעַ שֶׁהוּא נָבִיא בֶן נָבִיא; שְׁמוֹ וְלֹא שֵׁם אָבִיו – בְּיָדוּעַ שֶׁהוּא נָבִיא, וְלֹא בֶן נָבִיא.

כָּל שֶׁשְּׁמוֹ וְשֵׁם עִירוֹ מְפֹרָשׁ – בְּיָדוּעַ שֶׁהוּא נָבִיא מֵאוֹתָהּ הָעִיר; שְׁמוֹ וְלֹא שֵׁם עִירוֹ – בְּיָדוּעַ שֶׁהוּא נָבִיא מִירוּשָׁלַיִם.

בְּמַתְנִיתָא תָּנָא: כָּל שֶׁמַּעֲשָׂיו סְתוּמִין, וּמַעֲשֵׂה אֲבוֹתָיו סְתוּמִין, וּפֵרַט לְךָ הַכָּתוּב בְּאֶחָד מֵהֶם לְשֶׁבַח, כְּגוֹן: "דְּבַר ה' אֲשֶׁר הָיָה אֶל־צְפַנְיָה בֶּן־כּוּשִׁי בֶּן־גְּדַלְיָה, בֶּן־אֲמַרְיָה, בֶּן־חִזְקִיָּה", בְּיָדוּעַ שֶׁהוּא צַדִּיק בֶּן צַדִּיק. וְכָל שֶׁפֵּרַט לְךָ הַכָּתוּב בְּאֶחָד מֵהֶם לִגְנַאי, כְּגוֹן: "וַיְהִי בַּחֹדֶשׁ הַשְּׁבִיעִי בָּא יִשְׁמָעֵאל בֶּן נְתַנְיָה בֶן אֱלִישָׁמָע מִזֶּרַע הַמְּלוּכָה", בְּיָדוּעַ שֶׁהוּא רָשָׁע בֶּן רָשָׁע.

TRANSLATION

[15a] This [i.e., the tradition that Yirmiyahu, Chanamel, Baruch and Serayah were prophets] is appropriate, for they are specifically mentioned [as prophets]. But from where do we see [that] their fathers [i.e., Chilkiyah, Neriah, Mechasyah and Shalum were also prophets since they are not mentioned in Scripture as having prophesied]? [The answer is] as Ula [explained], for Ula taught: Everywhere where his [the prophet's] name and his father's name [are recorded when Scripture recounts] the prophecy, it is known that he is a prophet [who is] the son of a prophet. [If] his name [is recorded] and his father's name is not, it is known that he is a prophet but he is not the son of a prophet.

All [those] whose name and the name of the city [where he lived] are recorded — it is known that he is a prophet from that city. [If his] name [is mentioned] but the name of his city is not — it is known that he is a prophet from Jerusalem.

In a *beraisa* we learned: All whose actions are unrecorded and whose father's actions are unrecorded and Scripture offered praiseworthy details regarding one of them [i.e., either the person himself or one of his antecedents]; for example, [in the verse (*Tzefaniah* 1:1)] *The word of God spoken to Tzefaniah, son of Cushi, son of Gedalyah, son of Amaryah, son of Chizkiyah* — it is known that he was a righteous man, the son of a righteous man [i.e., all of those mentioned were righteous].[347] [But] all [those] who Scripture offered degrading details regarding one of them; for example, [in the verse (*Yirmiyahu* 41:1)] *And it was in the seventh month, Yishmael, son of Nesanyah, son of Elishamah of the royal seed* — it is known that he was a wicked man the son of a wicked man [i.e., all those mentioned were wicked].

COMMENTARY

Maharsha points out that Scripture is not a historical record of Israel. The prophets of Israel were famous and there was no need to trace their genealogies so as to etablish their worthiness. Hence, if a verse recounting a prophetic message adds the name of the prophet's father, the information must have been added to indicate that the father was also a prophet. However, the addition of the father's name when the prophet is first introduced does not indicate that the former was also a prophet.[348]

Ula added that when the prophet came from Jerusalem, there was no point in mentioning the name of his city, for Jerusalem is especially conducive to prophetic vision and the mention of the city thus teaches us nothing new.[349] The *beraisa* adds that if a wicked person's antecedents are listed, we can assume that they too were wicked people, for otherwise Scripture would have had no reason to include their names. Moreover, we can assume that the evil that the subject person did was rooted in those antecedents listed in Scripture.[350]

TALMUD

אָמַר רַב נַחְמָן: "מַלְאָכִי" - זֶה מָרְדְּכַי, וְלָמָה נִקְרָא שְׁמוֹ "מַלְאָכִי"? מִפְּנֵי שֶׁהוּא שֵׁנִי לַמֶּלֶךְ. מֵיתִיבֵי, בָּרוּךְ בֶּן נֵרִיָּה, וּשְׂרָיָה בֶּן מַחְסֵיָה, וְדָנִיֵּאל וּמָרְדְּכַי בִּלְשָׁן, וְחַגַּי, זְכַרְיָה וּמַלְאָכִי. כֻּלָּם נִתְנַבְּאוּ בִּשְׁנַת שְׁתַּיִם לְדָרְיָוֶשׁ, תִּיוּבְתָּא.

---

347 - Since we know that Tzefaniah was righteous, for he was a Prophet, we also know that all of his antecedents were also righteous. Otherwise, Scripture would not mention them as being part of his genealogy. Conversely, when we know that the person mentioned was wicked, as in the example of Yishmael son of Nesanyah who killed Gedaliah ben Achikam, we can extrapolate that the antecedents mentioned in the verse must have also been wicked. See *Rashi* to *Bereishis* 49:6.

348 - E.g., Hoshea ben B'eri (*Hoshea* 1:1) or Zefaniah ben Kushi (*Zefaniah* 1:1).

349 - See the commentary of *Siforno* to *Bereishis* 28:17.

350 - See *Rashi* to *Bersihis* 49:6, s.v. בקהלם.

תַּנְיָא, רַבִּי יְהוֹשֻׁעַ בֶּן קָרְחָה אוֹמֵר: "מַלְאָכִי" – זֶה עֶזְרָא. וַחֲכָמִים אוֹמְרִים: "מַלְאָכִי" שְׁמוֹ. אָמַר רַב נַחְמָן מִסְתַּבְּרָא כְּמַאן דַּאֲמַר: "מַלְאָכִי" – זֶה עֶזְרָא, דִּכְתִיב בִּנְבוּאָתֵיה דְּמַלְאָכִי: "בָּגְדָה יְהוּדָה, וְתוֹעֵבָה נֶעֶשְׂתָה בְיִשְׂרָאֵל וּבִירוּשָׁלַיִם, כִּי חִלֵּל יְהוּדָה קֹדֶשׁ ה' אֲשֶׁר אָהֵב, וּבָעַל בַּת אֵל נֵכָר". וּמַאן אַפְרֵישׁ נָשִׁים נָכְרִיּוֹת מִיִּשְׂרָאֵל? עֶזְרָא, דִּכְתִיב: "וַיַּעַן שְׁכַנְיָה בֶן יְחִיאֵל מִבְּנֵי עֵילָם, וַיֹּאמֶר לְעֶזְרָא: אֲנַחְנוּ מָעַלְנוּ בֵאלֹהֵינוּ, וַנֹּשֶׁב נָשִׁים נָכְרִיּוֹת מֵעַמֵּי הָאָרֶץ".

TRANSLATION

Rav[351] taught: [The prophet] Malachi is Mordechai [i.e., they are the same person]. Why was he called Malachi? Because he was second to the king.[352] It was asked: [The *beraisa* states that] Baruch ben Neriyah, Serayah ben Mechasyah, Daniel, Mordechai Balshan, Chagai, Zechariah and Malachi all prophesied in the second year of Darius. [This is a] refutation [of that which Rav taught]![353]

We learned in a *beraisa*: R. Yehoshua ben Karcha taught: Malachi is Ezra. The Sages held: Malachi was his name.[354] R. Nachman said: It is logical [to accept the opinion of] the one who said that Malachi is Ezra, for in the prophecy of Malachi the verse (*Malachi* 2:11) states: *Yehudah has been unfaithful and an abomination has been done in Israel and Jerusalem, for Yehudah has desecrated the holiness of God that he loved, he has cohabited with the daughter of a strange god.* Who was it that drove out the gentile women from Israel? Ezra, as the verse (*Ezra* 10:2) states: *And Shechanyah ben Yechiel from Eilam answered: We have sinned against our Lord, for we have taken gentile women from the people of the land.*[355]

---

351 - The parallel text in the Talmud quotes this statement in the name of R. Nachman, but *Mesores ha-Shas* points out that the *Ein Yaakov's* text quotes Rav as being the *amora* who held that Mordechai and Malachi were the same person. This would seem to be logical in that the Talmud goes on to quote R. Nachman as offering proof that Malachi and Ezra were the same person.

352 - *Maharsha* explains that the name Malachi — derived from the Hebrew מלאך — *angel* or *messenger* — implies that the reference is to a person of great importance.

353 - I.e., since both Mordechai and Malachi are mentioned in the *beraisa*, they could not be the same person.

354 - I.e., there was a prophet whose name was Malachi.

355 - Since the works of both Malachi and Ezra speak about the problem of intermarriage with gentile women, there are grounds to assume that they are the same person.

COMMENTARY

The Talmud seems to take it as a matter of course that Malachi was not the name of a prophet, but a pseudonym for someone else.[356] *Tosafos*[357] writes that Malachi was Ezra, offering contextual proof and discounting the opinion of the Sages cited here. We can conjecture that aside from the opinion of R. Yehoshua ben Korcha, he based his certainty on the *Targum* of Yonasan ben Uziel who translates the first verse in *Malachi* by writing: ביד מלאכי דיתקרי שמיה עזרא ספרא — *through Malachi who was called Ezra the Scribe.* As we have previously seen, the *Targum* of Yonasan was based on a tradition handed down from Chagai, Zechariah and Malachi.

We might add that the prophecy of Ezra/Malachi was separated from the historical record of Israel contained in the Book of *Ezra* and written as a separate work in the same way that David's psalms and Shlomo's works of wisdom were separated from the historical accounts of their times cited in the Books of *Shmuel* and *Melachim*.

TALMUD

תָּנוּ רַבָּנָן: אַרְבַּע נָשִׁים יְפֵיפִיּוֹת הָיוּ בָעוֹלָם. וְאֵלּוּ הֵן: שָׂרָה, רָחָב, אֲבִיגַיִל וְאֶסְתֵּר. וּלְמָאן דַּאֲמַר: אֶסְתֵּר יְרַקְרֶקֶת הָיְתָה, אַפִּיק אֶסְתֵּר, וְעַיֵּיל וַשְׁתִּי.

TRANSLATION

The Sages taught: There were four outstandingly beautiful women in the world: Sarah, Rachav, Avigail and Esther. According to the one who said that Esther was green,[358] remove Esther and replace her with Vashti.[359]

---

356 - *Metzudas David (Malachi* 1:1) translates Malachi as *my angel* rather than seeing it as a name. We might add that the context of that verse would suggest that *Malachi* is used as a description or pseudonym. Moreover, the name itself is not mentioned elsewhere which would also suggest that it was not the name of a prophet.

357 - יבמות פו: ד״ה מפני מה

358 - See page 127.

359 - *Tosafos* (s.v. ארבע נשים) points out that Chava is not included — even though the Talmud (*Bava Basra* 58a) writes that in comparison to her, Sarah resembeled a monkey — for Chava was created by God and was not born to a mortal. The purpose of the Talmud's statement here should be seen as teaching us that just as mortal man can achieve a level of physical perfection, so too can he achieve spiritual perfection.

COMMENTARY

There are two ways that the appreciation of physical beauty can be viewed: as a means of arousing one's sexual desires or as a means of expressing one's awe for the perfection of God's creation. Those who limit God's presence in the world to the realm of spirituality find it impossible to see physical beauty as a manifestation of God's powers and go so far as to characterize it as the work of sinister powers attempting to lead man to stray from the true path. Thus, when they seek to achieve a permanent level of holiness, they see no recourse but to insist upon celibacy. Those who deny God's presence in this world altogether, see beauty as an end unto itself. They permit themselves anything and everything, for they owe no fealty to an authority other than their own or to the minimal restrictions that their society establishes as a means of self-protection.

The Torah and its Sages, on the other hand, understand that the physical world is also a manifestation of God — a manifestation that is to be appreciated and enjoyed.[360] Indeed, man's mission in the physical world is to elevate the physical so that it has spiritual application as well. He is to express his appreciation for beauty and relate to it as part of God. It is for this reason that when one sees something of outstanding beauty, he is dutybound to recite a blessing.[361]

It is in this sense that we must understand the Talmud's statement here regarding Sarah, Rachav, Avigail and Esther. Aside from the spiritual greatness of these women, they possessed physical beauty that was also remarkable and the Sages therefore pointed it out.

TALMUD

תָּנוּ רַבָּנָן: רָחָב – בִּשְׁמָהּ זִנְּתָה. יָעֵל – בְּקוֹלָהּ. אֲבִינֵיִל – בִּזְכִירָתָהּ – מִיכַל בַּת שָׁאוּל – בִּרְאִיָּתָהּ.

TRANSLATION

The Sages taught: Rachav — the mention of her name [can lead one to]

---

360 - See *Nazir* 3a. *Ramban* to *Bamidbar* 6:11 notes that a *nazir* is required to offer a sacrifice at the end of his period of *nezirus* because he was not spiritually strong enough to withstand the temptations that are the lot of man but found it necessary to impose additional restrictions upon himself. Note also that even the *nazir* was never forbidden to marry.

361 - See *Berachos* 58b and *Avodah Zarah* 20a.

immorality. Yael — hearing her voice [can lead one to immorality]. Avigail — mentioning her [can lead one to immorality]. Michal the daughter of Shaul — seeing her [can lead one to immorality].

TALMUD

אָמַר רַבִּי יִצְחָק: כָּל הָאוֹמֵר: "רָחָב", "רָחָב" – מִיָּד נִקְרֵי. אָמַר לֵיהּ רַב נַחְמָן: אֲנָא אֲמִינָא: "רָחָב", "רָחָב", וְלָא מִקְרִינָא, וְלָא אִיכְפַת לִי מִינָהּ! אָמַר לֵיהּ: כִּי אֲמִינָא – בְּיוֹדְעָהּ וּמַכִּירָהּ קָאֲמִינָא.

TRANSLATION

R. Yitzchak said: Anyone who says "Rachav, Rachav" has an immediate seminal emission. R. Nachman said to him: I said "Rachav, Rachav" and did not have a seminal emission and I do not care about her. He answered him: I was referring to one who knew and saw her.

COMMENTARY

The Talmud[362] expounds on the verse (Devarim 6:5) that states: and you shall love God, your Lord, with all of your heart — all of your heart, with your good and your evil inclinations. R. Tzadok ha-Kohen of Lublin[363] explains that even if one finds that he is drawn toward the pleasures of the physical world, he should not be discouraged nor should he abandon hope of achieving spiritual fulfillment. Rather, the very drive that he has toward temporal pleasure should be channeled toward the service of God.[364]

Based on this premise, we can perhaps understand the intent of the Talmud's statement regarding Rachav, Yael, Avigail and Michal.[365] Each of these women had the potential of leading men astray, for each had an alluring quality that could well have led to immorality. Yet through their strength, the potential immorality that they might well have brought forth was not only avoided, but was transformed into holiness, for each of these women used their physical

---

362 - ברכות נד.

363 - See Tzidkos ha-Tzaddik, pg. 6.

364 - See also Reishis Chochmah (שער האהבה, פרק ד) where the author writes: and one who has no desires is less than a donkey, for from the sensual urges one can bring himself to the service of God.

365 - Maharsha adds that it would seem that Michal was aware of the effect that she had on men and she therefore stood by the window when the aron kodesh was returned by the Phillistines rather than joining with the people outside — see Shmuel II 6:15.

qualities in the service of God. By extension, then, man can learn from their example that he too possesses the inherent ability to transform his urges and desires into vehicles that can be used in the service of God.

Having digressed from its exegesis on the verses of the *Megillah* to discuss the subject of prophecy in general and specific prophets in detail, the Talmud now returns to its original discussion of the meaning of the verses.

TALMUD

"וּמָרְדֳּכַי יָדַע אֶת כָּל אֲשֶׁר נַעֲשָׂה" וְגוֹ'. מַאי אָמַר? רַב אָמַר: שֶׁגָּבַהּ לִבּוֹ שֶׁל הָמָן מֵאֲחַשְׁוֵרוֹשׁ. (אִיכָּא דְאָמְרִי: עַל אֲחַשְׁוֵרוֹשׁ) וּשְׁמוּאֵל אָמַר: גָּבַר מַלְכָּא עִילָאָה מִמַּלְכָּא תַּתָּאָה,

TRANSLATION

And Mordechai knew all that had happened [and Mordechai ripped his clothing ... and he cried out loudly and bitterly] (*Esther* 4:1) — What did he say [when he cried out]? Rav said: That Haman's heart had become prouder than Achashverosh. Shmuel said: That the heart of the King on High had overcome the heart of the king below.[366]

COMMENTARY

When Haman and Achashverosh reached agreement regarding the plan to annihilate the Jews on the 13th of Adar that was to follow, messengers were dispatched throughout the kingdom to inform the populace to prepare themselves for further details which would be issued at that time. The commentators raise a number of questions regarding the verse that the Talmud discusses.

First of all, everyone was aware of Haman's letter, for it was made public. Why then was it Mordechai alone who raised the bitter cry seeking salvation? Additionally, the verse states that Mordechai cried because *he knew all that had happened*. Would it not make more sense to say that he cried because he knew what was going to happen? Furthermore, why did Mordechai choose to demonstrate in the public square rather than attempting to immediately use his influence in the court to have the decree repealed?

Indeed, everyone was aware of the decree and the impending doom that faced

---

366 - The phrase is used euphemistically and the intended meaning is the opposite; i.e., the heart of the mortal king has overcome the will of God, as it were.

the Jews. But only Mordechai *knew what had happened* — i.e., he alone was aware of the causes of the decree. Because he was privy to this information, he knew that it was pointless to use his influence in the court before he first brought the Jews to repent.

In the text quoted in *Ein Yaakov*, Shmuel's statement — *the heart of the King on High had overcome the heart of the king below* — has the following addition in parantheses: *and He did not do justice*. The upshot of this addition is that because the Jews had sinned by taking part in Achashverosh's feast, God, as it were, had decided not to intervene on their behalf and Achashverosh and Haman were therefore able to plot against the Jews. It was this realization that led Mordechai to cry, for he knew that the decree of annihilation could not be averted without God's intercession. If God had decided not to intervene, then the fate of the Jews was sealed.

TALMUD

(דְלֹא עֲבִיד דִּינָא) "וַתָּבוֹאנָה נַעֲרוֹת אֶסְתֵּר וְסָרִיסֶיהָ וַיַּגִּידוּ לָהּ, וַתִּתְחַלְחַל". מַאי "וַתִּתְחַלְחַל"? רַב אָמַר: שֶׁפֵּרְסָה נִדָּה. וְרַבִּי יִרְמְיָה אָמַר: שֶׁהֻצְרְכָה לִנְקָבֶיהָ.

"וַתִּקְרָא אֶסְתֵּר לַהֲתָךְ", אָמַר רַב: "הֲתָךְ" – זֶה דָנִיֵּאל. וְלָמָּה נִקְרָא שְׁמוֹ "הֲתָךְ"? שֶׁחֲתָכוּהוּ מִגְּדֻלָּתוֹ. וּשְׁמוּאֵל אָמַר: שֶׁכָּל דִּבְרֵי מַלְכוּת נֶחְתָּכִין עַל פִּיו.

TRANSLATION

Esther's maidservants and chamberlains came to her and told her. And the queen became very distraught (ibid. :4) — What is meant by she became distraught?[367] Rav said: She began to menstruate. R. Yirmiyahu said: She needed to defecate.

And Esther called for Hasach (ibid. :5) — Rav said: Hasach is [another name for] Daniel. And why was he called Hasach? [Because] they cut[368] him [down] from his [previous] greatness. Shmuel said: [Because] all of the orders of the kingdom were enforced by him.

---

367 - The Hebrew ותתחלחל implies physical distress.

368 - Rav maintained that the name התך is etymologically related to the Hebrew חתך — *to cut*. Shmuel agreed that this was the source of his name but held that Daniel still had considerable influence in the court in the time of Achashverosh. He therefore explains the name idiomatically — i.e., all of the court orders were *cut by his mouth*.

COMMENTARY

Maharsha points out that the dialogue between Mordechai and Esther that the Talmud proceeds to quote was replete with references to the Torah. Hence, the messenger who went between them must have been a Jew. Daniel was the only Jew who occupied the position of chamberlain in the royal court, serving during the reigns of Belshatzar, Koresh and Daryavesh. The Talmud therefore assumed that Daniel and Hasach are identical, with the disagreement between Rav and Shmuel only concerned with the basis for referring to him by that name.

TALMUD

"וַתְּצַוֵּהוּ עַל מָרְדֳּכָי, לָדַעַת מַה זֶּה וְעַל מַה זֶּה". אָמַר רַבִּי יִצְחָק שָׁלְחָה לֵיהּ: שֶׁמָּא עָבְרוּ עַל חֲמִשָּׁה חֻמְשֵׁי תוֹרָה, דִּכְתִיב בֵּיהּ: "מִזֶּה וּמִזֶּה הֵם כְּתוּבִים"?

TRANSLATION

[Esther called for Hasach, one of the chamberlains who the king had provided for her,] and she told him to go to Mordechai to find out what this was and for what this was — R. Yitzchak said: She asked him: Perhaps they [the Jews] have transgressed the Five Books of the Torah regarding which the verse (*Shemos* 32:15) states: *And they were written from this [side] and from that [side].*[369]

COMMENTARY

The verse states מה זה ועל מה זה which would seem to be redundant. R. Yitzchak explains that Esther phrased her question in this form as a code, with the veiled reference to the Tablets alluding to the possibility that the sequence of events was a result of the Jews failure to live according to its dictates.

TALMUD

"וַיַּגִּידוּ לְמָרְדֳּכַי אֶת דִּבְרֵי אֶסְתֵּר", וְאִלּוּ אִיהוּ, לָא אָזִיל לְגַבֵּיהּ, מִכָּאן שֶׁאֵין מְשִׁיבִין עַל הַקַּלְקָלָה.

---

369 - The tablets that Moshe brought down from Sinai are described as being written מזה ומזה —*from this side and that side.* According to tradition. the letters on the Tablets were engraved completely through the stone (see page 15 regarding the miraculous ability of the middle of the letters *samech* and *mem sofis* not to collapse). If the letters were engraved competely through the stone, they should have appeared as a mirror image on the reverse side. Supernaturally, however, they did not and they could be read from either side.

"לֵךְ כְּנוֹס אֶת כָּל הַיְּהוּדִים הַנִּמְצָאִים בְּשׁוּשָׁן" וְגוֹ', עַד: "אֲשֶׁר לֹא כַדָּת",
מַאי: "אֲשֶׁר לֹא כַדָּת"? אָמַר רַבִּי אַבָּא: שֶׁלֹּא כְדָת שֶׁבְּכָל יוֹם וָיוֹם בְּאוֹנֶס,
וְעַכְשָׁיו בְּרָצוֹן.

"וְכַאֲשֶׁר אָבַדְתִּי – אָבָדְתִּי", כְּשֵׁם שֶׁנֶּאֱבַדְתִּי מִבֵּית אַבָּא, כָּךְ אֹבַד מִמֶּךָ.

TRANSLATION

And they told Mordechai what Esther had said (ibid. :12) — But he [Hasach] did
not go to him [to Mordechai].[370] From this we see that one should not report
bad news directly.

*Go and assemble all of the Jews who are in Shushan [and I shall go to the king]
in violation of the law* (ibid. :17) — What is meant [by the phrase] *in violation
of the law*? R. Aba explained: In violation of the law [of the Torah], for every
day [i.e., until this point Esther went to the king] because she was forced [to do so]
and now [she was going to him] willingly.

And if I perish, I perish (ibid.) — Just as I have become lost to my father's
house [when I became part of Achashverosh's court], so shall I be lost to you.[371]

COMMENTARY

As we have already noted,[372] Esther and Mordechai were husband and wife.
Until this point, Esther's relationship to Achashverosh did not render her
prohibited to Mordechai as an unfaithful wife, for she had been forced to live
with the king and was an unwilling participant in their union — a situation that
gave her the status of a wife who was raped and who remains permitted to her
husband. Now she would be submitting herself willingly to Achashverosh and
she would not be able to return to Mordechai.

While the *halachah* is clear[373] that one must sacrifice his life rather than engage in a forbidden sexual union, why was Esther's voluntary consent to submit

---

370 - Mordechai informed Hasach of Haman's plot and told him to instruct Esther to
go to the king and plead that he rescind the decree. After Hasach did so, Esther
answered that she was unable to appear before Achashverosh without being called
(verses 6-11). From the fact that the verse (12) states that *they* told Mordechai, we
see that Hasach did not personally deliver the message to Mordechai but sent others
instead.

371 - The Talmud's exegesis is based on interpreting the word אבדתי in its literal
sense — becoming lost.

372 - See page 129.

373 - See *Sanhedrin* 74a and *Rambam, Hilchos Yesodei ha-Torah* 5:2.

herself to Achashverosh not considered to be forced since she only did so because of the danger that her people were in? *Rambam* seems to differentiate between rape and consent that is a result of forced circumstance, viewing the latter as more serious than the former.[374]

Conversely, one might ask how Esther was permitted to submit herself to Achashverosh since the *halachah* would seem to have called upon her to sacrifice her life? Some authorities maintain that there is would be no such requirement if the person to whom she submitted herself was a gentile acting in his own interests rather than in an attempt to force the Jew to transgress a Torah prohibition.[375] Moreover, even according to those authorities who do not differentiate between a gentile and a Jew, we can conjecture that the fact that Esther was acting so as to save many lives negated the requirement to sacrifice her own life. However, according to both opinions, while the extenuating circumstances might have been sufficient grounds not to sacrifice herself rather than to submit to Achashverosh, they would not be sufficient grounds to allow her to return to Mordechai afterwards.

TALMUD

"וַיַּעֲבֹר מָרְדֳּכָי", אָמַר רַב: שֶׁהֶעֱבִיר יוֹם טוֹב הָרִאשׁוֹן שֶׁל פֶּסַח בְּתַעֲנִית. וּשְׁמוּאֵל אָמַר: עַרְקוּמָא דְמַיָּא עֲבַר.

TRANSLATION

And Mordechai traversed — Rav said: He traversed [the *halachah*] and fasted on the first festival day of Pesach. Shmuel said: He traversed the canal [that separated the palace from the city of Shushan].

---

374 - *Ohr Somayach* to *Yesodei ha-Torah* 5:6 explains that this is the basis for an apparent contradiction in *Rambam's* rulings. While one who fails to sacrifice his life when forced to transgress one of the three cardinal sins is not punished, one who engages in a prohibited relationship because of illness is culpable. According to *Ohr Somayach*, the former case is considered to be total force whereas the latter has an element of consent.

375 - See *Rama* to *Yoreh Deah* 157:1 quoting *Ramban*. *Shach* (ad loc.) writes that even according to *Ramban*, the woman would be required to give up her life if she was married. *Biur Heitev* (ad loc.) therefore adds that according to *Ramban*, Esther must not have been married to Mordechai. *Rabbenu Tam* (quoted by *Shach*) maintains that there is no difference between a married and an unmarried woman.

COMMENTARY

Haman's decree, calling for the annihilation of the Jews was issued on the 13th of Nisan. Mordechai began his public demonstrations on the very next day and, in consultation with Esther, ordered a three day public fast to begin immediately. Their call meant that instead of participating in the Pesach *seder*, the Jews would refrain from eating, a violation of Torah law. *Maharal* explains that Mordechai based his ruling permitting the fast on simple logic. The Torah was given for the Jews to fulfill. If Haman's plot was successful and there were no Jews left, it would not be fulfilled in any case.[376]

Ya'aros Devash notes that Shmuel's comment does not necessarily disagree with the opinion of Rav. Rather, Shmuel pointed out that Mordechai did much more than rule that the law prohibiting fasting on Pesach could be temporarily abrogated because of the great danger — a ruling that was not new. Mordechai also endangered himself by swimming across the canal that separated the royal court — located in the area referred to as *Shushan ha-Birah* — to join his brethren in the city of Shushan and inform them of Haman's plot. The full decree calling for the annihilation of the Jews was only publicized in the palace area. The Jews, who lived in Shushan, were only aware of Haman's letter telling the populace to be ready for further instructions that would be issued at a later date. Mordechai, understanding that the only means of saving the Jews from their fate was to assemble them and bring them to repent, crossed the canal surreptitiously — for the palace guard would obviously not have allowed him to cross over the bridges given the nature of his mission — despite the fact that he was more than eighty years old at this time.

TALMUD

"וַיְהִי בַּיּוֹם הַשְּׁלִישִׁי, וַתִּלְבַּשׁ אֶסְתֵּר מַלְכוּת", "בִּגְדֵי מַלְכוּת" מִיבָּעֵי לֵיהּ! אָמַר רַבִּי אֶלְעָזָר, אָמַר רַבִּי חֲנִינָא: מְלַמֵּד שֶׁלְּבָשַׁתָּה רוּחַ הַקֹּדֶשׁ, כְּתִיב הָכָא: "וַתִּלְבַּשׁ", וּכְתִיב הָתָם: "וְרוּחַ לָבְשָׁה אֶת עֲמָשַׂי".

TRANSLATION

And it was on the third day, and Esther clothed herself in royalty (ibid. 5:1) — It should say *in royal clothing*? R. Chanina explained: This teaches us that she

---

376 - Compare to *Yoma* 85b: *Violate one Shabbos on his [a sick person's] behalf so that he might observe many Shabbosos.*

clothed herself in the spirit of holiness. The verse here states: *And she clothed herself* and there (*Divrei ha-Yamim* I 12:19) it states: *and the spirit was clothed upon Amasa* [and we thus see that the term *clothed* can be used as a means of describing the assumption of the spirit of holiness — i.e., prophecy].[377]

Having quoted a statement of R. Chanina, the Talmud digresses and quotes other statements of his even though they are not relevant to the *Megillah*.

TALMUD

וְאָמַר רַבִּי אֶלְעָזָר, אָמַר רַבִּי חֲנִינָא: לְעוֹלָם אַל תְּהִי בִּרְכַּת הֶדְיוֹט קַלָּה בְּעֵינֶיךָ, שֶׁהֲרֵי שְׁנֵי גְדוֹלֵי הַדּוֹר, בֵּרְכוּם שְׁנֵי הֶדְיוֹטוֹת, וְנִתְקַיְּמָה בָּהֶם, וְאֵלּוּ הֵן: דָּוִד וְדָנִיֵּאל. דָּוִד - דְּבָרְכֵיהּ אֲרַוְנָה, דִּכְתִיב: "וַיֹּאמֶר אֲרַוְנָה אֶל הַמֶּלֶךְ: ה' אֱלֹהֶיךָ יִרְצֶךָ". דָּנִיֵּאל - דְּבָרְכֵיהּ דָּרְיָוֶשׁ, דִּכְתִיב: "אֱלָהָךְ דִּי אַנְתְּ פָּלַח לֵהּ" וְגוֹ'.

וְאָמַר רַבִּי אֶלְעָזָר, אָמַר רַבִּי חֲנִינָא: אַל תְּהִי קִלְלַת הֶדְיוֹט קַלָּה בְּעֵינֶיךָ, שֶׁהֲרֵי אֲבִימֶלֶךְ קִלֵּל אֶת שָׂרָה: "הִנֵּה הוּא לָךְ כְּסוּת עֵינַיִם", וְנִתְקַיֵּם בְּזַרְעָהּ, שֶׁנֶּאֱמַר: "וַיְהִי כִּי זָקֵן יִצְחָק, וַתִּכְהֶיןָ עֵינָיו".

TRANSLATION

R. Elazar taught in the name of R. Chanina: The blessing of a simple person should never be taken lightly by you, for two leaders of the generation were blessed by two simple people and it [the blessing] was fulfilled. And these are the two: David and Daniel. [Regarding] David, [we find that] he was blessed by Aravnah,[378] as the verse (*Shmuel* II 24:23) states: *And Aravnah said to the king: God, your Lord, shall desire you.* [Regarding] Daniel, [we find that] he was blessed by Daryavesh,[379] as the verse (*Daniel* 6:17) states: *The God to whom you always pray [He will save you].*

And R. Elazar taught in the name of R. Chanina: The curse of a simple person should not be taken lightly, for Avimelech cursed Sarah [as the verse (*Bereishis* 20:16) states:] *Behold it is for you as a covering for your eyes* and this was

---

377 - See page 164.

378 - Aravnah, the Yevusi, blessed David when he came to purchase the site of the altar on Mt. Moriah.

379 - Daniel was arrested for violating the law that outlawed all prayer other than that directed to Bel, the local deity. Daryavesh tried to protect him but was unable to intervene. As he cast him into the lion's pit, he blessed him.

fulfilled in her descendents, as the verse *(Bereishis* 27:1) states: *And it was when Yitzchak became old, and his eyes became covered [he became blind].*

COMMENTARY

Kuzari explains that the physical world can be divided into four classes: inanimate objects, animate objects, the animal world and those who speak. Each of these classes represents a more developed level within Creation. Man, who is considered to be the epitome of God's work, is referred to as "one who speaks", for it is the power of expressing ideas that sets man above the rest of creation.[380] *Maharal*[381] explains that man's ability to speak is the physical manifestation of the interdependence of the body and soul; i.e., speech represents the soul communicating through the body. *Ramchal*[382] adds that this can help us understand how the spoken word can have affect on the supernal world, for it is the power of speech that is the link between the world of the spirit and the physical world.

Malbim[383] explains that *berachah* — Divine bounty — exists in potential at all times in the supernal world and can be summoned to the physical world through speech — the link between the two worlds. Thus, the *berachah* of even a simple person should not be taken lightly, for it might well be the means through which the Divine bounty is to be channeled to the recepient.[384] For the very same reason the curse of a simple person should also not be taken lightly.

TALMUD

וְאָמַר רַבִּי אֶלְעָזָר, אָמַר רַבִּי חֲנִינָא: בֹּא וּרְאֵה, שֶׁלֹּא כְמִדַּת הַקָּדוֹשׁ בָּרוּךְ הוּא, מִדַּת בָּשָׂר וָדָם; מִדַּת בָּשָׂר וָדָם – אָדָם שׁוֹפֵת אֶת הַקְּדֵרָה, וְאַחַר כָּךְ נוֹתֵן לְתוֹכָהּ מַיִם. וְהַקָּדוֹשׁ בָּרוּךְ הוּא – נוֹתֵן מַיִם, וְאַחַר כָּךְ שׁוֹפֵת אֶת הַקְּדֵרָה, לְקַיֵּם מַה שֶּׁנֶּאֱמַר: "לְקוֹל תִּתּוֹ הֲמוֹן מַיִם בַּשָּׁמַיִם".

---

380 - See *Onkelos* to *Bereishis* 2:7 where he translates the verse *and man became a living soul — a spirit that speaks.*

381 - גבורות ה' פרק כ"ח.

382 - דרך ה' ח"א פ"ג.

383 - הכרמל, ערך ברכה.

384 - See *Siforno* to *Bereishis* 32:1 who explains that Lavan's *berachah* to his daughters is recorded in the Torah because he said it with full conviction and it thus represented the spark of Divinity that was within him.

TRANSLATION

And R. Elazar taught in the name of R. Chanina: Come and see that the manner of the Holy One, blessed is He, is not like the manner of man. The manner of man is that one first prepares the pot and then places water inside. But the Holy One, blessed is He, gives water and then prepares the pot, in fulfillment of the verse (*Yirmiyahu* 10:13) that states: *By the sound of His giving abundant waters in the heavens.*

COMMENTARY

The means through which man can begin to fathom God's greatness is by examining the world around him. *Rambam*[385] writes: *What is the path through which one can [come to] love and fear Him? At the time when man looks at His wondrous creations and acts, and sees the endless wisdom that they manifest, he immediately loves Him and praises Him and desparately seeks to know God.* *Chovos ha-Levavos*[386] writes that one who does not ponder God's wisdom as evidenced in Creation is worse than an animal, for he fails to use the intellectual powers that He invested within him.

The Sages were cognizant of the role that nature can play in bringing man to recognize God's power. R. Chanina, in this statement, points to the cycle of water as a means of recognizing God's hand, for the natural cycle that God implemented in this world stands in contrast to the way that man does things. While man first prepares the pot before he cooks, God creates the mists that rise from the ground and only then brings the clouds that store the rains. As *Rambam* concludes: *When one consider these things, he immediately retreats and is filled with fear, realizing that he is but a small and insignificant creation.*

TALMUD

וְאָמַר רַבִּי אֶלְעָזָר, אָמַר רַבִּי חֲנִינָא: צַדִּיק אָבַד – לְדוֹרוֹ אָבַד. מָשָׁל לְאָדָם שֶׁאָבְדָה מִמֶּנּוּ מַרְגָּלִית, כָּל מָקוֹם שֶׁהִיא, מַרְגָּלִית שְׁמָהּ. וְהִיא לֹא אָבְדָה אֶלָּא לְבְעָלָהּ.

וְאָמַר רַבִּי אֶלְעָזָר, אָמַר רַבִּי חֲנִינָא: כָּל הָאוֹמֵר דָּבָר בְּשֵׁם אוֹמְרוֹ, מֵבִיא גְּאֻלָּה לָעוֹלָם, שֶׁנֶּאֱמַר: "וַתֹּאמֶר אֶסְתֵּר לַמֶּלֶךְ בְּשֵׁם מָרְדְּכָי".

.יסודי התורה ב:א-ב - 385

.שער הבחינה פרק ב' - 386

TRANSLATION

And R. Elazar taught in the name of R. Chanina: [When] a righteous person perishes, he perishes for his generation [i.e., the generation suffers a loss, but the righteous person himself suffers no loss].[387] This can be compared to a man who lost a precious jewel. Wherever it is, it is still a precious jewel and it is only lost to its owner.

And R. Elazar taught in the name of R. Chanina: All who repeat something quoting the one who said it bring salvation to the world,[388] for the verse (*Esther* 2:22) states: *And Esther told the king in the name of Mordechai.*

COMMENTARY

Maharal[389] explains that exile and punishment come about when man fails to attribute all that happens in this world to the hand of God but rather sees himself as being solely responsible for all that transpires. The antidote to this is for man to transcend his natural egoistic tendency to ascribe everything to his own power and give credit where it is due.

Esther could well have told Achashverosh about the plot to assassinate him without informing the king that Mordechai was her source of information. By quoting Mordechai, she showed that she had no intention of taking personal credit for that which should rightfully be given to others. She thus paved the way for the salvation of the people, for God saw this as evidence that she would also make it known that the impending salvation was due to God's intercession rather than her personal efforts.

TALMUD

וְאָמַר רַבִּי אֶלְעָזָר, אָמַר רַבִּי חֲנִינָא: מַאי דִּכְתִיב: "וְכָל זֶה אֵינֶנּוּ שׁוֶה לִי". מְלַמֵּד שֶׁכָּל גְּנָזָיו שֶׁל אוֹתוֹ רָשָׁע הָיוּ חֲקוּקִים לוֹ עַל לִבּוֹ, וּכְשֶׁרָאָה אֶת מָרְדֳּכַי יוֹשֵׁב בְּשַׁעַר הַמֶּלֶךְ, הָיָה אוֹמֵר: "וְכָל זֶה אֵינֶנּוּ שׁוֶה לִי". וְכִי מִשּׁוּם דְּרוֹאֶה מָרְדֳּכַי יוֹשֵׁב בְּשַׁעַר הַמֶּלֶךְ, אוֹמֵר: "וְכָל זֶה אֵינֶנּוּ שׁוֶה לִי"? אִין, כִּדְאָמַר רַב חִסְדָּא: זֶה בָּא בִּפְרוּזְבּוּלֵי, וְזֶה בָּא בִּפְרוּזְבּוּטֵי. (״בּוּלֵי״ – אֵלּוּ

---

387 - Rav Dessler (מכתב מאליהו ד׳ ד״ה עולם הגמול) points out that the righteous person feels no loss when he leaves the material world, for his ambition while there was to achieve spiritual perfection and the world of the spirit is therefore more appropriate for him.

388 - Compare to *Avos* 6:7.

389 - *Derech Chaim* to *Avos*, pg. 301 and *Or Chadash*, pg. 124.

עֲשִׁירִים, שֶׁנֶּאֱמַר: "וְשָׁבַרְתִּי אֶת גְּאוֹן עֻזְּכֶם", וְתָנֵי רַב יוֹסֵף: אֵלּוּ בּוּלָאוֹת
שֶׁבִּיהוּדָה. "בּוּטֵי", אֵלּוּ עֲנִיִּים, וְכֵן הוּא אוֹמֵר: "וְהָעֲבֵט תַּעֲבִיטֶנּוּ". אָמַר רַב
פָּפָּא: וְקָארוּ לֵיהּ: עַבְדָּא דְּאִזְדַּבַּן בְּטוּלְמֵי דְנַהֲמָא.

TRANSLATION

And R. Elazar taught in the name of R. Chanina: What is the meaning of the
verse (ibid. 5:13): *But none of this is of any value.* This teaches us that all of
the treasures of this wicked person [Haman] were engraved upon his heart. But
when he saw Mordechai sitting at the entrance to the king's palace, he said: *But
none of this is of any value.* Because he saw Mordechai sitting at the entrance to
the palace he said: *But none of this is of any value?* Yes, as R. Chisda
explained: For this one [Mordechai] came as a rich man and this one [Haman]
came as a poor man.[390] **[15b]** R. Papa said: They called him [Haman], "a slave
who sold himself for a loaf of bread."

COMMENTARY

The *Midrash*[391] recounts that in the beginning of his reign, Achashverosh
was faced with a revolt in the province of Hindiki. He dispatched two armies of
60,000 soldiers each, commanded by Haman and Mordechai, providing them
with funds and provisions sufficient for three years. Haman wasted his army's
allocation and by the end of the first year did not have funds to pay his soldiers
or purchase food for them. Fearing for his life, Haman turned to Mordechai and
asked him for a loan, offering to pay an exorbitant rate of interest which
Mordechai could keep since the return of the capital would be sufficient to allow
Mordechai to feed his own soldiers. Mordechai refused Haman's offer, explaining
that he had no desire to become rich through public funds that had been entrusted
to him.

However, Mordechai continued, he was not insensitive to the predicament of
the soldiers under Haman's command. He was therefore willing to share his
army's rations with them provided that Haman would sell himself as a slave to

---

390 - Though Haman was extraordinarily wealthy, he felt like a poor man whenever
he was confronted by Mordechai.
In the text of the *Ein Yaakov*, there is a bracketed addition that explains the source of
the words פרוזבולי and פרוזבוטי. This text does not appear in the Talmud and has
therefore been left untranslated.
391 - *Yalkut Shimoni* to *Esther*, 1056. See also *Menos ha-Levi* to *Esther* 5:13.

Mordechai. With no choice other than death at the hands of his own angry army, Haman agreed. When they could not find a piece of paper to write a proper document attesting to their agreement, Haman wrote a document on the sole of Mordechai's shoe stating: I, Haman, the son of Hamdasa, from the family of Agag, hereby sell myself as a slave to Mordechai the Jew and I — both personally as well as my descendents — hereby agree to serve him for all times. When the war ended, the two commanders returned to Shushan and their ways parted.

Later, when Haman advanced in the hierarchy of the Persian court, he saw fit to engrave an amulet of his personal god which he wore on his chest to show that he attributed his success and new found fortune to the intervention of this god. He insisted that all of the palace officials pay homage to him and his god by prostrating themselves whenever he passed by. The only one who refused was Mordechai, who would show him the sole of his shoe and remind Haman that he was his slave.

TALMUD

וְאָמַר רַבִּי אֶלְעָזָר, אָמַר רַבִּי חֲנִינָא: עָתִיד הַקָּדוֹשׁ בָּרוּךְ הוּא לִהְיוֹת עֲטָרָה בְּרֹאשׁ כָּל צַדִּיק וְצַדִּיק, שֶׁנֶּאֱמַר: "בַּיּוֹם הַהוּא יִהְיֶה ה' צְבָאוֹת לַעֲטֶרֶת צְבִי" וְגוֹ', מַאי "לַעֲטֶרֶת צְבִי"? לָעוֹשִׂים צִבְיוֹנוֹ; "וְלִצְפִירַת תִּפְאָרָה" – לַמְצַפִּים תִּפְאַרְתּוֹ. יָכוֹל לַכֹּל? תַּלְמוּד לוֹמַר: "לִשְׁאָר עַמּוֹ", מַאי "לִשְׁאָר עַמּוֹ"? לַמֵּשִׂים עַצְמוֹ כִּשְׁיָרַיִם.

"וּלְרוּחַ מִשְׁפָּט" – זֶה הַדָּן אֶת יִצְרוֹ. "לַיּוֹשֵׁב עַל הַמִּשְׁפָּט" – זֶה הַדָּן דִּין אֱמֶת לַאֲמִתּוֹ. "וְלִגְבוּרָה" – זֶה הַמִּתְגַּבֵּר עַל יִצְרוֹ. "מְשִׁיבֵי מִלְחָמָה" – אֵלּוּ שֶׁנּוֹשְׂאִין וְנוֹתְנִין בְּמִלְחַמְתָּהּ שֶׁל תּוֹרָה. "שָׁעְרָה" – אֵלּוּ תַּלְמִידֵי חֲכָמִים שֶׁמַּשְׁכִּימִין וּמַעֲרִיבִין לְבָתֵּי כְנֵסִיּוֹת וּלְבָתֵּי מִדְרָשׁוֹת.

אָמְרָה מִדַּת הַדִּין לִפְנֵי הַקָּדוֹשׁ בָּרוּךְ הוּא: רִבּוֹנוֹ שֶׁל עוֹלָם: מַה נִּשְׁתַּנּוּ אֵלּוּ מֵאֵלּוּ? אָמַר לָהּ הַקָּדוֹשׁ בָּרוּךְ הוּא: יִשְׂרָאֵל עָסְקוּ בַּתּוֹרָה, גּוֹיִם (וְעוֹבְדֵי כּוֹכָבִים) לֹא עָסְקוּ בַּתּוֹרָה. אָמְרָה לוֹ: "וְגַם אֵלֶּה בַּיַּיִן שָׁגוּ, וּבַשֵּׁכָר תָּעוּ וְגוֹ', פָּקוּ פְּלִילִיָּה". וְאֵין "פָּקוּ" אֶלָּא גֵּיהִנָּם, שֶׁנֶּאֱמַר: "וְלֹא תִהְיֶה זֹאת לְךָ לְפוּקָה". וְאֵין "פְּלִילִיָּה" אֶלָּא דַיָּנִים, שֶׁנֶּאֱמַר: "וְנָתַן בִּפְלִלִים".

TRANSLATION

And R. Elazar taught in the name of R. Chanina: The Holy One, blessed is He, is destined to serve as a crown on the head of every righteous person, as the verse (*Yeshayahu* 28:5) states: *And on that day, the God of Hosts shall be a crown of glory and a turban of splendor*. What is [i.e., for whom will He be] a *crown of glory*? To those who fulfill His desire. *And a turban of splendor* — to those who await His splendor.[392] I might think that this applies to all [of Israel]. [The verse continues and] teaches us: *to the remnant of His people*. What is meant by *the remnant of His people*? For those who make themselves like a remnant [i.e., for those who are self-effacing].

[The next verse continues:] *A spirit of judgement* — this refers to one who judges his spirit [i.e., who controls his inclinations] — *for those who sit in judgement* — this refers to one who judges truthfully — *and as a hero* — this refers to one who overcomes his inclinations — *who do battle* — this refers to those who take part in the battle [i.e., the dialogue] of Torah [study] — *in the gates* — this refers to the scholars who arise [are the first to come] and [are the last to] leave the synagogues and study halls.[393]

The trait of judgement said to the Holy One, blessed is He: Master of the World! Why are these [the Jews] different than these [the other nations]? The Holy One, blessed is He, responded: Israel occupied herself in the Torah and the nations did not occupy themselves in the Torah. She [the trait of judgement] retorted: [The verse (ibid. :7) states:] *And also these [the righteous] erred through wine and were mistaken because of drink ... they stumbled in judgement*. [The word] *stumbled* is surely a reference to Gehinnom [i.e., punishment], as the verse (*Shmuel* I 25:31) states: *let this not be a [cause for] stumbling for you*.[394] And the word *judgement* surely refers to judges, as the verse (*Shemos* 21:22) states: *and it was*

---

392 - The Talmud's first exegesis is based upon the similarity between the words צבי — *glory* [compare to *Shmuel* II 1:19] — and צביון — *character* or *desire*. The second exegesis is based on the similarity between the words צפירה — *turban* [see *Metzudas Zion* ad loc.] — and צפיה — *awaiting* or *anticipating*.

393 - Thus, the upshot of the verse is that God will glorify those who are self-effacing, who control their inclinations, who judge truthfully, who overcome their inclinations and the scholars. The Talmud then quotes the spirit of judgement as having asked God why He shows favoritism.

394 - When Avigail pleaded with David to spare Naval, she also used the term פקו, warning David that he would be subject to punishment for having killed him. The verse is brought to point out that the righteous will also be subject to punishment for they too are not free of sin.

given [over to] the judges.[395]

COMMENTARY

In a parallel text quoted elsewhere in the Talmud,[396] the verse from Yeshayahu stating: *And also these [the righteous] erred through wine and were mistaken because of drink ... they stumbled in judgement* is quoted as God's answer to the trait of judgement. No mention is made there of a difference between Israel and the nations. Rather the trait of judgement asks God why He shows favoritism toward certain elements within Israel. God answers that He does so because even among the righteous there are those who sin.

The text in our Talmud and that brought in *Ein Yaakov* — which refers to a question that asks why God differentiates between Israel and the nations — is somewhat more difficult to understand, for there is no contextual continuity between the last paragraph and the preceding two. Moreover, in our text, God does not respond to the final question posed by the trait of judgement.

TALMUD

"וַתַּעֲמֹד בַּחֲצַר בֵּית הַמֶּלֶךְ הַפְּנִימִית", אָמַר רַבִּי לֵוִי: כֵּיוָן שֶׁהִגִּיעָה לְבֵית הַצְּלָמִים, נִסְתַּלְּקָה מִמֶּנָּה שְׁכִינָה. וְאָמְרָה: "אֵלִי, אֵלִי, לָמָה עֲזַבְתָּנִי?" וְגוֹ'. שֶׁמָּא אַתָּה דָן עַל שׁוֹגֵג כְּמֵזִיד, וְעַל אֹנֶס כְּרָצוֹן?! אוֹ שֶׁמָּא עַל שֶׁקְּרָאתִיו "כֶּלֶב" - שֶׁנֶּאֱמַר: "הַצִּילָה מֵחֶרֶב נַפְשִׁי, מִיַּד כֶּלֶב יְחִידָתִי"?! חָזְרָה וּקְרָאַתּוּ "אֲרִיֵּה", שֶׁנֶּאֱמַר: "הוֹשִׁיעֵנִי מִפִּי אַרְיֵה, וּמִקַּרְנֵי רֵמִים עֲנִיתָנִי".

TRANSLATION

And she stood in the inner courtyard of the king's palace (Esther 5:1) — R. Levi explained: Once she [Esther] reached the house [where Achashverosh kept his] idols, the *Shechinah* left her. She prayed: *My God, my God, why have You left me (Tehillim 22:2)*. [Esther said to herself,] perhaps You judge inadvertent actions like premeditated ones, forced actions like willful ones?[397] Or perhaps [You have

---

395 - The exegesis is based on the use of the word פלילה in the first verse and פלילים in the second.

396 - סנהדרין קי״א.

397 - I.e., perhaps the *Shechinah* has left me because I can no longer be seen as having been coerced to join Achashverosh's court, for I am now approaching him on my own volition.

left me] because I called him a dog,[398] as the verse [(ibid. :21) that Esther quoted in her prayer] states: *save my soul from the sword, my single [soul] from the hand of the dog.* But she recanted and called him a *lion* as the verse (ibid. :22) states: *Deliver me from the mouth of the lion, You have answered me [i.e., my prayers to be saved] from the horns of the ram.*

COMMENTARY

As we have already seen, Esther prepared herself for her meeting with Achashverosh by clothing herself in royalty — i.e., the spirit of holiness. However, when she reached the inner court, she suddenly felt that this spirit had left her and she began to examine her actions to try to determine why she was no longer clothed in prophecy. At first she thought that the Divine spirit had left her because she had agreed to approach Achashverosh voluntarily. She quickly discounted this possibility, for she had done so at Mordechai's specific order. She attributed her plight to the fact that she had referred to Achashverosh disrespectfully as a dog and she therefore re-referred to him as a lion.

Rav Shlomo Bravda[399] poses an interesting question. Why is Esther's reference to Achashverosh as a lion deemed to be more respectful than her reference to him as a dog? He answers that there is a fundamental difference between the two animals. When a person is confronted by a dog, he may well be frightened but he is usually convinced that he can handle the situation. On the other hand, were he suddenly faced by a lion, he would quickly reach the conclusion that he is helpless and totally dependent upon outside intervention.

Thus, Esther — realizing that the Divine spirit had left her — thought to herself that the cause might very well be that she had related to Achashverosh as a dog — i.e., as a situation that she could handle on her own. Her previous prayers to God were therefore no more than lip service. She thereupon recanted and referred to Achashverosh as a lion, acknowledging that alone she was powerless and needed God's assistance. Having determined the reason why the Divine spirit had left her, and having rectified the fault within her that had caused this to happen, she was now able to proceed toward the king.

---

398 - I.e., perhaps the *Shechinah* has departed because I referred to Achashverosh disrespectfully. I might be seen as having been disrespectful to God, since Achashverosh is no more than an instrument of the Divine will.

399 - עי' ספר קיימו וקבלו על מגילת אסתר.

TALMUD

"וַיְהִי כִרְאוֹת הַמֶּלֶךְ" וְגוֹ', אָמַר רַבִּי יוֹחָנָן: שְׁלֹשָׁה מַלְאֲכֵי הַשָּׁרֵת נִזְדַּמְּנוּ לָהּ בְּאוֹתָהּ שָׁעָה; אֶחָד שֶׁהִגְבִּיהַּ אֶת צַוָּארָהּ, וְאֶחָד שֶׁמָּשַׁךְ עָלֶיהָ חוּט שֶׁל חֶסֶד, וְאֶחָד שֶׁמָּתַח שַׁרְבִיטוֹ שֶׁל אֲחַשְׁוֵרוֹשׁ. וְכַמָּה מְתָחוֹ? אָמַר רַבִּי יִרְמְיָה: שְׁתֵּי אַמּוֹת הָיָה, וְהֶעֱמִידוֹ עַל שְׁתֵּים עֶשְׂרֵה. וְאָמְרִי לָהּ: עַל שֵׁשׁ עֶשְׂרֵה. (וְרַבִּי יהושׁע בֶּן לֵוִי אָמַר: עֶשְׂרִים וּשְׁמוֹנָה. וְרַב חִסְדָּא אָמַר: שִׁשִּׁים). וְאָמְרִי לָהּ: עַל עֶשְׂרִים וְאַרְבַּע. בְּמַתְנִיתָא תָּנָא: עַל שִׁשִּׁים. וְכֵן אַתָּה מוֹצֵא בָּאַמָּתָהּ שֶׁל בַּת פַּרְעֹה. וְכֵן אַתָּה מוֹצֵא בְּשִׁנֵּי רְשָׁעִים, דִּכְתִיב: "שִׁנֵּי רְשָׁעִים שִׁבַּרְתָּ", וְאָמַר רֵישׁ לָקִישׁ: אַל תִּקְרֵי "שִׁבַּרְתָּ", אֶלָּא "שֶׁרִבַּבְתָּ". רַבָּה בַּר עוֹפְרָן אָמַר מִשּׁוּם רַבִּי אֶלְעָזָר, שֶׁשָּׁמַע מֵרַבּוֹ, וְרַבּוֹ מֵרַבּוֹ: מָאתַיִם.

TRANSLATION

And when the king saw (Esther 5:2) — R. Yochanan taught: Three ministering angels came to her at that time: One lifted her neck, one spread a thread of grace upon her[400] and one extended Achashverosh's scepter. How far was it extended? R. Yirmiyah said: It was two *amos* long and he [the angel] extended it to reach twelve. And some say it reached sixteen. And some say it reached twenty-four. In the *beraisa* we learned: It reached sixty. We find the same concerning the *amos* of Pharaoh's daughter[401] and one finds the same regarding the teeth of the wicked,[402] as the verse (*Tehillim* 3:8) states: *You have broken the teeth of the*

---

400 - *Maharsha* notes that the verse states: ויהי כראות המלך את אסתר המלכה עומדת בחצר — *and when the king saw Esther the queen standing in the courtyard,* נשאה חן בעיניו — *she bore favor in his eyes.* The form נשאה חן — *she bore favor* — is rare and one would have expected the phrase מצאה חן — *she found favor* — as in *Bereishis* 6:8 — *and Noach found favor in God's eyes.* The Sages understood that the use of this form indicated that Esther *bore* favor because of the angel's intervention.

401 - I.e., her normal reach was miraculously extended. The Talmud bases this on an allusion from the verse (*Shemos* 2:8) that states: *And the daughter of Pharaoh went to bathe in the river ... and she sent her* אמה *and took it.* The word אמה can be translated either as *maidservant* or *arm.* Since the verse first refers to her maidservants as נערותיה, the Talmud viewed the change of terminology as an allusion that her arm was miraculously extended so that she could reach the box. See *Sotah* 12a.

402 - The Talmud (*Berachos* 54a) relates that Og, king of Bashan, stood with an enormous boulder on his shoulders, intending to cast it down upon Israel. God performed a miracle and ants began to make the boulder crumble, forming a hole in which Og's head became stuck. When he attempted to pick the boulder up so as to extricate himself, his teeth became extended and he was unable to lift it off his neck.

wicked, on which Resh Lakish expounded: Do not read *broken*, read *extended*. Raba bar Efron said in the name of R. Elazar who heard it from his teacher, who heard it [in turn] from his teacher: [The angel extended the scepter until it reached] two hundred [amos]!

TALMUD

"וַיֹּאמֶר לָהּ הַמֶּלֶךְ וְגוֹ', עַד חֲצִי הַמַּלְכוּת", "עַד חֲצִי הַמַּלְכוּת", וְלֹא כָל הַמַּלְכוּת, וְלֹא דָבָר שֶׁחוֹצֵץ בַּמַּלְכוּת. וּמַאי הוּא? זֶה בִּנְיַן בֵּית הַמִּקְדָּשׁ.

TRANSLATION

And the king said to her ... until half my kingdom (Esther 5:3) — *half my kingdom* and not my whole kingdom and not something that divides my kingdom. And what is that [i.e., what request would divide Achashverosh's kingdom]? Building the *Beis ha-Mikdash*.

COMMENTARY

As we previously noted,[403] capture of Jerusalem was always considered to be *prima-facie* evidence of world domination. While Koresh had permitted the Jews to return to Jerusalem and begin construction of the second *Beis ha-Mikdash* in fulfillment of a prophetic message, Achashverosh had — at the urging of Vashti — stopped construction and ordered the end of the emigration to the Land of Israel, for he became convinced that the renewal of the Divine service — even in a vassal state subservient to the Persian ruler in Shushan — would lessen the power of his throne. To his mind, world rule meant that no manifestation of fealty to an authority other than his could be permitted. Thus, even though he did not yet know that Esther was Jewish, he predicated his agreement to fulfill Esther's request on the stipulation that she not ask that construction of the *Beis ha-Mikdash* be renewed.

We see that the question of the construction of the *Beis ha-Mikdash* weighed heavily on the minds of the rulers of Bavel and later Persia. Both Belshatzar and Achashverosh made feasts when, according to their calculations, the seventy years prophesied by Yirmiyahu passed and the Jews remained in exile.

R. Yonasan Eybeschutz[404] writes that Achashverosh, having consulted with his astrologers as to who would succeed him on his throne, knew that he would

---

403 - See page 94.

404 - יערות דבש, חלק ראשון, דרש יז.

be followed by a king of Jewish origin.[405] Unaware that Esther was Jewish, he assumed that he was destined to be overthrown and he thus hated the Jews even more than Haman did. Moreover, he knew that the responsibilities of a Jewish king called for him to destroy the remnant of Amalek and build the *Beis ha-Mikdash*. He therefore elevated Haman — a descendent of Amalek — to an important position within his court and agreed to Vashti's request that he stop the construction of the *Beis ha-Mikdash*.

When Esther suddenly approached him with a personal request, risking her life in doing so by contravening palace law, he was shocked and immediately began to suspect that she was an instrument in the hands of those who sought to replace him with a Jewish king. Moreover, her relationship with Mordechai was well known and he had every reason to suspect that she might be seeking something on his behalf. He therefore immediately stipulated that he would be prepared to grant her anything except the building of the *Beis ha-Mikdash*, for he saw that request as spelling the beginning of the end of his rule.

TALMUD

"וַתֹּאמֶר אֶסְתֵּר: אִם עַל הַמֶּלֶךְ טוֹב, יָבוֹא הַמֶּלֶךְ וְהָמָן אֶל הַמִּשְׁתֶּה", תָּנוּ רַבָּנָן: מָה רָאֲתָה אֶסְתֵּר שֶׁזִּמְּנָה אֶת הָמָן? רַבִּי אֱלִיעֶזֶר אוֹמֵר: פַּחִים טָמְנָה לְכַלְכְּדוֹ, שֶׁנֶּאֱמַר: "יְהִי שֻׁלְחָנָם לִפְנֵיהֶם לְפָח". רַבִּי יְהוֹשֻׁעַ אוֹמֵר: מִבֵּית אָבִיהָ לָמְדָה, שֶׁנֶּאֱמַר: "אִם רָעֵב שֹׂנַאֲךָ, הַאֲכִילֵהוּ לָחֶם" וְגוֹ', רַבִּי מֵאִיר אוֹמֵר: כְּדֵי שֶׁלֹּא יִטּוֹל עֵצָה וְיִמְרֹד. רַבִּי יְהוּדָה אוֹמֵר: כְּדֵי שֶׁלֹּא יַכִּירוּ בָהּ שֶׁהִיא יְהוּדִית. רַבִּי נְחֶמְיָה אוֹמֵר: כְּדֵי שֶׁלֹּא יֹאמְרוּ יִשְׂרָאֵל: אָחוֹת לָנוּ בְּבֵית הַמֶּלֶךְ, וְיַסִּיחוּ דַעְתָּם מִן הָרַחֲמִים. רַבִּי יוֹסֵי אוֹמֵר: כְּדֵי שֶׁיְּהֵא מָצוּי לָהּ בְּכָל עֵת. רַבִּי שִׁמְעוֹן בֶּן מְנַסְיָא אוֹמֵר: אוּלַי יַרְגִּישׁ הַמָּקוֹם וְיַעֲשֶׂה לָנוּ נֵס. רַבִּי יְהוֹשֻׁעַ בֶּן קָרְחָה אוֹמֵר: הַסְבִּירָה לוֹ פָּנִים, כְּדֵי שֶׁיֵּהָרֵג הוּא וָהִיא. אָמַר רַבָּן גַּמְלִיאֵל: אֲחַשְׁוֵרוֹשׁ מֶלֶךְ הַכַּכְפֵּד הָיָה. וְאָמַר רַבָּן גַּמְלִיאֵל: עֲדַיִן צְרִיכִין אָנוּ לַמּוּדָעִי, דְּתַנְיָא: רַבִּי אֱלִיעֶזֶר הַמּוֹדָעִי אוֹמֵר: קִנְאָתוֹ בַּמֶּלֶךְ, קִנְאָתוֹ בַשָּׂרִים.

TRANSLATION

And Esther replied: If it is pleasing to the king, let the king and Haman come to the party (ibid. :4). Our Sages taught: Why did Esther see fit to invite Haman? R. Eliezer said: She prepared traps to ensnare him, as the verse (*Tehillim* 69:23)

---

405 - Darius II, who succeeded Achashverosh, was his son from Esther.

states: *may their tables be traps before them.*[406] R. Yehoshua said: She learned this [strategy] in her father's home, as the verse (*Mishlei* 25:21) states: *If your enemy is hungry, feed him bread* [*and God shall pay you* — do not read *pay you*, rather read *will make him subservient to you*].[407] R. Meir said: [Esther invited Haman] so that he would not seek counsel [when she accused him of plotting to kill the Jews] and rebel.[408] R. Yehudah explained: So that they would not know that she was a Jewess.[409] R. Nechemyah taught: So that the Jews would not say, "We have a sister in the king's palace" and thereby they would remove their thoughts from [seeking] mercy.[410] R. Yosi taught: So that he would be available at all times. R. Shimon ben Menasya taught: [Esther invited Haman, hoping that] perhaps God would feel [her plight][411] and would perform a miracle. R. Yehoshua ben Karcha taught: She was kind to him so that both she and he

---

406 - *Maharsha* points out that Esther knew that Achashverosh had a habit of drinking heavily at parties and losing his self-control as per the previous feast when he had impulsively ordered Vashti's execution. She therefore wanted Haman to be present so that the king's anger with Haman — when she informed Achashverosh that she too would be a victim of Haman's plans — could be immediately acted upon.

407 - The bracketed addition does not appear in the text of the Talmud, but does appear in both *Ein Yaakov* and in the parallel version quoted by *Yalkut Shimoni*. *Maharal* explains that when one is unexpectedly generous to an enemy, he causes the enemy to be confused. Instead of acting according to his evil design, he finds himself subservient to the person whom he sought to destroy.

408 - By inviting Haman to dine with her and the king, Esther effectively prevented him from seeking allies to overthrow the king which he might have done had he been given the opportunity. By accusing him in the king's presence, she assumed that Achashverosh would immediately order that Haman be killed.

409 - By inviting Haman to her party, Esther removed any suspicion that people might have that she was Jewish, for obviously no Jew would invite his arch-enemy to a party.

410 - Some of the commentators maintain that this was also one of the reasons why Mordechai did not want Esther to reveal her background to Achashverosh and thus make her Jewishness public knowledge.

411 - *Rashi* (ד״ה אולי ירגיש) explains that Esther felt that if God would see the extent to which she was prepared to belittle herself — extending an invitation to Haman to dine with her — He might see fit to miraculously save Israel. *Maharal* adds that Esther based herself on the verse (*Tehillim* 147:6) that states: *He humiliates the wicked until they sink to the ground* — i.e., when the wicked reach the epitome of their power, it is then that God humiliates them.

would be killed.[412] Rabban Gamliel taught: Achashverosh was a fickle king.[413] Rabban Gamliel added: We still need the [reason that was taught by the] Modai, for we are taught in a *beraisa*: R. Eliezer ha-Modai taught: [Esther invited Haman to the party and she thereby] made the king jealous and she made the officials [who were not invited] jealous.[414]

TALMUD

רָבָה אָמַר: "לִפְנֵי שֶׁבֶר – גָּאוֹן". אַבַּיֵי וְרָבָא דְּאָמְרֵי תַרְוַיְיהוּ: "בְּחֻמָּם אָשִׁית אֶת מִשְׁתֵּיהֶם". אַשְׁכְּחֵיהּ רַבָּה בַר אֲבוּהּ לְאֵלִיָּהוּ, אָמַר לֵיהּ: כְּמָאן חַזְיָא אֶסְתֵּר וְעָבְדָה הָכֵי? אָמַר לֵיהּ: כְּכוּלְהוּ תַנָּאֵי, וּכְכוּלְהוּ אָמוֹרָאֵי.

TRANSLATION

Raba taught: *Before the downfall there is pride* (*Mishlei* 16:19). Abbaye and Rava both taught: *[At the time] when they are warm, I shall make them a party [which will lead to their downfall]* (*Yirmiyahu* 51:39).[415] Raba bar Avahu met Eliyahu and asked him: In agreement with whom did Esther see fit to act as she did

---

412 - The *Midrash* relates that Esther did all that was possible to arouse Achashverosh's jealousy at the party so as to provide him with a reason to kill Haman and thus foil the plot against the Jews. Additionally, she hoped that in his rage, Achashveroh would kill her as well and she would thus be saved from the necessity to continue serving as his queen.

413 - *Rashi* (ד"ה מלך הפכפך) explains that Esther knew that Achashverosh was fickle. If she told him about the plot in Haman's presence, he would order him killed immediately. If Haman was not present, Achashverosh might well change his mind.

414 - By inviting Haman alone, Esther cleverly destroyed Haman's power base, for she caused both the king and his officers to detest him.

415 - *Rashi* notes that the verse refers to the party made by Belshetzar when he had successfully prevented Daryavesh and Koresh from capturing Babylonia. [*Rashi's* explanation, however, is difficult to understand, for Balshetzar made a party to celebrate the fact that the Babylonian kingdom remained intact even though the seventy years prophesied by Yirmiyahu seemed to have passed. Indeed, after Balshetzer's death, Daryavesh and Koresh successfully overthrew the Babylonian kingdom and established the kingdom of the Medes and Persians. See *Daniel* 5.]

At the party, a mysterious hand wrote on the wall and Daniel was called to interpret the meaning of the words. That same night, Balshetzar died. Esther thus hoped that history would repeat itself and Haman would also be killed following the party that seemed to have been given in his honor. *Radak* (ad loc.) adds that Vashti's downfall also occurred after a party. Thus, Esther had ample historical precedent upon which she based her invitation to Haman.

[i.e., which of the opinions cited is correct in describing her motivation in inviting Haman]? Eliyahu answered: Like all of the *tannaim* and all of the *amoraim*.

COMMENTARY

Maharal explains that since Esther acted under the influence of the Divine spirit, all of the reasons offered by the *tannaim* and *amoraim* quoted are correct in describing her motivation. Any reason that is logical was taken into account when God gave Esther the idea to invite Haman.

TALMUD

"וַיְסַפֵּר לָהֶם הָמָן אֶת כְּבוֹד עָשְׁרוֹ, וְרֹב בָּנָיו". וְכַמָּה "רֹב בָּנָיו"? רַב אָמַר: שְׁלֹשִׁים - עֲשָׂרָה מֵתוּ, וַעֲשָׂרָה נִתְלוּ, וַעֲשָׂרָה שֶׁמְּחַזְרִים עַל הַפְּתָחִים. רַבָּנָן אָמְרִי: אוֹתָם שֶׁמְּחַזְרִים עַל הַפְּתָחִים, שִׁבְעִים הָיוּ, שֶׁנֶּאֱמַר: "שְׂבֵעִים בַּלֶּחֶם נִשְׂכָּרוּ", אַל תִּקְרֵי "שְׂבֵעִים", אֶלָּא "שִׁבְעִים".

וְרָמֵי בַּר אַבָּא אָמַר: כֻּלָּן מָאתַיִם וּשְׁמוֹנָה הָיוּ, שֶׁנֶּאֱמַר: "וְרֹב בָּנָיו", "וְרֹב", בְּגִימַטְרִיָּא הָכֵי הֲוֵי. "וְרֹב" בְּגִימַטְרִיָּא מָאתָן וְאַרְבֵּיסַר הֲוֵי? אָמַר רַב נַחְמָן בַּר יִצְחָק: "וְרֹב" כְּתִיב.

"בַּלַּיְלָה הַהוּא נָדְדָה שְׁנַת הַמֶּלֶךְ", אָמַר רַבִּי תַּנְחוּם: נָדְדָה שְׁנַת מַלְכּוֹ שֶׁל עוֹלָם. וְרַבָּנָן אָמְרִי: נָדְדוּ עֶלְיוֹנִים וְתַחְתּוֹנִים.

TRANSLATION

And Haman told them about the glory of his wealth and of his many sons (*Esther 5:11*) — How *many sons* did he have? Rav said: Thirty! Ten died, ten were hanged and ten went begging in the doorways. The Sages said: There were seventy who went begging in the doorways. [How do we know this?] The verse (*Shmuel I 2:5*) states: *Those sated by bread were hired [as slaves — i.e., forced to beg]*. Do not read [the word as] *sated*. Rather, [read it as if it says] *seventy*.[416]

Rami bar Abba taught: In all there were two hundred and eight, for the verse (op. cit.) states: *verov banav* and the numerical value of the word] *verov* is such [i.e., two hundred and eight]. But the numerical value of *verov* is two hundred and fourteen? R. Nachman bar Yitzchak answered: The verse states *verov* [without a

416 - I.e., the verse from Chanah's prophetic prayer of thanksgiving is interpreted to be referring to the sons of Haman who were reduced to begging for a piece of bread. *Maharsha* points out that the exegesis is based on the difficulty of understanding the phrase literally, for if they were sated, why would they hire themselves out as servants? The Sages therefore deduced that the word שבעים should be read as *shiv'im* — *seventy* — rather than as *s'vei'im* — *sated*.

vav between the *reish* and the *beis* and the numerical value is thus two hundred and eight].[417]

That night the sleep of the king was disturbed (*Esther* 6:1) — R. Tanchum explained: The sleep of the King of the world. The Sages explained: There were disturbances in the higher and lower [worlds].[418]

COMMENTARY

How is it possible to say that the sleep of the Almighty was disturbed? The verse (*Tehillim* 121:4) specifically states: *Behold, the Guardian of Israel does not sleep or rest!*

The episode of Esther and Mordechai took place at a time of *hester panim* — when the Divine countenance that guides the world is hidden. When Mordechai and Esther decreed the three days of public prayer and fast, the Jews repented and once again placed their trust solely in the Almighty, recognizing that their only chance for survival rested upon His active intervention.[419] These prayers and fast atoned for the sins of those who had joined Achashverosh's feast and who had thus symbolically linked their fortunes with the Persian king. Having accomplished this, the Divine presence could once again be revealed, and it is in this sense that R. Tanchum noted that the sleep of the King of the world was disturbed.

TALMUD

אָמַר רָבָא: נָדְדָה שְׁנַת הַמֶּלֶךְ אֲחַשְׁוֵרוֹשׁ מַמָּשׁ. נָפְלָה לֵיהּ מִילְתָא בְּדַעְתֵּיהּ, אָמַר: מַאי דְּקַמָּן, דְּזַמִּנְתֵּיהּ אֶסְתֵּר לְהָמָן בַּהֲדַאי? דִּילְמָא עֵצָה קָא שָׁקְלֵי עֲלֵיהּ דְּהַהוּא גַּבְרָא לְמִקְטְלֵיהּ? הֲדַר אָמַר: אִי הָכֵי הֲוָה, לָא הֲוָה אִינִישׁ דְּרָחֵים לִי, וַהֲוָה מוֹדַע לִי? הֲדַר אָמַר: דִּילְמָא אִיכָּא אִינִישׁ דְּעָבִיד בִּי טִיבוּתָא, וְלָא פְּרַעְתֵּיהּ, מִשּׁוּם הָכֵי מִימְּנְעֵי אֱנָשֵׁי וְלָא מְגַלּוּ לִי. מִיָּד - "וַיֹּאמֶר לְהָבִיא אֶת סֵפֶר הַזִּכְרֹנוֹת, וְגוֹ'. וַיִּהְיוּ נִקְרָאִים", מְלַמֵּד שֶׁנִּקְרָאִים מֵאֲלֵיהֶם.

---

417 - The numerical value of the letter *vav* is six, the letter *reish* is two hundred and the letter *beis* is two.

418 - *Rashi* (ד"ה נדדו עליונים) explains that the ministering angels disturbed Achashverosh's sleep, accusing him of being ingrateful for the assistance that Mordechai had rendered in foiling the assasination plot of Bigsan and Seresh.

419 - See also *Sotah* 48a.

"וַיִּמָּצֵא כָתוּב", "כְּתָב" מִיבָּעֵי לֵיהּ! מְלַמֵּד שֶׁשִּׁמְשַׁי מוֹחֵק, וְגַבְרִיאֵל כּוֹתֵב.
אָמַר רַבִּי אַסִּי, דָּרַשׁ רַבִּי שֵׁילָא אִישׁ כְּפַר תָּמַרְתָּא: וּמַה כְּתָב שֶׁל מַטָּה – שֶׁל
זְכוּתָן שֶׁל יִשְׂרָאֵל, אֵינוֹ נִמְחָק. כְּתָב שֶׁל מַעְלָה, עַל אַחַת כַּמָּה וְכַמָּה?

TRANSLATION

Rava explained: Achashverosh's sleep was disturbed for a thought had entered his mind. He said to himself: "What is going on? Why did Esther invite Haman together with me? Perhaps she is seeking counsel from that man to kill me?" He then said: "If this is so, there is no one who will have mercy upon me and inform me [of their plot]." He then said: "Perhaps there is someone who did me a favor and I have not repaid him? Perhaps that is why people avoid me and did not reveal it to me?" As a result, *He called to bring the chronicles ... and they were read before him* (ibid.). This teaches us that they read themelves.[420]

And they found writing (ibid. :2) — it should say *written!*[421] This indicates **[16a]** that [Haman's son] Shimshi erased [the section about Mordechai] and [the angel] Gavriel wrote it. R. Asi said: R. Shila from Kfar Tamrasa expounded [based on this]: If human records [that recount the] merit of Israel are not erasable, then Heavenly records are surely [not erasable].

COMMENTARY

Targum Sheni to the *Megillah* records that there were two chronicles: a complete version called *Divrei ha-Yamim* and a condensed version called *Sefer ha-Zichronos*. Haman's son, Shimshi, in his position as court archivist, erased all mention of Mordechai in the former version, substituting his father's name instead. But Shimshi had no access to the latter work which was kept at the king's bedside. When Achashverosh found that he could not sleep, he asked that the condensed version be read to him. Shimshi attempted to skip the portion but the pages kept on turning back to the section recounting Mordechai's role in

420 - *Maharsha* explains that grammatically the verse should state ויקראו לפניו — *that they be read before him.* The construction ויהיו נקראים — *and they were read* — in present tense suggests that the chronicles read themselves.

The *Midrash* recounts that the chamberlain called to read the chronicles was Shimshi, Haman's son. He attempted to skip the part that described Mordechai's role in foiling the assasination plot, but miraculously, the chronicles would not allow the pages to be turned to any other subject and he was forced to read that section.

421 - Rashi (ד״ה כתוב) explains that the verse uses the term כתוב rather than כתב which would imply that it was already written.

foiling the plot against Achashverosh. He then tried to erase Mordechai's name but the angel Gavriel appeared and rewrote it.[422]

TALMUD

"וַיֹּאמֶר הַמֶּלֶךְ: מַה נַּעֲשָׂה יְקָר וּגְדוּלָה, וְגוֹ'. לֹא נַעֲשָׂה עִמּוֹ דָבָר". אָמַר רָבָא: לֹא מִפְּנֵי שֶׁאוֹהֲבִים אֶת מָרְדְּכַי, אֶלָּא מִפְּנֵי שֶׁשּׂוֹנְאִים אֶת הָמָן.

"הֵכִין לוֹ", תָּנָא "לוֹ" הֵכִין.

TRANSLATION

And the king asked: What honor and dignity [were granted to Mordechai for this? And the king's servants who served him replied:] Nothing was done for him. (ibid. :3) — Rava explained: [All of the servants answered together] not because they loved Mordechai but because they hated Haman.

[Haman had arrived at the outer courtyard of the palace to speak to the king about hanging Mordechai on the gallows] which he had prepared for him (ibid. :4) — We learned in a *beraisa:* [The phrase *for him* teaches us that Haman] had prepared it for himself.[423]

COMMENTARY

The parallel version cited in the *Midrash* continues: Regarding him [Haman] the verse (*Tehillim* 7:14-16) states: *And for himself he prepared the instrument of his execution, his sharpened his arrows. He dug a pit and they deepened it, and he fell into the abyss which he had made.* When the gallows was brought to Haman to inspect, he tried it out on himself so as to demonstrate to his servants what he planned for Mordechai. A Divine voice then issued forth and declared: "The gallows suits you, it has been ready for you since the Six Days of Creation."

TALMUD

"וַנַעֲשֵׂה כֵן לְמָרְדְּכַי", אָמַר לוֹ: מַנּוּ מָרְדְּכַי? אָמַר לוֹ: מָרְדְּכַי הַיְהוּדִי. אָמַר לוֹ:

---

422 - *Maharal* explains that Shimshi might have attempted to erase Mordechai's name without substituting Haman's, for Achashverosh would have been suspicious had he seen Shimshi writing. If there was no name recorded, Achashverosh would probably have asked who was responsible for saving him and Shimshi could have then suggested that they consult the complete chronicles which he had previously doctored.

423 - I.e., the verse could have simply said *on the gallows that he had prepared.* The additional phrase *for him* indicates that, without realizing it, Haman had actually prepared the very gallows on which he would be hung.

טוּבָא אִיכָּא מָרְדְּכַי בִּיהוּדָאֵי! אָמַר לוֹ: הַיּוֹשֵׁב בְּשַׁעַר הַמֶּלֶךְ. אָמַר לוֹ: סַגִּי
בַּחֲדָא דְסְקַרְתָּא, אִי נַמִי, בַּחֲדָא נַהֲרָא. אָמַר לוֹ: "אַל תַּפֵּל דָּבָר מִכֹּל אֲשֶׁר
דִּבַּרְתָּ", גְּמַר וְהַב לֵיהּ! "וַיִּקַּח הָמָן אֶת הַלְּבוּשׁ וְאֶת הַסּוּס". אֲזַל, וְאַשְׁכַּח
רַבָּנָן דְּיָתְבֵי קַמֵּי מָרְדְּכַי, וְקָא מַחְוֵי לְהוּ הִלְכוֹת קְמִיצָה לְרַבָּנָן. כֵּיוָן דְּחַזְיֵיהּ
מָרְדְּכַי, דְּאָפֵיק לְקָבְלֵיהּ וְסוּסֵיהּ מֵיחַד בִּיָדֵיהּ, מִירְתַת, אָמַר לְהוּ לְרַבָּנָן:
הַאי רְשִׁיעָא, לְמִקְטַל נַפְשִׁי קָא אָתֵי, זִילוּ מִקַּמֵּיהּ, דִּי לָא תִכָווּ בְּגַחַלְתִּי.

TRANSLATION

Do this for Mordechai (ibid:10) — Haman asked him: Which Mordechai? The
king answered: Mordechai the Jew. He asked: There are many Mordechais among
the Jews? The king answered: The one who sits at the gate of the palace. Haman
said: It is sufficient to give him one village or one river [as a reward and there is
no reason to award him such great honor]. The king answered: *Do not leave out a
detail of anything that you have said* (ibid.) — Do it and give it to him [i.e, give
Mordechai all that you had previously suggested as well as what you suggested now]!
And Haman took the clothing and the horse (ibid. :11) — Haman went out and
found the rabbis sitting in front of Mordechai who was demonstrating the laws
of *kemitza*[424] for the rabbis. When Mordechai saw him approaching with the
reins of a horse in his hand, he became afraid. He told the rabbis: This wicked
man has come to kill me! Flee so that you not be burned in my flame.[425]

COMMENTARY

As we have already seen, Achashverosh suspected that Esther's invitation to
Haman indicated that the two of them planned to kill him. When Haman
suddenly appeared in the courtyard in the middle of the night, his suspicions
became even stronger. He therefore sought a means to humiliate Haman
publicly and thus foil his plot. He allowed Haman to believe that he sought a
means of honoring him and only after Haman had gone on and on advising the

---

424 - The fistful of grain that the *kohen* took from the *omer* — see *Vayikra* 23:11.
425 - This occurred on the 16th of Nisan, the day when the *omer* sacrifice was offered
in the *Beis ha-Mikdash*. Mordechai was therefore teaching the laws applicable to that
day, in fulfillment of the dictum of Moshe (*Megillah* 4a) that one should study the
laws of the holiday on the day of the holiday.
The parallel version in the *Midrash* adds that Haman asked Mordechai what the point
of their studies was since the *Beis ha-Mikdash* was no longer in use and their studies
were academic. Mordechai answered that when Israel studies the laws of the sacrifices,
God considers it as if they had offered them.

king as to the honor due one of his station did he tell him to honor Mordechai. Haman was crushed and desparately tried to avoid fulfilling the king's instructions, offering a variety of excuses. But Achashverosh would not be put off and forced Haman to fulfill his instructions without exception.

TALMUD

בְּהַהִיא שַׁעְתָּא, נִתְעַטֵּף מָרְדְּכַי וְקָם לֵיהּ לִצְלוֹתָא. אֲתָא הָמָן, וְיָתִיב לֵיהּ קַמַּיְיהוּ, וְאוֹרִיךְ עַד דְּסָלִיק מָרְדְּכַי לִצְלוֹתֵיהּ. אֲמַר לוֹ: בְּמַאי עַסְקִיתוּ? אֲמַר לֵיהּ: דְּכִי הֲוָה בֵּית מַקְדְּשָׁא קַיָּם, רַחֲמָנָא אָמַר: מָאן דִּמְנַדֵּב מִנְחָה, לֵיתִי מַלְיָא קוּמְצֵיהּ מִמֶּנָּה, וְלִיקְטַר עַל גַּבֵּי מַדְבְּחָא, וְלִיכַפֵּר לֵיהּ. אֲמַר לֵיהּ: אֲתָא מְלָא קוּמְצָא דְּקַמְחָא דִּידְכוּ, וְדָחֵי עַשְׂרָא אַלְפָא כְּכָרֵי כַסְפָּא דְּהַהוּא גַּבְרָא.

אֲמַר לֵיהּ: רָשָׁע, עַבְדָּא דְּקָנָה נְכָסִים, עַבְדָּא דְּמָאן? נְכָסִים דְּמָאן?

אֲמַר לֵיהּ: קוּם לְבוּשׁ הַנֵּי מָאנֵי, וּרְכִיב הַאי סוּסְיָא, דְּקָא בָּעֵא לָךְ מַלְכָּא. אֲמַר לֵיהּ: לָא יָכִילְנָא, עַד דְּאָזְלִינָא לְבֵי בָנֵי, וְאֶשְׁקוֹל לְמֵיזָאי, דְּלָא אוֹרַח אַרְעָא לְאִשְׁתַּמּוּשֵׁי בְמָאנֵי דְמַלְכוּתָא הָכֵי. אַדְּהָכֵי וְהָכֵי, שָׁדְרָה אֶסְתֵּר, וַאֲסַרְתִּינְהוּ לְכוּלְהוּ בֵּי בָנֵי, וּלְכוּלְהוּ אוּמְנֵי. עַיְּילֵיהּ אִיהוּ לְבֵי בָנֵי, וְאַסְחֵיהּ. וְאֲזַל וְאַיְּיתֵי זוּזָא מִבֵּיתֵיהּ, וְקָא שָׁקִיל לְמַזְיֵיהּ. בָּתַר דְּקָא שָׁקִיל לֵיהּ, אִינְגִּיד וְאִתְנַח. אֲמַר לֵיהּ: אַמַּאי קָא מִתְנַחַת? אֲמַר לֵיהּ: גַּבְרָא דַּחֲשִׁיב לֵיהּ לְמַלְכָּא מִכּוּלְהוּ רַבְרְבָנוֹהִי, הַשְׁתָּא לְשַׁוְּיֵיהּ בַּלָּאנִי וְסַפָּר?! אֲמַר לֵיהּ: רָשָׁע! לָאו סַפָּר בִּכְפַר קַרְצוּם הָיֵיתְ?! תָּנָא: הָמָן סַפָּר שֶׁל כְּפַר קַרְצוּם הֲוָה, עֶשְׂרִים וּשְׁתַּיִם שָׁנָה.

TRANSLATION

At this time, Mordechai donned [his *tallis*] and rose to pray. Haman approached, sat down in front of him and waited for Mordechai to finish praying. He asked him: "What were you discussing?" Mordechai answered: "When the *Beis ha-Mikdash* stood, the Torah ordained that one who brought a grain-offering was required to take a fistful of it and offer it on the altar and this was his atonement." Haman responded: "Your fistful of grain is more powerful than the ten thousand measures of silver of this man [i.e., the money that Haman had offered the king's treasury in return for the right to kill the Jews]."

Mordechai said to him: "Wicked man! A servant who purchases property — who owns the servant and who owns the property [i.e., the money that you offered the treasury is mine since you are my servant]?"[426]

426 - See page 184.

Haman then said to him: "Arise and put on this clothing and mount this horse, for the king desires [to honor] you." Mordechai answered: "I can't until I go to the bath house and cut my hair, for it is improper to use the royal clothing in this manner." In the meantime, Esther sent [agents] to close all of the bath houses and all the barbershops. Haman [therefore] took him to the bath house himself and washed him and then went to his house and brought scissors to cut his hair. After he had cut Mordechai's [hair], he sighed. Mordechai asked him: "Why are you sighing?" Haman answered: "A man whom the king considered more important than all of the other officials has now become a bath house attendant and a barber!" Mordechai said: "Wicked man! Were you not a barber in the village of Kartzum?" We learned in a *beraisa*: Haman was the barber in the village of Kartzum for twenty-two years.[427]

COMMENTARY

Gaon Yaakov offers an interesting analysis of the conversation between Mordechai and Haman. The Talmud quotes Mordechai as calling Haman a wicked man, whereas based on the fact that Haman had served as the barber in Kartzum, he should have called him a liar!

When Haman sighed about his fate, he tried to justify his previous actions and told Mordechai that he was born under the influence of Mars and the stars forced him to be a person who shed blood. He thus had no choice but to plan to annihilate the Jews and Mordechai should not hold it against him. Mordechai replied that Haman's astrological prediliction had already been fulfilled when he served as a barber[428] and his plans for the Jews were not a result of his being forced by the stars but were a result of his wickedness.

---

427 - *Rambam* (הלכות מלכים א:ו) writes that a barber or a bath house attendant should not be appointed as a king, for these positions are considered to be degraded and the people do not respect those who engage in these professions. While Achashverosh did not make his palace appointments contingent upon the criteria for office delineated by the *Rambam*, it is obvious that these positions were always held as being less than honorable. Haman therefore was aghast when he was forced to serve as Mordechai's barber and bath attendant.

428 - See *Shabbos* 156a: *One born under Mars will shed blood. R. Ashi said: [He will either be] a bloodletter [a function performed by barbers], a thief, a butcher or a mohel.*

TALMUD

בָּתַר דְּאַשְׁקֵיל לֵיהּ לְמַזְיֵיהּ, אַלְבְּשֵׁיהּ. אֲמַר לֵיהּ: סְלִיק רְכִיב. אֲמַר לֵיהּ: לָא
יָכֵילְנָא, דִּכְחִישׁ חֵילָאי מִתַּעֲנִיתָא. גָּחֵין לֵיהּ וְרָכֵיב, וְכִי הֲוָה סָלֵיק, בָּטֵישׁ
בֵּיהּ, אֲמַר לֵיהּ: וְלָא כְּתִיב: "בִּנְפֹל אוֹיִבְךָ אַל תִּשְׂמָח"?! אֲמַר לֵיהּ: רָשָׁע! הַנֵּי
מִילֵי בְּיִשְׂרָאֵל, אֲבָל בְּדִידְכוּ כְּתִיב: "וְאַתָּה עַל בָּמוֹתֵימוֹ תִדְרֹךְ".

TRANSLATION

After he cut his hair, he dressed him. Haman told him: "Mount and ride [the horse]." Mordechai said: "I can't because I am weak from fasting." Haman bent down and [Mordechai stepped on his back] to mount. As he began to ride, he kicked him. Haman said: "Does the verse (*Mishlei* 24:17) not say: *when your adversary falls do not be happy*?" Mordechai answered: "Wicked one! That refers to [an adversary who is from] Israel! Regarding you the verse (*Devarim* 33:29) states: *And you shall tread on their platforms*."

COMMENTARY

Ramban[429] writes that before a miracle begins to transpire, it is possible that it will be delayed if circumstances arise — e.g., the unworthiness of the beneficiaries — and will only take place later when the time is more conducive. On the other hand, once the miracle begins, it is completed even if the circumstances change. Mordechai was concerned that Haman's miraculous fall from grace might be delayed because of the precarious state of the Jews who had but now repented. He therefore decided to have the miracle begin, by humiliating Haman publicly, so that it would be brought to fruition.

TRANSLATION

"וַיִּקְרָא לְפָנָיו: כָּכָה יֵעָשֶׂה לָאִישׁ", כִּי הֲוָה נָקֵיט וְאָזֵיל בִּשְׁבִילָא דְּבֵי הָמָן,
חַזְיְתֵיהּ בְּרַתֵּיהּ דַּהֲוַת קַיְּימָא בְּאִיגְּרָא, סָבְרָה: הַאי דִּרְכֵיב - אֲבוּהּ הוּא,
וְהַאי דְּמַסְגֵי קַמֵּיהּ - מָרְדְּכַי. שָׁקְלָה עֲצִיצָא דְּבֵית הַכִּסֵּא, וְשַׁדְיָא לֵיהּ אַרֵישֵׁהּ
דַּאֲבוּהּ. דְּלֵי עֵינֵיהּ וְחַזְיֵיהּ דַּאֲבוּהָא הֲוֵי, נָפְלָה מֵאִיגְּרָא וּמֵתָה. וְהַיְינוּ
דִּכְתִיב: "וַיָּשָׁב מָרְדְּכַי אֶל שַׁעַר הַמֶּלֶךְ". אֲמַר רַב שֵׁשֶׁת: שֶׁשָׁב לְשַׂקּוֹ
וּלְתַעֲנִיתוֹ. "וְהָמָן נִדְחַף אֶל בֵּיתוֹ אָבֵל וַחֲפוּי רֹאשׁ", "אָבֵל" עַל בִּתּוֹ. "וַחֲפוּי
רֹאשׁ" מִדָּבָר שֶׁאֵרְעוֹ.

---

429 - Commentary to *Bereishis* 12:6.

TRANSLATION

And he called out before him: Thus is done to the man (Esther 6:11) — When they were walking and reached the street of Haman's house, his daughter, who was standing on the roof, saw them. She thought that the rider was her father and the one leading him was Mordechai. She took the toilet pot and spilled it on her father's head. He looked up and she saw that it was her father [whereupon] she fell from the roof and died. And this is what the verse is referring to [when it says (ibid. :12)]: *And Mordechai returned to the palace gate* — he returned to his sackcloth and fasting[430] — *and Haman hurried home, in mourning and with his head covered* — *in mourning* for his daughter *and with his head covered* because of what happened to him.

TALMUD

"וַיְסַפֵּר הָמָן לְזֶרֶשׁ אִשְׁתּוֹ" גו', מַאי שְׁנָא הָתָם דְּקָרֵי לְהוּ: "אוֹהֲבָיו"? וּמַאי שְׁנָא הָכָא, דְּקָרֵי לְהוּ: "חֲכָמָיו"? אָמַר רַבִּי יוֹחָנָן: מְלַמֵּד שֶׁכָּל הָאוֹמֵר דְּבַר חָכְמָה, אֲפִילוּ בַּגּוֹיִם (עוֹבְדֵי כּוֹכָבִים) נִקְרָא ,חָכָם'.

"אִם מִזֶּרַע הַיְּהוּדִים מָרְדֳּכַי" וְגוֹ', אָמְרוּ לוֹ: אִם מִשְּׁאָר שִׁבְטֵי יִשְׂרָאֵל קָא אָתֵי, יָכֹלְתְּ לֵיהּ. וְאִם מִשֵּׁבֶט יְהוּדָה, מְנַשֶּׁה וְאֶפְרַיִם, וּבִנְיָמִין, קָא אָתֵי, לָא יָכֹלְתְּ לֵיהּ. "יְהוּדָה", דִּכְתִיב: "יָדְךָ בְּעֹרֶף אֹיְבֶיךָ", וּ"בִנְיָמִין", וּ"מְנַשֶּׁה", דִּכְתִיב: "לִפְנֵי אֶפְרַיִם וּבִנְיָמִן וּמְנַשֶּׁה, עוֹרְרָה אֶת גְּבוּרָתֶךָ, וּלְכָה לִישֻׁעָתָה לָּנוּ".

TRANSLATION

And Haman told Zeresh, his wife, and all of his loved ones all that had happened to him. And his wise advisers and Zeresh, his wife, said to him (ibid. :13) — Why is it different in the verse there [in the beginning] where they are called *his loved ones* and why is it different here where they are called *his wise advisers*? R. Yochanan explained: This [the change of expression] teaches us that anyone who says something wise — even among the gentiles — is referred to as wise.[431]

---

430 - See *Rambam* (הלכות תענית א:טו): *If an individual was fasting on behalf of a sick person and that person became healthy, he still must complete his fast.* Although Mordechai understood that the episode marked the beginning of Haman's downfall, he knew that he was still required to continue his fasts and prayers.

431 - I.e., the author changed phrases to indicate that the advice offered was wise and that those who gave it were worthy of being described as wise men.

If Mordechai is a descendent of the Jews (ibid. :14) — They told him: "If Mordechai is a descendent of one of the other tribes, you will be able to overcome him. But if he is a descendent of the tribes of Yehudah, Efraim, Menashe or Binyamin, you will be unable to overcome him."[432] [Why would he be unsuccessful if Mordechai was from the tribe of] Yehudah? The verse (*Bereishis* 49:8) states [in reference to the tribe of Yehudah]: *Your hand is in your enemy's back.* [And if Mordechai was from the] tribes of Efraim, Binyamin and Menashe [why was Haman bound to fail]? The verse (*Tehillim* 80:3) states: *Before Efraim, Binyamin and Menashe arouse Your strength and go and [bring] salvation for us.*[433]

COMMENTARY

Haman, as a truly wicked person, was determined not to abandon his plans and attributed his setbacks to a combination of unfortunate circumstances, refusing to recognize the hand of God. He turned again to his wife and advisers seeking a new means of bringing his plans to annihilate the Jews to fruition.

But Zeresh and the advisers were wiser than Haman and were quite capable of interpreting the sequence of events correctly. They told him that his sudden downfall must be a result of his having entered into battle with a scion of one of the tribes of Israel to whom God had promised success in overcoming the plots of Amalek. They understood that if Mordechai was a descendent of one of the other tribes, Haman could still be successful, for the battle between them had no cosmic significance and could be won on natural terms by the strongest. However, if Mordechai was a descendent of one of the four tribes mentioned, then the battle between Mordechai and Haman was a part of the Divine plan and the latter stood no chance of success. Based on their correct analysis of the situation, the author of the *Megillah* refers to them as being wise.

The four tribes delineated — Yehudah, Efraim, Menashe and Binyamin —

---

432 - Haman, as well as those close to him, knew that Mordechai was Jewish even before he began his plans to destroy him. Thus, telling Haman now that he would be unsuccessful if Mordechai was Jewish would be meaningless and could hardly be characterized as wise advice. The Talmud therefore interprets their statement as referring to specific tribes.

433 - I.e., these tribes had a Divine promise, as we see from Scripture, that they would be capable of overcoming Israel's enemies. If Mordechai was a descendent of one of these tribes, Haman could not be successful.

can be divided into two groups: the latter three are descendents of Rachel while the first is the child of Leah. *Maharal*[434] explains that the descendents of Rachel — who excelled in her trait of modesty[435] — are particularly suited to lead the ongoing war against Amalek/Esav whose trait is unmitigated conceit. Yehudah, who killed Esav,[436] was also suited to lead the battle against Amalek. We might add that Yehudah also excelled in modesty as evidenced by his confession in the incident with Tamar.

Rav Dessler[437] writes that evil character traits have their source in one of two factors — overwhelming desire or vanity. Actions whose roots are in the former can eventually be overcome, for desire is limited in scope and can eventually be sated. Vanity, on the other hand, has no natural boundaries and the desire of the person who exhibits this trait can never be satisfied.

Among the nations, there is a difference between those who made Israel subservient to serve their own interests — e.g., Egypt and Bavel — and those who tormented Israel because through doing so they were able to feed their own egos — e.g., the exile of Esav. While the former nations will find their downfall once their desires have been fulfilled and Israel can thus be delivered from their hands through a variety of instruments or people, the latter nation has an unsatiable appetite that can only be overcome when the part of Israel that represents the diametric opposite — pure modesty — stands up to do battle. Thus, Amalek — the most extreme example of Esav's vanity — could only be defeated when faced by a descendent of Rachel or a scion of the tribe of Yehudah, for they represent the epitome of modesty.

TALMUD

"כִּי נָפוֹל תִּפּוֹל לְפָנָיו", דָּרַשׁ רַבִּי יְהוּדָה בְּרַבִּי אִלְעָאי: שְׁתֵּי נְפִילוֹת אֵלּוּ, לָמָּה? מְלַמֵּד שֶׁאָמְרוּ לוֹ: אֻמָּה זוֹ מְשׁוּלָה לֶעָפָר, וּמְשׁוּלָה לַכּוֹכָבִים. כְּשֶׁהֵן יוֹרְדִין - יוֹרְדִין עַד עָפָר, וּכְשֶׁהֵן עוֹלִין - עוֹלִין עַד לַכּוֹכָבִים.

"עוֹדָם מְדַבְּרִים עִמּוֹ וְסָרִיסֵי הַמֶּלֶךְ" וְגוֹ'. מְלַמֵּד שֶׁהֱבִיאוּהוּ בְּבֶהָלָה. "כִּי אֵין הַצַּר שׁוֶֹה בְּנֶזֶק הַמֶּלֶךְ", אָמְרָה לֵיהּ: צַר זֶה אֵינוֹ שׁוֶֹה בְּנִזְקֵי הַמֶּלֶךְ! אִיקְנֵי בָּהּ בְּנַשְׁתִּי, וְקָטְלָהּ; הַשְׁתָּא אִיקְנֵי בְּדִידִי, וּבָעֵי לְמִקְטְלִי.

---

434 - *Chiddushei Aggados* to *Bava Basra* 123b.

435 - See page 133.

436 - See *Yerushalmi*, *Kesubos* 1:5 and *Tosafos*, *Gittin* 55b, s.v. *b'Yehudah*.

437 - מכתב מאליהו, חלק ב', page 50.

TRANSLATION

For you will surely fall before him (ibid.) — R. Yehuda b'R. Ilai expounded: Why does the [verse] twice speak of falling?[438] This [the doubled word] teaches us that they told him [Haman]: "This nation [the Jews] are compared to the dust and are compared to the stars. When they are falling, they fall unto the dust. But when they are rising, they rise until the stars."[439]

They were still talking to him when the king's chamberlains arrived and they hastened to bring Haman to the party that Esther had made (ibid. :14) — This teaches us that they brought him in a state of panic.[440]

For the enemy is not worthy enough to cause damage to the king (ibid. 7:4) — She told him: "This enemy [Haman] is not worthy enough compared to the damages to the king [that he has already caused]. He was jealous of Vashti and had her killed. Now he is jealous of me and seeks to kill me."

COMMENTARY

Haman's advisers told him that Mordechai's sudden rise to glory and his own humiliation signified that the end of his ascendancy was near. They began to outline a plan of action for him that would enable him to make the best of the situation and told him that he should prostrate himself before Mordechai — נפול תפול לפניו — *fall before him.* But their conversation abruptly ended when the king's servants arrived to take him to the feast. Not knowing what to do, Haman became even more panicked.

Maharal explains that Esther cleverly accused Haman of not having the king's interests at heart. She knew that Achashverosh was no great friend of the Jews and were she to accuse Haman of plotting to kill the Jews, Achashverosh

---

438 - The Hebrew states נפול תפול. The repetititon of a word, which is quite common in Scripture, is used as a means of emphasis. Thus, we have translated the words as *you will surely fall.*

439 - Haman's advisers were telling him that he had no chance of success. He would *surely fall* before Mordechai since Mordechai's stature was ascending. This meant that all of the Jews were in a state of ascendancy that would bring them to the stars.

440 - The Hebrew בהלה can be translated either as *in haste* or *in panic.* The Talmud explains that Haman panicked when the chamberlains hastened to bring him to Esther's party, not even giving him an opportunity to bathe. The rapid sequence of events that he no longer controlled filled him with trepidation as he wondered what disaster loomed next.

might well find grounds to spare Haman. She therefore attacked Haman as being self-serving, accusing him of killing Vashti so as to usurp her position of influence in the court. She then went on to accuse him of not being a true enemy of the Jews, explaining that his plot was no more than a ruse to kill her because she too had found favor in the king's eyes and threatened his power base.

TALMUD

"וַיֹּאמֶר הַמֶּלֶךְ אֲחַשְׁוֵרוֹשׁ, וַיֹּאמֶר לְאֶסְתֵּר הַמַּלְכָּה". "וַיֹּאמֶר", "וַיֹּאמֶר", לָמָּה לִי? אָמַר רַבִּי אַבָּהוּ: בַּתְּחִלָּה עַל יְדֵי תַרְגְּמָן, כֵּיוָן דְּאָמְרָה לֵיהּ: בַּת מְלָכִים אֲנָא, וּמִשָּׁאוּל מַלְכָּא קָא אָתִינָא, אִשְׁתָּעֵי מִיָּד בַּהֲדָהּ.

"וַיֹּאמֶר לְאֶסְתֵּר הַמַּלְכָּה: מִי הוּא זֶה וְגוֹ'? וַתֹּאמֶר אֶסְתֵּר: אִישׁ צַר וְאוֹיֵב הָמָן הָרָע הַזֶּה", אָמַר רַבִּי אֶלְעָזָר: מְלַמֵּד שֶׁהָיְתָה מַחֲוָה כְּלַפֵּי אֲחַשְׁוֵרוֹשׁ, וּבָא מַלְאָךְ וְסָטַר יָדָהּ כְּלַפֵּי הָמָן.

"וְהַמֶּלֶךְ קָם בַּחֲמָתוֹ וְגוֹ', וְהַמֶּלֶךְ שָׁב מִגִּנַּת הַבִּיתָן", מַקִּישׁ "שִׁיבָה" לְ"קִימָה", מַה "קִימָה" בְּחֵמָה, אַף "שִׁיבָה" בְּחֵמָה. דַּאֲזַל וְאַשְׁכַּח מַלְאֲכֵי הַשָּׁרֵת, דְּאִידְּמוּ לֵיהּ לְגַבְרֵי דְּקָא מְקָרֵי וְעָקְרֵי אִילָנֵי דְּבוּסְתְּנָא וְשָׁדוּ. אָמַר לְהוּ: מַאי עֲבִידְתַּיְיכוּ? אָמְרוּ לֵיהּ: דְּפַקְּדִינַן הָמָן. אָתָא לְבֵיתֵיהּ. "וְהָמָן נֹפֵל עַל הַמִּטָּה", "נָפַל" מִבָּעֵי לֵיהּ! אָמַר רַבִּי אֶלְעָזָר: מְלַמֵּד שֶׁבָּא מַלְאָךְ וְהִפִּילוֹ עָלֶיהָ. אָמַר: וַי מִבֵּיתָא, וַי מִבָּרָא. "וַיֹּאמֶר הַמֶּלֶךְ: הֲגַם לִכְבּוֹשׁ אֶת הַמַּלְכָּה עִמִּי בַּבָּיִת?!".

"וַיֹּאמֶר חַרְבוֹנָה אֶחָד מִן הַסָּרִיסִים" וְגוֹ'. אָמַר רַבִּי אֶלְעָזָר: אַף חַרְבוֹנָה הָרָשָׁע בְּאוֹתָהּ עֵצָה הָיָה. כֵּיוָן שֶׁרָאָה שֶׁלֹּא נִתְקַיְּמָה עֲצָתוֹ, מִיָּד בָּרַח. וְהַיְינוּ דִכְתִיב: "וַיַּשְׁלֵךְ עָלָיו, וְלֹא יַחְמֹל, מִיָּדוֹ – בָּרוֹחַ יִבְרָח".

TRANSLATION

And Achashverosh the king said, and he said to Esther the queen (ibid. :5) — Why does the verse use the word *said* twice? R. Abahu explained: At first [Achashverosh spoke to her using] an interpreter.[441] When she told him, "I am the daughter of kings and am descended from King Shaul," he immediately began to address her [directly].

And he said to Esther, the queen. Who is the person ... and Esther replied: A

---

441 - Achashverosh was unaware of Esther's background, for she had always concealed it from him. He therefore assumed that she was from common stock and would therefore not address her directly as it would demean his position to be seen

talking to a woman of no stature.

man who is an oppressor and an enemy, this wicked Haman (ibid.) — R. Elazar explained: This teaches us that she was pointing to Achashverosh, but an angel came and pushed her hand toward Haman.[442]

And the king arose in anger ... and the king returned from the palace garden (ibid. :7-8) — His return is compared to his leaving.[443] Just as he left in anger, so too did he return in anger. He went out [when he left Esther's party in fury] and found the ministering angels, who appeared in the guises of men, standing and removing trees from the palace garden and discarding them. He asked them: "What are you doing?" They answered: "Haman ordered us [to do this]." He [then] went back to the house and *Haman was falling on the couch [on which Esther was sitting]* (ibid. :8) — Why does the verse say *falling*? It should say *had fallen.* R. Elazar explained: This teaches us that an angel came and pushed Haman onto her. He [Achashverosh] said [to himself when he saw what was happening]: "Woe to my house and woe to what is happening outside." *The king then said: Do you even intend to capture the queen while I am in the house?!* (ibid.).

And Charvonah, one of the chamberlains, said (ibid. :9) — R. Elazar said: Charvonah, the wicked, was part of the plot [to hang Mordechai]. When he saw that the plot was unsuccessful, he immediately fled [from Haman's camp — i.e., he switched allegiances]. This is what the verse was referring to when it states (*Iyov* 27:22) — *When He punishes him [the wicked] without mercy, those who*

---

442 - R. Elazar derives his exposition from the phrasing of the verse. Esther first spoke of *an oppressor and an enemy* and then identified him as *this Haman*. The fact that she found it necessary to add *this Haman* implies that he might not have been the subject of her previous description. R. Elazar therefore explains that Esther was pointing to Achashverosh — no small enemy of the Jews himself — and an angel came and moved her hand.

Eitz Yosef explains that Esther did not intend to accuse Achashverosh of being a partner to Haman's plot, for had she done so who knows what the king's reaction would have been. Rather, she pointed toward Achashverosh to indicate that Haman was as much an enemy of his as he was of hers. However, Achashverosh might well have misunderstood her intentions and the angel therefore came and moved her hand.

443 - The exegesis is based on the seemingly superfluous use of king in the second phrase since we already know that Achashverosh is the subject of the sentence. The Talmud therefore explains that the author's purpose was to indicate that the king's exit and entrance were equivalent.

benefit from him flee quickly.

COMMENTARY

Why does R. Elazar refer to Charvonah as being wicked? In other instances we find that people who have a change of heart and switch sides are praised — e.g., Basya, daughter of Pharoah, or Rachav. It would seem that when the change of heart is a result of recognizing the truth, as in the case of Basya or Rachav, they are worthy of praise. But when the change of allegiance is no more than a means of saving one's own position or disguising one's role — as in the case of Charvonah — the categorization of that person as being wicked is still appropriate.

Maharal points out that even though Charvonah is characterized by R. Elazar as being wicked, the *Yerushalmi* states that one should remember Charvonah for the good advice he provided. Thus, the author of the song *Shoshanas Yaakov* that is recited on Purim after the *Megillah* reading saw fit to add his name. He explains, based on the parallel version in the *Midrash*, that Charvonah fled when Haman's plot began to crumble and Eliyahu appeared in his guise and it was he who offered Achashverosh the information regarding the gallows that Haman had prepared for Mordechai. Thus, when we mention Charvonah's name we are actually remembering Eliyahu.[444]

Rav Shlomo Bravda points out that Charvonah's advice that Haman be immediately hung on the gallows that he prepared is another example of the Divine attribute of מדה כנגד מדה — punishment suited to the crime. Aside from the fact that Haman met his death through an instrument that he had prepared, the fact that Achashverosh was able to immediately order his execution without having to first bring him to trial was a result of the precedent that Haman had himself established in the case of Vashti. Charvonah had been one of the palace officials who had been sent to bring Vashti and was undoubtedly

---

444 - *Anaf Yosef*, quoted in *Siddur Otzar ha-Tefillos*, writes that there were actually two Charvonahs; the one mentioned here and the one mentioned previously (1:10) as one of Achashverosh's palace officials. He notes that the former is spelled חרבונא whereas the latter is spelled חרבונה. The second Charvonah was actually Eliyahu, who assumed the role of one of the palace officals so as not to make Achashverosh suspicious by the sudden disappearance of his underling. Thus, חרבונא was indeed wicked, but חרבונה/Eliyahu is remembered for good.

aware of Haman's advice that she be immediately executed for having refused.

TALMUD

"נָחֲמַת הַמֶּלֶךְ שָׁכָכָה", שְׁתֵּי שְׁכִיכוֹת הַלָּלוּ לָמָּה? אַחַת שֶׁל מַלְכוּ שֶׁל עוֹלָם.
וְאַחַת שֶׁל אֲחַשְׁוֵרוֹש. אִיכָּא דְּאָמְרִי: אַחַת שֶׁל אֶסְתֵּר, וְאַחַת שֶׁל וַשְׁתִּי.

"לְכֻלָּם נָתַן לָאִישׁ חֲלִפוֹת שְׂמָלֹת, וּלְבִנְיָמִן נָתַן וְגוֹ', וְחָמֵשׁ חֲלִיפֹת שְׂמָלֹת".
אֶפְשָׁר, דָּבָר שֶׁנִּצְטַעֵר בּוֹ אוֹתוֹ צַדִּיק, יִכָּשֵׁל בּוֹ?

דַּאֲמַר רָבָא בַּר מַחְסְיָה, אָמַר רַב חָמָא בַּר גּוּרְיָא, אָמַר רַב: בִּשְׁבִיל מִשְׁקַל
שְׁנֵי סְלָעִים מֵילַת שֶׁהוֹסִיף יַעֲקֹב לְיוֹסֵף מִשְׁאָר בָּנָיו, נִתְקַנְּאוּ בוֹ אֶחָיו,
וְנִתְגַּלְגֵּל הַדָּבָר, וְיָרְדוּ אֲבוֹתֵינוּ לְמִצְרַיִם,

אָמַר רַבִּי בִּנְיָמִין בַּר יֶפֶת: רָמַז לוֹ, שֶׁעָתִיד לָצֵאת מִמֶּנּוּ בֵּן שֶׁיֵּצֵא מִלְּפְנֵי
הַמֶּלֶךְ בַּחֲמִשָּׁה לְבוּשֵׁי מַלְכוּת. וּמַנּוּ? מָרְדֳּכַי, דִּכְתִיב: "וּמָרְדֳּכַי יָצָא מִלִּפְנֵי
הַמֶּלֶךְ" וְגוֹ'.

TRANSLATION

And the king's anger subsided (ibid.) — Why [does the verse refer] to a double subsiding?[445] One [anger that subsided] was the anger of the King of the World and one was the anger of Achashverosh. Others say: One was [Achashverosh's anger over what Haman had planned to do to] Esther and one was [his anger over what Haman had done to] Vashti.

To each man he gave a suit of clothing and to Binyamin he gave three hundred measures of silver and five suits of clothing (Bereishis 45:22) — Is it possible that something which brought that righteous person [Yosef] torment, **[16b]** he himself would stumble because of it!?[446]

As Rava bar Machsaya taught in the name of R. Chama bar Gurya who taught in the name of Rav: Because of two *selaim's* weight of fine wool that Yaakov gave Yosef above that of his other sons, his sons became jealous of him [Yosef] and a chain of events transpired [which culminated] in our forefathers going down to Egypt.

R. Binyamin bar Yefes explained: [Why did Yosef give Binyamin five suits of clothing?] He [did so to] hint to him that a descendent of his was destined to leave the king's presence wearing five royal suits. And who is this [descendent]?

---

445 - The Hebrew term is שככה, from the root שכה — see *Bereishis* 8:1. The repetition of the כ alludes to two sources of anger that subsided.

446 - I.e., based on his own experience, Yosef should have known better.

Mordechai, regarding whom the verse (*Esther* 8:15) states: *And Mordechai left the king's presence [wearing royal clothing of blue and white, a large gold crown and a robe of linen and purple].*

TALMUD

"וַיִּפֹּל עַל צַוְּארֵי בִנְיָמִן אָחִיו" וְגוֹ', כַּמָּה צַוָּארֵי הֲווֹ לֵיהּ לְבִנְיָמִין? אָמַר רַבִּי
אֶלְעָזָר: מְלַמֵּד שֶׁבָּכָה יוֹסֵף עַל מִקְדָּשׁ רִאשׁוֹן, וְעַל מִקְדָּשׁ שֵׁנִי, שֶׁעֲתִידִין
לִהְיוֹת בְּחֶלְקוֹ שֶׁל בִּנְיָמִין, וַעֲתִידִין לֵיחָרֵב.

"וּבִנְיָמִן בָּכָה עַל צַוָּארָיו", בָּכָה עַל מִשְׁכַּן שִׁילֹה שֶׁעֲתִיד לִהְיוֹת בְּחֶלְקוֹ שֶׁל
יוֹסֵף וְעָתִיד לֵיחָרֵב.

"וְהִנֵּה עֵינֵיכֶם רֹאוֹת, וְעֵינֵי אָחִי בִנְיָמִין", אָמַר רַבִּי אֶלְעָזָר: אָמַר לָהֶם: כְּשֵׁם
שֶׁאֵין בְּלִבִּי כְּלוּם עַל בִּנְיָמִין אָחִי, שֶׁלֹּא הָיָה בִמְכִירָתִי. כָּךְ אֵין בְּלִבִּי עֲלֵיכֶם,
שֶׁהֱיִיתֶם בִּמְכִירָתִי.

"כִּי פִי הַמְדַבֵּר אֲלֵיכֶם", כְּפִי - כָּךְ לִבִּי.

"וּלְאָבִיו שָׁלַח כְּזֹאת, עֲשָׂרָה חֲמֹרִים נֹשְׂאִים מִטּוּב מִצְרָיִם", מַאי "מִטּוּב
מִצְרָיִם"? אָמַר רַבִּי בִּנְיָמִין בַּר יֶפֶת, אָמַר רַבִּי אֶלְעָזָר: שִׁגֵּר לוֹ יַיִן יָשָׁן שֶׁדַּעַת
זְקֵנִים נוֹחָה הֵימֶנּוּ.

TRANSLATION

And he [Yosef] fell on Binyamin's necks and wept (*Bereishis* 45:14) — How many necks did Binyamin have?[447] R. Elazar explained: This [the plural form] teaches us that Yosef wept over the first *Beis ha-Mikdash* and over the second *Beis ha-Mikdash* that were destined to be in the portion of Binyamin and that were destined to be destroyed.[448]

And Binyamin cried on his neck (ibid.) — [This teaches us that Binyamin] cried over the Tabernacle at Shiloh which was destined to be in the portion of Yosef and was destined to be destroyed.

And behold your eyes see and the eyes of my brother Binyamin (ibid. :12) — [Why did Yosef speak of the brothers and of Binyamin separately?] R. Elazar explained: He [Yosef] said to them: Just as I have nothing in my heart against

---

447 - The Hebrew צוארי is plural.

448 - The comparison of the *Beis ha-Mikdash* to the neck is based on *Shir ha-Shirim* 4:4 — *Your neck is like the Tower of David.* The *Midrash* (ad loc.) explains: *Why is it compared to the neck? During the entire period when the Beis ha-Mikdash stood, Israel's necks were higher than the other nations. When it was destroyed, it was as if their necks were bowed.*

my brother Binyamin, for he was not [involved] in my sale [as a slave], so too I
have nothing in my heart against you [who were involved] in my sale.

That it is my mouth that speaks to you (ibid.) — that my mouth is like my
heart.[449]

And to his father he sent as follows: ten donkeys carrying the best of Egypt
(ibid. :23) — What is [meant by] *the best of Egypt*? R. Binyamin bar Yefes
explained in the name of R. Elazar: He sent him old wine, for the elderly find
that pleasurable.[450]

TALMUD

"וַיֵּלְכוּ גַּם אֶחָיו, וַיִּפְּלוּ לְפָנָיו", אָמַר רַבִּי בִּנְיָמִין בַּר יֶפֶת, אָמַר רַבִּי אֶלְעָזָר:
הַיְינוּ דְּאָמְרִי אֱנָשֵׁי: תַּעֲלָא בְּעִידָּנֵיהּ סְגִיד לֵיהּ. "תַּעֲלָא"?! מַאי בְּצִירוּתֵיהּ
מֵאֲחוּהִי? אֶלָּא אִי אִיתְּמָר, הָכֵי אִיתְּמָר: "וַיִּשְׁתַּחוּ יִשְׂרָאֵל עַל רֹאשׁ הַמִּטָּה",
אָמַר רַבִּי בִּנְיָמִין בַּר יֶפֶת, אָמַר רַבִּי אֶלְעָזָר: תַּעֲלָא בְּעִידָּנֵיהּ סְגִיד לֵיהּ.

"וַיְנַחֵם אוֹתָם, וַיְדַבֵּר עַל לִבָּם", אָמַר רַבִּי בִּנְיָמִין בַּר יֶפֶת, אָמַר רַבִּי אֶלְעָזָר:
מְלַמֵּד שֶׁאָמַר לָהֶם דְּבָרִים הַמִּתְקַבְּלִים עַל הַלֵּב – וּמָה עֲשָׂרָה נֵרוֹת, לֹא יָכְלוּ
לְכַבּוֹת נֵר אֶחָד. הֵיאַךְ נֵר אֶחָד יָכוֹל לְכַבּוֹת עֲשָׂרָה נֵרוֹת?

TRANSLATION

And his brothers also went and bowed before him (ibid. 50:18) — R. Binyamin
bar Yefes explained in the name of R. Elazar: This is what people say: When
the fox enjoys success, bow down to him. [Was Yosef] a fox? In what way was
he less deserving than his brothers?[451] Rather, if this was said [i.e., if the
parable has application], this is what is said [it can be applied to this situation].
[The verse (ibid. 47:31) states:] *And Yisrael bowed at the head of the bed.* R.
Binyamin bar Yefes explained in the name of R. Elazar: When the fox enjoys

---

449 - I.e., there is no reason to suspect that I say one thing but mean another.

450 - *Rashi* (*Bereishis* 45:27) explains that during the entire period of his separation
from Yosef, Yaakov did not have the Divine spirit rest upon him because he was
depressed — see *Shabbos* 30b. Yosef therefore sent him wine, in fulfillment of the
verse (*Tehillim* 104:15): *And wine gladdens the heart of man.*

451 - I.e., why would the Talmud use a disparaging term when comparing Yosef to his
brothers?

success, bow down to him.[452]

And he consoled them and spoke to their hearts (ibid. :21) — R. Binyamin bar Yefes explained in the name of R. Elazar: This[453] teaches us that he told them things which are acceptable. [What did he say?] If ten candles [the brothers] could not extinguish one candle [i.e., you were unsuccessful when you tried to destroy me by selling me into servitude], how can one candle [Yosef] extinguish ten candles [by attempting to seek revenge]?[454]

TALMUD

"לַיְהוּדִים הָיְתָה אוֹרָה וְשִׂמְחָה וְשָׂשׂן וִיקָר", אָמַר רַב יְהוּדָה: "אוֹרָה" – זוֹ תּוֹרָה, וְכֵן הוּא אוֹמֵר: "כִּי נֵר מִצְוָה וְתוֹרָה אוֹר". "שִׂמְחָה" – זֶה יוֹם טוֹב, וְכֵן הוּא אוֹמֵר: "וְשָׂמַחְתָּ בְּחַגֶּךָ". "וְשָׂשׂן", זוֹ מִילָה, וְכֵן הוּא אוֹמֵר: "שָׂשׂ אָנֹכִי עַל אִמְרָתֶךָ". "וִיקָר" – אֵלּוּ תְּפִלִּין, וְכֵן הוּא אוֹמֵר: "וְרָאוּ כָּל עַמֵּי הָאָרֶץ כִּי שֵׁם ה' נִקְרָא עָלֶיךָ, וְיָרְאוּ מִמֶּךָּ", וְתָנֵי, רַבִּי אֱלִיעֶזֶר הַגָּדוֹל אוֹמֵר: אֵלּוּ תְּפִלִּין שֶׁבָּרֹאשׁ.

TRANSLATION

And the Jews had light, happiness, joy and honor (Esther 8:16) — R. Yehudah expounded: *light* refers to Torah, as the verse (*Mishlei* 6:23) states: *For mitzvos are lanterns and the Torah is light. Happiness* refers to the festivals, as the verse (*Devarim* 16:13) states: *And you shall be happy on your festivals. Joy* refers to [the mitzvah of] circumcision, as the verse (*Tehillim* 119:162) states: *I am*

---

452 - The fact that Yosef's brothers bowed down to him should not be seen as an undeserved act of respect, performed only because he was enjoying a period of success, for Yosef was their equal. Yaakov, however, had no reason to show Yosef such respect and must have done so in fulfillment of the popular proverb cited.

453 - Yosef first told his brothers *do not be afraid* (ibid.). The Torah continues and says that *he consoled them and spoke to their hearts*. The latter phrase would seem to be superfluous since he had already assured them that they need not fear that he would take revenge after their father's death. R. Binyamin bar Yefes therefore explains that Yosef not only promised them that he would not seek revenge, but convinced them that there was no purpose since he stood no chance of being successful.

454 - *Maharsha* adds that Yosef used the example of a candle because the nature of a candle is to create light and not to extinguish it. He thus stressed to his brothers that they all should seek to help each other rather than to seek revenge.

joyous because of your sayings.[455] *Honor* refers to [the mitzvah] of *tefillin*, for
the verse (*Devarim* 28:10) states: *And all of the nations of the earth shall see that
the name of God is apparent upon you and they will fear you.* And we learned in
a *beraisa*: R. Eliezer ha-Gadol taught: This[456] refers to the *tefillin* worn on the
head.

COMMENTARY

Sfas Emes asks why the *Megillah* does not simply state that the Jews had
Torah, the holidays, *tefillin* and circumcision rather than alluding to them. He
answers that the characterization of Torah as being light, the festivals as being a
time of happiness, circumcision as being a source of joy and *tefillin* as being a
source of honor only became clear to the Jews in the aftermath of the Purim
miracle. Until that point in history — when the Jews reaffirmed their acceptance
of the Torah — the mitzvos were often tasks that had no real meaning to them.
It was only when they saw that the hidden Divine presence could be brought to
reveal itself through their efforts that they began to appreciate the essence of
these commandments.

TALMUD

"וְאֵת פַּרְשַׁנְדָּתָא, וְאֵת דַּלְפוֹן וְגוֹ', עֲשֶׂרֶת בְּנֵי הָמָן", אָמַר רַבִּי אַדָּא דְּמִן יָפוֹ:
"עֲשֶׂרֶת בְּנֵי הָמָן", וְ"עֲשֶׂרֶת" צָרִיךְ לְמֶימְרִינְהוּ בִּנְשִׁימָה אַחַת, מַאי טַעְמָא?
דְּכוּלְהוּ בַּהֲדֵי הֲדָדֵי נַפְקָא נִשְׁמַתְיְיהוּ.

אָמַר רַבִּי יוֹחָנָן: וָא"ו דְּ"וַיְזָתָא" - צָרִיךְ לְמִמְתְּחָה בִּזְקִיפָא, כְּמוֹרְדְיָא
דְּלַבְרוּת, מַאי טַעְמָא? דְּכוּלְהוּ בַּחֲדָא זְקִיפָא אִזְדַּקִּיפוּ.

---

455 - *Rashi* (ד״ה אמרתך) explains that the Talmud understood that the reference was to
the mitzvah of circumcision — even though any of the mitzvos could be the subject
of the verse — from the use of the word אמרתך — *your sayings.* Most of the mitzvos
are prefixed with the phrase וידבר ה' — *and God spoke* — whereas the mitzvah of
circumcision (*Bereishis* 17:9) is preceded by the phrase ויאמר אלקים — *and God said.*
Rashi adds that there is a special joy connected to the mitzvah of circumcision. Thus,
the Talmud (*Menachos* 43b) notes that when David went into the bath-house, he was
ashamed because he saw himself as being devoid of mitzvos, for he was wearing
neither *tzitzis* nor *tefillin*. However, when he remembered his circumcision, he
became happy and it was then that he said: *I am joyous because of your sayings.*
456 - I.e., God's name is apparent upon the Jews by virtue of the *tefillin* that they
wear. One can conjecture that the exegesis might be based on the similarity in sound
between ויקר — *honor* — and נקרא — *apparent.*

אָמַר רַבִּי חֲנִינָא בַּר פַּפָּא: דָּרַשׁ רַבִּי שִׁילָא אִישׁ כְּפַר תָּמַרְתָּא: כָּל הַשִּׁירוֹת כֻּלָּן נִכְתָּבוֹת - אָרִיחַ עַל גַּבֵּי לְבֵנָה, וּלְבֵנָה עַל גַּבֵּי אָרִיחַ, חוּץ מִשִּׁירָה זוֹ, וּמַלְכֵי כְּנַעַן, שֶׁהִיא - אָרִיחַ עַל גַּבֵּי אָרִיחַ, וּלְבֵנָה עַל גַּבֵּי לְבֵנָה. מַאי טַעְמָא? מִפְּנֵי שֶׁלֹּא תִהְיֶה תְּקוּמָה לְמַפַּלְתָּן שֶׁל רְשָׁעִים.

TRANSLATION

And Parshandasa and Dalfon ... the ten sons of Haman (Esther 9:7-10) — R. Ada of Yaffo taught: [The names of] the ten sons of Haman and [the word] ten must be said with a single breath. What is the reason [for this *halachah*]? Because they all died at one time.

R. Yochanan taught: The *vav* of *Vayzasa* must be elongated [when writing the *Megillah*] like the oar of a raft. What is the reason [for this *halachah*]? Because they were all hung on a single pole.[457]

R. Chanina bar Pappa taught: R. Shila of the village of Tamarta expounded: All of the songs [of praise in Scripture][458] are written as a brick atop a white space except for this song of praise [i.e., the list of the ten sons of Haman whose death is also a song of praise to God] and the kings of Canaan[459] which are written as bricks atop bricks and white spaces atop white spaces.[460] What is the reason [for this *halachah*]? So that there not be revival when the enemies of Israel [who

---

457 - *Vayzasa* is the only name that begins with the letter *vav* which is the only letter that can be stretched to look like an oar.

458 - E.g., *Shemos* 15:1-19, *Shoftim* 5:1-31 and *Shmuel* II 22:1-51. *Maharsha* explains that the *parashah* of האזינו (*Devarim* 32:1-43) is not written in the interlaced form because it also speaks of the fall of the wicked.

459 - See *Yehoshua* 12:9-24.

460 - The song sung by the sea (אז ישיר) is written as if the words were bricks and empty spaces are interlaced as one would were he building a wall. Thus, in Torah scrolls one finds the following:

אז ישיר משה ובני ישראל את השירה הזאת לה׳ ויאמרו

סוס	אשירה לה׳ כי גאה גאה	לאמר
עזי וזמרת י-ה ויהי לי	ורוכבו רמה בים	

On the other hand, when writing the names of the ten sons of Haman, the names are written one atop the other:

ואת	פרשנדתא
ואת	דלפון
ואת	אספתא

This latter format is similar to a wall where the bricks are layed atop each other without being interlaced and it thus lacks strength.

are mentioned in the verses in *Esther* and *Yehoshua*] fall.[461]

TALMUD

"וַיֹּאמֶר הַמֶּלֶךְ לְאֶסְתֵּר הַמַּלְכָּה: בְּשׁוּשַׁן הַבִּירָה הָרְגוּ הַיְּהוּדִים", אָמַר רַבִּי אַבָּהוּ: מְלַמֵּד שֶׁבָּא מַלְאָךְ וּסְטָרוֹ עַל פִּיו.

"וּבְבֹאָהּ לִפְנֵי הַמֶּלֶךְ, אָמַר עִם הַסֵּפֶר". "אָמַר"?! "אָמְרָה" מִבָּעֵי לֵיהּ! אָמַר רַבִּי יוֹחָנָן: אָמְרָה לוֹ: יֵאָמֵר בַּפֶּה מַה שֶּׁכָּתוּב בַּסֵּפֶר.

"דִּבְרֵי שָׁלוֹם וֶאֱמֶת", אָמַר רַבִּי תַּנְחוּם: וְאָמְרֵי לָהּ אָמַר רַבִּי אַסִי: מְלַמֵּד שֶׁצְּרִיכָה כַּאֲמִתָּהּ שֶׁל תּוֹרָה. "וּמַאֲמַר אֶסְתֵּר קִיַּם דִּבְרֵי הַפֻּרִים הָאֵלֶּה". "מַאֲמַר אֶסְתֵּר" אִין, "דִּבְרֵי הַצּוֹמוֹת וְזַעֲקָתָם" לֹא?! אָמַר רַבִּי יוֹחָנָן: "דִּבְרֵי הַצּוֹמוֹת וְזַעֲקָתָם וּמַאֲמַר אֶסְתֵּר, קִיַּם דִּבְרֵי הַפֻּרִים הָאֵלֶּה".

"כִּי מָרְדֳּכַי הַיְּהוּדִי מִשְׁנֶה לַמֶּלֶךְ אֲחַשְׁוֵרוֹשׁ, וְגָדוֹל לַיְּהוּדִים, וְרָצוּי לְרֹב אֶחָיו" "לְרֹב אֶחָיו", וְלֹא "לְכָל אֶחָיו"?! מְלַמֵּד שֶׁפָּרְשׁוּ מִמֶּנּוּ מִקְצָת סַנְהֶדְרִין. וְאָמַר רַב יוֹסֵף: גָּדוֹל תַּלְמוּד תּוֹרָה יוֹתֵר מֵהַצָּלַת נְפָשׁוֹת, דְּאִלּוּ מֵעִיקָּרָא, קָא חָשִׁיב לְמָרְדֳּכַי בָּתַר אַרְבָּעָה, וּלְבַסּוֹף בָּתַר חֲמִשָּׁה; מֵעִיקָּרָא כְּתִיב: "אֲשֶׁר בָּאוּ עִם זְרֻבָּבֶל - יֵשׁוּעַ, נְחֶמְיָה, שְׂרָיָה, רְעֵלָיָה, מָרְדֳּכַי בִּלְשָׁן". וּלְבַסּוֹף כְּתִיב: "הַבָּאִים עִם זְרֻבָּבֶל - יֵשׁוּעַ, נְחֶמְיָה, עֲזַרְיָה, רַעַמְיָה, נַחֲמָנִי, מָרְדֳּכַי בִּלְשָׁן".

TRANSLATION

And the king said to Esther the Queen: In the capital Shushan the Jews killed ... (*Esther* 9:12) — R. Abahu taught: This[462] teaches us that an angel came and slapped him [Achashverosh] on the mouth.

And when she approached the king, he said with the letters (ibid. :25) — [Why does the verse state] *he said*? It should say *she said* [since the speaker in the verse is Esther]! R. Yochanan explained: She told him: Express verbally that which is written in the letters.[463]

---

461 - I.e., their names are symbolically weakened when recorded so that when they fall, as they did, there is no chance that the inherent strength of the structure allow it to be even partially reconstructed.

462 - I.e., the continuation of the verse, where Achashverosh asks Esther: *What did they do in the other provinces of the king* seems to imply that Achashverosh was annoyed. Yet, in the very next verse, he is once again solicitous, asking her: *What is your request and it shall be granted you*? R. Abahu therefore explained that Achashverosh was indeed angry but changed his tone when the angel slapped him.

463 - Esther asked Achashverosh to acknowledge the contents of the *Megillah* — even those parts that were uncomplimentary. The verse should thus be understood: *And when she approached the king, he said what was in the letters [of the Megillah].*

Letters of peace and of truth (ibid. :31) — R. Tanchum taught and some say that it was R. Ami who taught: This teaches us that it [the *Megillah*] requires [drawn] lines [on the parchment on which the letters are written] like the Torah itself.[464]

And Esther's command confirmed these days of Purim (ibid. :32) — [Was it] Esther's command [that led to the miracle] and not the fasts and prayers? R. Yochanan taught: [Both] the fasts and prayers and Esther's command confirmed these days of Purim.

For Mordechai the Jew was second in greatness to King Achashverosh, and he was great among the Jews and was accepted by most of his brethren (ibid. 10:2) — Most of his brethren but not all of his brethren?! This teaches us that a minority of the *sanhedrin* disassociated themselves from him [i.e., from Mordechai's actions].[465] As R. Yosef taught: [We can deduce that] the study of Torah is greater than the saving of lives, for previously [i.e., before Mordechai battled Haman] Mordechai is mentioned after the fourth [person who accompanied Zerubavel to Jerusalem to rebuild the *Beis ha-Mikdash*] and at the end [after the Purim miracle] he is mentioned after the fifth. Previously the verse (*Ezra* 2:2) states: *[The ones] who came with Zerubavel — Yeshua, Nechemiah, Serayah, R'elyah and Mordechai Balshan.* And at the end [i.e., after the Purim miracle] the verse (*Nechemiah* 7:7) states: *[The ones] who came with Zerubavel — Yeshua, Nechemiah, Azariah, Ra'amiah, Nachmani and Mordechai Balshan.*

COMMENTARY

Riaf asks why R. Yosef didn't derive that Torah study is greater than the saving of lives from the fact that part of the *Sanhedrin* disassociated themselves from Mordechai's actions. He answers that while the *Sanhedrin* may well have disapproved of what Mordechai did, there is no means of knowing whether the heavenly tribunals agreed with them. However, the Book of *Nechemiah* — which was written with *ruach ha-kodesh* — is indicative of what the attitude of

---

464 - The exposition is based on the use of the term אמת, which the verse (*Mishlei* 23:23) uses when characterizing the Torah. Torah scrolls are only fit for use if lines are etched into the parchment to enable the scribe to write upon them. The lines are not made with ink but are embossed directly onto the parchment. These lines must also be drawn onto the parchment used for the writing of a *Megillah*. See *Rambam, Hilchos Sefer Torah* 1:7.

465 - *Rashi* (ד"ה שפירשו) explains that they took exception to his agreement to accept public office.

heaven was vis-à-vis Mordechai's actions. Thus, if he was demoted from fifth to sixth in the list of those who accompanied Zerubavel, we can conclude that heaven also disapproved of what he did. What must be clarified, however, is why there was any disapproval of Mordechai's actions since the *halachah* clearly holds that saving lives takes precedence over all the mitzvos of the Torah.

The key to understanding the issue would seem to be *Rashi's* comment that those members of the *sanhedrin* who disassociated themselves from Morechai did so because he accepted public office. Obviously, Mordechai did not accept the appointment from Achashverosh as first deputy to the king because he sought personal gain. Rather, he saw it as a means through which he could protect and further the interests of his brethren. It was this decision that the minority of the *sanhedrin* disapproved of, for this could have been accomplished by others and Mordechai could have reassumed his role as one of the rabbinic leaders of the generation. For the very same reason, Mordechai was demoted in the list of those who accompanied Zerubavel, for he could have left public office in the hands of others who did not have his ability as a scholar.

R. Yosef's statement that Torah study is greater than saving lives should also be understood in the same vein. Distinction muust be drawn between actually saving lives which takes precedence and accepting office which has the potential of saving lives in which case, according to R. Yosef, Torah study takes precedence.[466]

Having completed the *aggadah* on the verses of the *Megillah*, *Ein Yaakov* quotes a Talmudic section of mostly halachic material that appears earlier in the tractate. Perhaps because much of the material is accompanied by examples of the manner in which the Sages fulfilled these *halachos*, the author saw fit to include the material. Note that the material appears earlier in the tractate and for reasons unknown to us, *Ein Yaakov* saw fit to include it after the exegesis on the verses of the *Megillah*. We can conjecture that he might have thought that this was its proper place since the verses cited appear at the end of the *Megillah* or that he did so because its content is primarily halachic and he therefore saw fit to separate it from the *aggadic* materials.

---

466 - See also *Taz* to *Yoreh Deah* 251:6 and *Rambam, Hilchos Talmud Torah* 3:3-4.

TALMUD

"וּמַתָּנוֹת לָאֶבְיוֹנִים", תָּנֵי רַב יוֹסֵף: "וּמִשְׁלֹחַ מָנוֹת אִישׁ לְרֵעֵהוּ" – שְׁתֵּי מָנוֹת
לְאָדָם אֶחָד. "וּמַתָּנוֹת לָאֶבְיוֹנִים" – שְׁתֵּי מַתָּנוֹת לִשְׁנֵי בְּנֵי אָדָם.

TRANSLATION

[7a] *And gifts for the poor* (Esther 9:22) — R. Yosef taught: [The requirement derived from the first phrase of the verse which speaks of] *sending portions* [of food] *to each other* [is fulfilled by] sending two portions to one person. [The requirement of] *gifts for the poor* [is fulfilled by] giving two gifts to two poor people.[467]

COMMENTARY

As we have already seen, Mordechai and Esther ordained that the *Megillah* be read as a means of offering thanksgiving for the miracles that occurred — an ordinance that the Sages concurred with and made obligatory. They also ordained that Purim be celebrated as a holiday which in itself makes a festive meal a requirement.[468] Note, however, that they also required that foodstuffs be exchanged between friends and that gifts be given to the poor — enactments that bear further examination if we are to understand the connection between these requirements and the holiday of Purim.

R. S. R. Hirsch writes that the Jews were saved from Haman's plot because they were unified — when they prayed and fasted upon discovering his plans and when they joined together to do battle with their enemies. The basis of Israel's survival is unity — the acceptance of a shared national mission and of a shared destiny that transcends physical boundaries. To reinforce this sense of unity, Mordechai and Esther introduced two mitzvos — exchanging gifts and giving charity on Purim — so that Jews, no matter where or when they lived, would

---

467 - *Rashi* explains that R. Yosef based his teaching on the difference in grammatical structure between the first and second phrases of the verse. When referring to gifts to the poor, the verse uses the plural form for *poor* — אביונים. Thus, the use of the plural for *gifts* — מתנות — need not indicate that one is required to give more than one gift, since the plural form was necessary to match the subject which is plural. On the other hand, when speaking of the requirement to *send portions one to another*, the recipient is singular — איש. Thus, the use of the plural form for *portions* — מנות — must be understood as requiring one to send more than one portion.

468 - See *Sefer ha-Chinuch*, מצוה תרצ"ח.

see themselves as a part of the same nation sharing both past and future.

Rambam[469] writes: *It is preferable that one increase the amount that he gives to the poor rather than to make a more elaborate meal or send more lavish gifts to friends. There is no greater joy than to bring happiness to the poor, to orphans, to widows or converts, for one who brings happiness to these unfortunate people is compared to the Shechinah, as the verse (Yeshayahu 57:15) states: To give life to the spirit of the downtrodden, to give life to the heart of the oppressed.*

TALMUD

רַבִּי יְהוּדָה הַנָּשִׂיא שָׁלַח לֵיהּ לְרַבִּי אוֹשַׁעְיָא, אַטְמָא דְעִגְלָא תִילְתָּא, וְגַרְבָּא דְחַמְרָא. שָׁלַח לֵיהּ: קִיַּמְתְּ בָּנוּ רַבֵּנוּ "וּמִשְׁלֹחַ מָנוֹת אִישׁ לְרֵעֵהוּ, וּמַתָּנוֹת לָאֶבְיֹנִים".

TRANSLATION

R. Yehudah ha-Nasi sent R. Oshiya the thigh of a third-born calf and a jug of wine. He [R. Oshiya] sent him a message [in return]: **[7b]** "Our master has fulfilled [the requirement of] *sending portions one to another* [as well as the requirement of] *and gifts to the poor* [for R. Yehuda ha-Nasi's gift was far larger than what was required]."

COMMENTARY

In the text brought in the Talmud, the last phrase is omitted — i.e., that R. Yehudah's gift fulfilled both requirements. Rabbenu Chananel, based on the *Yerushalmi*, adds the final phrase and it would seem that it appeared in the text that *Ein Yaakov* used in his compilation.

TALMUD

רַבָּה שָׁדַר לֵיהּ לְמָרִי בַּר מַר, בִּיָדָא דְאַבַּיֵּי, מַלְיָא טַסְקָא דְקִישְׁבֵּי, וּמָלֵי כַּסָּא דְקִמְחָא דַאֲבִישׁוּנָא. אָמַר לֵיהּ אַבַּיֵּי: הַשְׁתָּא אָמַר מָרִי בַּר מַר: אִי חַקְלָאָה מַלְכָּא לִיהֱוֵי, דִּיקוּלָא מִצַּוָּארֵיהּ לָא נָחִית. הֲדַר שָׁדַר לֵיהּ אִיהוּ, מְלָא טַסְקָא דְזַנְגְּבִילָא, וּמְלָא כַּסָּא דְפִלְפְּלֵי אֲרִיכְתָּא. אָמַר אַבַּיֵּי: הַשְׁתָּא אָמַר מָרִי: אֲנָא שָׁדְרִית לֵיהּ חוּלְיָא, וְאִיהוּ שָׁדַר לִי חוּרְפָא.

TRANSLATION

Rabah sent Mari bar Mar [a gift of food to fulfill the requirement] with Abbaye

---

[and the gift that he sent was] a sackful of dates and a jug full of sweet flour. Abbaye told him [Rabah]: Now [i.e., when he receives your gift], Mari bar Mar will say, "When the farmer becomes king he does not remove the sack from around his neck." He [Mari] sent [Rabah] in return a sackful of ginger and a jug full of long [hot] peppers.[470] Abbaye said [to Mari]: Now the master [Rabah] will say, "I sent him sweets and he returned hot [spicy foods]."

COMMENTARY

It is customary, when sending gifts to a friend, that the gift be in proportion to both the station of the giver and the recepient. Rabah, who was a poor man before being selected to head the yeshiva in Pumbedisa, continued his previous practice of sending modest gifts — even when the recepient was a rich man like Mari bar Mar. *Maharsha* adds that Rabah's student, Abbaye, who was given the task of delivering the gift, respectfully chided him and told him that his gift was not elaborate enough, cleverly using a pun that compared the sack in which it was sent to the sack that a farmer wears around his neck to carry feed for his animal. Mari took advantage of Abbaye's presence and used him as a messenger to send gifts to Rabah in return. Here too we see that Abbaye commented upon the nature of the gift. Abbaye cleverly chided Mari that his gift was also inappropriate, again using a pun that compared his name Mari — bitter or sharp tasting — to the food that he sent to Rabah.

TALMUD

אָמַר אַבַּיֵי: כִּי נָפְקִי מְבֵּי מַר, הֲוַאי שָׂבַעְנָא, וְכִי מַטַּאי לְהָתָם, קָרִיבוּ לִי שִׁתִּין צָעֵי, דְּשִׁתִּין מִינֵי קְדֵרָה. וְאָכְלִי בְּהוֹן שִׁתִּין פְּלוּגֵי, וְצָעָא דְּבִישׁוּלָא בַּתְרָאָה, קָרוּ לֵיהּ: "צְלִי קְדֵרָה", בָּעֵאי לְמִכַּסְיֵיהּ לְצָעָא בַּתְרָאָה. אָמַר אַבַּיֵי: הַיְינוּ דְּאָמְרֵי אֱנָשֵׁי: כַּפְנָא עַנְיָא וְלָא יָדַע, אִי נַמֵי: רְוֹוחָא לִבְסוּמֵי שְׁכִיחָא.

אַבַּיֵי בַּר אַבִּין, וְרַב חֲנִינָא בַּר אַבִּין, מַחְלְפֵי סְעֻדָתַיְיהוּ לַהֲדָדֵי.

TRANSLATION

Abbaye said: When I left the master's home [to deliver his gift to Mari], I was sated. When I arrived there [at Mari's home], they brought me sixty plates with sixty types of food and I ate sixty portions! [At the end of the meal they brought

---

470 - See *Pesachim* 42b where the Talmud notes that these two spices have no adverse side effects and are good for one's health.

me] a plate with the last course which they called the "roasted portion" and [it was so tasty that] I wanted to eat the plate as well!

Abbaye added: This is [an example of] the popular expression, "The pauper is hungry but he is not aware of it." Alternatively, there is always room for sweet food.

Abbaye bar Avin and R. Chanina bar Avin exchanged [Purim] meals with each other.

COMMENTARY

Rashi[471] explains that one year one would prepare the Purim meal and send it to his friend and they would then eat together; the following year they would reverse the roles. *Ran*, on the other hand, maintains that they simply exchanged meals, with Abbaye eating the meal that R. Chanina prepared and R. Chanina eating the meal that Abbaye prepared. He explains that because they were both very poor, they did not have the wherewithall to send gifts and also prepare a festive meal. By exchanging meals with each other they were able to fulfill both requirements.

Riaf defends *Rashi's* explanation pointing out that if they simply exchanged meals, the Talmud would have had no reason to tell us about it. He adds that Abbaye and R. Chanina were so poor that they could only afford one meal between the two of them and did not have the means to also exchange gifts. They therefore hit upon a novel means of solving their predicament. Abbaye would prepare a meal and send it to R. Chanina to fulfill the requirement of sending gifts. R. Chanina would then send it back to Abbaye to fulfill his requirement of sending gifts and he and Abbaye would then eat the meal together. In the following year, they would reverse the roles.

TALMUD

אָמַר רָבָא: מִיחַיֵּיב אֱנָשׁ לִבְסוּמֵי בְּפוּרְיָא, עַד דְּלָא יָדַע בֵּין "בָּרוּךְ מָרְדֳּכַי", לְ"אָרוּר הָמָן". רַבָּה וְרַבִּי זֵירָא עָבְדוּ סְעֻדַת פּוּרִים בַּהֲדֵי הֲדָדֵי. בָּתַר דְּאִיבְסוּם, קָם רַבָּה וְשָׁחְטֵיהּ לְרַבִּי זֵירָא. לְמָחָר בָּעָא רַחֲמֵי עֲלֵיהּ וְאַחְיֵיהּ. לְשָׁנָה אָמַר לֵיהּ: לֵיתֵי מָר וְנַעֲבִיד סְעֻדַת פּוּרִים בַּהֲדֵי הֲדָדֵי. אָמַר לֵיהּ: לָאו כָּל שַׁעֲתָא וְשַׁעֲתָא מִיתְרַחֲישׁ נִיסָא.

TRANSLATION

Rava taught: One is required to drink on Purim until [he reaches the point where] he can not differentiate between "blessed is Mordechai" and "cursed is Haman". Rabah and R. Zeira made the Purim meal together. After he became intoxicated, Rabah arose and killed R. Zeira. The next day he asked for Divine mery for him [R. Zeira] and he revived him. The next year, he [Rabah] said to him [R. Zeira]: Come and let us make the Purim meal together. He responded: Miracles do not occur at every hour.

COMMENTARY

Avudraham asks how it is possible that the Sages would have ordained that one is required to drink until one becomes intoxicated given that the Torah and *Nevi'im* warn against becoming drunk. He answers that an exception was made in the case of Purim since almost all of the events that brought on the miraculous deliverance were associated with drinking — e.g., the downfall of both Vashti and Haman.

Chafetz Chaim[472] notes that although one is required to drink on Purim, one should not do so if he will not be able to pray, recite the Grace after Meals or if it will cause him to act irresponsibly.

TALMUD

רַב אַשִׁי הֲוָה יָתֵיב קַמֵּיהּ דְּרַב כַּהֲנָא, נָגַהּ, וְלָא אָתוּ רַבָּנָן, אֲמַר לֵיהּ: מַאי טַעְמָא לָא אָתוּ רַבָּנָן? דִּלְמָא טְרִידֵי בִּסְעָדַת פּוּרִים? אֲמַר לֵיהּ: וְלָא הֲוָה אֶפְשָׁר לְמִיכְלַהּ בְּאוּרְתָּא?! אֲמַר לֵיהּ: לָא שְׁמִיעַ לֵיהּ לְמָר הָא דְּאָמַר רָבָא: סְעֻדַּת פּוּרִים שֶׁאֲכָלָהּ בַּלַּיְלָה לֹא יָצָא יְדֵי חוֹבָתוֹ. אֲמַר לֵיהּ: אָמַר רָבָא הָכִי? אֲמַר לֵיהּ: אִין. תָּנָא מִנֵּיהּ אַרְבְּעִין זִמְנִין, וְדָמֵי לֵיהּ כְּמַאן דְּמַנַּח בְּכִיסֵיהּ.

TRANSLATION

R. Ashi was sitting before R. Kahana [his teacher]. It was getting dark and the students had not arrived. He [R. Kahana] asked him: Why have the students not arrived? [R. Ashi answered:] Perhaps they are busy with the Purim meal? [R. Kahana then said:] Couldn't they have eaten it at night [i.e., at the beginning of the holiday rather than during the day]? He [R. Ashi] responded: Has the master not

472 - ביאור הלכה, תרצ"ה. *Ba'al ha-Maor*, in his glosses to *Rif*, maintains that the Talmud cites the incident of Rabbah and R. Zeira to indicate that Rava's ruling that one must become intoxicated is not the accepted *halachah*.

heard that which Rava taught [that one] does not fulfill his requirement with a Purim meal that was eaten at night? He [R. Kahana] said: Did Rava say this? He [R. Ashi] answered: Yes! I learned this [halachah] from him and [repeated it to myself] forty times until it is as if it [this halachah] is in my pocket.

TALMUD

אָמַר רַב, וְאִיתֵימָא רַב שְׁמוּאֵל בַּר מַרְתָּא: גָּדוֹל תַּלְמוּד תּוֹרָה יוֹתֵר מִבִּנְיַן בֵּית הַמִּקְדָּשׁ, שֶׁכָּל זְמָן שֶׁהָיָה בָּרוּךְ בֶּן נֵרִיָּה קַיָּם, לֹא הִנִּיחוֹ עֶזְרָא וְעָלָה.

TRANSLATION

[16b] Rav taught, and some say [that this was taught by] R. Shmuel bar Marta: The study of Torah is greater than the building of the Beis ha-Mikdash, for as long as Baruch ben Neriah was alive, Ezra [who was his disciple] did not leave him and ascend [to the Land of Israel].

COMMENTARY

Interestingly, Rambam quotes the halachah that Torah study is not interrupted for the construction of the Beis ha-Mikdash in two places.[473] We can conjecture that while its proper place would seem to be in the laws of Torah study, Rambam saw fit to repeat it in the laws of building the Beis ha-Mikdash so as to emphasize that if the Beis ha-Mikdash was built at the expense of Torah study, the very structure would be lacking its necessary foundation, for Torah study is the unparalleled essence of Judaism. In a responsa he adds that this halachah also teaches us that one should not engage in community activities at the expense of Torah study unless there is absolutely no alternative.

TALMUD

אָמַר רַבָּה אָמַר רַבִּי יִצְחָק בַּר שְׁמוּאֵל בַּר מַרְתָּא גָּדוֹל תַּלְמוּד תּוֹרָה יוֹתֵר מִכְּבוֹד אָב וָאֵם. שֶׁכָּל אוֹתָן שָׁנִים שֶׁהָיָה יַעֲקֹב אָבִינוּ בְּבֵית עֵבֶר, לֹא נֶעֱנַשׁ. דְּאָמַר מַר: לָמָּה נִמְנוּ שְׁנוֹתָיו שֶׁל יִשְׁמָעֵאל? כְּדֵי לְיַחֵס בָּהֶן שְׁנוֹתָיו שֶׁל יַעֲקֹב. דִּכְתִיב: "וְאֵלֶּה שְׁנֵי חַיֵּי יִשְׁמָעֵאל, מְאַת שָׁנָה, וּשְׁלֹשִׁים שָׁנָה, וְשֶׁבַע שָׁנִים". כַּמָּה קָשִׁישׁ יִשְׁמָעֵאל מִיִּצְחָק? אַרְבַּע עֶשְׂרֵה שָׁנִים, דִּכְתִיב: "וְאַבְרָם בֶּן שְׁמֹנִים שָׁנָה וְשֵׁשׁ שָׁנִים, בְּלֶדֶת הָגָר אֶת יִשְׁמָעֵאל לְאַבְרָם". וּכְתִיב: "וְאַבְרָהָם בֶּן מְאַת שָׁנָה בְּהִוָּלֶד לוֹ אֵת יִצְחָק בְּנוֹ". וּכְתִיב: "וְיִצְחָק בֶּן שִׁשִּׁים שָׁנָה בְּלֶדֶת אֹתָם". בַּר כַּמָּה הֲוָה יִשְׁמָעֵאל כְּשֶׁנּוֹלַד יַעֲקֹב? בַּר שִׁבְעִים וְאַרְבַּע. כַּמָּה פַּיִישָׁן מִשְׁנֵיהּ? שִׁשִּׁים וְשָׁלֹשׁ.

---

473 - See Hilchos Talmud Torah 2:2 and Hilchos Beis ha-Bechirah 1:2.

TRANSLATION

Raba taught in the name of R. Yitzchok bar Shmuel bar Marta: The study of Torah is greater than honoring one's parents, for all of the years that our father Yaakov was in the house [of study] of Ever, he was not punished. As Mar taught: **[17a]** Why are the years [i.e., the age] of Yishmael recorded?[474] So that we can calculate the chronology of Yaakov. The verse (*Bereishis* 25:17) states: *And these are the years of Yishmael's life — one hundred years and thirty years and seven years.* How much older was Yishmael than Yitzchak? Fourteen years, for the verse (ibid. 16:16) states: *And Avram was eighty six years old when Hagar gave birth to Yishmael* and [later (ibid. 21:5) the Torah] states: *and Avraham was one hundred years old when Yitzchok was born to him.* [The Torah (ibid. 28:26) then] states: *and Yitzchak was sixty years old when she gave birth to them [to Yaakov and Esav].* How old was Yishmael when Yaakov was born? Seventy-four. How many years were left to his life? Sixty-three.

TALMUD

וְתַנְיָא: בֶּן שִׁשִּׁים וְשָׁלֹשׁ שָׁנִים הָיָה יַעֲקֹב אָבִינוּ בְּשָׁעָה שֶׁנִּתְבָּרֵךְ מֵאָבִיו. וּבְאוֹתוֹ פֶּרֶק מֵת יִשְׁמָעֵאל, דִּכְתִיב: "וַיַּרְא עֵשָׂו כִּי בֵרַךְ יִצְחָק אֶת יַעֲקֹב וְגוֹ', וַיִּשְׁמַע יַעֲקֹב אֶל אָבִיו וְגוֹ', וַיַּרְא עֵשָׂו כִּי רָעוֹת בְּנוֹת כְּנָעַן וְגוֹ', וַיֵּלֶךְ עֵשָׂו אֶל יִשְׁמָעֵאל, וַיִּקַּח אֶת מַחֲלַת בַּת יִשְׁמָעֵאל אֲחוֹת נְבָיוֹת" מִמַּשְׁמָע שֶׁנֶּאֱמַר: "מַחֲלַת בַּת יִשְׁמָעֵאל", אֵינִי יוֹדֵעַ שֶׁהִיא "אֲחוֹת נְבָיוֹת"?! מְלַמֵּד שֶׁקִּדְּשָׁהּ יִשְׁמָעֵאל אָבִיהָ וָמֵת, וְהִשִּׂיאָהּ נְבָיוֹת אָחִיהָ.

וְאַרְבַּע עֶשְׂרֵה דַהֲוָה בְּבֵית לָבָן עַד דְּאִתְיְלִיד יוֹסֵף, הָא שִׁבְעִים וְשֶׁבַע. וּכְתִיב: "וְיוֹסֵף בֶּן שְׁלֹשִׁים שָׁנָה בְּעָמְדוֹ לִפְנֵי פַּרְעֹה מֶלֶךְ מִצְרָיִם". הָא מֵאָה וְשֶׁבַע. וְשֶׁבַע דְּשַׂבְעָא, וּתְרָתֵי דְכַפְנָא, הָא מֵאָה וְשִׁתְּסְרֵי. וּכְתִיב: "וַיֹּאמֶר פַּרְעֹה אֶל יַעֲקֹב: כַּמָּה יְמֵי שְׁנֵי חַיֶּיךָ? וַיֹּאמֶר יַעֲקֹב אֶל פַּרְעֹה: יְמֵי שְׁנֵי מְגוּרַי שְׁלֹשִׁים וּמְאַת שָׁנָה". וְהָא מֵאָה וְשִׁתְּסְרֵי הַוְיָן? אֶלָּא שְׁמַע מִינָהּ אַרְבַּע עֶשְׂרֵה שְׁנִין דַהֲוָה בְּבֵית עֵבֶר לָא חָשִׁיב לְהוּ. דְּתַנְיָא: יַעֲקֹב אָבִינוּ הָיָה מַטְמָן בְּבֵית עֵבֶר וּמְשַׁמֵּשׁ, אַרְבַּע עֶשְׂרֵה שָׁנָה. וּלְאַחַר יְרִידָתוֹ שֶׁל יַעֲקֹב לַאֲרַם נַהֲרַיִם שְׁתֵּי שָׁנִים, מֵת עֵבֶר. יָצָא מִשָּׁם, וּבָא לוֹ לַאֲרַם נַהֲרַיִם. נִמְצָא כְּשֶׁעָמַד עַל הַבְּאֵר - בֶּן שִׁבְעִים וְשֶׁבַע שָׁנִים.

---

474 - We do not find that the Torah informs us of the age of the founders of other nations — e.g., of Lot or Esav. Hence, if an exception was made in the case of Yishmael, there must be some significance to his age which has other implications.

TRANSLATION

We learned in a *beraisa*: Yaakov, our father, was sixty-three years old when he received the blessing from his father Yitzchak, and at that same time Yishmael died. [This can be deduced from Scripture, for] the verse (ibid. 28:6-8) states: *and Esav saw that Yitzchak had blessed Yaakov ... and Yaakov listened to his father ... and Esav saw that the daughters of Canaan were evil ... and Esav went to Yishmael and took Machlas bas Yishmael, the sister of Nevayos [as a wife].* It can be inferred from that which it says *Machlas bas Yishmael* [who her brother was]. Do I not know that [she was] *the sister of Nevayos*? [Rather, the Torah adds this seemingly superflous information] to teach us that Yishmael, her father, betrothed her [to Esav] and died, and Nevayos, her brother, gave her in marriage [to Esav].

[To this calculation of Yaakov's age, add] the fourteen years that he spent in Lavan's home until Yosef was born — [Yaakov's age at this juncture] was seventy-seven. The verse (ibid. 41:46) states: *And Yosef was thirty years old when he stood before Pharaoh, king of Egypt* — [Yaakov's age at this juncture] was one hundred and seven. [Add] the seven years of plenty and two years of famine [that passed before Yosef revealed himself and was reunited with Yaakov] — [Yaakov's age at this juncture] was one hundred and sixteen. Yet, the verse (ibid. :47) states: *Pharaoh asked Yaakov, how many years have you lived? Yaakov answered Pharaoh, the years of my sojourning are one hundred and thirty.* But [according to our calculations] he was one hundred and sixteen! From this we can deduce that the fourteen years that he [Yaakov] spent in the [study] house of Ever were not counted.[475]

TALMUD

וּמְנָא לָן דְּלָא אִיעֲנַשׁ יַעֲקֹב אָבִינוּ? דְּתַנְיָא: נִמְצָא יוֹסֵף שֶׁפֵּרֵשׁ מֵאָבִיו, שֶׁלֹּא רָאָהוּ עֶשְׂרִים וּשְׁתַּיִם שָׁנָה, כְּשֵׁם שֶׁפֵּרֵשׁ יַעֲקֹב מֵאָבִיו עֶשְׂרִים וּשְׁתַּיִם שָׁנָה, דְּיַעֲקֹב תְּלָתִין וְשִׁתָּא הַוְיָין! אֶלָּא אַרְבַּע עֶשְׂרֵה דְּבֵית עֵבֶר לָא חָשִׁיב לְהוּ.

TRANSLATION

And how do we know that Yaakov was not punished [for the fourteen years that

---

475 - I.e., the discrepancy between the number that Yaakov told Pharaoh and that calculable based on Yishmael's chronology indicates that these years were not counted as part of Yaakov's life.

he spent at the yeshiva of Ever]?[476] We learned in a *beraisa*: We find that Yosef was separated from his father for twenty-two years, corresponding to the twenty-two years that Yaakov was separated from his father. But Yaakov [was separated from Yitzchak] for thirty-six years! [Why was his separation from Yosef — his punishment for having separated himself from Yitzchak — only twenty-two years?] Because the fourteen years [spent in the study] house of Ever were not counted.

TALMUD

סוֹף סוֹף, דְּבֵית לָבָן עֶשְׂרִים הֲוָיָין! אֶלָּא מִשּׁוּם דְּאִישְׁתַּהְי שְׁתֵּי שָׁנִים בְּאוֹרְחָא. דְּתַנְיָא: יָצָא מֵאֲרַם נַהֲרַיִם, וּבָא לוֹ לְסֻכּוֹת. וְעָשָׂה שָׁם שְׁמוֹנָה עָשָׂר חֹדֶשׁ, שֶׁנֶּאֱמַר: "וְיַעֲקֹב נָסַע סֻכֹּתָה, וַיִּבֶן לוֹ בָּיִת, וּלְמִקְנֵהוּ עָשָׂה סֻכֹּת". וּבְבֵית אֵל עָשָׂה שִׁשָּׁה חֳדָשִׁים, וְהִקְרִיב זְבָחִים לֵאלֹהֵי אָבִיו יִצְחָק.

TRANSLATION

But in the end, [the time that Yaakov spent in] Lavan's home was twenty years! [Why was he punished for separating himself from his father for twenty-two years?] Because he delayed [his return from Lavan's home for] two years [instead of returning immediately to Yitzchak]. Thus, we learned in a *beraisa*: He [Yaakov] left Aram Naharayim and came to Sukkos where he spent eighteen months, as the verse (ibid. 33) states: *And Yaakov travelled to Sukkos and built a home for himself. And for his cattle he built booths.*[477] [In addition,] he spent six months in Beis El and offered sacrifices to the God of his father, Yitzchak.[478]

---

476 - The Talmud now seeks to prove that Torah study is greater than the mitzvah of honoring one's parents. This halachah is derived from the fact that Yaakov was not punished for the period that he spent with Ever, even though he did not fulfill the mitzvah of honoring his parents during that entire period.

477 - *Rashi* (ד״ה ויבן לו בית) explains that the Talmud inferred that Yaakov spent a total of eighteen months in Sukkos from the verse which uses the plural form *sukkos* — *booths* — rather than the singular. Had Yaakov not spent two summers in Sukkos, he would have constructed a booth rather than booths to protect his cattle from the sun. Moreover, the verse informs us that he built himself a home which implies that he spent the winter there as well.

478 - Thus, Yaakov spent a total of twenty-two years separated from his father — twenty years with Lavan, eighteen months at Sukkos and six months at Beis El. In punishment for this, he was separated from Yosef for an equivalent period of time.

TALMUD

מִשְׁנָה. הַקּוֹרֵא אֶת הַמְּגִלָּה לְמַפְרֵעַ לֹא יָצָא כוּ'.

TRANSLATION

[17a] **MISHNAH:** One who reads the *Megillah* in reverse order has not fulfilled his obligation.

COMMENTARY

The Talmud derives the obligation of reading the text of the *Megillah* in the correct sequence from the verse (9:28) that states: *And these days shall be commemorated and celebrated* — just as the celebration cannot be made in reverse order, so too the commemoration cannot be in reverse order. *Meiri* writes that if one read a later verse or chapter before an earlier verse or chapter, he would not fulfill the requirement, for the reading would not follow the chronology in which the miracles occurred; hence, he would not publicize the miracles which is the primary purpose of the *Megillah* reading.

TALMUD

גְּמָרָא. תָּנָא: וְכֵן בְּהַלֵּל, וְכֵן בִּקְרִיאַת שְׁמַע, וּבִתְפִלָּה. הַלֵּל מְנָא לָן? רַבָּה אָמַר: דִּכְתִיב: "מִמִּזְרַח שֶׁמֶשׁ עַד מְבוֹאוֹ". רַב יוֹסֵף אָמַר: "זֶה הַיּוֹם עָשָׂה ה'". רַב אַוְיָא אָמַר: "יְהִי שֵׁם ה' מְבֹרָךְ". רַב נַחְמָן בַּר יִצְחָק, וְאִיתֵּימָא רַבִּי אַחָא בַּר יַעֲקֹב אָמַר, מֵהָכָא: "מֵעַתָּה וְעַד עוֹלָם".

TRANSLATION

TALMUD: We learned [in a *beraisa*]: The same is true of *Hallel*, and [as concerns] the [recital of] *Shema* and [as concerns] prayer [the *amidah*]. From where do we [derive that this is true of] *Hallel*? Rabah explained: The verse (*Tehillim* 113:3) states: *From the east of the sun until where it sets [the name of God is praised].*[479] R. Yosef taught: [The verse (ibid. 118:25) states:] *This is the day that God made.*[480] R. Avia taught: [The verse (ibid. 113:2) states:] *Thus shall*

---

479 - The verse cited by Rabah is part of *Hallel* and relates that the praise of God is recited from east to west. Rabah maintained that just as the order of the sun's rising and setting follows a set pattern that is never deviated from, so too, the order of the verses should not be deviated from when *Hallel* is recited.

480 - R. Yosef also quotes a verse from *Hallel* that implies that just as the hours of the day follow a set pattern, so too the verses of *Hallel* must be read according to their fixed pattern.

the name of God be blessed.[481] R. Nachman bar Yitzchak, and some say R. Acha bar Yaakov taught: [The verse (ibid.) states:] *from now and until eternity.*[482]

COMMENTARY

Interestingly, *Rambam* quotes the *halachah* that *Hallel* must be recited in the proper order in the laws of Chanukah, whereas in *Shulchan Aruch,* this *halachah* is cited in the laws of *Rosh Chodesh.* This would seem to suggest that *Rambam* differentiates between the recital of *Hallel* on Chanukah and its recital at other times, the former being a requirement linked to the concept of publicizing the miracle — similar to the reading of the *Megillah* — and the latter recital being a custom to express thanksgiving to God at specific times of the year.[483]

As we previously noted,[484] *Hallel* is a preset means of expressing praise of and thanksgiving to God. Were one to reverse the order of the verses or the chapters, the recital would lose much of its intended meaning as well as its efficacy, for it would no longer follow the chronology in which David wrote the verses and chapters — an order that best expresses the praise and thanks due God.[485]

TALMUD

קְרִיאַת שְׁמַע, דְּתַנְיָא: קְרִיאַת שְׁמַע כִּכְתָבָהּ, דִּבְרֵי רַבִּי. וַחֲכָמִים אוֹמְרִים: בְּכָל לָשׁוֹן. מַאי טַעְמָא דְּרַבִּי? אָמַר קְרָא: "וְהָיוּ", בַּהֲוָיָתָן יְהוּ. וְרַבָּנָן, מַאי טַעְמָא? אָמַר קְרָא: "שְׁמַע" – בְּכָל לָשׁוֹן שֶׁאַתָּה שׁוֹמֵעַ. וְרַבִּי, נַמִי הָא כְּתִיב: "שְׁמַע"? הַהוּא מִיבָּעֵי לֵיהּ: הַשְׁמַע לְאָזְנֶיךָ מַה שֶּׁאַתָּה מוֹצִיא מִפִּיךָ. וְרַבָּנָן סָבְרֵי כְּמַאן דְּאָמַר: הַקּוֹרֵא אֶת שְׁמַע, וְלֹא הִשְׁמִיעַ לְאָזְנוֹ, יָצָא. וְרַבָּנָן נַמִי, הָכְתִיב: "וְהָיוּ"? הַהוּא מִבָּעֵי לֵיהּ: שֶׁלֹּא יִקְרָא לְמַפְרֵעַ. וְרַבִּי. שֶׁלֹּא יִקְרָא לְמַפְרֵעַ', מְנָא לֵיהּ? מִ"דְּבָרִים", "הַדְּבָרִים". וְרַבָּנָן – "דְּבָרִים", "הַדְּבָרִים" לָא מַשְׁמַע לְהוּ.

---

481 - I.e., in this manner — the order in which they are written.

482 - Just as the present precedes the future, so too must the first verses of *Hallel* be read before the verses that follow.

483 - See *Berachos* 14a and *Pesachim* 117a.

484 - See page 149.

485 - *Beis Yosef,* in his commentary to *Tur Orach Chaim* 462, differentiates between reading the chapters of *Hallel* out of order — in which case one would not fulfill the obligation — and reading the chapters of *Shema* out of order. In the latter case, one would still fulfill the obligation since the order of their recital does not follow the order in which they are written in the Torah.

TRANSLATION

[How do we know that the] recital of *Shema* [must be in accordance with the order of the verses]? We learned in a *beraisa*:[486] The recital of *Shema* is according to the way it is written [i.e., in Hebrew] — this is the opinion of Rebbi. The Sages say: [It may be recited] in any language. What is Rebbi's reason [for insisting that the *Shema* can only be read in Hebrew]? The verse (*Devarim* 6:6) states: [17b] *And they shall be* — as they are, thus shall they be.[487] And what is the reason of the Sages [who permitted the *Shema* to be read in any language]? The verse (ibid. :4) states: *Hear* — in any language that you hear. According to Rebbi, the verse also states *Hear* [which would imply that one can fulfill the obligation in any language that can be heard]? [Rebbi answered] this [the word *Hear*] is required [to teach us] that one must let the ears hear what the mouth says.[488] The Sages share the opinion of the one who says that one who recited the *Shema* but did not allow his ears to hear has [nevertheless] fulfilled his obligation.[489] According to the Sages, the verse says *and they shall be* [which, as Rebbi expounded, would seem to imply that the words must be read as they were written]? [The Sages answered] that this [phrase] is required to teach us that one may not read it in reverse order. How did Rebbi derive that it may not be read in reverse order? [He derived this *halachah*] from the word הדברים [which is used in place of] דברים [i.e., the definite article ה — *the* — is superfluous and was added to teach us the *halachah* that *Shema* must be recited in the correct order]. As to the Sages, [the difference between] דברים and הדברים [i.e., the added ה] is not significant [i.e.,

---

486 - Although the *beraisa* deals with another subject entirely — reading *Shema* in another language — the Talmud deduces from the means through which both Rebbi and the Sages support their opinions that both held that the verses of *Shema* must be read in the correct order. The discussion does not concern itself with reading the paragraphs of *Shema* out of order — see previous note.

487 - I.e., in the manner that they are written, thus shall they be read.

488 - I.e., the word *Hear* teaches us another *halachah* — that one must enunciate the words in order to fulfill the obligation. Since the word is used to teach us one *halachah*, it can not be used to teach a different *halachah*, as the Sages sought to do.

489 - I.e., the Sages held that there is no requirement to enunciate the words of the *Shema*. Thus, the word *Hear* remains available for halachic exposition and they were able to derive that the *Shema* may be read in any language that one hears.

the definite article is not superfluous and is therefore not open for exposition].[490]

TALMUD

לֵימָא קָסָבַר רַבִּי: כָּל הַתּוֹרָה כֻּלָּהּ, בְּכָל לָשׁוֹן נֶאֶמְרָה, דְּאִי סַלְקָא דַעְתָּךְ –
בִּלְשׁוֹן הַקֹּדֶשׁ נֶאֶמְרָה, לָמָּה לִי לְמִכְתַּב: "וְהָיוּ"? אִיצְטְרִיךְ, סַלְקָא דַעְתָּךְ –
"שְׁמַע" כְּרַבָּנָן, כָּתַב רַחֲמָנָא: "וְהָיוּ".

לֵימָא קָסַבְרֵי רַבָּנָן: כָּל הַתּוֹרָה בִּלְשׁוֹן הַקֹּדֶשׁ נֶאֶמְרָה? דְּאִי סַלְקָא דַעְתָּ בְּכָל
לָשׁוֹן נֶאֶמְרָה, לָמָּה לִי לְמִכְתַּב "שְׁמַע"? אִיצְטְרִיךְ, סַלְקָא דַעְתָּךְ אֲמִינָא:
"וְהָיוּ" כְּרַבִּי, כָּתַב רַחֲמָנָא: "שְׁמַע".

TRANSLATION

Can we assume that Rebbi is of the opinion that all of the Torah [except for the *Shema*] may be read in any language? If you held that it was said [i.e., can only be read] in Hebrew, why did [the Torah] have to [specifically] write *and they shall be* [which teaches us that the *Shema* must be recited in Hebrew, since this law is true of all parts of the Torah and not only the *Shema*]. It is necessary [i.e., though Rebbi might well hold that the Torah can only be read in Hebrew, it was still necessary to specifically restate this *halachah* as regards *Shema*], for I might think that [the word] *Shema* [should be explained] as the Sages [did — i.e., in any language that one hears]. The Torah [therefore] writes: *and they shall be* [teaching us that the *Shema* can only be recited in Hebrew].

Can we assume that the Sages are of the opinion that the Torah may only be read in Hebrew? If you held that it can be read in any language, why did [the Torah] have to [specifically] write *hear* [which teaches us that the *Shema* may be read in any language, for if the entire Torah may be read in any language, why would one think that the *Shema* is different]? It is necessary [i.e., though the Sages might have held that the Torah may be read in any language, they still held that this law had to be specifically restated as regards the *Shema*], for I might think that [the words] *and they shall be* [should be explained] as Rebbi [did — i.e., in Hebrew only]. The Torah [therefore] writes: *Hear* [which teaches us that the *Shema* may be recited in any language that one hears].

---

490 - According to the Sages, no halachic exposition can be drawn from the use of the definite article ה, for it is used for stylistic purposes and is not open for exposition. Hence, the *halachah* that the *Shema* may not be read in reverse order had to be derived from another source.

COMMENTARY

The Talmud's discussion as to whether Rebbi and the Sages disagreement regarding the language in which the Torah is to be read applies to other Torah readings is not resolved — i.e., *Shema* might well be an exception. The dialogue is only cited to indicate why it was necessary to single out the law of *Shema*, both Rebbi and the Sages pointing out that there were grounds to think that they might have held differently in other cases.

Rashi comments that the question concerns reading the Torah in general while *Tosafos* maintains that the question only concerns those portions whose readings are a Torah requirement — e.g., *parashas Zachor* or the confession recited when bringing *ma'aser sheni*.[491]

TALMUD

תְּפִלָּה, מְנָלָן? דְּתַנְיָא: שִׁמְעוֹן הַפָּקוּלִי הִסְדִּיר שְׁמוֹנֶה־עֶשְׂרֵה בְּרָכוֹת לִפְנֵי רַבָּן גַּמְלִיאֵל עַל הַסֵּדֶר בְּיַבְנֶה. אָמַר רַבִּי יוֹחָנָן, וְאָמְרֵי לָהּ בְּמָתְנִיתָא תָּנָא: מֵאָה וְעֶשְׂרִים זְקֵנִים, וּמֵהֶם כַּמָּה נְבִיאִים, תִּקְּנוּ שְׁמוֹנֶה־עֶשְׂרֵה בְּרָכוֹת עַל הַסֵּדֶר.

TRANSLATION

How do we know [that the *halachah* of reading in the set order applies to] prayer [i.e., *Shemoneh Esrei*]? We learned in a *beraisa*: Shimon ha-Pakuli set the order of the eighteen blessings [of *Shemoneh Esrai*] in the presence of Rabban Gamliel at Yavne. R. Yochanan taught, and some say that we learned it in a *Mishnah*: One hundred and twenty elders,[492] among them some Prophets, ordained the order of the eighteen blessings [of *Shemoneh Esrai*].

COMMENTARY

Rambam[493] writes that it is an obligatory precept to pray daily, as the verse

---

491 - See *Tosafos*, s.v. כל התורה and *Berachos* 13a, *Rashi*, s.v. לימא קסבר and *Tosafos* s.v. בלשון הקדש. See also *Tosafos*, *Sotah* 33a, s.v. כל התורה כולה. *Rosh*, in his commentary to *Berachos*, adds *parashas Parah*.

492 - I.e., אנשי כנסת הגדולה — the Members of the Great Assembly, who met at the end of the Prophetic era and served as the supreme legislative body of Judaism for some one hundred and twenty years. As the Talmud shall point out, Shimon ha-Pakuli only re-established the order because it had been forgotten. This might explain why the parallel text in the Talmud (*Berachos* 28b) does not cite R. Yochanan's opinion that the order was established by the Members of the Great Assembly.

493 - הלכות תפילה א:א-ד.

(*Shemos* 23:25) states: *and you shall serve God, your Lord.* The Sages[494] derived that this service is fulfilled through prayer. The Torah, however, does not delineate the number, form or time for this required prayer.

Rambam then writes that when the Jews were exiled in the time of Nevuchadnezer, they became assimilated with the Persians and Greeks and were no longer able to express themselves in one language, as the verse (*Nechemiah* 13:24) states: *and their sons — half spoke Ashdodis and they could not speak the Jewish [language].* When Ezra and his court saw this, they established the order of the *Shemoneh Esrai.* The first three *berachos* were set as praise to God, the last three as thanks and the middle *berachos* were set as requests for one's needs, each serving as a heading for the needs of individuals and for the community as a whole.

In the period of Rabban Shimon ben Gamliel, the number of heretics increased and they were the greatest source of trouble for Israel. He therefore instituted a nineteenth *berachah* asking that the heretics be destroyed.

R. Chaim Volozhin[495] writes that the texts of these *berachos* were written with Divine inspiration. The words themselves were placed into the minds of the authors and they contain all of the necessary ingredients and formulas that makes Israel's prayer efficacious in all generations.

The decision to include eighteen *berachos* within the *amidah* was not arbitrary. The Talmud[496] notes that the number parallels the eighteen times that David mentioned the name of God in the twenty-ninth chapter of *Tehillim* which speaks of praising God. Based on this very same chapter, the members of the Great Assembly also established the order of the first three *berachos* as well as the *berachah* that ends the *amidah.*

TALMUD

תָּנוּ רַבָּנָן: מִנַּיִן שֶׁאוֹמְרִים "אָבוֹת"? שֶׁנֶּאֱמַר: "הָבוּ לַה' בְּנֵי אֵלִים". וּמִנַּיִן שֶׁאוֹמְרִים "גְּבוּרוֹת"? שֶׁנֶּאֱמַר: "הָבוּ לַה' כָּבוֹד וָעֹז". וּמִנַּיִן שֶׁאוֹמְרִים "קְדֻשּׁוֹת"? שֶׁנֶּאֱמַר: "הָבוּ לַה' כְּבוֹד שְׁמוֹ, הִשְׁתַּחֲווּ לַה' בְּהַדְרַת קֹדֶשׁ".

---

494 - ספרי, פרשת עקב. See also *Bris Moshe* to *Semag* (מצות עשה יט) regarding *Rambam's* source.

495 - נפש החיים, שער ב' פרק י"ג.

496 - *Berachos* 28b. See also *Yerushalmi, Berachos* 2:4.

TRANSLATION

The Sages taught: How do we know that we recite [a *berachah* that mentions] the Patriarchs[497] [in *Shemoneh Esrai*]? The verse (*Tehillim* 29:1) states: *Bring to God the sons of the strong.*[498] How do we know [that we are to mention] God's power?[499] The verse (ibid.) states: *Bring to God honor and strength.* How do we know [that we are to mention] His holiness? The verse (ibid.) states: *Bring to God the honor of His name, bow down to God with reverence [for His] holiness.*[500]

TALMUD

וּמָה רָאוּ לוֹמַר "בִּינָה" אַחַר "קְדֻשָּׁה"? שֶׁנֶּאֱמַר: "וְהִקְדִּישׁוּ אֶת קְדוֹשׁ יַעֲקֹב, וְאֶת אֱלֹהֵי יִשְׂרָאֵל יַעֲרִיצוּ", וְסָמִיךְ לֵיהּ: "וְיָדְעוּ תֹעֵי רוּחַ בִּינָה".

וּמָה רָאוּ לוֹמַר "תְּשׁוּבָה" אַחַר "בִּינָה"? דִּכְתִיב: "וּלְבָבוֹ יָבִין, וָשָׁב וְרָפָא לוֹ".

TRANSLATION

Why did they see fit to say [the *berachah* of] understanding after [the *berachah* of] holiness?[501] [The decision was based on] the verse (*Yeshayahu* 29:23) [that] states: *And they sanctified the holiness of Yaakov and esteemed the Lord of Israel* which is followed by [the phrase] *and those whose spirits are mistaken will know wisdom.*[502]

Why did they see fit to say [the *berachah* of] repentance[503] after [the *berachah* of] understanding? [The decision was based on] the verse (ibid. 6:10) [that] states: *and his heart will understand and he will [then] repent and be healed.*

---

497 - I.e., אלקי אברהם, אלקי יצחק ואלקי יעקב — the first *berachah* of the *amidah.*

498 - The Hebrew states בני אלים which the Talmud understands as a reference to the strong — see *Bereishis* 31:29 — יש לאל ידי which *Rashi* (ad loc.) interprets as meaning *I have the strength.*

499 - I.e., אתה גבור — the second *berachah* of the *amidah.*

500 - The first three *berachos*, which speak of the Patriarchs — מגן אברהם, God's power — מחיה המתים — and His holiness — הא-ל הקדוש, were inserted into the *amidah* because the verse in *Tehillim* mentions them in that order. The Sages interpreted the phrase הבו לה' — bring to God — as meaning that these are the blessings that one should bring to Him.

501 - I.e., why does אתה חונן follow the *berachah* of אתה קדוש?

502 - Thus, the Prophet establishes that the necessary prerequisite for true understanding is holiness. See also *Kuzari*, beginning of Chapter I, where the author contrasts this approach to that of the nations who see the two as being entirely unrelated elements.

503 - I.e., השבנו.

TALMUD

אִי הָכֵי לֵימָא "רְפוּאָה" בָּתַר "תְּשׁוּבָה"? לָא סַלְקָא דַעְתָּךְ, דִּכְתִיב: "וְיָשֹׁב אֶל
ה' וִירַחֲמֵהוּ, וְאֶל אֱלֹהֵינוּ כִּי יַרְבֶּה לִסְלוֹחַ". וּמַאי חָזֵית דְּסָמְכַתְּ אַהַאי? סְמוֹךְ
אַהָא! כְּתִיב קְרָא אַחֲרִינָא: "הַסֹּלֵחַ לְכָל עֲוֹנֵכִי, הָרֹפֵא לְכָל תַּחֲלוּאָיְכִי,
הַגּוֹאֵל מִשַּׁחַת חַיָּיְכִי". לְמֵימְרָא דִּ"גְאֻלָּה" וּ"רְפוּאָה" בָּתַר "סְלִיחָה" הִיא?
וְהָכְתִיב: "וְשָׁב וְרָפָא לוֹ". הַהוּא – לָאו רְפוּאָה דְּתַחֲלוּאִים הִיא, אֶלָּא רְפוּאָה
דִּסְלִיחָה הִיא.
וּמָה רָאוּ לוֹמַר "גְאֻלָּה" בַּשְּׁבִיעִית? אָמַר רָבָא: מִתּוֹךְ שֶׁעֲתִידִין לִיגָּאֵל
בַּשְּׁבִיעִית, לְפִיכָךְ קְבָעוּהָ בַּשְּׁבִיעִית. וְהָאָמַר מַר: בַּשִּׁשִׁית קוֹלוֹת, בַּשְּׁבִיעִית
מִלְחָמוֹת, בְּמוֹצָאֵי שְׁבִיעִית בֶּן־דָּוִד בָּא? מִלְחָמָה נַמִּי, אַתְחַלְתָּא דִּגְאֻלָּה
הִיא.

TRANSLATION

If so [i.e., based on this verse], the [*berachah* of] healing should follow [the *berachah* of] repentance?[504] This is not logical, for the verse (ibid. 55:2) states: *And he shall return to God who will have mercy upon him, and to the Lord who is great in forgiving.*[505] What did you see [i.e., what made the Sages decide] to base yourselves on this [latter verse which juxtaposes repentance and forgiveness], base yourselves on the other one [the verse that juxtaposes repentance and healing]? [They based their decision] on another verse (*Tehillim* 103:2-4) that states: *who forgives all of your sins, who cures all of yor ills, who redeems all of the guilty from punishment.*[506] Do you mean to say that redemption and healing follow forgiveness? Does the verse (op. cit.) not say: *and he will repent and be healed?*[507] That [verse] is not [referring to] healing from illness. Rather, [it is referring to] the healing of forgiveness [i.e., the healing of the spirit that comes from being forgiven by God].

---

504 - I.e., based on this verse, the *berachah* of רפאנו should follow השבנו since the subjects are juxtaposed in the verse. In the order established however, רפאנו follows סלח לנו.

505 - I.e., since the verse mentions repentance and then forgiveness, the order that was established was to first say השבנו and then סלח לנו

506 - I.e., since this verse also juxtaposes forgiveness and healing, it is logical that this order be followed in the *berachos* since we now have two verses — one in *Tehillim* and one in *Yeshayahu* — which follow this order.

507 - I.e., why did they decide to separate סלח לנו and רפאנו with the *berachah* of ראה נא — redemption — when the verse clearly links the two?

Why did they see fit to say [the *berachah* of] redemption as the seventh [*berachah*]? Rava explained: Since they are destined to be redeemed in the seventh [year of the Sabbatical cycle], they therefore established it as the seventh [*berachah*].[508] But did Mar not say that in the sixth year there will be sounds [of the shofar], in the seventh there will be wars and at the end of the seventh year the son of David [*mashiach*] will come? War too is the beginning of the redemption.

TALMUD

וּמָה רָאוּ לוֹמַר "רְפוּאָה" בַּשְׁמִינִית? אָמַר רַבִּי אַחָא: מִתּוֹךְ שֶׁנִּתְּנָה מִילָה בַּשְׁמִינִית – שֶׁצְּרִיכָה רְפוּאָה, לְפִיכָךְ קְבָעוּהָ בַּשְׁמִינִית.

TRANSLATION

Why did they see fit to say [the *berachah* of] healing as the eighth [*berachah*]? R. Acha explained: Since circumcision — which requires healing — was given on the eighth day, they therefore established it [the *berachah* of healing] as the eighth [*berachah* of the *amidah*].

COMMENTARY

Maharal[509] explains that all numbers used by the Sages have symbolic significance; thus, if the Sages deduced that the set time for the redemption was in the seventh year of the Sabbatical cycle, they did so because the coming of *mashiach* represents the end of the natural cycle of events that is symbolized by the number seven as in the days of the week. For this very same reason, the mitzvah of circumsicion was set for the eighth day because the number eight represents the ability of man to transcend natural order and link himself to the supernal world.

Healing, in that it is a gift from God, also represents a departure from natural order.[510] Based on natural law, one would be reluctant to inject a virus or

---

508 - Rava's statement should not be understood as denying the possibility of the redemption coming at any time. Rather, as the Talmud (*Sanhedrin* 97a) explains the redemption can come at its set time or can be brought on earlier through repentance.

509 - See נתיבות עולם, נתיב התורה.

510 - Note the similarity between the Hebrew words בריאה — *Creation* — and בריא — *healthy*; i.e., the natural order set in Creation calls for man to be healthy. When he is ill, this represents a departure from natural order and we therefore seek God's intervention.

bacteria into an otherwise healthy body to prevent disease. Yet, as our own experience has shown us in numerous examples, doing so spurs the body into forming antibodies that can ward off disease at a later date. This ability would seem to point toward the unnatural character of the healing arts. Thus, it is fitting that the *berachah* that expresses our request that God heal us was set as the eighth *berachah* of the *amidah*.

Chazon Ish[511] adds that while the body often has the ability to heal itself and defend itself from the onslaught of bacteria and viruses which threaten its well-being, there are times when outside intervention is necessary in the form of medicines and herbs that assist the body in its efforts. God in his wisdom saw fit to create all of these elements within Creation, as well as granting pharmacologists the wisdom to use them correctly. Hence, though natural law might seem to dictate that a body that does not have the ability to defend itself should perish, we ask God to bring us healing through the external means that He has created.

TALMUD

וּמָה רָאוּ לוֹמַר בִּרְכַּת "הַשָּׁנִים" בַּתְּשִׁיעִית? אָמַר רַבִּי אַלֶּכְּסַנְדְּרִי: כְּנֶגֶד מַפְקִיעֵי שְׁעָרִים, דִּכְתִיב: "שְׁבֹר זְרוֹעַ רָשָׁע" וְגוֹ', וְדָוִד כִּי אֲמָרָהּ, בַּתְּשִׁיעִית אֲמָרָהּ.

TRANSLATION

Why did they see fit to say the *berachah* of the seasons[512] as the ninth [*berachah* of the *amidah*]? R. Alexandri explained: [This *berachah* was made part of the *amidah*] as a protest against those who raise prices, as the verse (*Tehillim* 10:15) states: *break the arm of the wicked*, and David said this as the ninth [chapter of *Tehillim*].[513]

COMMENTARY

Rashi[514] explains that the reference is to the speculators who raise the prices

---

511 - אמונה ובטחון, פרק א' סימן ו'.

512 - I.e., ברך עלינו. The *berachah* asks God to provide precipitation at the appropriate times — rain in the winter and dew in the summer — so that the crops will be plentiful and thus there will be no fluctuations in grain prices.

513 - *Rashi* explains that though this chapter is the tenth according to our division of *Tehillim*, R. Alexandrai was of the opinion that chapters 1 and 2 — אשרי תמימי דרך and למה רגשו גוים — are one chapter.

514 - ד"ה שבור.

of grains in times of drought. In a previous verse (ibid. :9), David describes the wicked — *They lie in wait to snatch from the poor.* The reference is obviously not to thieves, for they steal from the rich. Rather, the reference is to those who unscrupulously take advantage of the poor by raising prices. The rich, who can afford to purchase grains and store them against possible shortages, are less affected. David therefore asked God to grant bounty to the world and thus *break the arm of the wicked* by removing the means whereby they take advantage of the poor.

Maharal[515] points out that speculators who withold their produce so as to cause prices to rise are referred to as being wicked because their actions go against the natural order of the world which had provided produce at the proper time. Evil, according to *Maharal*, is man acting according to his whims in place of acting as God ordains. The *berachah* of the seasons thus asks God to rule the world according to natural order — each season in its proper time — as well as to grant bounty to the world, for these factors will prevent the wicked speculators from prospering at the expense of others.

TALMUD

וּמָה רָאוּ לוֹמַר "קִבּוּץ גָּלִיּוֹת" לְאַחַר בִּרְכַּת "הַשָּׁנִים"? דִּכְתִיב: "וְאַתֶּם הָרֵי יִשְׂרָאֵל, עַנְפְּכֶם תִּתֵּנוּ, וּפֶרְיְכֶם תִּשְׂאוּ לְעַמִּי יִשְׂרָאֵל כִּי קֵרְבוּ לָבֹא".

וְכֵיוָן שֶׁנִּתְקַבְּצוּ גָלִיּוֹת, נַעֲשָׂה דִין בָּרְשָׁעִים, שֶׁנֶּאֱמַר: "וְאָשִׁיבָה יָדִי עָלַיִךְ, וְאֶצְרֹף כַּבֹּר סִיגָיִךְ". וּכְתִיב:"וְאָשִׁיבָה שֹׁפְטַיִךְ כְּבָרִאשֹׁנָה".

TRANSLATION

Why did they see fit to say [the *berachah*] of the ingathering of the exiles[516] after the *berachah* of the seasons? The verse (*Yechezkel* 36:8) states: *And you, oh mountains of Israel — give your branches and carry your fruits for My people Israel, for they are soon to come.*[517]

And once the exiles are gathered [and returned], judgement will be rendered against the wicked [and the *berachah* of judgement[518] therefore follows the *berachah* of the ingathering of the exiles], as the verse (*Yeshayahu* 1:25) states:

---

515 - דרך חיים, אבות ב:יג.

516 - I.e., תקע בשופר.

517 - I.e., when the land begins to give abundant produce, it is a sign that the end of the exile is near. See *Sanhedrin* 98a.

518 - I.e., השיבה שפטינו.

And I shall return My hand upon you and I will cleanse your impurities with soap and [the next verse] states: *and I shall return your judges as before.*

COMMENTARY

The reference in this *berachah* is to the coming of *mashiach*, for it is only then that true judgement will once again be rendered. As *Rambam*[519] writes: *And if a king shall come from the House of David, a scholar of Torah who busies himself in Torah like his father, David, in both the written Torah and the orally transmitted Torah, and he shall bend [the will] of Israel to go according to it and strengthen that which needs strengthening and wage the wars of God, then he is assumed to be the mashiach.*

If he is successful and rebuilds the *Beis ha-Mikdash* in its place and gathers the exiled of Israel, he is then certainly *mashiach*. And he shall correct the entire world to serve God together, as the verse (*Zefaniah* 3:9) states: *For then I shall transform the nations [so that they speak] a clear language, all of them calling in the name of God, serving Him together.*

Thus, *mashiach's* mission is to bring the entire world to follow the path of Torah — a mission that was the responsibility of the Judges in Israel. Hence, this *berachah* follows the *berachah* that refers to the ingathering of the exiles.

TALMUD

וְכֵיוָן שֶׁנַּעֲשָׂה דִין מִן הָרְשָׁעִים, כָּלוּ "הַמִּינִין", וְכוֹלֵל זֵדִים עִם הַמִּינִין, שֶׁנֶּאֱמַר: "וְשֶׁבֶר פֹּשְׁעִים וְחַטָּאִים יַחְדָּו וְגוֹ' יִכְלוּ".

TRANSLATION

And once judgement has been rendered against the wicked, all of the heretics [who are mentioned in the next *berachah*][520] will be destroyed and the insolent are included among the heretics, as the verse (ibid. :28) states: *And the destruction of the guilty and the sinners shall be together.*

---

519 - הלכות מלכים יא:ד.

520 - I.e., ולמלשינים. The Talmud (*Berachos* 28b) records that the text of this *berachah* was written at the conclave of Yavneh by Shmuel ha-Katan at the request of Rabban Gamliel. While it would seem that this *berachah* was a new addition to the *amidah* and was thus not part of the order established by the Members of the Great Assembly, it is also possible that a similar *berachah* had previously been included but the text had been forgotten. The question is dealt with in great length in the prefatory commentary to *Shemoneh Esrai* in the *Siddur Otzar ha-Tefillos*.

TALMUD

וְכֵיוָן שֶׁכָּלוּ הַמִּינִין – מִתְרוֹמֶמֶת קֶרֶן צַדִּיקִים, דִּכְתִיב: "וְכָל קַרְנֵי רְשָׁעִים
אֲגַדֵּעַ, תְּרוֹמַמְנָה קַרְנוֹת צַדִּיק". וְכוֹלֵל גֵּרֵי הַצֶּדֶק עִם הַצַּדִּיקִים, שֶׁנֶּאֱמַר:
"מִפְּנֵי שֵׂיבָה תָּקוּם, וְהָדַרְתָּ פְּנֵי זָקֵן", וּסְמִיךְ לֵיהּ: "וְכִי יָגוּר אִתְּךָ גֵּר".
וְהֵיכָן מִתְרוֹמֶמֶת קַרְנָם? בִּירוּשָׁלַיִם, שֶׁנֶּאֱמַר: "שַׁאֲלוּ שְׁלוֹם יְרוּשָׁלָיִם, יִשְׁלָיוּ
אֹהֲבָיִךְ".

TRANSLATION

And once the heretics are destroyed, the prestige of the righteous will be raised [and the *berachah* of the righteous[521] therefore follows the *berachah* of the destruction of the non-believers], as the verse (*Tehillim* 75:11) states: *And I shall uproot the prestige of the wicked and the prestige of the righteous will be uplifted.* And they included the righteous converts among the righteous, as the verse (*Vayikra* 19:32) states: *You shall rise for the elderly and give honor to the aged* and in proximity [in the next verse, the Torah states:] *and if a convert shall live among you.*[522]

And where will their prestige be uplifted? In Jerusalem [and the *berachah* of Jerusalem[523] therefore follows], as the verse (*Tehillim* 122:6) states: *Seek the peace of Jerusalem, that Your loved ones find serenity [there].*

COMMENTARY

The rebuilding of Jerusalem, at the time of the final redemption, refers to the time when all of mankind will once again follow the dictates of God without falling prey to their own narrow self-interests and the satisfaction of their personal desires. It is for this that the righteous pray, for as *Rambam*[524] writes:

---

521 - I.e., על הצדיקים.

522 - I.e., since the Torah saw fit to juxtapose the verses that speak of the honor due the elderly and the prohibition of taking advantage of a convert, the Talmud assumes that there is a connection between the two. The text of the *berachah* that speaks of the righteous was therefore expanded to include a reference to righteous converts as well and the *berachah* therefore mentions both גרי הצדק and זקני עמך בית ישראל.

Maharal (גבורות ה' פרק טי) adds that wisdom in the temporal world can be considered to be a גר — a stranger — for most people act according to the dictates of their hearts rather than their minds. It is thus fitting that the *berachah* refering to the righteous, who act according to the dictates of the mind, also includes a reference to גרים.

523 - I.e., ולירושלים עירך.

524 - הלכות מלכים יב:ד. See also *Rambam's* Commentary to the *Mishnah*, *Sanhedrin* 11:1.

The Sages and Prophets did not desire the period of mashiach so as to rule the world or so as to be able to gorge themselves and be happy. Rather, so that they might be free [of their dependence upon the temporal world so that they might occupy themselves] in the Torah and its wisdom, for then they shall have no oppressors or interruptions.

TALMUD

וְכֵיוָן שֶׁנִּבְנֵית יְרוּשָׁלַיִם, בָּא דָוִד, שֶׁנֶּאֱמַר: "אַחַר יָשֻׁבוּ בְּנֵי יִשְׂרָאֵל וּבִקְשׁוּ אֶת ה' אֱלֹהֵיהֶם, וְאֵת דָּוִיד מַלְכָּם".

וְכֵיוָן שֶׁבָּא דָוִד, בָּאת "תְּפִלָּה", שֶׁנֶּאֱמַר: "וַהֲבִיאוֹתִים אֶל הַר קָדְשִׁי, וְשִׂמַּחְתִּים בְּבֵית תְּפִלָּתִי".

וְכֵיוָן שֶׁבָּאת תְּפִלָּה, בָּאת "עֲבוֹדָה", שֶׁנֶּאֱמַר: "עוֹלֹתֵיהֶם וְזִבְחֵיהֶם לְרָצוֹן עַל מִזְבְּחִי".

וְכֵיוָן שֶׁבָּאת "עֲבוֹדָה", בָּאת "הוֹדָאָה", שֶׁנֶּאֱמַר: "זֹבֵחַ תּוֹדָה יְכַבְּדָנְנִי".

וּמָה רָאוּ לוֹמַר "בִּרְכַּת כֹּהֲנִים" אַחַר "הוֹדָאָה"? דִּכְתִיב: "וַיִּשָּׂא אַהֲרֹן אֶת יָדָיו אֶל הָעָם וַיְבָרְכֵם, וַיֵּרֶד מֵעֲשׂת הַחַטָּאת וְהָעֹלָה וְהַשְּׁלָמִים". אֵימָא קֹדֶם עֲבוֹדָה? לָא סַלְקָא דַעְתָּךְ, דִּכְתִיב: "וַיֵּרֶד מֵעֲשׂת הַחַטָּאת וְגו'. מִי כְּתִיב: "לַעֲשׂת"? "מֵעֲשׂת" כְּתִיב.

TRANSLATION

And when Jerusalem is rebuilt, then David [i.e., *mashiach*] will come [and the *berachah* regarding *mashiach*[525] therefore follows], as the verse (*Hoshea* 3:8) states: [18a] *And the children of Israel will then return and seek God, their Lord, and David their king.*

And when David [*mashiach*] will come, then [fully efficacious] prayer [will again be possible],[526] as the verse (*Yeshayahu* 56:7) states: *And I shall bring them to My holy mountain, and I shall bring them joy in the house of My prayer.*

And when [efficacious] prayer comes, then Divine service will come,[527] as the verse (ibid.) states: *their burnt-offerings and sacrifices will be acceptable upon My altar.*

And when the Divine service comes, then thanks come,[528] as the verse (*Tehillim* 50:22) states: *[He who] offers a thanksgiving sacrifice brings Me honor.*

---

525 - I.e., את צמח דוד.

526 - The *berachah* of שמע קלנו therefore follows את צמח דוד.

527 - The *berachah* of רצה therefore follows שמע קלנו.

528 - The paragraph of מודים therefore follows רצה.

Why did they see fit to say the priestly blessing after [the *berachah* of] thanks?[529] The verse (*Vayikra* 9:22) states: *And Aharon raised his hands toward the people and blessed them and he descended from offering the sin-offering, the burnt-offering and the peace-offering.* Say [the priestly blessing] before the Divine service?[530] It is not logical [to do so], for the verse states: *and he descended from offering the sin offering.* The verse does not state *to offer* — it states *from offering* [which implies that Aharon had already offered the sacrifices before blessing the people].

COMMENTARY

The verse (*Bamidbar* 6:23-27) states: *Speak to Aharon and his sons and say to them. Thus shall you bless the people of Israel ... and they shall place My name upon the children of Israel and I shall bless them.*

Sefer ha-Chinuch[531] explains: *God, in His goodness, sought to bless His people through the servants who are always in His home, whose thoughts are constantly linked to His service and whose souls are always bound to His awe. In their [the kohanim's] merit, the [Divine] blessing shall be manifested upon them [Israel] and all their actions will be blessed.*

TALMUD

וְאֵימָא אַחַר הָעֲבוֹדָה? לָא סַלְקָא דַעְתָּךְ, דִּכְתִיב: "זֶבַח תּוֹדָה". מַאי חָזִית דְּסָמַכְתְּ אֲהָא? סְמוֹךְ אֲהָא! מִסְתַּבְּרָא, עֲבוֹדָה וְהוֹדָאָה חֲדָא מִלְתָא הִיא. וּמָה רָאוּ לוֹמַר "שִׂים שָׁלוֹם" אַחַר "בִּרְכַּת כֹּהֲנִים"? דִּכְתִיב: "וְשָׂמוּ אֶת שְׁמִי עַל בְּנֵי יִשְׂרָאֵל, וַאֲנִי אֲבָרְכֵם". בְּרָכָה דְּהַקָּדוֹשׁ בָּרוּךְ הוּא – "שָׁלוֹם", שֶׁנֶּאֱמַר: "ה' יְבָרֵךְ אֶת עַמּוֹ בַשָּׁלוֹם".

TRANSLATION

Say it [the priestly blessing] after the Divine service?[532] It is not logical [to do so], for the verse (op. cit.) states: *[He who] offers a thanksgiving sacrifice brings Me honor* [and it is therefore logical to juxtapose the Divine service — רצה

---

529 - I.e., why did they insert ברכת כהנים after the *berachah* of הטוב שמך which is the end of מודים?

530 - I.e., why was ברכת בכהנים placed after רצה? From the order of the verse cited, it should precede רצה, for the verse first mentions Aharon's blessing and then mentions the Divine service.

531 - מצוה שע"ח.

532 - Based on the verse cited, why do we not say ברכת כהנים immediately after רצה?

— to thanksgiving — מודים]. Why did you see fit to base yourself on this verse [that connects thanksgiving and the Divine service] — base yourself on that verse [that connects the priestly blessing with the Divine service]? It is more logical [to connect thanksgiving and the Divine service], for the Divine service and thanksgiving are one concept.[533]

Why did they see fit to say bring peace after the priestly blessing?[534] The verse [that follows the priestly blessing] (*Bamidbar* 6:28) states: *And they [the kohanim] shall place My name upon the children of Israel, and I shall bless them.* The blessing of the Holy One, blessed is He, is peace, as the verse (*Tehillim* 29:11) states: *God shall bless His people with peace.*

TALMUD

וְכִי מֵאַחַר דְּמֵאָה וְעֶשְׂרִים זְקֵנִים, וּמֵהֶם כַּמָּה נְבִיאִים, תִּקְנוּ תְּפִלָּה עַל הַסֵּדֶר, שִׁמְעוֹן הַפָּקוּלִי מַאי הִסְדִּיר? שְׁכָחוּם, וְחָזַר וְסִדְּרָם. מִכָּאן וְאֵילָךְ אָסוּר לְסַפֵּר בְּשִׁבְחוֹ שֶׁל הַקָּדוֹשׁ בָּרוּךְ הוּא, דְּאָמַר רַבִּי אֶלְעָזָר: מַאי דִּכְתִיב: "מִי יְמַלֵּל גְּבוּרוֹת ה', יַשְׁמִיעַ כָּל תְּהִלָּתוֹ", לְמִי נָאֶה לְמַלֵּל גְּבוּרוֹת ה'? לְמִי שֶׁיָּכוֹל לְהַשְׁמִיעַ כָּל תְּהִלָּתוֹ.

TRANSLATION

Once one hundred and twenty sages — among them some prophets — ordained the order of prayer [i.e., the *amidah*], what order did Shimon ha-Pakuli ordain? They had forgotten it [the order of the *amidah*] and he re-established it.

From this point on [i.e., once the order of the *amidah* was set], it is forbidden to speak in praise of the Holy One, blessed is He.[535] As R. Elazar explained: What is the meaning of the verse (ibid. 106:2): *Who shall speak of the power of God, enunciate all of His glory*? Who is worthy of speaking of the power of God? He who can enunciate all of His glory.[536]

---

533 - *Rashi* (ד״ה חדא מילתא) explains that offering thanks is also a form of Divine service.

534 - I.e., why does the *berachah* of שים שלום follow ברכת כהנים?

535 - *Rashi* (ד״ה אסור לספר) explains that it is forbidden to add *berachos* to the *amidah*.

536 - The Sages and Prophets who established the text of the *amidah* were capable of enunciating all of God's glory. But, later generations are incapable and it is therefore forbidden to add *berachos* to *Shemoneh Esrei*.

COMMENTARY

Ramchal[537] writes: *Every Jew must believe and know that there is a first being, without beginning and without end and it is He who brought all things into existence and it is He who sustains them. This being is God. Furthermore, he must know that the true nature of this being, may His name be blessed, cannot be fathomed at all by anyone but Himself. Only this is known: that He is complete in every way and He has absolutely no deficiency.*

Admittedly, this is far beyond our understanding and imagination and we have almost no means of explaining it or putting it into words, for our understanding and imagination is limited by the boundaries of nature that He created ... but, as we already noted, His true nature is beyond our comprehension and no comparison can be drawn between that which we see among the created and between the Creator Himself, for the nature and essence of the two is not at all equal that we might be able to draw a parallel between them.

Based on *Ramchal*, we can see that any attempt to offer praise and thanks to the Creator will be deficient, for we can only offer praise and thanks based on our limited understanding. Indeed, this would seem to point to the possibility that one should desist from offering praise and thanks to Him because of the paucity of our comprehension and expression. However, the Sages — basing themselves on the prophetic vision of the Prophets who were among them — were able to provide us with a means of expression that enables us to offer suitable praise and thanks. It is for this reason that we are dutybound in all of our prayers not to change their text and, as the Talmud teaches us here, not to add prayers of our own composition into the set text of the *amidah*.

TALMUD

אָמַר רַבָּה בַּר בַּר חָנָה, אָמַר רַבִּי יוֹחָנָן: הַמְסַפֵּר בְּשִׁבְחוֹ שֶׁל הַקָּדוֹשׁ בָּרוּךְ הוּא יוֹתֵר מִדַּאי, נֶעֱקָר מִן הָעוֹלָם, שֶׁנֶּאֱמַר: "הַיְסֻפַּר לוֹ כִּי אֲדַבֵּר?! אִם אָמַר אִישׁ כִּי יְבֻלָּע?!".

דָּרַשׁ רַבִּי יְהוּדָה. אִישׁ כְּפַר גְּבוֹרַיָא, וְאָמְרֵי לָהּ, אִישׁ כְּפַר גִּבּוֹר חַיִל: מַאי דִּכְתִיב: "לְךָ דֻמִיָּה תְהִלָּה"? סַמָּא דְכוּלָּא – מַשְׁתּוּקָא. כִּי אָתָא רַב דִּימִי אָמַר: אָמְרִי בְּמַעְרְבָא: "מִלָּה – בְּסֶלַע, מַשְׁתּוּקָא – בִּתְרֵין".

---

537 - דרך ה', פרק ראשון.

TRANSLATION

Raba bar bar Chana taught in the name of R. Yochanan: One who overly speaks in praise of the Holy One, blessed is He, is uprooted from the world, as the verse (*Iyov* 37:20) states: *Need it be told to Him if I speak [His praise]? If man speaks, he will be swallowed.*

R. Yehudah, a resident of Kfar Giboraya — and some say a resident of Kfar Gibor Chayil — expounded: What is the meaning of the verse (*Tehillim* 65:2) that states: *to You silence is praise*? The choicest of all spices is silence. When R. Dimi came, he taught: In the west [the Land of Israel] they say: A word [is worth] a *sela* and silence is [worth] two.

TALMUD

אָמַר רַבִּי אַחָא, אָמַר רַבִּי אֶלְעָזָר: מִנַּיִן שֶׁקְּרָאוֹ הַקָּדוֹשׁ בָּרוּךְ הוּא לְיַעֲקֹב "אֵ־ל"? שֶׁנֶּאֱמַר: "וַיַּצֶּב שָׁם מִזְבֵּחַ, וַיִּקְרָא לוֹ: אֵל אֱלֹהֵי יִשְׂרָאֵל". דְּאִי סַלְקָא דַעְתָּךְ, לַמִּזְבֵּחַ קָרִי לֵיה יַעֲקֹב "אֵל", "וַיִּקְרָא לוֹ יַעֲקֹב", מִיבָּעֵי לֵיה? אֶלָּא וַיִּקְרָא לוֹ לְיַעֲקֹב: "אֵ־ל"? וּמִי קְרָאוֹ: "אֵ־ל"? – אֱלֹהֵי יִשְׂרָאֵל. מֵהֵיכָן קוֹרֵא אָדָם אֶת הַמְּגִלָּה? וכו'. תַּנְיָא, רַבִּי שִׁמְעוֹן בַּר יוֹחַאי אוֹמֵר: מ"בַּלַּיְלָה הַהוּא".

TRANSLATION

R. Acha taught in the name of R. Elazar: From where do we see that The Holy One, blessed is He, referred to Yaakov as God? The verse (*Bereishis* 33:20) states: *And he established an altar there and he called it, God, the Lord of Israel.* If you would think that [the verse means that] Yaakov called the altar *God*, it should state, *and Yaakov called it.* Rather, [the verse should be interpreted in the following manner:] *and He called Yaakov, God.* And who was it that called him [God]? The Lord of Israel.

[19a] **MISHNAH:** From what point must one read the Megillah to fulfill his obligation?[538] **TALMUD:** We learned in a *beraisa*: R. Shimon bar Yochai taught: From [the verse (*Esther* 6:1) that states:] *On that night.*

---

538 - In the text brought in the *Ein Yaakov*, the author omits the opinions cited in the *Mishnah*; i.e., R. Meir who maintains that the entire *Megillah* must be read, R. Yehudah who maintains that the reading begins from the verse (2:5) *there was a Jewish* man, and R. Yosi who maintains that one must begin from the verse (3:1) *after these things [happened].*

TALMUD

אָמַר רַבִּי יוֹחָנָן: וְכֻלָּן מִקְרָא אֶחָד דָּרְשׁוּ: "וַתִּכְתֹּב אֶסְתֵּר הַמַּלְכָּה וְגוֹ',
וּמָרְדֳּכַי הַיְּהוּדִי אֵת כָּל תֹּקֶף". מָאן דַּאֲמַר: ,כֻּלָּהּ' - תָּקְפוֹ שֶׁל אֲחַשְׁוֵרוֹשׁ.
וּמָאן דַּאֲמַר: מֵ"אִישׁ יְהוּדִי" - תָּקְפוֹ שֶׁל מָרְדֳּכַי. וּמָאן דַּאֲמַר: מֵ"אַחַר
הַדְּבָרִים הָאֵלֶּה" - תָּקְפוֹ שֶׁל הָמָן. וּמָאן דַּאֲמַר: מִ"בַּלַּיְלָה הַהוּא" - תָּקְפוֹ שֶׁל
נֵס.
רַב הוּנָא אָמַר מֵהָכָא: "וּמָה רָאוּ עַל כָּכָה, וּמָה הִגִּיעַ אֲלֵיהֶם" מָאן דַּאֲמַר:
,כֻּלָּהּ', "מָה רָאָה" אֲחַשְׁוֵרוֹשׁ שֶׁנִּשְׁתַּמֵּשׁ בְּכֵלִים שֶׁל בֵּית הַמִּקְדָּשׁ? "עַל כָּכָה" -
מִשּׁוּם דְּחָשִׁיב שִׁבְעִים שָׁנִין וְלָא אִיפְרוּק. "וּמָה הִגִּיעַ אֲלֵיהֶם", דְּקָטַל וַשְׁתִּי.

TRANSLATION

R. Yochanan taught: All of them [i.e., R. Shimon bar Yochai as well as the *tannaim* quoted in the *Mishnah*] based their deductions on one [i.e., the same] verse (ibid. 9:29): *And Esther the queen ... and Mordechai the Jew wrote all of the relevant [miracles that occurred so as to give authority to this letter of Purim].*[539] The opinion that maintains that [the *Megillah* must be read] in entirety [holds that] the relevant [part of the *Megillah*] is [all that which concerns] Achashverosh [thus, all of the *Megillah* must be read since he is discussed throughout]. The opinion that maintains that [we need only begin the reading from] *there was a Jewish man* [i.e., from the introduction of Mordechai, holds that] the relevant [part of the *Megillah*] is [all that which concerns] Mordechai. The opinion that maintains that [we need only begin the reading from] *after these events* [i.e., from the introduction of Haman, holds that] the relevant [part of the *Megillah*] is Haman. The opinion that maintains that [we need only begin the reading from] *on that night* [holds that] the relevant [part of the *Megillah*] is the miracle [i.e., the miraculous chain of events that led to Haman's downfall].

R. Huna taught [that they all based themselves on different interpretations of this verse (ibid. 9:26):] *because of what they did see happen and what they had*

---

539 - I.e., Mordechai and Esther recorded the events that occurred and ordained that the *Megillah* be read so as to publicize the miracles that occurred. As the Talmud noted earlier, it is by virtue of their authority that we are dutybound to read the *Megillah*. The discussion in the Talmud concerns the difference of opinion between the *tannaim* as to which specific portion of the *Megillah* is relevant to the miracles that Esther and Mordechai sought to publicize through their enactment.

experienced.[540] The opinion that maintains [that the *Megillah* must be read in its] entirety [explains the verse as follows:] *what did he see*[541] — [what did] Achashverosh see that brought him to use the vessels from the *Beis ha-Mikdash*? *Happen* — he calculated the seventy years [that Yirmiyahu had prophesied would be the length of the exile][542] and they were not redeemed [which he took as a sign that the prophecy would not be fulfilled]. *And what they had experienced* — that Vashti was killed [as punishment for his having used the vessels, and Esther took her place which ultimately led to the deliverance of the Jews].[543]

TALMUD

וּלְמָאן דַּאֲמַר מֵ"אִישׁ יְהוּדִי", "מָה רָאָה", מָרְדְּכַי דְּאִיקְנֵי בְהָמָן? "עַל כָּכָה" – דְּשַׁוֵּי נַפְשֵׁיהּ עֲבוֹדָה זָרָה. "וּמָה הִגִּיעַ אֲלֵיהֶם" – דְּאִתְרְחִישׁ נִיסָא.

וּמָאן דַּאֲמַר: מֵ"אַחַר הַדְּבָרִים הָאֵלֶּה" – "מָה רָאָה", הָמָן שֶׁנִּתְקַנֵּא בְּכָל הַיְּהוּדִים. "עַל כָּכָה" – מִשּׁוּם דְּמָרְדְּכַי לֹא יִכְרַע וְלֹא יִשְׁתַּחֲוֶה. "וּמָה הִגִּיעַ אֲלֵיהֶם" – "וְתָלוּ אוֹתוֹ וְאֶת בָּנָיו עַל הָעֵץ".

וּמָאן דַּאֲמַר: מִ"בַּלַּיְלָה הַהוּא" – "מָה רָאָה", אֲחַשְׁוֵרוֹשׁ לְהָבִיא אֶת סֵפֶר הַזִּכְרוֹנוֹת? "עַל כָּכָה" – דְּזַמִּינְתֵּיהּ אֶסְתֵּר לְהָמָן בַּהֲדֵיהּ. "וּמָה הִגִּיעַ אֲלֵיהֶם" – דְּאִתְרְחִישׁ נִיסָא.

TRANSLATION

According to the opinion that maintains [that the *Megillah* only need be read] from *there was a Jewish man,* [the verse should be interpreted in the following manner:] *What did he see* — [what reason did] Mordechai have to make Haman jealous? *Happen* — [Mordechai saw that] he [Haman] made himself into an object of worship. *And what they experienced* — that a miracle occurred.

---

540 - According to R. Huna, it would appear that Esther and Mordechai added this verse as an explanation for their having written their historical account. Thus, each opinion cited in the *Mishnah* and *beraisa* would have to interpret this verse as being consistent with their viewpoint. The verse can best be understood in English by explaining it as follows: *What was it that Esther and Mordechai saw happen that led them to write their account and what was the result of what they had seen*

541 - Although the verse uses the plural מה ראו — *what did they see* — the Talmud nevertheless explains the verse as if it was written in singular.

542 - See page 95.

543 - According to this interpretation of the verse, the entire *Megillah* must be read since these events are recorded in the very beginning.

According to the opinion that maintains [that the *Megillah* only need be read] from *after these events,* [the verse should be interpreted in the following manner:] *What did he see* — [what reason did] Haman have to become jealous of all of the Jews [and therefore plot their deaths]? *Happen* — [Haman saw] that Mordechai would not bow down or prostrate himself. *And what they experienced* — he and his children were hung on the tree.

According to the opinion that maintains [that the *Megillah* only need be read] from *on that night,* [the verse should be interpreted in the following manner:] *What did he see* — [what reason did] Achashverosh have to call for the Book of Chronicles? *Happen* — [Achashverosh saw] that Esther had invited Haman along with him. *And what they experienced* — that a miracle transpired.

TALMUD

אָמַר רַבִּי חִיָּא בַר אַבָּא, אָמַר רַבִּי יוֹחָנָן: אִלְמָלֵי נִשְׁתַּיֵּר בַּמְּעָרָה שֶׁעָבַר בָּהּ מֹשֶׁה וְאֵלִיָּהוּ, כִּמְלֹא נֶקֶב מַחַט סִדְקִית, לֹא הָיוּ יְכוֹלִין לַעֲמֹד מִפְּנֵי הָאוֹרָה. דִּכְתִיב: "כִּי לֹא יִרְאַנִי הָאָדָם וָחָי".

TRANSLATION

[19b] R. Chiya bar Abba taught in the name of R. Yochanan: Had there remained in the cave in which the Shechinah passed over Moshe and Eliyahu a crack as wide as a sewing needle, they would have been unable to bear the light, as the verse (*Shemos* 33:20) states: *for man cannot see Me and live.*

COMMENTARY

When Moshe ascended to the heavens, he asked God (*Shemos* 33:18): *Show me Your essence.* The commentators[544] explain that Moshe sought a perception of God that was unfiltered and unlimited in scope. Through this request Moshe sought to achieve the level of true understanding. But God replied: *Man cannot see Me and live* — i.e., man cannot achieve this level and still remain human. However, God granted Moshe a level of prophetic understanding that was just below that which he sought — a level which the verse (ibid.) characterizes as: *Behold there is place with Me and you shall stand upon the rock. And when My essence shall pass over, I shall place you in the cave within the rock and My hands shall cover you until I pass.*

Hundreds of years later, Eliyahu merited a similar prophetic exposure after

544 - See *Ramban* and *Malbim* ad loc.

having prepared himself by denying himself food for forty days. He too was placed within the cave within the rock as the Divine essence passed over him, and he too was protected from the light which, if seen, would have precluded his continued existence as a man.

TALMUD

וְאָמַר רַבִּי חִיָּא בַּר אַבָּא, אָמַר רַבִּי יוֹחָנָן: מַאי דְּכְתִיב: "וַעֲלֵיהֶם כְּכָל הַדְּבָרִים" וְגוֹ'. מְלַמֵּד שֶׁהֶרְאָה הַקָּדוֹשׁ בָּרוּךְ הוּא לְמֹשֶׁה בְּסִינַי, דְּקְדּוּקֵי תוֹרָה, וְדְקְדּוּקֵי סוֹפְרִים, וּמַה שֶּׁסוֹפְרִים עֲתִידִים לְחַדֵּשׁ. וּמַאי נִיהוּ? מִקְרָא מְגִלָּה.

TRANSLATION

R. Chiya bar Abba also taught in the name of R. Yochanan: What is the meaning of the verse (*Devarim* 9:10): *And upon them [the second tablets] were all of the things*? This teaches us that the Holy One, blessed is He, showed Moshe at Sinai all of the deductions from the Torah and [those made by] the Sages and all that the *soferim*[545] were destined to enact. And what is this [i.e., what enactments were made by the *soferim*]? The reading of the *Megillah*.

---

545 - The *tannaim* and *amoraim* of the Talmud are sometimes referred to as *soferim* — literally scribes. See *Kidushin* 30a.

TALMUD

מִשְׁנָה. הַקּוֹרֵא אֶת הַמְּגִלָּה עוֹמֵד וְיוֹשֵׁב, יָצָא. גְּמָרָא. תָּנָא, מַה שֶּׁאֵין כֵּן
בַּתּוֹרָה. מְנָא הַנֵּי מִילֵי? אָמַר רַבִּי אַבָּהוּ: דַּאֲמַר קְרָא: "וְאַתָּה, פֹּה עֲמֹד
עִמָּדִי", וְאָמַר רַבִּי אַבָּהוּ: אִלְמָלֵא מִקְרָא כָּתוּב, אִי אֶפְשָׁר לְאָמְרוֹ, כִּבְיָכוֹל,
שֶׁאֲפִלּוּ הַקָּדוֹשׁ בָּרוּךְ הוּא בַּעֲמִידָה. וְאָמַר רַבִּי אַבָּהוּ: מִנַּיִן לְרַב שֶׁלֹּא יֵשֵׁב עַל
גַּבֵּי מִטָּה, וְיִשְׁנֶה לְתַלְמִידָיו עַל גַּבֵּי קַרְקַע? שֶׁנֶּאֱמַר: "וְאַתָּה פֹּה עֲמֹד עִמָּדִי".

TRANSLATION

[21a] **MISHNAH:** One who reads the *Megillah* [either] standing or sitting has fulfilled the obligation. **TALMUD:** We learned in a *beraisa*: This [ruling that the *Megillah* may be read either while standing or sitting] is not [the case] as concerns [the reading of] the Torah. From where do we derive this [that the Torah may not be read while sitting]? R. Avahu explained: The verse (*Devarim* 5:28) states: *And you [Moshe], stand here with Me*. R. Avahu added: Were this not a written verse, it could not be said. It is as though even the Holy One, blessed is He, is standing.[546] R. Avahu also taught: From where [do we know] that a teacher should not sit on a couch and teach his students [who are seated] on the ground? The verse states: *And you [Moshe], stand here with Me*.

COMMENTARY

Iyun Yaakov points out that the *Megillah* may be read while sitting because the reading is compared to the recital of *Shema*[547] which may also be read while sitting, as per Hillel's ruling.[548] Had the Sages compared the *Megillah* reading to the reading of the Torah, then it would have to be read while standing. It would seem that there is a fundamental difference between the Torah reading, which was enacted as an educational tool, and the recital of *Shema* or the reading of the *Megillah* which have commemorative nuances. The former, because it is the essence of Judaism, demands a symbolic expression of respect — even

---

546 - While it is not unusual to find anthropomorphic references to God throughout the Talmud without the accompanying disclaimer that were it not written it could not be said, it would seem that R. Avahu felt it necessary to make this statement in this case because the teaching would seem to imply that God too is required to show respect to the Torah by standing.

547 - See *Tosafos* 19a, s.v. אלא הא דתניא.

548 - See *Berachos* 1:3.

though the Torah reading is a Rabbinic[549] ordinance — that transcends even the recital of *Shema* which is a Torah obligation.

Magen Avraham[550] rules that even though the *Megillah* may be read while sitting, the *berachah* that precedes the reading must be recited while standing.

TALMUD

תָּנוּ רַבָּנָן: מִימוֹת מֹשֶׁה, עַד רַבָּן גַּמְלִיאֵל, הָיוּ לְמֵדִין תּוֹרָה מְעֻמָּד. מִשֶּׁמֵּת רַבָּן גַּמְלִיאֵל יָרַד חֹלִי לָעוֹלָם, וְהָיוּ לְמֵדִין תּוֹרָה מְיֻשָּׁב. וְהַיְנוּ דִתְנַן: מִשֶּׁמֵּת רַבָּן גַּמְלִיאֵל בָּטֵל כְּבוֹד תּוֹרָה.

כָּתוּב אֶחָד אוֹמֵר: "וָאֵשֵׁב בָּהָר". וּכְתִיב: "וְאָנֹכִי עָמַדְתִּי בָהָר". אָמַר רַב: עוֹמֵד וְלוֹמֵד, יוֹשֵׁב וְשׁוֹנֶה. רַבִּי חֲנִינָא אָמַר: לֹא עוֹמֵד, וְלֹא יוֹשֵׁב, אֶלָּא שׁוֹחֶה. רַבִּי יוֹחָנָן אָמַר: אֵין "יְשִׁיבָה", אֶלָּא לְשׁוֹן עֲכָבָה, שֶׁנֶּאֱמַר: "וַתֵּשְׁבוּ בְקָדֵשׁ יָמִים רַבִּים". רָבָא אָמַר: רַכּוֹת – מְעֻמָּד, קָשׁוֹת – מְיֻשָּׁב.

TRANSLATION

The Sages taught: From the days of Moshe until Rabban Gamliel,[551] the Torah was studied while standing. When Rabban Gamliel died, illness descended to the world and the Torah was studied while seated. And this is what we learned: From the death of Rabban Gamliel the honor of the Torah ceased.

One verse (*Devarim* 9:9) states: *and I [Moshe] sat on the mountain* and [another] verse (ibid. 10:10) states: *and I [Moshe] stood on the mountain*. [How can this apparent contradiction be resolved?] Rav answered: He stood and learned and sat and reviewed. R. Chanina explained: He neither stood or sat — rather he was bent over [and both terms can therefore be applied to Moshe and there is no contradiction]. R. Yochanan explained: The word *sat* should be understood as stayed, as the verse (ibid. 1:46) states: *and they [Israel] sat at Kadesh many days* [i.e., they encamped and stayed there]. Rava explained: [For] the easy [parts] he

---

549 - I.e., the sources of the obligation are the *takanos* of Moshe and Ezra who enacted them to insure a minimum of Torah learning.

550 - *Orach Chaim* 690:1.

551 - Some texts read Rabban Gamliel *ha-Zaken* (the elder) who was a grandson of Hillel, in contradistinction to his grandson who is sometimes referred to as Rabban Gamliel of Yavne. The former was a contemporary of R. Akiva while the latter followed him. This change is consistent with the parallel text in the *Mishnah* (*Sotah* 49a) and explains how that *Mishnah* could associate the cessation of honor for the Torah with the deaths of both R. Akiva and Rabban Gamliel.

stood, [for] the hard parts, he sat.[552]

COMMENTARY

Chidushei Gaonim poses an interesting question. The Talmud[553] notes that when Moshe taught Aharon the Torah, Aharon would come to Moshe's tent. When they had finished, Aharon would sit to Moshe's left and Aharon's sons would then enter. When they had finished, Elazar would sit to Moshe's right and Itamar would sit to the left of Aharon. *Rashi*[554] states specifically that they were seated while studying. Thus, the practice of sitting while learning would seem to date back to Moshe rather than to the period following the death of Rabban Gamliel.

TALMUD

פִּיסְקָא. בְּשֵׁנִי וּבַחֲמִישִׁי וּבְמִנְחָה בְּשַׁבָּת, קוֹרִין שְׁלֹשָׁה. כְּנֶגֶד מִי? אָמַר רַב אַסִי: כְּנֶגֶד תּוֹרָה, נְבִיאִים וּכְתוּבִים. רָבָא אָמַר: כְּנֶגֶד כֹּהֲנִים, לְוִיִּם וְיִשְׂרְאֵלִים.

TRANSLATION

MISHNAH: On Monday, Thursday and at *Minchah* on Shabbos, three people are called [up to the Torah]. **[21b] TALMUD:** To whom do they correspond?[555] R. Asi taught: [The number] corresponds to the Torah, *Nevi'im* and *Kesuvim*. Rava explained: [The number] corresponds to *kohanim*, Levites and Israelites.

COMMENTARY

The Talmud[556] explains that the reading of the Torah was a *takanah* of both Moshe and Ezra. Originally, Moshe ordained that the Torah be read on Mondays and Thursdays so that three days not pass without Torah study. This reading was

---

552 - R. Chaim Volozhin (נפש החיים שער ד' פ״ג) comments that when the Sages saw that the generation was weak, they permitted them to be seated while studying, for they were more concerned with the quality of Torah study than external signs of respect.

553 - עירובין נד:.

554 - שם ד״ה נכנס אהרון.

555 - The Talmud predicates the ensuing discussion on the axiom that the number of people called up to the Torah was not chosen arbitrarily. It therefore seeks to determine on what basis it was decided to call up three people for the readings on Monday, Thursday and at *Minchah* on Shabbos.

556 - בבא קמא פב:.

done by one person who read three verses or possibly by three people who read three verses each. Later, Ezra ordained that the Torah also was to be read at *Minchah* on Shabbos and that the reading be expanded to a minimum of ten verses read by three people. Interestingly, the Talmud there does not cite the reason offered by R. Asi but does cite the explanation offered by Rava as an anonymous opinion.

We might conjecture that the Talmud does not cite R. Asi's opinion there since there is an opinion cited that the practice of calling three people to the Torah dates back to Moshe. According to this opinion, the practice of calling three people could not have been instituted to correspond to the three parts of *Tanach* since in the time of Moshe there was only Torah. Our text however might well hold that the practice of calling three people was introduced by Ezra who might have done so to correspond to the three parts of *Tanach* that were established by the Great Assembly of which he was a member.

TALMUD

אֶלָּא הָא דְּתָנֵי רַב שִׁימִי: אֵין פּוֹחֲתִין מֵעֲשָׂרָה פְּסוּקִים בְּבֵית הַכְּנֶסֶת, "וַיְדַבֵּר" עוֹלֶה מִן הַמִּנְיָן. הַנֵי עֲשָׂרָה כְּנֶגֶד מִי? אָמַר רַבִּי יְהוֹשֻׁעַ בֶּן לֵוִי: כְּנֶגֶד עֲשָׂרָה בַּטְלָנִין שֶׁבְּבֵית הַכְּנֶסֶת. רַב יוֹסֵף אָמַר: כְּנֶגֶד עֲשֶׂרֶת הַדִּבְּרוֹת שֶׁנֶּאֶמְרוּ לְמֹשֶׁה בְּסִינַי. רַבִּי לֵוִי אָמַר: כְּנֶגֶד עֲשָׂרָה הִלּוּלִין שֶׁאָמַר דָּוִד בְּסֵפֶר תְּהִלִּים. וְרַבִּי יוֹחָנָן אָמַר: כְּנֶגֶד עֲשָׂרָה מַאֲמָרוֹת שֶׁבָּהֶן נִבְרָא הָעוֹלָם, וְהֵי נִינְהוּ? "וַיֹּאמֶר" דִּבְרֵאשִׁית, הַנֵי – תִּשְׁעָה הֲווּ? "בְּרֵאשִׁית" נַמֵּי מַאֲמָר הוּא, דִּכְתִיב: "בִּדְבַר ה' שָׁמַיִם נַעֲשׂוּ, וּבְרוּחַ פִּיו כָּל צְבָאָם".

TRANSLATION

What of that which we learned in a *beraisa* taught by R. Simi: We do not [read] less than ten verses [when reading the Torah] in the synagogue. To what do these ten correspond? R. Yehoshua ben Levi explained: They correspond to the ten *batlanim*[557] in the synagogue. R. Yosef explained: They correspond to the ten statements that were said to Moshe at Sinai. R. Levi explained: They correspond

---

557 - *Batlanim* are literally people who do not work. The Talmud (*Bava Kama* 82a) writes that every town should have a *minyan* of *batlanim* who sacrifice their own work and are supported by communal funds so that they might be available at all times to deal with the community's spiritual needs. Since ten is the minimum number that can be called an important congregation, Ezra ordained that the minimum number of verses read also be ten to emphasize the importance of the reading.

to the ten *hallelus* that David said in *Tehillim* [i.e., in Psalm 150]. R. Yochanan explained. They correspond to the ten declarations through which the world was created.[558] And what are these [ten declarations]? [The ten times that the Torah states] *And He said in* [*parashas*] *Bereishis*. There are only nine? [The word] *Bereishis* is also a declaration [of Creation], for the verse (*Tehillim* 33:6) states: *With the word of God the heavens were made and with the spirit of His breath all of its hosts.*[559]

TALMUD

אָמַר רָבָא: רִאשׁוֹן שֶׁקָּרָא אַרְבָּעָה - מְשֻׁבָּח. שֵׁנִי שֶׁקָּרָא אַרְבָּעָה - מְשֻׁבָּח. שְׁלִישִׁי שֶׁקָּרָא אַרְבָּעָה - מְשֻׁבָּח.

רִאשׁוֹן שֶׁקָּרָא אַרְבָּעָה מְשֻׁבָּח, דִּתְנַן: בְּשָׁלֹשׁ קֻפּוֹת שֶׁל שָׁלֹשׁ סְאִין, שֶׁבָּהֶן תּוֹרְמִין אֶת הַלִּשְׁכָּה, וְהָיָה כָתוּב עֲלֵיהֶן: א' ב' ג', לֵידַע אֵיזוֹ מֵהֶן נִתְרְמָה רִאשׁוֹן, לְהַקְרִיב מִמֶּנָּה רִאשׁוֹן, שֶׁמִּצְוָה בָּרִאשׁוֹן.

אֶמְצָעִי שֶׁקָּרָא אַרְבָּעָה מְשֻׁבָּח, דִּתְנַיָא: "אֶל מוּל פְּנֵי הַמְּנוֹרָה יָאִירוּ", מְלַמֵּד שֶׁמְּצַדֵּד פְּנֵיהֶם כְּלַפֵּי נֵר מַעֲרָבִי, וְנֵר מַעֲרָבִי כְּלַפֵּי שְׁכִינָה. וְאָמַר רַבִּי יוֹחָנָן: מִכָּאן שֶׁאֶמְצָעִי מְשֻׁבָּח.

וְאַחֲרוֹן שֶׁקָּרָא אַרְבָּעָה מְשֻׁבָּח, מִשּׁוּם - "מַעֲלִין בַּקֹּדֶשׁ וְלֹא מוֹרִידִין".

רַב פַּפָּא אִיקְלַע לְבֵי כְּנִישְׁתָּא דְּאַבֵּי גּוּבַר, וְקָרָא רִאשׁוֹן - אַרְבָּעָה, וְשַׁבְּחֵיהּ רַב פַּפָּא.

TRANSLATION

Rava taught: [If] the first [person called to read from the Torah] read four [verses],

---

558 - See *Avos* 5:1.

559 - The first verse states בראשית ברא אלקים את השמים וכו' — *In the beginning God created the heavens* ... Based on the verse in *Tehillim*, we see that this act of creation was also accomplished through the word of God. Thus, the word בראשית is to be understood as a declaration of creation as well.

In his commentary to Avos (דרך חיים), *Maharal* asks why the Torah does not state *And God said let there be a heaven and an earth* since the Talmud holds that the first act of Creation was also accomplished through the word of God. He answers that since we can not comprehend that which preceded Creation, the Torah saw fit to present Creation as an accomplished fact. Compare to *Chagigah* 11b — *One who dwells upon one of these four things, it is better that he not have come into the world: that which is above and that which is below, that which is before [Creation] and that which is after.*

that is praiseworthy.[560] [If] the second [person called to the Torah] read four verses, that is praiseworthy. [If] the third [person called to the Torah] read four verses, that is praiseworthy.

[If] the first [person called to read from the Torah] read four [verses], that is praiseworthy — [what is the source for this?] We learned in a *Mishnah*:[561] The *shekalim* [taken from] the office [of the *Beis ha-Mikdash*] were placed in three baskets of three *sa'im*. They [the baskets] were marked as *aleph, beis* and *gimmel* so that it could be determined which [*shekalim*] had been donated first so as to [purchase an animal] for the [public] sacrifices from the one [that had been donated] first, for it is a mitzvah [to take from the] first.[562]

[If] the middle [person called to the Torah] read four verses, that is praiseworthy — [what is the source for this?] We learned in a *beraisa*: [The verse (*Bamidbar* 8:2) states:] *Facing the middle of the menorah they shall illuminate* — this teaches us that he [the *kohen*] bends the wicks to face the western [i.e., the middle] lamp, and the western lamp was bent to face the *Shechinah*. R. Yochanan taught: From this [we see] that the middle is praiseworthy.[563]

[If] the last [person called to the Torah] read four verses, that is praiseworthy — [what is the source for this?] Because we ascend in sanctification and do not descend.[564]

R. Pappa happened [to come] to the synagogue in Abei Gubar and the first

---

560 - I.e., there is a basis for honoring the first person called to the Torah. A minimum of ten verses must be read every time the Torah is read publicly. Since three people are called up on Mondays, Thursdays and at *Minchah* on Shabbos, one of those called will read at least one verse more than the other two.

561 - שקלים ג:ב.

562 - We see from this *Mishnah* that the first of a series has special status. We can thus assume that in the case of reading from the Torah, the first one called also enjoys special status and should be honored by being given four verses to read.

563 - The seven branched *menorah* used in the *Beis ha-Mikdash* was placed on the southern side of the Sanctuary. The middle branch was referred to as the western lamp since its wick was pointed towards the *kodesh ha-kedoshim* — the Holy of Holies — which was on the west side of the Sanctuary. Thus the three wicks on the left and the three wicks on the right all faced toward the middle which shows that something that is in the middle has special status.

564 - I.e., when we have a number of acts to perform, we perform the most sanctified act last. There are thus grounds to save the reading of four verses for the last person called to read the Torah.

[person called to the Torah there] read four verses and R. Pappa praised him.

COMMENTARY

In discussing the concept of מעלין בקדש — performing a more sanctified act after a less sanctified one — Ramchal[565] explains that if one exercises self-control and cleaves to God, he will be in a continuous state of ascension and will raise his surroundings with him. Thus, if one performs a mitzvah, he raises the level of the world to a greater level of sanctity. Hence, when faced with a number of opportunities, one should also perform them in ascending order.

If the Talmud provided sources that supported the practice of honoring any one of the three people called up to the Torah with the reading of four verses, why did R. Pappa praise the man in the synagogue in Abei Gubar?

Maharsha explains that there is an additional reason for honoring the first person called, the Talmudic dictum[566] of זריזים מקדימים למצוות — *the diligent fulfill mitzvos as quickly as possible.* Though grounds can be found for giving this honor to anyone of the three, R. Pappa was pleased that the members of the synagogue in Abei Gubar chose to fulfill this dictum.

TALMUD

אָמַר רַבִּי אֶלְעָזָר: אֵין אָדָם חָשׁוּב רַשַּׁאי לִפֹּל עַל פָּנָיו, אֶלָּא אִם כֵּן נַעֲנָה כִּיהוֹשֻׁעַ בֶּן נוּן, דִּכְתִיב: "וַיֹּאמֶר ה' אֶל יְהוֹשֻׁעַ" קָם לָךְ" וְגוֹ'. תָּנוּ רַבָּנָן: "קִדָּה" - עַל אַפַּיִם, שֶׁנֶּאֱמַר: "וַתִּקֹּד בַּת שֶׁבַע אַפַּיִם אָרֶץ". "כְּרִיעָה" - עַל בִּרְכַּיִם, וְכֵן הוּא אוֹמֵר: "מִכְּרֹעַ עַל בִּרְכָּיו". "הִשְׁתַּחֲוָאָה" - זוֹ פְשׁוּט יָדַיִם וְרַגְלַיִם, שֶׁנֶּאֱמַר: "הֲבוֹא נָבוֹא אֲנִי וְאִמְּךָ וְאַחֶיךָ לְהִשְׁתַּחֲוֹת לְךָ אָרְצָה?!".

TRANSLATION

[22b] R. Elazar taught: An important person is not permitted to prostrate himself [in prayer] unless he is certain that he will be answered as was Yehoshua bin Nun, as the verse (*Yehoshua* 7:10) states: *And God said to Yehoshua, arise ...*
The Sages taught: [Wherever the term] קידה — bowing [is used, it refers to] facing downwards, as the verse (*Melachim* I 1:31) states: *And Bas-sheva bowed her face toward the ground.* [Wherever the term] כריעה— kneeling [is used, it refers to standing on] the knees, as the verse (ibid. 8:54) states: *kneeling on his*

---

565 - מסילת ישרים פי"א.
566 - See *Pesachim* 4a.

knees. [Wherever the term] השתחואה — prostration [is used, it refers to] laying completely face down, as the verse (*Bereishis* 37:10) states: *Will I, your mother and your brothers come and prostrate ourselves on the ground before you?*

TALMUD

פִּיסְקָא. בְּשֵׁנִי וּבַחֲמִישִׁי וּבְשַׁבָּת בְּמִנְחָה קוֹרִין שְׁלֹשָׁה כו'. בְּרֹאשׁ חֹדֶשׁ וּבְחֻלּוֹ שֶׁל מוֹעֵד, קוֹרִין אַרְבָּעָה כו'. בְּיוֹם טוֹב חֲמִשָּׁה, בְּיוֹם הַכִּפּוּרִים שִׁשָּׁה, בְּשַׁבָּת שִׁבְעָה כו'.

הָנֵי: שְׁלֹשָׁה, חֲמִשָּׁה, שִׁבְעָה, כְּנֶגֶד מִי? פְּלִיגֵי בָּהּ רַבִּי יִצְחָק בַּר נַחֲמָנִי וְחַד דְּעַמֵּיהּ, וּמַנּוּ? רַבִּי שִׁמְעוֹן בֶּן פָּזִי, וְאָמְרִי לָהּ: רַבִּי שִׁמְעוֹן בֶּן פָּזִי וְחַד דְּעַמֵּיהּ, וּמַנּוּ? רַבִּי יִצְחָק בַּר נַחֲמָנִי. וְאָמְרִי לָהּ: רַבִּי שְׁמוּאֵל בַּר נַחֲמָנִי. חַד אָמַר: כְּנֶגֶד "בִּרְכַּת כֹּהֲנִים". וְחַד אָמַר: כְּנֶגֶד "שְׁלֹשָׁה שׁוֹמְרֵי הַסַּף", "חֲמִשָּׁה מֵרוֹאֵי פְנֵי הַמֶּלֶךְ", "וְשִׁבְעָה רוֹאֵי פְנֵי הַמֶּלֶךְ".

TRANSLATION

MISHNAH: On Monday, Thursday and at *Minchah* on Shabbos three people are called [to the Torah]. On *Rosh Chodesh* and on *Chol ha-Moed*, four people are called. On Holidays, five people are called. On Yom Kippur, six people are called. On Shabbos, seven people are called.

[23a] TALMUD: These three, five and seven [people called to the Torah on weekdays, on Holidays and on Shabbos respectively] — to what do [these numbers] correspond?[567] R. Yitzchak bar Nachmani and one of the people disagreed [on this subject]. And who was this [person referred to as one of the people]? R. Shimon ben Pazi. Some say [that the dispute was between] R. Shimon ben Pazi and one of the people. And who was this [person referred to as one of the people]? R. Yitzchak bar Nachmani and some say R. Shmuel bar Nachmani. One said: [The numbers] correspond to the priestly blessing.[568] One said: [The numbers] correspond to the three guards of the gate,[569] five of those [officials] who attend

567 - The Talmud goes on to ask to what the six people called on Yom Kippur correspond. *Tosafos* (ד״ה הני שלשה) notes that regarding the four people called on *Rosh Chodesh* and *Chol ha-Moed*, however, the Talmud does not raise this question. He explains that the Talmud assumed that since *Musaf* is added on these days, it is obvious that they are more sanctified than regular weekdays and it is therefore logical that an additional person be called up to the Torah.

568 - The priestly blessing (*Bamidbar* 6:24-26) is made up of three verses. The first verse has three words, the second has five and the last has seven.

569 - See *Melachim* II 25:18.

the king[570] and the seven [officials] who attend the king.[571]

COMMENTARY

As we have noted, the numbers used in halachic requirements or in describing events are not arbitrarily chosen but have meanings of their own. Thus, not only do the words of the priestly blessing have cosmic significance; so do the number of sentences, the number of words in each sentence and even the number of letters in each word. The first opinion cited links the priestly blessing and the Torah reading and maintains that the number of the latter should follow those used in the former.

The second opinion in the Talmud links the number of the people called to the Torah to the number of officials that serve mortal kings. The least important officials — those who guard the gate and control entrance to the king — are linked to the weekday Torah reading which is considered to be less important than the reading on Festivals or Shabbos since the weekdays are less holy.

Ritva writes that the Talmud assumed that an additional person should be called to the Torah corresponding to the increased sanctity of the days. Thus, once it was established that a minimum of three people must be called up, it was obvious that four should be called on *Rosh Chodesh* or *Chol ha-Moed* which have more sanctity than weekdays, five should be called on the Festivals which have even more sanctity, six on Yom Kippur which has more sanctity and seven on Shabbos which has the highest degree of sanctity. The linkage of these numbers to either the priestly blessing or the number of officers who serve a king was simply a means of providing a Scriptural allusion to support an already known practice that is based on common sense.[572]

TALMUD

תָּנֵי רַב יוֹסֵף: שְׁלֹשָׁה, חֲמִשָּׁה, וְשִׁבְעָה. שְׁלֹשָׁה שׁוֹמְרֵי הַסַּף. חֲמִשָּׁה מֵרוֹאֵי פְּנֵי הַמֶּלֶךְ. שִׁבְעָה רוֹאֵי פְּנֵי הַמֶּלֶךְ. אָמַר לוֹ אַבַּיֵי: עַד הָאִידָנָא מַאי טַעְמָא לֹא

---

570 - Ibid.

571 - According to *Rashi*, the reference is to *Esther* 1:14. *Tosafos* questions why the Talmud would link the number of people called to the Torah to the number of officials who served a wicked king. He therefore maintains that the reference is to the seven mentioned in *Yirmiyahu* 52:25. According to the *Yerushalmi,* the additional two officials mentioned there were the palace scribes.

572 - *Tosafos Rid* adds that the Talmud was therefore not troubled by the fact that thre is no allusion to the practice of caling four people up on *Rosh Chodesh.*

פָּרִישׁ לָן מָר? אָמַר לוֹ: לָא הֲוָה יָדַעְנָא דִּצְרִיכִיתוּ לִי, וּמִי בָּעֵיתוּ מִינַּאי מִלְתָא
וְלָא אָמְרֵי לְכוּ?!

אָמַר לוֹ יַעֲקֹב מִינָאָה לְרַב יְהוּדָה: הַנֵּי שִׁשָּׁה דְיוֹם הַכִּפּוּרִים כְּנֶגֶד מִי? אָמַר
לוֹ: כְּנֶגֶד שִׁשָּׁה שֶׁעָמְדוּ מִימִינוֹ שֶׁל עֶזְרָא, וְשִׁשָּׁה מִשְּׂמֹאלוֹ, שֶׁנֶּאֱמַר: "וַיַּעֲמֹד
עֶזְרָא הַסֹּפֵר עַל מִגְדַּל עֵץ אֲשֶׁר עָשׂוּ לַדָּבָר, וַיַּעֲמֹד אֶצְלוֹ: מַתִּתְיָה, וְשֶׁמַע,
וַעֲנָיָה, וְאוּרִיָּה, וְחִלְקִיָּה, וּמַעֲשֵׂיָה עַל יְמִינוֹ. וּמִשְּׂמֹאלוֹ: פְּדָיָה, וּמִישָׁאֵל,
וּמַלְכִּיָּה, וְחָשֻׁם, וְחַשְׁבַּדָּנָה, זְכַרְיָה, מְשֻׁלָּם". הַנֵּי, שִׁבְעָה הֲווּ! הַיְינוּ "זְכַרְיָה",
הַיְינוּ "מְשֻׁלָּם", וְאַמַּאי קָרֵי לֵיהּ "מְשֻׁלָּם"? דִּמְשַׁלָּם בְּעוֹבָדֵיהּ.

TRANSLATION

R. Yosef taught: The three, five and seven [called to the Torah on weekdays,
Festivals and Shabbos respectively] correspond to the three guards of the gate, the
five [officials] who attend the king and the seven [officials] who attend the king.

Abbaye said to him: Why didn't the master explain this to us until now? He
answered: I didn't know that you needed me to explain this. Did you ever ask me
something and I did not explain it?

Yaakov Mina'a[573] asked R. Yehudah: The six [people called to the Torah] on
Yom Kippur — to what [does that number] correspond? He answered: To the six
[important people] who stood at Ezra's right and to the six who stood at his left
[when he read the Torah to the people]. As the verse (*Nechemiah* 8:4) states: *And
Ezra stood on a wood platform which was made for this purpose, and [the
following people] stood beside him — Matisyah, Shema, Anayah, Uriah,
Chilkiyah and Ma'aseyah on his right and on his left, Pedayah, Mishael,
Malkiyah, Chusham, Chashbadanah, Zecharyah and Meshulam.* There are seven
[people listed on his left, not six]! This is Zecharyah and this is Meshulam [i.e.,
they are the same person].[574] And why was he called Meshulam [if his name was

---

573 - The name מינאה implies that he was a מין — a heretic. *Tosafos* changes the text
to read יעקב מצעה, noting that were he truly a heretic, he would not have been
mentioned by name.

574 - Previously (page 170), the Talmud proved that Mordechai and Malachi could
not be identical since both are mentioned in a *beraisa*. Here the Talmud finds no
problem in identifying Zecharyah as Meshulam though both are listed. *Maharsha*
writes that in this case, the two names are brought without a conjunctive *vav* between
them.

Zecharyah]? Because he was complete in his acts.[575]

TALMUD

מִשְׁנָה. סוּמָא פּוֹרֵס עַל שְׁמַע, וּמְתַרְגֵּם. רַבִּי יְהוּדָה אוֹמֵר: כָּל מִי שֶׁלֹּא רָאָה מְאוֹרוֹת מִיָּמָיו, לֹא יִפְרֹס עַל שְׁמָע.

גְּמָרָא. תַּנְיָא: אָמְרוּ לוֹ לְרַבִּי יְהוּדָה: וַהֲלֹא הַרְבֵּה צָפוּ לִדְרֹשׁ בַּמֶּרְכָּבָה, וְלֹא רָאוּ אוֹתָהּ מִימֵיהֶם?! וְרַבִּי יְהוּדָה? הָתָם – בַּאֲבַנְתָּא דְּלִבָּא תַּלְיָא מִילְּתָא, וְהָא קָא מְכַוֵּין וְיָדַע. הָכָא – מִשּׁוּם הֲנָאָה הוּא, וְהָא לֵית לֵיהּ הֲנָאָה. וְרַבָּנַן? אִית לֵיהּ הֲנָאָה, כִּדְרַבִּי יוֹסֵי, דְּתַנְיָא, אָמַר רַבִּי יוֹסֵי כָּל יָמַי הָיִיתִי מִצְטַעֵר עַל מִקְרָא זֶה: "וְהָיִיתָ מְמַשֵּׁשׁ בַּצׇּהֳרַיִם, כַּאֲשֶׁר יְמַשֵּׁשׁ הָעִוֵּר בָּאֲפֵלָה", וְכִי מַאי אִיכְפַּת לֵיהּ לָעִוֵּר בֵּין אֲפֵלָה לְאוֹרָה? עַד שֶׁבָּא מַעֲשֶׂה לְיָדִי, פַּעַם אַחַת הָיִיתִי מְהַלֵּךְ בְּאִישׁוֹן לַיְלָה וַאֲפֵלָה, וְרָאִיתִי סוּמָא שֶׁהָיָה מְהַלֵּךְ בַּדֶּרֶךְ, וַאֲבוּקָה בְּיָדוֹ. אָמַרְתִּי לוֹ: בְּנִי, אֲבוּקָה זוֹ לָמָּה לְּךָ? אָמַר לִי: כָּל זְמַן שֶׁאֲבוּקָה בְּיָדִי, בְּנֵי אָדָם רוֹאִים אוֹתִי, וּמַצִּילִין אוֹתִי מִן הַפְּחָתִים, וּמִן הַקּוֹצִים, וּמִן הַבַּרְקָנִים.

TRANSLATION

[24a] MISHNAH: A blind person may [recite the] *berachos* that precede the *Shema*[576] and may translate [the Torah reading into Aramaic]. R. Yehudah said: One who has never seen light may not [recite the] *berachos* that precede the *Shema*.[577]

[24b] TALMUD: We learned in a *beraisa*: They said to R. Yehudah: But did

---

575 - I.e., he was also referrred to as Meshulam since he was מושלם — *complete* or *without imperfection* — in his actions.

576 - The literal translation of פורס על שמע is to divide the *berachos* of the *Shema*. For clarity's sake, we have chosen to use an explanation instead of a translation in this case. It should be noted that *Hagaos Maimonis* (הלכות תפילה ח:ה) writes that the word פורס in Aramaic means to bless.

In Talmudic times, if ten people came into the synagogue after the *Shema* had been recited, the custom was for one person to recite the *berachah* of יוצר המאורות that precedes the *Shema* on behalf of the entire congregation. This person was referred to as the one who was פורס על השמע.

577 - R. Yehudah maintained that since a blind person cannot see light, he cannot recite the *berachah* so as to fulfill someone else's obligation. See *Rosh Hashanah* 29a — *One who is not obligated in an action, cannot fulfill the obligation of the congregation [to perform that action]*.

not many see fit to expound on the [Celestial] chariot[578] and they had never seen it [i.e., they expounded though they lacked prophetic vision]?[579] [How did] R. Yehudah [explain the difference, since this would seem to imply that one can speak about events or things that one has not personally experienced]? There [i.e., the prophetic vision of Yechezkel] the matter depends on one's understanding, and they [the Sages who expounded] could concentrate and [thereby] understand. Here [regarding the *berachah* on light which precedes the *Shema*, the purpose of the *berachah* is to express thanks for] the benefit [that one has from light]. He [a blind man] has no benefit [and thus cannot recite the *berachah*]. [How then do the] Sages [maintain that a blind man can recite the *berachah*]? He [a blind man] has benefit [from light] as we see from [the teching of] R. Yosi. We learned in a *beraisa*: R. Yosi said: My whole life I was troubled by this verse (*Devarim* 28:29): *And you shall grope in the afternoon like the blind man gropes in the dark*. What difference does it make to a blind man if it is light or dark [i.e., why does the verse specify *as a blind man gropes in the dark*]? [I could not understand] until [I had] the following experience. I was once walking in the middle of a dark night and I saw a blind man walking on the road with a torch in his hand. I asked him: "My child, of what use is the torch to you?" He answered: "As long as the torch is in my hand, people see me and save me from openings [in the road], thorns and briars."

TALMUD

אָמַר רַב אַסִי: חֵיפָנֵי וּבֵישָׁנֵי לֹא יִשָּׂא אֶת כַּפָּיו. תַּנְיָא נַמִי הָכֵי: אֵין מוֹרִידִין לִפְנֵי הַתֵּבָה, לֹא אַנְשֵׁי בֵית שְׁאָן, וְלֹא אַנְשֵׁי בֵית חֵיפָה, וְלֹא אַנְשֵׁי טִבְעוֹנִין, מִפְּנֵי שֶׁקּוֹרִין לְ"אָלְפִין" "עַיְנִין", וּלְ"עַיְנִין" "אָלְפִין".

TRANSLATION

R. Asi taught: One [i.e., a *kohen*] who comes from Haifa or from Beis Shean should not raise his hands [for the priestly blessing]. There is a *beraisa* that also says this: We do not send before the [prayer] stand people from Beis Shean nor

---

578 - I.e., the prophetic vision of Yechezkel. *Rambam* (הלכות יסודי התורה ב:יא) writes that the term מעשה מרכבה is used as a general description for all discussions related to the essence of God.

579 - *Ritva* explains that just as the Sages were able to expound upon the vision of Yechezkel without themselves having witnessed it, so too can a blind man recite the blessing on light even though he has never seen it.

from Haifa nor from Tivonin because they read *aleph* as *ayin* and *ayin* as *aleph*.

COMMENTARY

The efficacy of the priestly blessing is dependent upon the people hearing the blessing of God as transmitted through the *kohanim*. If the *kohen* were to mispronounce these blessings — e.g., by failing to differentiate between an *aleph* and an *ayin* for example — the congregation would be distracted. For this very reason, a *kohen* who has a physical imperfection may also not ascend to recite the priestly blessing, for the congregation might well focus on his imperfections and thus fail to concentrate on the words of the blessing.[580]

Chafetz Chaim[581] writes that the Talmud's limitation only applies to *kohanim* from Haifa or Beis Shean who sought to ascend in other cities. In Haifa or Beis Shean, where the failure to properly enunciate the letters was common, there would be no grounds for ruling that they should not recite the priestly blessing, for their mispronunciations would not cause people to be distracted since everyone there made the same mistakes. He adds that today, when people are no longer careful to enunciate Hebrew correctly, *kohanim* may recite the priestly blessing even if they make mistakes in pronunciation.

TALMUD

מִשְׁנָה. הָאוֹמֵר: "יְבָרְכוּךְ כו'. עַל קַן צִפּוֹר יַגִּיעוּ רַחֲמֶיךָ" כו', מְשַׁתְּקִין אוֹתוֹ. גְּמָרָא. מַאי טַעְמָא? פְּלִיגֵי בָהּ תְּרֵי אֲמוֹרָאֵי בְּמַעֲרָבָא, רַבִּי יוֹסֵי בַּר אָבִין, וְרַבִּי יוֹסֵי בַּר זְבִידָא. חַד אֲמַר: מִפְּנֵי שֶׁמַּטִּיל קִנְאָה בְּמַעֲשֵׂה בְרֵאשִׁית, וְחַד אֲמַר: מִפְּנֵי שֶׁעוֹשֶׂה מִדּוֹתָיו שֶׁל הַקָּדוֹשׁ בָּרוּךְ הוּא רַחֲמִים, וְאֵינָן אֶלָּא גְּזֵרוֹת.

TRANSLATION

[24b] **MISHNAH:**[582] One who says **[25a]** that good men shall bless you —

---

580 - The *Mishnah* (24b) rules specifically that *kohanim* who have physical defects on their hands are not to ascend for the priestly blessing. R. Yehudah adds that this includes *kohanim* whose hands are stained, explaining that the people will stare at them.

581 - משנה ברורה, סי' קכ"ח ס"ק קי"כ.

582 - *Ein Yaakov* only quotes part of the text of this *Mishnah* and omits the Talmud's opening statement which explains why this is considered heretical.

[this is heresy].[583] [One who says] Your mercy extends to a bird's nest — he is silenced. **TALMUD:** What is the reason [that we silence him if he makes the second statement]? It [the reason] was the source of a dispute between two *tannaim* in the west [i.e., in the Land of Israel] — R. Yosi bar Abin and R. Yosi bar Zvida. One said: Because he creates jealousy among those created.[584] One said: Because he makes God's traits mercy and they are decrees.[585]

COMMENTARY

God's aim, as it were, in creating man is to bring mankind to believe in His unity. The mission of the Jewish people is to further that aim by leading man to recognize and accept this fundamental truth. Hence, the major effort of the power of evil in this world is to distort this truth and lead man astray by filling his heart with doubts regarding God's unity, by leading him to believe that good and evil represent two separate forces, by bringing him to deny the existence of Providence, to accept the materialistic theory that the world is governed by natural law and that there is no guiding hand directing history.[586]

It is for this reason that the Sages were extremely careful to silence any statement that might reflect these views — even if they were innocently included as part of heartfelt prayer.

Ran[587] explains that the first statement cited in the *Mishnah* is considered to be heretical for it reflects the Zorastrian belief in two separate Divine authorities: one that guides good people and one that guides the wicked. *Rabbenu Yonah* writes that it is considered heretical because it implies that only the righteous may bless God, whereas the wicked are also required to do so.

---

583 - Compare the text here with the similar text in *Berachos* 5:3 where the *Mishnah* adds "he is silenced." In the text brought in editions of the *Mishnah* and Talmud, the text here states "this is heresy" and we have therefore added it in brackets. Some editions of the *Mishnah* state "this is the way of the Sadducees."

584 - *Rashi* (ד״ה מטיל קנאה) explains that he implies that God has mercy on birds but does not have mercy on other animals. He is thus accusing God of maintaining a double standard.

585 - *Rashi* (ד״ה ואינן אלא גזירות) explains that he implies that the reason why we are obligated to fulfill the mitzvos is not because they are Divine decrees, but rather because we can attribute a moral value to them.

586 - See דעת תבונות סימן ל״ו.

587 - See also *Pnei Moshe* on the *Mishnah* as cited in the *Yerushalmi*.

Meiri adds that the Sages objected to this statement because it suggests that God seeks the service of the righteous alone and has no desire for the wicked to change their ways.[588]

As regards the second statement, *Rambam*[589] writes: *If one says, as part of his pleading [to God for mercy]: He who has mercy on the bird's nest and ordained that the children not be taken while their mother is present [may He have mercy on me] or if he says, He who commanded us not to slaughter an animal and its child on the same day shall have mercy upon us or similar statements, he is silenced. [The reason is] because these mitzvos are Divine decrees and [their source is] not mercy. If they were [ordained] because of mercy, He would not have permitted us to slaughter at all.*

Ramban[590] comments that we are permitted to derive moral lessons from the commandments — e.g., by assuming that the fulfillment of this mitzvah teaches us to be merciful. However, we have no right to claim that God's motivation in commanding us to fulfill this mitzvah is because He wanted to be merciful. Our perception of mercy or morality has no bearing on God. Were we to attribute human values to Him, we would be guilty of heresy, for we would then allow ourselves to violate or ignore those mitzvos that are inconsistent with our perception.

TALMUD

הָאוֹמֵר: "וּמִזַּרְעֲךָ לֹא תִתֵּן לְהַעֲבִיר" וכו'. תָּנָא דְּבֵי רַבִּי יִשְׁמָעֵאל: בְּיִשְׂרָאֵל הַבָּא עַל הַגּוֹיָה וְהוֹלִיד מִמֶּנָּה בֵן לַעֲבוֹדָה זָרָה, הַכָּתוּב מְדַבֵּר.

TRANSLATION

MISHNAH: One who says [that the verse (*Vayikra* 18:21) that states:] *And you shall not give your children over to Molech* ... **TALMUD:** It was taught in the school of R. Yishmael: [He is silenced if he explains] that the verse is referring to an Israelite who has relations with a gentile and bears a son from her who

---

588 - *Tosafos ha-Rosh* maintains that the statement is only silenced if it is said in prayer, for then it might be misconstrued. He notes that *Rabbenu Tam* used this statement at the conclusion of his personal correspondence.

589 - הלכות תפילה ט:ז.

590 - Commentary to *Devarim* 22:6.

worships idolatry.[591]

COMMENTARY

Rashi explains that this statement is silenced because his distortion of the text will cause him to rule that one who has relations with a gentile woman is guilty of a capital crime which is halachically untrue. *Maharsha*, quoting *Aruch*, explains that the school of R. Yishmael added that he is silenced because his distortion will lead him to conclude that relations with a gentile woman are only forbidden if she will bear children who worship idolatry.

TALMUD

תָּנוּ רַבָּנָן: יֵשׁ נִקְרָאִים וְלֹא מִתַּרְגְּמִין. יֵשׁ נִקְרָאִין וּמִתַּרְגְּמִין. וְיֵשׁ לֹא נִקְרָאִין וְלֹא מִתַּרְגְּמִין.

TRANSLATION

Our Sages taught: There are [portions of Scripture] that are read but not translated and there are [portions] that are read and translated and there are [portions] that are neither read nor translated.

COMMENTARY

When the Jews returned to the Land of Israel after their exile in Bavel, many had forgotten Hebrew and spoke a variety of dialects and languages.[592] In order to faciliate their understanding of the Torah reading, it became customary to translate the verses into Aramaic — their primary language. As Rambam[593] writes: *From the time of Ezra, it became customary to have a translator translate that which the Torah reader read so that they might understand the meaning. The reader would read one verse and would remain silent until it was translated ... the reader was not allowed to read more than one verse [at a time] for the translator.*

Given that any translation of the Torah can be a source for misunderstanding and based on the premise that this Aramaic translation was enacted to benefit the

591 - The *Mishnah* explains that he says: *and you shall not give of your seed to impregnate a gentile woman* — i.e., he translates זרע as seed rather than as referring to one's child. The *Mishnah* adds that this statement is silenced and the person making it is rebuked. It would seem that the reference is to the *meturgaman* — the person in the synagogue who translated the Torah verses into Aramaic.

592 - See *Nechemiah* 13:24 — *And their children, half spoke Ashdodis and did not know Yehudis.*

593 - הלכות תפילה יב:י.

common people who did not have the time or ability to delve deeply into the subject being read, the Sages decided that certain portions of the Torah should be read without being translated.

TALMUD

מַעֲשֵׂה־בְרֵאשִׁית', נִקְרָא וּמִתַּרְגֵּם. פְּשִׁיטָא! מַהוּ דְּתֵימָא, אָתוּ לְשַׁיּוּלֵי: מַה לְמַעְלָה? וּמַה לְמַטָּה? מַה לְפָנִים? וּמַה לְאָחוֹר? קָא מַשְׁמַע לָן.

מַעֲשֵׂה לוֹט וּשְׁתֵּי בְנוֹתָיו, נִקְרָא וּמִתַּרְגֵּם. פְּשִׁיטָא! מַהוּ דְּתֵימָא, נֵיחוֹשׁ לִכְבוֹדוֹ דְּאַבְרָהָם, קָמַשְׁמָע לָן.

מַעֲשֵׂה תָּמָר וִיהוּדָה, נִקְרָא וּמִתַּרְגֵּם. פְּשִׁיטָא? מַהוּ דְּתֵימָא, לֵיחוֹשׁ לִכְבוֹדוֹ דִּיהוּדָה, קָמַשְׁמַע לָן – שֶׁבַח הוּא לוֹ דְּאוֹדִי.

מַעֲשֵׂה הָעֵגֶל הָרִאשׁוֹן, נִקְרָא וּמִתַּרְגֵּם. פְּשִׁיטָא! מַהוּ דְּתֵימָא לֵיחוֹשׁ לִכְבוֹדָן שֶׁל יִשְׂרָאֵל, קָא מַשְׁמַע לָן – כָּל שֶׁכֵּן דְּנִיחָא לְהוּ, דְּהָוְיָא לְהוּ כַּפָּרָה.

קְלָלוֹת וּבְרָכוֹת, נִקְרָאִין וּמִתַּרְגְּמִין. פְּשִׁיטָא! מַהוּ דְּתֵימָא, נֵיחוֹשׁ דִּילְמָא פָּיְיגָא דַּעְתַּיְיהוּ דְּצִבּוּרָא, קָא מַשְׁמַע לָן.

אַזְהָרוֹת וַעֲנָשִׁים – נִקְרָאִין וּמִתַּרְגְּמִין. פְּשִׁיטָא! מַהוּ דְּתֵימָא, נֵיחוֹשׁ דִּילְמָא אָתוּ לְמֶעְבַּד מִיּרְאָה, קָא מַשְׁמַע לָן.

TRANSLATION

The acts of Creation[594] are read and translated [into Aramaic]. This is obvious! I might have thought [they should not be read or translated] because one might come to ask what is above and what is below [the universe], what was before [the Creation] and what is at the end [what will follow].[595] He [the *tanna*] therefore taught us this.

The incident of Lot and his two daughters[596] is read and is translated [into Aramaic]. This is obvious! I might have thought we should be concerned with Avraham's honor [and we should therefore omit reading or translating the incident that concerned his nephew]. He [the *tanna*] therefore taught us this.

The incident of Yehudah and Tamar[597] is read and is translated [into Aramaic]. This is obvious! I might have thought that we should be concerned with Yehuda's honor [since the incident casts him in a disparaging light]. He [the *tanna*]

594 - See *Bereishis* 1.
595 - See *Chagigah* 11b.
596 - See *Bereishis* 19:30-38.
597 - See *Bereishis* 38:1-26.

therefore taught us this — it is to his credit that he admitted [that he was culpable].

The first incident of the [golden] calf[598] is read and translated. This is obvious! I might have thought that we should be concerned with Israel's honor. He [the *tanna*] therefore taught us this — they [Israel] are surely willing [that the incident be read and translated for future generations], for they were forgiven [and subsequent generations will learn that they too can be forgiven their sins if they repent].[599]

The curses and blessings[600] are read and translated [into Aramaic]. This is obvious! I might have thought that we should be concerned that the congregation might become discouraged.[601] He [the *tanna*] therefore taught us this.

The warnings and punishments[602] are read and translated [into Aramaic]. This is obvious! I might have thought that they might be led to perform them [the mitzvos] out of awe [for God rather than out of love for God].[603] He [the *tanna*] therefore taught us this.

TALMUD

מַעֲשֵׂה אַמְנוֹן וְתָמָר, נִקְרָא וּמִתַּרְגֵּם, מַעֲשֵׂה אַבְשָׁלוֹם, נִקְרָא וּמִתַּרְגֵּם, פְּשִׁיטָא! מַהוּ דְּתֵימָא, לֵיחוּשׁ לִיקָרֵיהּ דְּדָוִד, קָא מַשְׁמַע לָן. מַעֲשֵׂה פִּילֶגֶשׁ בַּגִּבְעָה, נִקְרָא וּמִתַּרְגֵּם, פְּשִׁיטָא! מַהוּ דְּתֵימָא מַהוּ לֵיחוּשׁ לִכְבוֹדוֹ דְּבִנְיָמִין, קָא מַשְׁמַע לָן.

---

598 - See *Shemos* 32:1-6.

599 - The Talmud (עבודה זרה ד:) writes: *R. Yehoshua ben Levi taught: Israel only made the golden calf so as to provide a basis for those who repent.* Rashi explains that God allowed, as it were, Israel to sin so grievously so that people in future generations would not be overwhelmed by the enormity of their own shortcomings and conclude that repentance was impossible.

600 - See *Vayikra* 26 and *Devarim* 28.

601 - The *Midrash* (תנחומא, פרשת נצבים) recounts that when the Jews heard this *parashah* in the desert they indeed became discouraged, saying: Who can stand up to these curses? Moshe then came and reassured them that they would be capable.

602 - The reference would seem to be to all of the portions of the Torah where Scripture warns against sin and describes the punishment due one who transgresses rather than to a specific portion.

603 - Our bracketed edition follows *Rashi's* explanation. *Rahba* maintains that the reference must be to fear of punishment and love of reward, for one who serves God out of awe is considered to be completely righteous.

TRANSLATION

The incident of Amnon and Tamar[604] is read [as a *haftarah*] and translated.[605]
The incident of Avshalom[606] is read and translated. This is obvious! I might
have thought that we should be concerned with David's honor [since both
incidents are disparaging]. He [the *tanna*] therefore taught us this.

The incident of the concubine at Givah[607] is read [as a *haftarah*] and translated.
This is obvious! I might have thought that we should be concerned with the
honor of [the tribe of] Binyamin. He [the *tanna*] therefore taught us this.

TALMUD

"הוֹדַע אֶת יְרוּשָׁלַיִם אֶת תּוֹעֲבֹתֶיהָ", נִקְרָא וּמִתַּרְגֵּם, פְּשִׁיטָא! לַאֲפוּקֵי
מִדְּרַבִּי אֱלִיעֶזֶר, דְּתַנְיָא: מַעֲשֶׂה בְּאָדָם אֶחָד שֶׁהָיָה קוֹרֵא לְמַעְלָה מֵרַבִּי
אֱלִיעֶזֶר: "הוֹדַע אֶת יְרוּשָׁלַיִם אֶת תּוֹעֲבֹתֶיהָ", אָמַר לוֹ: עַד שֶׁאַתָּה בּוֹדֵק
בְּתוֹעֲבוֹת יְרוּשָׁלַיִם, צֵא בְּדֹק בְּתוֹעֲבוֹת אִמֶּךָ. בָּדְקוּ אַחֲרָיו, וּמָצְאוּ בּוֹ שֶׁמֶץ
פְּסוּל.

TRANSLATION

[The verses (*Yechezkel* 16) beginning with] *inform Jerusalem of her abominations*
are read [as a *haftarah*] and translated. This is obvious! This [teaching is brought]
to exclude the opinion of R. Eliezer, for we learned in a *beraisa*: It once
happened that a man was reading [from Yechezkel from the *bimah* which was]
above [the place of] R. Eliezer [and read] *inform Jerusalem of her abominations*.
He [R. Eliezer] told him: Before you examine Jerusalem's abominations, go out
and examine the abominations of your mother! They [the congregation]
examined his past [i.e., his lineage] and found a trace of impropriety.[608]

COMMENTARY

How did R. Eliezer know that the lineage of the person reading was tainted?

---

604 - See *Shmuel* II 13.

605 - This statement, as well as the ones regarding Avshalom, the concubine at
Giv'ah and the verse from Yechezkel, implies that it was customary for the
meturgeman to translate both the Torah reading *haftarah* and the *haftarah*.

606 - Ibid. 14.

607 - See *Shoftim* 20-21.

608 - See *Soferim* 9:11 where the Talmud informs us that they discovered that he was
a bastard.

We might conjecture that he based himself on the Talmudic[609] dictum that one who describes the faults of others, mentions the faults that he has. Because this person chose to publicly read the verses from the Book of *Yechezkel* which cast a disparaging light upon Jerusalem, R. Eliezer surmised that he was subconsciously giving voice to faults that he had as well. R. Eliezer therefore castigated him publicly, for he should have been more careful, as the subsequent investigation proved. Alternatively, R. Eliezer might have noticed that the man was emphasizing certain phrases and therefore understood that he was of less than pure lineage himself.[610] Rav Shlomo Volbe[611] adds that the man was obviously unaware of his tainted lineage, for had he known, he would have been extremely careful to prevent people from discovering the truth. His soul, however, knew and in a mysterious manner that we cannot understand, expressed its anguish by bringing him to read these verses from Yechezkel in public.

TALMUD

וְאֵלּוּ נִקְרָאִים וְלֹא מִתַּרְגְּמִין: מַעֲשֵׂה רְאוּבֵן, נִקְרָא וְלֹא מִתַּרְגֵּם. מַעֲשֶׂה בְּרַבִּי חֲנִינָא בֶּן גַּמְלִיאֵל שֶׁהָלַךְ לְכָבוּל, וְהָיָה קוֹרֵא חַזַּן הַכְּנֶסֶת: "וַיְהִי בִּשְׁכֹּן יִשְׂרָאֵל וְגו', וַיִּהְיוּ בְנֵי יַעֲקֹב שְׁנֵים עָשָׂר", אָמַר לוֹ לַמְּתַרְגְּמָן: אַל תְּתַרְגֵּם אֶלָּא אַחֲרוֹן, וְשִׁבְּחוּהוּ חֲכָמִים.

TRANSLATION

And these [portions] are read but are not translated: The incident of Reuven[612] is read but is not translated. It once happened that R. Chanina ben Gamliel went to Cabul and the reader for the congregation was reading [the verses (*Bereishis* 35:22-23)]: *And it was when Israel [Yaakov] encamped ... and Yaakov had twelve sons.* He [R. Chanina] told the translator: Only translate the latter verse, and the Sages praised him [for having instructed him to delete the translation of the first verse].

COMMENTARY

Previously,[613] we learned that the *meturgeman* was not permitted to translate more than one verse at a time. Yet, here it would seem that the reader

---

609 - ‏קדושין ע.‏

610 - Compare to *Pesachim* 3b where the Talmud recounts the story of an Aramean whose identity was discovered because he mis-spoke.

611 - ‏עלי שור חלק א' עמוד קס״ג.‏

612 - See *Bereishis* 35:22.

613 - See page 264.

read two verses and it was then that R. Chanina told the *meturgeman* not to translate the first verse. We can conjecture that verses 22 and 23 were actually one verse and R. Chanina told the translator to refrain from interpreting the first portion which mentioned Reuvane's action. Support for this can be drawn from the cantillation, for verse 22 ends with an *esnachta* note — which is usually used as a pause in mid-sentence — rather than a *sof pasuk* which would indicate that it is separate from verse 23.[614]

TALMUD

מַעֲשֵׂה הָעֵגֶל הַשֵּׁנִי נִקְרָא וְלֹא מִתַּרְגֵּם. וְאֵיזֶהוּ מַעֲשֵׂה הָעֵגֶל הַשֵּׁנִי? מִן: "וַיֹּאמֶר מֹשֶׁה" עַד "וַיַּרְא מֹשֶׁה".

"בִּרְכַּת כֹּהֲנִים", נִקְרָא וְלֹא מִתַּרְגֵּם, מַאי טַעְמָא? מִשּׁוּם דִּכְתִיב: "יִשָּׂא".

מַעֲשֵׂה דָוִד וְאַמְנוֹן, לֹא נִקְרִין, וְלֹא מִתַּרְגְּמִין. וְהָאָמַרְתְּ: מַעֲשֵׂה אַמְנוֹן וְתָמָר, נִקְרָא וּמִתַּרְגֵּם? לָא קַשְׁיָא, הָא דִּכְתִיב: "אַמְנוֹן בֶּן דָּוִד", הָא דִּכְתִיב: "אַמְנוֹן" סְתָמָא.

TRANSLATION

The second incident of the [golden] calf is read but is not translated. What is the second incident of the [golden] calf? [The verses] from (*Shemos* 32:21-25) *and Moshe said* until *and Moshe said* [which quote Moshe's dialogue with Aharon and are left untranslated out of respect for the latter].[615]

The priestly blessing is read but is not translated. What is the reason? Because the verse (*Bamidbar* 6:24) states: *and He shall turn [His face toward you].*

The incident of David and Amnon[616] is neither read [as a *haftarah*] nor translated. Did you not say [previously] that the incident of Amnon and Tamar is read and translated? This is not a question. This [i.e., the portion that is neither read nor translated] refers to the verses that state *Amnon the son of David* and that [the verses that are read and translated] refers to the verses where it states *Amnon* generally [i.e., without referring to him as being David's son].

COMMENTARY

Rashi, in his commentary to *Bamidbar*, explains that this phrase means that God will be lenient and will overcome, as it were, His anger with you when you

614 - *Rashi* notes that the second verse is separated from the first by a פ indicating that it is a new *parashah*. However, this would not resolve the question we posed.

615 - The brackets reflect the explanation of *Tosafos* (ד"ה מעשה של עגל) based on the parallel text in the *Yerushalmi*. *Rashi* offers another explanation — see note 614.

616 - See *Shmuel* II 13.

sin. This concept would seem to contradict the verse in *Devarim* (10:17) that states: *For God, your Lord, shall not show favor nor accept bribes* — i.e., God does not yield when judging any evil act. This latter verse was reinforced by the Sages[617] who declared: One who says that God is lenient — i.e., that He does not punish sin — deserves to have his limbs cut apart. This statement is considered reprehensible because it can lead people not to take sin seriously.

According to the *Sifri*, the resolution of this apparent contradiction is that God is lenient with those who fulfill His will.[618] However, when a person consistently fails to fulfill God's will, then *God, your Lord, shall not show favor nor accept bribes.*[619]

TALMUD

תַּנְיָא, רַבִּי שִׁמְעוֹן בֶּן אֶלְעָזָר אוֹמֵר: לְעוֹלָם יְהֵא אָדָם זָהִיר בִּתְשׁוּבָתוֹ, שֶׁמִּתּוֹךְ תְּשׁוּבָה שֶׁהֱשִׁיבוּ אַהֲרֹן לְמֹשֶׁה, פָּקְרוּ הַמִּינִין, שֶׁנֶּאֱמַר: "וָאַשְׁלִכֵהוּ בָאֵשׁ, וַיֵּצֵא הָעֵגֶל הַזֶּה".

TRANSLATION

We learned in a *beraisa*: R. Shimon ben Elazar taught: One should always be careful in answering, for through the answer that Aharon gave Moshe, the heretics [found support for their] heresy. The verse (*Shemos* 32:24) states: *and I [Aharon] cast it [the gold] into the fire and this calf came forth.*[620]

COMMENTARY

In *Pirkei Avos*,[621] Avtalyon is quoted as teaching: *Scholars! Be careful with your words lest you be liable to exile and be exiled to the place of foul waters*

בבא קמא נ. - 617

618 - I.e., with those whose sins are a temporary failing and do not represent a conscious denial of God.

619 - *Rashi* (ד״ה משום ישא) explains that the Talmud maintains that the priestly blessing should not be translated because it could be misinterpreted to imply that God shows favoritism to Israel. Quoting the Talmud in *Berachos* (27a) he adds: [God says,] Is it not right that I show them favoritism. I told them *and you shall eat and be sated and bless [Me]* and they are strict with themselves [and recite the Grace after Meals] after [eating] food the size of an egg!

620 - I.e., Aharon's answer to Moshe could be misinterpreted to mean that the calf had powers of its own and created itself. *Rashi,* in his commentary to the *Mishnah,* maintains that this is the reason why the Talmud said earlier that the second incident of the golden calf should not be translated.

פרק א׳ משנה י״א - 621

and the students who follow you will drink from them and die and it will turn out that the name of Heaven will be desecrated through you. In his commentary to that Mishnah, *Rambam* explains that *foul waters* is a euphemism for heresy. Scholars must take care when speaking in public that nothing that they say be misconstrued, for if there are heretics present, they will interpret what is said as supporting their mistaken beliefs and the simple people will assume that this was the scholars intent.

When Aharon told Moshe about the series of events that led to the golden calf, he used the phrase *and this calf came forth.* His intention was to emphasize that the Jews were not culpable for having made a golden calf, for they had not sought to build an idol. The calf *came forth* due to the magical incantations of those Egyptians who accompanied them. However, though Aharon's intentions were good, his choice of phrases could easily be misinterpreted as lending support to the heretics who claimed that idols have powers of their own.[622]

TALMUD

תָּנוּ רַבָּנָן: כָּל הַמִּקְרָאוֹת הַכְּתוּבִים בַּתּוֹרָה לִגְנַאי, קוֹרִין אוֹתָן לְשֶׁבַח, כְּגוֹן: "יִשְׁגָּלֶנָה" – "יִשְׁכָּבֶנָה"; "בַּעְפוֹלִים" – "בַּטְּחוֹרִים"; "חַרְיוֹנִים" – "דִּבְיוֹנִים". "לֶאֱכֹל אֶת חוֹרֵיהֶם, וְלִשְׁתּוֹת אֶת שִׁינֵיהֶם" – "לֶאֱכֹל אֶת צוֹאָתָם, וְלִשְׁתּוֹת אֶת מֵימֵי רַגְלֵיהֶם". "לְמַחֲרָאוֹת" – "לְמוֹצָאוֹת". רַבִּי יְהוֹשֻׁעַ בֶּן קָרְחָה אוֹמֵר: "לְמַחֲרָאוֹת" כִּשְׁמָן, מִפְּנֵי שֶׁהוּא גְנַאי לַעֲבוֹדַת כּוֹכָבִים.

TRANSLATION

The Sages taught: All of the verses in the Torah that are written disparagingly are read favorably.[623] For example: [Instead of] *shall cohabit with her,*[624] [we read] *shall lie with her.* [Instead of] *hemorrhoids,* [we read] *piles.*[625] [Instead of]

622 - *Maharitz Chayes* comments that Aharon's answer to Moshe was the basis for Yeravam's construction of two calves as idols — see *Melachim* I 12:28.
623 - I.e., in a less disparaging or direct manner. In the examples cited, the substitute phrase also has a disparaging connotation, but is less forthright than the word or phrase written. For the most part, קרי and כתיב — reading a word differently than spelled — is limited to substituting a *vav* for a *yud*, a *yud* for a *vav* or omitting a written letter. In the examples cited, the word read is completely different than the word written. All cases of קרי and כתיב are *halachos* transmitted by Moshe at Sinai.
624 - *Devarim* 28:30.
625 - Ibid. :27. In English the two terms are interchangeable, but in Hebrew, the latter is considered to be a less graphic description.

droppings, [we read] *emissions.*[626] [Instead of] *to eat from their rectums and drink their diahrrea*, [we read] *to eat their feces and drink their urine.*[627] [Instead of] *their places of defecation*, [we read] *their outhouses.*[628]

R. Yehoshua ben Korcha taught: *Places of defecation* as they are called [i.e., we do not read the word differently than written], for it [the term] disparages idolatry [and it is therefore not considered to be vulgar].

TALMUD

אָמַר רַב נַחְמָן: כָּל לֵיצָנוּתָא אֲסִירָא, בַּר מִלֵּיצָנוּתָא דַּעֲבוֹדַת כּוֹכָבִים, דְּשַׁרְיָא. דִּכְתִיב: "כָּרַע בֵּל קֹרֵס נְבוֹ", וּכְתִיב: "קָרְסוּ כָרְעוּ יַחְדָּו, לֹא יָכְלוּ מַלֵּט מַשָּׂא" וְגוֹ'.

רַבִּי יַנַּאי אָמַר, מֵהָכָא: "לְעֶגְלוֹת בֵּית אָוֶן, יָגוּרוּ שְׁכַן שֹׁמְרוֹן. כִּי אָבַל עָלָיו עַמּוֹ, וּכְמָרָיו עָלָיו יָגִילוּ, עַל כְּבוֹדוֹ כִּי גָלָה מִמֶּנּוּ". אַל תִּקְרֵי "כְּבוֹדוֹ", אֶלָּא "כְּבֵדוֹ".

TRANSLATION

R. Nachman taught: [All forms of] ridicule are prohibited except for ridiculing idolatry which is permitted, as the verse (*Yeshayahu* 46:1-2) states: *Bal kneels and Nevo stoops ... they bow and stoop together for they cannot carry the burden.*[629]

R. Yannai deduced [that ridicule is permitted] from here: [The verse (*Hoshea* 10:5) states:] *Those who dwell in Shomron will be fearful [because] of the calves of Beis Aven [that were taken into captivity]. For the people mourn for her and the priests who were joyful [also mourn] for his honor which has been taken from*

---

626 - See *Melachim* II 6:28. The verse describes the famine that took place during Ben Haddad of Aram's siege of Shomron. People were so desparate for food that they ate bird-droppings — חריונים. The word is read as דביונים which means emissions from doves, a less graphic description.

627 - See *Melachim* II 18:27. The reference is to Ravsheka's taunt to the watchmen on the walls of Jerusalem. The form read is still graphic in its description but is considered to be less vulgar than the terms that Ravsheka used.

628 - See *Melachim* II 10:27. The reference is to the places of worship of Ba'al which were destroyed and turned into public bathrooms.

629 - The Hebrew terms קרסו and כרעו implies people who are stooped over because they have to defecate. If Yeshayahu did not hesitate to use this kind of description, we can deduce that the prohibition of ridiculing does not apply to idolatry.

her.[630] Do not read כבודו — *his honor* — but כבדו — *his burden.*[631]

TALMUD

אָמַר רַב הוּנָא בַּר מָנוֹחַ מִשְּׁמֵיהּ דְּרַב אַחָא בְּרֵיהּ דְּרַב אִיקָא: שָׁרֵי לֵיהּ לְבַר יִשְׂרָאֵל לְמֵימַר לְגוֹי (עוֹבֵד כּוֹכָבִים): שָׁקְלֵיהּ לַעֲבוֹדַת כּוֹכָבִים, וְאַנְחֵיהּ בְּשִׁי"ן תָּי"ו שֶׁלָּךְ.

אָמַר רַב אַשִׁי: הַאי מָאן דְּסָאנֵי שׁוּמְעָנֵיהּ, שָׁרֵי לֵיהּ לְבַזּוּיֵיהּ בְּגִימֶ"ל וְשִׁי"ן. וְהַאי מָאן דְּשַׁפִּיר שׁוּמְעָנֵיהּ, שָׁרֵי לֵיהּ לְשַׁבּוּחֵיהּ. וּמָאן דְּשַׁבְּחֵיהּ, יָנוּחוּ לוֹ בְּרָכוֹת עַל רֹאשׁוֹ.

TALMUD

R. Huna bar Manoach taught in the name of R. Acha son of R. Ika: A Jew may tell a gentile:[632] Take your idol and place it in your *shin taf.*[633]

R. Ashi taught: [Regarding] one about whom hateful stories are spread,[634] one may mock him [and refer to him as a] *gimmel shin.*[635] And one about whom favorable stories are told, one may praise him and he who praises him will have blessings placed upon him.

---

630 - The Prophet is referring to the statues of calves that Yeravam ben Nevat built as idols when he established the breakaway kingdom of Israel. According to *Radak*, Beis Aven is a cynical euphemism for Beis El, the site of one of the calves. See also *Yehoshua* 7:2 where Beis Aven is mentioned as being in proximity to Beis El.

631 - I.e., the burden of his bowels.

632 - Some texts state an idol worshipper.

633 - *Rashi* explains that the reference is to the buttocks, as in *Yechezkel* 20:4.

634 - *Rashi* (ד"ה דסני שומעניה) adds that he is accused of being an adulterer. Obviously the Talmud is referring to stories that are corroborated and not baseless rumors or slander. See *Chafetz Chaim* 7:4-5 and *Be'er Mayim Chaim* ad loc.

635 - *Rashi* explains ג"ש as an abbreviation for גיופא שטייא — stupid prostitute. Others maintain that it is an acronym for בן גויה, בן שפחה — son of a gentile, son of a maidservant. It should be noted that in this statement as well as in the previous statement, abbreviations were used rather than the words themselves.

TALMUD

כְּתִיב: "לְבִנְיָמִן אָמַר: יְדִיד ה', יִשְׁכּוֹן לָבֶטַח עָלָיו, חוֹפֵף עָלָיו כָּל הַיּוֹם". וּבַגְּמָרָא הֵבִיאוּ פְּלוּגְתָּא דְּתַנָּאֵי בְּעִנְיָן אִם יְרוּשָׁלַיִם נִתְחַלְּקָה לַשְּׁבָטִים אוֹ לֹא). תַּנָּא אֶחָד סוֹבֵר שֶׁנִּתְחַלְּקָה לְשֵׁבֶט יְהוּדָה וּלְשֵׁבֶט בִּנְיָמִין, דְּתַנְיָא: מֶה הָיָה בְּחֶלְקוֹ שֶׁל יְהוּדָה? הַר הַבַּיִת, וְהַלְּשָׁכוֹת, וְהָעֲזָרוֹת. וּמֶה הָיָה בְּחֶלְקוֹ שֶׁל בִּנְיָמִין? אוּלָם, וְהֵיכָל, וּבֵית קָדְשֵׁי הַקֳּדָשִׁים. וּרְצוּעָה הָיְתָה יוֹצֵאת מֵחֶלְקוֹ שֶׁל יְהוּדָה, וְהָיְתָה נִכְנֶסֶת בְּחֶלְקוֹ שֶׁל בִּנְיָמִין, וּבָהּ מִזְבֵּחַ בָּנוּי, וְהָיָה בִּנְיָמִין הַצַּדִּיק מִצְטַעֵר עָלֶיהָ בְּכָל יוֹם לְבָלְעָהּ, שֶׁנֶּאֱמַר: "חוֹפֵף עָלָיו כָּל הַיּוֹם". וּלְפִיכָךְ זָכָה בִנְיָמִין וְנַעֲשָׂה אוּשְׁפִּיזְכָאן לַשְּׁכִינָה, שֶׁנֶּאֱמַר: "וּבֵין כְּתֵפָיו שָׁכֵן".

TRANSLATION

[26a] The verse (*Devarim* 33:12) states: *And to Binyamin he said: Friend of God — He shall dwell serenely upon him. He hovers above him at all times.*[636] [The Talmud cites a difference of opinion between two *tannaim* as to whether Jerusalem was divided among the tribes or not.] One *tanna* is of the opinion that it [the Temple Mount] was divided between the tribe of Yehudah and the tribe of Binyamin, as we learn in a *beraisa*: What [part] was in the area of Yehudah? The Temple mount, the offices and the [three] courtyards. And what [part] was in the area of Binyamin? The building [of the *Beis ha-Mikdash*], the Sanctuary and the Holy of Holies.[637] There was a strip of land that extended from the area of Yehudah and it went into the area of Binyamin and upon it the altar[638] was constructed. Binyamin the righteous suffered constantly because of it [the strip belonging to Yehudah upon which the altar was constructed] and sought to swallow it [make it part of his area] as the verse (ibid.) states: *He hovers above it at all*

---

636 - The text in the Talmud does not quote this verse, which is the basis for the opinion that the *Beis ha-Mikdash* was built within the territory of the tribe of Binyamin. The Talmud begins its discussion with a difference of opinion between the *tanna kamma* — the anonymous opinion cited — and R. Yehudah as to whether the area of the city of Jerusalem was divided between the tribes or whether it was never allotted to a specific tribe.

637 - The building of the *Beis ha-Mikdash* (referred to as the אולם) included warehouses and closets. The Sanctuary (referred to as the קדש) was further inside and was the site of the *menorah*, the *shulchan* and the golden altar. Further inside was the Holy of Holies (the קדש הקדשים) which was the site of the *aron*.

638 - The reference is to the earthen altar that was located outside the *Beis ha-Mikdash*.

times.[639] Because of this [i.e., his anguish and desire that the *Beis ha-Mikdash* be entirely in his area], Binyamin was rewarded and was made the host for the *Shechinah*, as the verse (ibid.) states: *and It [the Shechinah] reposes between his shoulders.*

COMMENTARY

R. Samson Rafael Hirsch explains that the *Beis ha-Mikdash* was destined to be located in the area allotted to the youngest and weakest of the tribes, for Binyamin had three attributes that made him particularly suited to act as host for the Sanctuary. He was the only one of the tribes born in Eretz Yisrael, he was the only one of the brothers who was not involved in the sale of Yosef and it was he who served as a source of comfort to his father Yaakov in his old age.

TALMUD

וְתַנָּא אֶחָד סוֹבֵר: לֹא נִתְחַלְּקָה יְרוּשָׁלַיִם לִשְׁבָטִים, דְּתַנְיָא: אֵין מַשְׂכִּירִין בָּתִּים בְּתוֹךְ יְרוּשָׁלַיִם, לְפִי שֶׁאֵינָן שֶׁלָּהֶם. רַבִּי אֶלְעָזָר בְּרַבִּי צָדוֹק אוֹמֵר: אַף לֹא מִטּוֹת. לְפִיכָךְ עוֹרוֹת קָדָשִׁים, בַּעֲלֵי אוּשְׁפִּיזִין נוֹטְלִין אוֹתָן בִּזְרוֹעַ. אָמַר אַבַּיֵּי: שְׁמַע מִינָּהּ – אוֹרַח אַרְעָא לְמִשְׁבַּק אִינִישׁ גּוּלְפָא וּמַשְׁכָא בְּאוּשְׁפִּיזֵיהּ.

TRANSLATION

The other *tanna* is of the opinion that Jerusalem was not divided among the tribes [but remained the property of the nation as a whole]. As we learned in a *beraisa*: They [the residents of Jerusalem] cannot rent out houses within Jerusalem because they are not theirs.[640] R. Elazar b'R. Tzadok taught: [They may] not [even charge] for beds.[641] Therefore, the hosts may insist on being given the skins of [the animals brought as] sacrifices [as recompense].[642] Abbaye taught: We learn from this that it is customary for guests to give their

---

639 - According to this *tanna*, the word He refers to Binyamin rather than to God.

640 - I.e., since the land does not belong to them, for it was not parcelled out to any individual tribe, the residents of Jerusalem cannot charge rent to the pilgrims who ascended to Jerusalem but must host them in their homes for free.

641 - R. Elazar adds that since the land does not belong to them, the residents of Jerusalem have no right to even charge for the use of the beds in their homes.

642 - *Tosafos* (ד"ה אף לא המטות) explains that even though they could not charge their guests rent since the beds were placed on public lands, they could demand recompense for use of their property.

hosts the [empty] barrels and the skins [of the animals that they slaughtered].

TALMUD

אָמַר מַר זוּטְרָא: מִטְפְּחוֹת סְפָרִים שֶׁבָּלוּ, עוֹשִׂין אוֹתָן תַּכְרִיכִין לְמֵת מִצְוָה,
וְזוּ הִיא גְּנִיזָתָן.

TRANSLATION

[26b] Mar Zutra taught: The mantles of Torah scrolls that are worn out are made into shrouds for a *meis mitzvah*[643] and this is the means through which they are stored.[644]

COMMENTARY

The sanctity of a Torah scroll extends to the articles that are used with it — e.g., the *atzei chaim* — the wooden handles around which it is rolled, the *aron kodesh* where it is stored or the mantle used to cover it, as in the case here. Since this mantle was used to cover a Torah scroll, it would be forbidden to use it for any purpose that is less sanctified.

From the Talmud's ruling that it may be used to make burial shrouds for a *meis mitzvah*, we can see the importance that was attached to burying a *meis mitzvah* as well as the sanctity that the Sages attached to man himself. They compared every Jew to a Torah scroll, for it is through man's fulfillment of the Torah that it is transformed from a parchment document into a sacred heritage. Thus, when a Jew dies, it is as if the Torah itself has been lost. The Sages[645] said: *One who stands beside a dying man at the time when his soul leaves him is required to tear his clothing. To what may this be compared? To seeing a*

---

643 - *Meis mitzvah* refers to a corpse that is found and which no one claims. Since there are no known relatives who would be obligated to take care of the burial, the responsibility devolves upon the community and it is a mitzvah to bury the corpse. The importance of this mitzvah is so great, that even a *kohen* — who is forbidden to come into contact with a corpse — is dutybound to bury a *meis mitzvah*.

644 - While the word גניזה is literally translatable as stored, it refers to the means through which sacred articles are disposed of when they are no longer of use. Because of their sanctity, they cannot be thrown away. Rather, they must either be buried or used for some other sacred function that is no less holy than their former function. See *Yoreh Deah* 282:11-13.

645 - מועד קטן כה. — see also *Michtav Mi'Eliyahu*, Vol. IV, pg. 91 who writes: *When a person sins, it is as if he has ripped the Torah.*

Torah scroll being burnt where he is also required to tear his clothing.

Mar Zutra's ruling, as well as the subsequent statements, is another example of the concept of מעלין בקדש ואין מורידין — *we ascend in sanctity but do not descend.*[646] Thus, whenever we seek to use an item that has any degree of sanctity for a use other than its original purpose, we must first determine that the new use does not represent a lesser degree of sanctity, for such use would be considered a desecration and would be forbidden.

TALMUD

וְאָמַר רָבָא: סֵפֶר תּוֹרָה שֶׁבָּלָה, גּוֹנְזִין אוֹתוֹ אֵצֶל תַּלְמִיד חָכָם. וַאֲפִלּוּ שׁוֹנֶה הֲלָכוֹת. אָמַר רַב אַחָא בַּר יַעֲקֹב: וּבִכְלִי חֶרֶס, שֶׁנֶּאֱמַר: "וּנְתַתָּם בִּכְלִי חָרֶשׂ, לְמַעַן יַעַמְדוּ יָמִים רַבִּים".

דָּרַשׁ בַּר קַפָּרָא, מַאי דִכְתִיב: "וַיִּשְׂרֹף אֶת בֵּית ה', וְאֶת בֵּית הַמֶּלֶךְ, וְאֵת כָּל בָּתֵּי יְרוּשָׁלַיִם, וְאֵת כָּל בֵּית גָּדוֹל שָׂרַף בָּאֵשׁ". "בֵּית ה'" - זֶה בֵּית הַמִּקְדָּשׁ. "בֵּית הַמֶּלֶךְ" - אֵלּוּ פַּלְטְרִין שֶׁל מֶלֶךְ. "וְאֵת כָּל בָּתֵּי יְרוּשָׁלַיִם" - כְּמַשְׁמָעוֹ. "וְאֵת כָּל בֵּית גָּדוֹל", (וּפְלִיגִי בָהּ) רַבִּי יוֹחָנָן וְרַבִּי יְהוֹשֻׁעַ בֶּן לֵוִי, חַד אָמַר: מָקוֹם שֶׁמְּגַדְּלִין בּוֹ תוֹרָה. וְחַד אָמַר: מָקוֹם שֶׁמְּגַדְּלִין בּוֹ תְפִלָּה. מָאן דַּאֲמַר: תּוֹרָה, דִכְתִיב: "יַגְדִּיל תּוֹרָה וְיַאְדִּיר". וּמָאן דַּאֲמַר: מָקוֹם שֶׁמְּגַדְּלִין בּוֹ תְפִלָּה, דִכְתִיב: "סַפְּרָה נָא לִי אֵת כָּל הַגְּדֹלוֹת אֲשֶׁר עָשָׂה אֱלִישָׁע". וֶאֱלִישָׁע כִּי עָבַד, בְּרַחֲמֵי הוּא דְעָבַד.

TRANSLATION

Rava taught: A Torah scroll that is worn out is stored [i.e., buried][647] next to a Torah sage, even one who was [only] a teacher of *halachah.*[648] Rav Acha bar Yaakov taught: [It is placed before burial] in an earthen jug [rather than buried as

---

646 - See מנחות צט. and note 563.

647 - Since the scroll can not be used for any other purpose, for any other use would of necessity be less sacred, it is buried.

648 - I.e., one who did not develop new ideas or explanations of his own but taught that which was already known. One might think that he is less worthy and the Torah scroll should be buried next to someone of greater importance. Rava therefore taught that since he occupied himself in Torah study, he is considered to be worthy.

It should be noted that just as we are required to give people the respect due them while they are alive, we are also required to do so when they die. Thus, the *halachah* rules that we do not bury a wicked person next to a Sage and we even refrain from burying a totally wicked person next to a person who was only occasionally evil. See *Yoreh Deah* 362:5.

is], for the verse (*Yirmiyahu* 32:14) states: *And you shall place it in an earthen jug so that it shall last for many days.*

[27a] Bar Kappara expounded: What is [the meaning of the verse (*Melachim* II 25:9)] that states: *And he [Nevuchadnezer] burned the house of God, and the house of the king and all of the houses of Jerusalem and every great house he set on fire? The house of God —* this [refers to the] *Beis ha-Mikdash. The house of the king —* this [refers to the] palace of the king. *And all of the houses of Jerusalem —* [this should be understood] literally. [As regards] *and every great house —* [the meaning of this was the subject of a difference of opinion between] R. Yochanan and R. Yehoshua ben Levi. One said: [This refers to] a place where the Torah is made great [i.e., the study halls]. One said: [This refers to] a place where prayer is made great [i.e., the synagogues]. The one who says [that *great houses* refers to the study halls of] Torah [based himself on the verse (*Yeshayahu* 42:21) that] states: *Let the Torah become great and precious.*[649] The one who says [that *great houses* refers to the houses of] prayer [based himself on the verse (*Melachim* II 8:4) that] states: *Tell me please all of the great things that Elisha has done.* That [the great things] which Elisha did, he did through prayer.

TALMUD

תִּסְתַּיֵּם דְּרַבִּי יְהוֹשֻׁעַ בֶּן לֵוִי הוּא דַּאֲמַר: מָקוֹם שֶׁמְּגַדְּלִין בּוֹ תּוֹרָה, דַּאֲמַר רַבִּי יְהוֹשֻׁעַ בֶּן לֵוִי: בֵּית הַכְּנֶסֶת, מֻתָּר לַעֲשׂוֹתוֹ בֵּית הַמִּדְרָשׁ. תִּסְתַּיֵּם. אִיבַּעְיָא לְהוּ: מַהוּ לִמְכֹּר סֵפֶר תּוֹרָה יָשָׁן, לִקַּח בּוֹ חָדָשׁ? וְכוּ'. תָּא שְׁמַע: דַּאֲמַר רַבִּי יוֹחָנָן מִשּׁוּם רַבִּי מֵאִיר: אֵין מוֹכְרִין סֵפֶר תּוֹרָה, אֶלָּא לְלִמּוּד תּוֹרָה, וְלִשָּׂא אִשָּׁה. שְׁמַע מִינָהּ – תּוֹרָה בְתוֹרָה – שַׁפִּיר דָּמֵי! דִּילְמָא, שָׁאנֵי תַלְמוּד, שֶׁהַתַּלְמוּד מֵבִיא לִידֵי מַעֲשֶׂה? אִשָּׁה נַמִּי – "לֹא תֹהוּ בְרָאָהּ לָשֶׁבֶת יְצָרָהּ"! אֲבָל תּוֹרָה בְתוֹרָה לא.

TRANSLATION

Let it be clear that it was R. Yehoshua ben Levi who said [that the verse is referring to] the places where Torah is made great, for R. Yehoshua ben Levi said a synagogue may be made into a study hall. This is proof.[650]

649 - I.e., since the verse uses the term *great* in reference to the Torah, we can infer that the *great houses* referred to in the verse in *Melachim* refers to the study halls.

650 - We see that R. Yehoshua ben Levi was of the opinion that study halls have a greater degree of sanctity than synagogues, for otherwise we would not be permitted to make the synagogues into study halls.

It was asked: Is it permitted to sell an old Torah scroll in order to purchase a new one? Come and hear: R. Yochanan taught in the name of R. Meir: One may not sell an old Torah scroll except [if one does so to use the funds] to study Torah or to marry a woman. From this we see that [to exchange] the Torah for the Torah is permissible [i.e., it follows that just as one may sell a Torah scroll to study Torah, one may also sell an old Torah scroll to purchase a new one]. [Perhaps Torah] study is different [i.e., perhaps it represents a higher degree of sanctity than does a Torah scroll] since it brings one to act [correctly, and that is why one may sell a Torah scroll in order to finance one's study]. [Additionally, perhaps] marrying a woman [also represents a higher degree of sanctity than does a Torah scroll and one is therefore permitted to sell the former to finance the latter, for the verse (*Yeshayahu* 48:18) states:] *Do not sit idly, you were created to propogate* [and marrying a woman is thus a mitzvah that one must fulfill]. [As regards exchanging an old] Torah [scroll] for a [new] Torah [scroll, this might] be forbidden!

COMMENTARY

The writing of a Torah scroll is an obligatory precept. *Sefer ha-Chinuch* writes: *The reason for this mitzvah is so that each one might have a Torah of his own that he can study from at all times. Even if he inherited a scroll from his father, he is required to write a new scroll, for he may be less than enthusiastic in reading from an old scroll.*[651]

Interestingly, *Ein Yaakov* does not quote the difference of opinion in the Talmud as to whether one may sell an old scroll to purchase a new one. The opinion that forbids one to do so maintains that the reason is because the funds received from the sale cannot be judged to have ascended in sanctity. According

---

651 - מצוה תרי"ג. In the preface to his responsa, R. Akiva Eiger wrote to his son praising the invention of the printing press: *Study from newly and nicely printed books brings wonder to the soul and expands the mind and awakens one's intent.*
Beis Yosef (*Yoreh Deah* 270:2) rules that in our times, it is also obligatory to write (or print) other religious works. *Taz* (ad loc.) explains that in *tannaic* times, when it was forbidden to record the orally transmitted Torah, the mitzvah of writing a Torah scroll was limited. Today, however, when this prohibition no longer applies, the mitzvah includes all works that enhance Torah study. *Drishah*, however, rules that the obligation to write a Torah scroll no longer applies, for we do not study from scrolls. Rather, he maintains that the obligation is to provide printed works for study.

to this opinion, use of funds for a purpose of equal sanctity would be forbidden. The opinion that permits the sale maintains that since there is no greater degree of sanctity than a Torah scroll, there is no need to ascend. The Talmud then goes on to cite a ruling by Rabban Shimon ben Gamliel who maintains that the sale is forbidden, but explains that no inference can be drawn from there since he may have forbidden the practice because he was afraid that the funds secured from the sale would be used for other community purposes before the new scroll was written. The Talmud — and *Ein Yaakov* — then proceeds to quote R. Yochanan, seeking to draw evidence that such a sale would be permitted, but determines that no proof can be drawn from his ruling either and the question is left unresolved.[652]

TALMUD

תָּנוּ רַבָּנָן: לֹא יִמְכֹּר אָדָם סֵפֶר תּוֹרָה, אַף עַל פִּי שֶׁאֵינוֹ צָרִיךְ לוֹ. יָתֵר עַל כֵּן אָמַר רַבָּן שִׁמְעוֹן בֶּן גַּמְלִיאֵל: אֲפִלּוּ אֵין לוֹ מַה יֹּאכַל, וּמָכַר סֵפֶר תּוֹרָה, אוֹ בִּתּוֹ, אֵינוֹ רוֹאֶה סִימָן בְּרָכָה לְעוֹלָם.

שָׁאֲלוּ תַלְמִידָיו אֶת רַבִּי זַכַּאי: בַּמֶּה הֶאֱרַכְתָּ יָמִים? אָמַר לָהֶם: מִיָּמַי לֹא הִשְׁתַּנְתִּי מַיִם בְּאַרְבַּע אַמּוֹת שֶׁל תְּפִלָּה, וְלֹא כִּנִּיתִי שֵׁם לַחֲבֵרִי, וְלֹא בִּטַּלְתִּי קִדּוּשׁ הַיּוֹם. אִמָּא זְקֵנָה הָיְתָה לִי, פַּעַם אַחַת לֹא הָיָה לִי קִדּוּשׁ, מָכְרָה כִּפָּה שֶׁעַל רֹאשָׁהּ, וְהֵבִיאָה לִי קִדּוּשׁ הַיּוֹם. תָּנָא, כְּשֶׁמֵּתָה הִנִּיחָה לוֹ שְׁלֹשׁ מֵאוֹת גַּרְבֵּי יַיִן. כְּשֶׁמֵּת הוּא, הִנִּיחַ לְבָנָיו שְׁלֹשֶׁת אֲלָפִים גַּרְבֵּי יַיִן.

TRANSLATION

The Sages taught: One may not sell a Torah scroll even if he does not need it. More than this, R. Shimon ben Gamliel taught: Even if one has nothing to eat, and he sold a Torah scroll or his daughter, he will see no sign of blessing ever [from the money that he receives].

[27b] R. Zakai's students asked him: How did you [merit to] live long? He answered them: During my entire life, I never urinated within four *amos* of [a place of] prayer and I never called a friend by a nickname and I never missed

---

652 - See *Yoreh Deah* 270:1. *Beis Yosef* rules that the sale would be permitted if the new Torah scroll was ready when the old one was sold, since there is no reason to fear that the funds might be squandered. *Shach*, quoting *Ran* among others, maintains that it would still be forbidden, for the funds secured from the sale could not be seen as having ascended in sanctity.

reciting the *kiddush* of the day [i.e., using wine for the *kiddush* recited on Shabbos morning]. I had an elderly mother and once I did not have [wine for] *kiddush*. She sold the scarf on her head [and used the proceeds] and brought me [wine for] *kiddush* of the day. We learned in a *beraisa*: When she died, she left him three hundred jugs of wine. And when he died, he left his sons three thousand jugs of wine.

COMMENTARY

Maharsha comments that even though the Talmud[653] maintains that שכר מצוה בהאי עלמא ליכא — the reward for mitzvos is not paid in this world — it was obvious to R. Zakai's students that his longevity must have been a result of his exemplary life and they therefore asked him to explain the source of his merit. *Ramban*[654] explains that though the reward for mitzvah performance is paid in the World to Come, if one is especially careful to fulfill mitzvos in the most exemplary fashion and adds to their performance from the goodness of his heart, he receives reward in this world as well.

R. Eliezer Pappo,[655] in his ethical work יעלזו חכמים writes: *If one sees a Torah scholar who has reached [extreme] old age know that it is because he was more careful than were others in fulfilling mitzvos that are not written in the Torah, as the verse (Mishlei 3:2) states: For long days and years of life will be added to you.*

Chafetz Chaim[656] adds that though the Torah calls upon us to be modest and discrete in our service of God, *when dealing with common people or with students one should publicize his good deeds so that they might learn to act in the same manner. However, one should be careful to act in the name of Heaven and not, God forbid, to show off in front of them.*

In all three of the examples cited by R. Zakkai, he pointed to practices of his that went beyond the requirement of the law. In the first example, he was obviously not referring to the fact that he did not urinate inside a synagogue. Rather, as *Tosafos* explains, he was referring to a place of private prayer, and he

---

653 - קידושין לט: לט.

654 - כתבי הרמב"ן, אמונה ובטחון.

655 - The author of the ethical work, פלא יועץ.

656 - אורח חיים א:א ס"ק ו.

would have been permitted to urinate there once it was no longer being used for prayer. However, because of his sensitivity he still refrained from doing so.

In the second example that he cited, he stressed that out of his respect for his colleagues, he never addressed them by nicknames or dimunitives even when those names were by no means disrespectful, for he was sensitive to the need to show the utmost respect for Torah scholars.

In the third example, he told his students that though his financial status would have allowed him to fulfill his obligation of kiddush by using challos, he nevertheless sought wine out of his great desire to fulfill mitzvos in the optimal fashion.

TALMUD

רַב הוּנָא הֲוָה אֲסַר רִיתָא, וְקָאֵי קַמֵּיהּ דְּרַב. אֲמַר לֵיהּ: מַאי הַאי? אֲמַר לֵיהּ: לָא הֲוָה לִי לְקִדּוּשָׁא, וּמִשְׁכַּנְתֵּיהּ לְהֶמְיָנָאי וְאֵיתִיתִי בֵּיהּ קִדּוּשָׁא. אֲמַר לֵיהּ: יְהֵא רַעֲוָא דְּתִיטּוֹם בְּשִׁירָאֵי.

כִּי אִכְּלַל רַבָּה בְּרֵיהּ. רַב הוּנָא - אִינִישׁ גּוּצָא הֲוָה, גָּנָא אַפּוּרְיָא, אָתְאָן בְּנָתֵיהּ וְכַלָּתֵיהּ, שַׁלְחָן וְשַׁדְיָין מָאנֵי עִילָוֵיהּ, עַד דְּאִיטּוֹם בְּשִׁירָאֵי. (כִּי אֲתָא רַב יוֹסֵף אַשְׁכְּחֵיהּ אֲמַר לֵיהּ: אַקַּיֵּים בָּךְ בִּרְכָתֵיהּ דְּרַב). כִּי שְׁמַע רַב - אִיקְּפַּד, אֲמַר: מַאי טַעְמָא לֹא אֲמַרְתְּ לִי כִּי בֵּרַכְתִּיךְ: "וְכֵן לְמַר"?

TRANSLATION

R. Huna was girdled with a straw belt and was standing in front of Rav. He [Rav] asked him: What is this [i.e., why are you wearing a belt of straw]? He answered him: I did not have [wine for] kiddush so I pawned my belt and used [the funds] that I borrowed [to purchase wine] for kiddush. He told him: May it be His will that you be completely covered in silk.

[Rav's blessing was fulfilled] when his [R. Huna's] son Raba was married. R. Huna was a very short man and he went [during the wedding] to rest on a sofa. His daughters and daughters-in-law came [and did not notice that he was sleeping on the sofa since he was so short]. They placed their [silk] wraps on top of him until he was completely covered in silk. When R. Yosef came, he found him and said: Rav's blessing to you has been fufilled. When Rav heard [what had happened], he was annoyed [with R. Huna] and said: Why did you not say when I blessed you, "The same to the master?"

TALMUD

שָׁאֲלוּ תַלְמִידָיו אֶת רַבִּי אֶלְעָזָר בֶּן שַׁמּוּעַ: בַּמֶּה הֶאֱרַכְתָּ יָמִים? אָמַר לָהֶם:
מִיָּמַי לֹא עָשִׂיתִי בֵּית הַכְּנֶסֶת, קַפֶּנְדַרְיָא. וְלֹא פָּסַעְתִּי עַל רָאשֵׁי עַם קֹדֶשׁ. וְלֹא
נָשָׂאתִי כַּפַּי בְּלֹא בְרָכָה.

TRANSLATION

R. Elazar ben Shamua's students asked him: How did you [merit to] live long?
He answered them: During my entire life I never made a synagogue a
shortcut[657] and I never stepped over the heads of the holy nation [i.e., the
students in the study hall][658] and I never lifted up my hands [to recite the preistly
blessing] without reciting a *berachah*.[659]

COMMENTARY

Maharal[660] explains that R. Elazar ben Shamua pointed out to his students
that his longevity was a result of his having been careful to show respect for
God, for his fellow man and for himself. In refraining from using the synagogue
as a shortcut, he evidenced his recognition of God's sanctity. In refraining from
stepping over his students heads, he showed that he respected them. *Anaf Yosef,*
quoting the *Rif's* commentary to *Sotah,* explains that in being careful to always

657 - I.e., he never went through a synagogue in order to shorten the way when
travelling, for doing so would be a sign of disrespect. Halachically, if the shortcut
was in use before the synagogue was built, there would be no prohibition of
continuing to use it — see *Orach Chaim* 151:5. R. Elazar, however, was stringent and
did not take advantage of this *halachah.*

658 - The custom was for the students to sit on the floor in front of their teacher. Had
R. Elazar ben Shamua come into the study hall after his students, he would have had
to step over them in order to reach his seat in the front, an act which might be
misconstrued as showing a lack of respect for them. He therefore was always careful
to be the first one in the study hall so that he would not have to do so.

659 - This last example of R. Elazar's behavior bears further examination, for all
kohanim are dutybound to recite the *berachah* when ascending for the priestly
blessing. *Maharal*, in his commentary to the parallel text in *Sotah*, comments that
R. Elazar was especially careful to recite the priestly blessing with a feeling of love
for his fellow man, for the *berachah* recited by the *kohanim* is one of the means
through which God provides the world with bounty. R. Elazar pointed out to his
students that when he recited the *berachah*, he did so because of his selfless desire to
bring benefit to others and he was therefore rewarded with long life.

660 - חידושי אגדות לסוטה לט.

recite the *berachah* before reciting the priestly blessing, he showed that he recognized that he was an instrument through which God would shower the world with bounty and he therefore expressed his appreciation to God for having seen fit to use him in this manner. Though there may well have been numerous other examples of exemplary behavior that could have been his source of merit, R. Elazar attributed his longevity to the care that he took to be respectful to all facets of the Creation.

TALMUD

שָׁאֲלוּ תַלְמִידָיו אֶת רַבִּי פְּרִידָא: בַּמֶּה הֶאֱרַכְתָּ יָמִים? אָמַר לָהֶם: מִיָּמַי לֹא קְדָמַנִי אָדָם לְבֵית הַמִּדְרָשׁ, וְלֹא בֵּרַכְתִּי לִפְנֵי כֹהֵן, וְלֹא אָכַלְתִּי מִבְּהֵמָה שֶׁלֹּא הוּרְמוּ מַתְּנוֹתֶיהָ דְּאָמַר רַבִּי יִצְחָק, אָמַר רַבִּי יוֹחָנָן: אָסוּר לֶאֱכֹל מִבְּהֵמָה שֶׁלֹּא הוּרְמוּ מַתְּנוֹתֶיהָ. וְאָמַר רַבִּי יִצְחָק: כָּל הָאוֹכֵל מִבְּהֵמָה שֶׁלֹּא הוּרְמוּ מַתְּנוֹתֶיהָ, כְּאִלּוּ אוֹכֵל טְבָלִים. וְלֵית הִלְכְתָא כְּוָתֵיהּ.

וְלֹא בֵּרַכְתִּי לִפְנֵי כֹהֵן. לְמֵימְרָא: דְּמַעֲלְיוּתָא הִיא? וְהָאָמַר רַבִּי יוֹחָנָן: כָּל תַּלְמִיד חָכָם שֶׁמְּבָרֵךְ לְפָנָיו אֲפִלּוּ כֹהֵן גָּדוֹל עַם הָאָרֶץ, אוֹתוֹ תַּלְמִיד חַיָּב מִיתָה, שֶׁנֶּאֱמַר: "כָּל מְשַׂנְאַי אָהֲבוּ מָוֶת", אַל תִּקְרֵי "מְשַׂנְאַי", אֶלָּא "מַשְׂנִיאַי". כִּי קָאָמַר אִיהוּ בְּשָׁוִין.

TRANSLATION

R. Preida's students asked him: How did you [merit to] live long? He answered them: During my entire life no one ever was in the study hall before me, **[28a]** and I never recited [the introductory] blessing [of the Grace after Meals][661] in the presence of a *kohen*[662] and I never ate [meat] from an animal whose gifts [the shank, cheeks and stomach][663] had not been separated. As R. Yitzchak taught in the name of R. Yochanan: One may not eat [meat] from an animal whose gifts were not separated. R. Yitzchak also taught: One who eats [meat] from an animal whose gifts were not separated is equavilent to one who eats untithed grain. But the *halachah* is not in accordance with his opinion [i.e., eating meat

---

661 - The bracketed addition reflects *Rashi's* explanation. *Tosafos Rid* adds that he also did not recite *ha-motzi* in the presence of a *kohen*.

662 - See *Gittin* 59b where the Talmud derives that a *kohen* is given precedence in all sanctified matters.

663 - See *Devarim* 18:3. These parts of the animal were given to a *kohen*.

whose gifts were not separated is not equivalent to eating untithed produce].[664]
I never recited [the introductory] blessing [of the Grace after Meals] in the presence
of a *kohen* — is this to say that this is something advantageous? Didn't R.
Yochanan teach: A Torah scholar who [allows] someone else to recite the
blessing before him [i.e., when he is present] — even [if that person is] a n
ignorant[665] *kohen gadol* — is worthy of death, for the verse (*Mishlei* 8:36)
states: *All those who hate Me love death* — do not read [the verse as stating]
those who hate Me, read it [as if it stated] *who make Me hated* [i.e., those who
through their actions prevent the people from properly appreciating Torah scholars].
He [R. Preida] was referring to those [*kohanim*] who were of equal stature.

COMMENTARY

Tosafos notes that elsewhere,[666] R. Preida's longevity was attributed to the
fact that he reviewed his lesson with a single student four hundred times. A *bas
kol* issued forth and asked: Do you prefer that you and your entire generation
merit the World to Come or to live for four hundred years? R. Preida answered: I
prefer that I and my generation merit the World to Come. God then said: Let
him have both [rewards]. *Tosafos* answers that R. Preida might have been
unaware of God's response and attributed his longevity to his acts of piety.

Rabbenu Yonah[667] explains the importance of honoring Torah scholars and
writes: *By showing them respect and giving them precedence, their words are
listened to and the entire people seeks to accompany them. When people see the*

---

664 - Thus, since the meat may be eaten before the gifts to the *kohen* are separated,
R. Preida's refusal to do so was a stringency that he accepted out of piety.
Rambam (הלכות ביכורים ט:יד) explains that the gifts given to the *kohen* are different
than untithed grain — which also require the separation of a portion that is given to
the *kohen* — because the meat portions are distinguishable even before they are
separated, whereas the gifts — *terumah* and *terumas ma'aser* — that must be separated
from grain are only recognizable once separated.
665 - If the *kohen* was himself a scholar, he would obviously take precedence. The
Talmud seeks to prove from R. Yochanan's ruling that a Torah scholar is considered
more important than a *kohen*. Thus, how could R. Preida — a great scholar — have
claimed that he was given long life because he never recited the blessing in the
presence of a *kohen*.
666 - עירובין נד:.
667 - שערי תשובה ג' קמ"ז.

respect given them, they learn to also give respect and knowledge is thereby increased. Many whose hearts are asleep are awakened when they see the honor and prestige given the Torah and they then recognize its stature and desire enters their hearts to occupy themselves in its study and serve Him with a pure heart.

TALMUD

שָׁאֲלוּ תַלְמִידָיו אֶת רַבִּי נְחוּנְיָא בֶּן הַקָּנָה: בַּמֶּה הֶאֱרַכְתָּ יָמִים? אָמַר לָהֶם: מִיָּמַי לֹא נִתְכַּבַּדְתִּי בִּקְלוֹן חֲבֵרִי, וְלֹא עָלְתָה עִמִּי קִלְלַת חֲבֵירִי עַל מִטָּתִי, וּוַתְּרָן הָיִיתִי בְמָמוֹנִי.

לֹא נִתְכַּבַּדְתִּי בִּקְלוֹן חֲבֵירִי, כִּי הָא דְרַב הוּנָא דָּרֵי מָרָא אַכַּתְפֵּיהּ, אָתָא רַב חָנָא בַר חֲנִילָאִי וְקָא שָׁקִיל מִינֵּיהּ, אָמַר לֵיהּ: אִי רְגִילַת דְּדָרִית בְּמָאתִיךְ - דָּרִי. וְאִי לָא - אִיתְיַיקּוּרֵי אֲנָא בְּזִילוּתָא דִּידָךְ, לָא נִיחָא לִי.

TRANSLATION

R. Nechunya ben ha-Kana's students asked him: How did you [merit to] live long? He answered them: During my entire life I never took honor from my friend's embarrassment and I never went to bed with my friend's curse upon me [i.e., I never retired before first pacifying those who were angry with me] and I was lenient with my funds.

I never took honor from my friend's embarrassment — as in the example of R. Huna who was once carrying a scythe on his shoulder. R. Chana bar Chanilai came and took it from him [to carry it in his stead]. He [R. Huna] said to him: If you are used to carrying [implements] in your town, you may carry it. But if not, I am not willing to be honored through your embarrasment.

COMMENTARY

R. Nechunyah's first statement describing the type of behavior that earned him long life bears examination, for it would not seem to be an act of piety but an obvious requirement. As *Rambam*[668] writes: *It is a positive precept to love everyone in Israel, as the verse (Vayikra 19:18) states: And you shall love your friend as yourself. One is therefore dutybound to speak favorably of him and to be as careful in guarding his money as he is with his own [and honor him] as he would want to be honored. And one who accepts honor through the embarrassment of another has no portion in the World to Come.*

---

668 - הלכות דעות ו:ד.

However, through the example that the Talmud offers, we can understand the extreme length that Sages like R. Nechunya went to avoid being honored through someone else's embarrassment. Even though R. Huna could have allowed R. Chanilai to carry the implement, for he was a greater scholar and deserved the honor, he would not permit him to do so if there was any possibility of the act causing him embarrassment.

TALMUD

וְלֹא עָלְתָה עַל מִטָּתִי קִלְלַת חֲבֵרִי, כִּי הָא דְּמַר זוּטְרָא, כִּי הֲנָה סָלִיק לְפוּרְיֵיה, אָמַר: שָׁרֵי לֵיה לְכָל מָאן דְּצַעֲרָן.

וּוַתְּרָן בְּמָמוֹנִי הָיִיתִי, דְּאֲמַר מַר: אִיּוֹב וַתְּרָן בְּמָמוֹנֵיה הֲנָה, שֶׁהָיָה מַנִּיחַ פְּרוּטָה לְחֶנְוָנִי מִמָּמוֹנֵיה.

TRANSLATION

I never went to bed with my friend's curse upon me — as in the example of Mar Zutra. When he went to bed, he would say: I forgive all those who caused me anguish.

I was lenient with my funds — as Mar taught: Iyov was lenient with his funds, for he would leave the change [due him from his purchases] with the storekeeper.

COMMENTARY

Maharal[669] explains that because R. Nechunya forgave others for any wrong that they may have done them, God forgave him for any sins that he might have done. Similarly, because he was lenient in dealing with others, God was lenient in dealing with him and he therefore merited long life.

TALMUD

שָׁאַל רַבִּי עֲקִיבָא אֶת רַבִּי נְחוּנְיָא הַגָּדוֹל: בַּמֶּה הֶאֱרַכְתָּ יָמִים? אֲתוּ גְּווֹזָאֵי קָא מָחוּ לֵיה. סָלִיק, יָתִיב אַרֵישָׁא דְּדִיקְלָא, אָמַר לוֹ: רַבִּי, אִם נֶאֱמַר: "כֶּבֶשׂ", לָמָה נֶאֱמַר: "אֶחָד" אָמַר לֵיה: "אֶחָד" – מְיֻחָד שֶׁבְּעֶדְרוֹ. אָמַר לְהוּ: צוּרְבָּא מֵרַבָּנָן הוּא, שָׁבְקוּהוּ!

אָמַר לוֹ: מִיָּמַי לֹא קִבַּלְתִּי מַתָּנוֹת, דִּכְתִיב: "וְשׂוֹנֵא מַתָּנוֹת יִחְיֶה" וְלֹא עָמַדְתִּי עַל מִדּוֹתַי. וּוַתְּרָן בְּמָמוֹנִי הָיִיתִי;

TRANSLATION

R. Akiva asked R. Nechunya the Great: How did you merit long life? The

---

669 - נתיבות עולם, נתיב הנדיבות פ"א and חידושי אגדות בבא בתרא טו.

servant came in and struck him [for asking an impudent question].[670] He [R. Akiva] left and sat on the top of a palm tree and asked him: Teacher! If [the verse (*Bamidbar* 28:4)] states: *a sheep* [using the singular form], why does it [also] state *one* [i.e., the number is superfluous]? He answered him: [The word] *one* [teaches us that he is to offer] the best of his flock. He then said to him [to his servant, based on R. Akiva's question]: He is a Torah scholar. Let him be.

He [R. Nechunya] told him [in answer to his question as to how he had merited to live so long]: During my entire life I did not accept gifts, as the verse (*Mishlei* 15:27) states: *He who detests gifts shall live*, I did not insist upon that which was due me and I was lenient with my funds.

TALMUD

לֹא קִבַּלְתִּי מַתָּנוֹת, כִּי הָא דְרַבִּי אֶלְעָזָר, כִּי הֲווֹ מְשַׁדְּרֵי לֵיה מַתָּנוֹת מִבֵּי־
נְשִׂיאָה, לָא הֲוָה שָׁקִיל. כִּי הֲווֹ מְזַמְּנֵי לֵיה, לָא הֲוָה אָזִיל, אָמַר לְהוּ: לָא נִיחָא
לְכוּ דְאֶחְיֶה?! דִכְתִיב: "וְשׂוֹנֵא מַתָּנוֹת יִחְיֶה". רַבִּי זֵירָא, כִּי הֲווֹ מְשַׁדְּרֵי לֵיה
מִבֵּי־נְשִׂיאָה, לָא הֲוָה שָׁקִיל. כִּי הֲווֹ מְזַמְּנֵי לֵיה, אָזִיל. אָמַר: אִתְיַיקּוּרֵי
דְמִתְיַיקְּרֵי בִי.

וְלֹא עָמַדְתִּי עַל מִדּוֹתַי, דְּאָמַר רָבָא: כָּל הַמַּעֲבִיר עַל מִדּוֹתָיו, מַעֲבִירִין לוֹ עַל
כָּל פְּשָׁעָיו, שֶׁנֶּאֱמַר: "נֹשֵׂא עָוֹן וְעֹבֵר עַל פֶּשַׁע", לְמִי "נוֹשֵׂא עָוֹן"? לְמִי שֶׁהוּא
"עֹבֵר עַל פֶּשַׁע".

TRANSLATION

I did not accept gifts — as in the example of R. Elazar. When he would be sent [a gift] from the house of the *nasi*, he would not accept [it]. When he was invited [to the home of the *nasi*], he would not go. He would tell them: Do you not want me to live? The verse states: *He who detests gifts shall live.* When R. Zeira would be sent [gifts] from the houe of the *nasi*, he would not accept [them]. When he was invited [to the home of the *nasi*], he would go. He explained [his reason]: They are honored by me [i.e., my presence brings them honor and I

---

thus have no right to refuse their invitation, for I receive nothing in return].[671]
I did not insist upon that which was due me — as Rava said: One who is forebearing, all of his sins are waived, as the verse (*Michah* 7:18) states: *He bears sin and waives inequity* — for whom does He bear sin? For one who waives inequity [done against him].

COMMENTARY

The dialogue between R. Nechunya and R. Akiva bears further explanation, for we find that the reasons that he offered R. Akiva to explain his longevity differ from those that he had given his own students.

Iyun Yaakov explains that R. Akiva was not a student of R. Nechunya; thus, R. Nechunya did not feel obligated to explain his source of merit and did not intervene when the servant banished him.[672] When R. Akiva climbed the tree and asked him a seemingly innocuous question, he was really asking R. Nechunya how he — the singular sheep in R. Akiva's question — merited longevity when, as the leading scholar of the era, he should have been held culpable for the sins of the generation. We might suggest that this might also be the reason why the Talmud here refers to R. Nechunya as the Great whereas previously the Talmud does not refer to him by this title, for R. Akiva's question related directly to R. Nechunya's greatness.

R. Nechunya answered that he was not held liable for the sins of the generation because he had always acted with forebearance and because he had never accepted gifts which would have made him beholden to them.

Netziv[673] explains that a community leader can be held responsible for the sins of the generation because the generation's shortcomings may well be a

---

671 - Why did R. Zeira, an *amora*, not follow the example set by R. Elazar and refuse the invitation? We might suggest that in R. Elazar's time the office of the *nasi* was occupied by men of stature, whereas in R. Zeira's time, the prestige associated with the office of the exilarch who served as *nasi* for the Jews of Bavel had slipped greatly. Thus, R. Elazar refused the invitation for accepting it would have brought him honor. R. Zeira, however, recognized that the exilarch's invitation was meant to lend prestige to the office and he therefore had no grounds to refuse it.

672 - Had he been a disciple, he would have told him that he wanted to know so that he might emulate his example, as per the subsequent dialogue between Rebbi and R. Yehoshua ben Korcha.

673 - רנה של תורה לשיר השירים ה:ג.

result of the leader's failure to admonish the people due to his own self-interests or because of his reluctance to forego his own prestige and deal with the day-to-day problems of the community. By explaining to R. Akiva that he had never accepted gifts and had always been self-effacing in his dealings, R. Nechunya provided him with the answer to his specific question.

TALMUD

שָׁאַל רַבִּי, אֶת רַבִּי יְהוֹשֻׁעַ בֶּן קָרְחָה: בַּמֶּה הֶאֱרַכְתָּ יָמִים? אָמַר לוֹ: קַצְתָּ בְחַיַּי? אָמַר לוֹ: רַבִּי, תּוֹרָה הִיא, וְלִלְמֹד אֲנִי צָרִיךְ! אָמַר לוֹ: מִיָּמַי לֹא נִסְתַּכַּלְתִּי בְּצֶלֶם דְּמוּת אָדָם רָשָׁע. דְּאָמַר רַבִּי יוֹחָנָן אָסוּר לְאָדָם לְהִסְתַּכֵּל בְּצֶלֶם דְּמוּת אָדָם רָשָׁע, שֶׁנֶּאֱמַר: "כִּי לוּלֵי פְּנֵי יְהוֹשָׁפָט מֶלֶךְ יְהוּדָה אֲנִי נֹשֵׂא, אִם אַבִּיט אֵלֶיךָ, וְאִם אֶרְאֶךָּ". רַבִּי אֶלְעָזָר אָמַר: עֵינָיו כֵּהוֹת, שֶׁנֶּאֱמַר: "וַיְהִי כִּי זָקֵן יִצְחָק, וַתִּכְהֶיןָ עֵינָיו מֵרְאֹת", מִשּׁוּם דְּאִסְתַּכֵּל בֵּיהּ בְּעֵשָׂו הָרָשָׁע. וְהָא גְּרָמָא לֵיהּ?! וְהָאָמַר רַבִּי יִצְחָק: לְעוֹלָם אַל תְּהִי קִלְלַת הֶדְיוֹט קַלָּה בְעֵינֶיךָ, שֶׁהֲרֵי אֲבִימֶלֶךְ קִלֵּל אֶת שָׂרָה, וְנִתְקַיֵּם בְּזַרְעָהּ, שֶׁנֶּאֱמַר: "הִנֵּה הוּא לָךְ כְּסוּת עֵינַיִם", אַל תִּקְרֵי "כְּסוּת", אֶלָּא "כַּסְיוּת". הָא וְהָא גְּרָמָא לֵיהּ.

רָבָא אָמַר, מֵהָכָא: "שְׂאֵת פְּנֵי רָשָׁע לֹא טוֹב".

TRANSLATION

Rebbi asked R. Yehoshua ben Karcha: How did you [merit to] live long? He answered him: Are you disgusted with my life? He told him: My teacher! This [my question] is Torah and I must learn [i.e., the secret of your longevity so that I might apply it to myself as well]. He [R. Yehoshua ben Karcha] told him: During my entire lifetime I never looked[674] at the image of a wicked person, as R. Yochanan taught: It is forbidden to look at the image of a wicked person, for the verse (*Melachim* II 3:14) states: *For the countenance of Yehoshafat, king of Yehudah, I bear. But I will not look at you or see you.*[675] R. Elazar taught: [One who looks at an evil person] becomes blind, as the verse (*Bereishis* 27:1) states: *And it was when Yitzchak became old, his eyes became dim [and could*

674 - R. Akiva Eiger, quoting *Magen Avraham*, explains that the Talmud is referring to closely examining the essence of a wicked person rather than glancing at him.
675 - Yehoram, king of Israel, formed an alliance with Yehoshafat, king of Yehudah, to wage war against Moav. Yehoshafat suggested that they consult with the prophet Elisha, but the prophet refused to even look at Yehoram, admonishing him that he should consult with the false gods of his father Achav.

not see] — [Why did this happen?] Because he looked at Esav the wicked. Is this what caused it [Yitzchak's blindness]? Did R. Yitzchak not teach: The curse of a common person should never be taken lightly,[676] for Avimelech cursed Sarah and it [his curse] was fulfilled in her progeny. The verse (*Bereishis* 20:16) states: *Behold it shall be a covering for your eyes* — do not read the word as כסות — *cover* — rather כסיות — *blindness*. [We see, then, that Yitzchak's blindness was a result of Avimelech's curse and was not the result of his looking at Esav.] [R. Elazar answered:] Both were the cause.

Rava taught: [The prohibition of looking at a wicked person can be derived from this verse (*Mishlei* 18:5):] *To see the face of the wicked is not good.*

COMMENTARY

One of the more difficult concepts to understand is that which we refer to as עין הרע — the evil eye. How is it possible that one can simply look at something and cause an event to transpire or a change to occur? While it is beyond the scope of this work — and surely beyond the ability of this writer — to explain the true manner in which the temporal world functions, the subject cannot be totally ignored.

Chazon Ish[677] writes: *One of the secrets of the Creation is that man, through his thought processes, can release hidden forces in the physical world. His limited capabilities can act as the catalyst for the destruction and desolation of material elements ... Everything is in the hands of Heaven, and as long as God has not decreed that something be destroyed, it will remain in existence. Nevertheless when it is decreed that something be destroyed, it sometimes happens that by looking at something and expressing amazement, it is then that it is brought to destruction. Our Sages tell us that ninety-nine percent of those who die perish because of the evil eye — i.e., when it is decreed on Yom Kippur that they are to die, it is the evil eye that brings this about. It is possible that the greater the person, the greater the sensitivity of his eye ... Although no one dies without being judged by Heaven, it is known that Satan prosecutes at the time of danger. Similarly, it is said that man is judged daily. Moreover, in the judgement rendered on Yom Kippur, the sentence is sometimes*

---

676 - See page 180.

677 - ליקוטים סימן כ״א. See also the commentary of *Malbim* to *Shmuel* II 24:1.

issued that man be left to the whims of nature and no miracle be performed on his behalf and he is therefore harmed by the evil eye.

TALMUD

בִּשְׁעַת פְּטִירָתוֹ, אָמַר לוֹ: בָּרְכֵנִי, אָמַר לוֹ: יְהִי רָצוֹן שֶׁתַּגִּיעַ לַחֲצִי יָמַי. וּלְכוּלְהוּ לֹא?! אָמַר לוֹ: הַבָּאִים אַחֲרֶיךָ בְּהֵמָה יִרְעוּ?!

אָבוּהַ בַּר אִיהִי, וּמִינְיָמִין בַּר אִיהִי, חַד אָמַר: תֵּיתֵי לִי דְּלָא אִסְתַּכְּלֵי בְּגוֹי וְחַד אָמַר: תֵּיתֵי לִי דְּלָא עָבְדֵי שְׁתָּפוּת בַּהֲדֵי גוֹי.

שָׁאֲלוּ תַּלְמִידָיו אֶת רַבִּי זֵירָא: בַּמֶּה הֶאֱרַכְתָּ יָמִים? אָמַר לָהֶם: מִיָּמַי לֹא הִקְפַּדְתִּי בְּתוֹךְ בֵּיתִי. וְלֹא צָעַדְתִּי בִּפְנֵי מִי שֶׁגָּדוֹל מִמֶּנִּי. וְלֹא הִרְהַרְתִּי בַּמְּבוֹאוֹת הַמְטֻנָּפוֹת. וְלֹא הָלַכְתִּי אַרְבַּע אַמּוֹת בְּלֹא תּוֹרָה וּבְלֹא תְפִלִּין, וְלֹא יָשַׁנְתִּי בְּבֵית הַמִּדְרָשׁ, לֹא שְׁנַת קֶבַע וְלֹא שְׁנַת עֲרַאי. וְלֹא שַׂשְׂתִּי בְּתַקָּלַת חֲבֵרִי. וְלֹא קָרִיתִי לַחֲבֵרִי בַּחֲכִינָתוֹ; וְאָמְרֵי לָהּ: בַּחֲנִיכָתוֹ.

TRANSLATION

At the time of his [R. Yehoshua ben Korcha's] death, he [Rebbi] asked him: Bless me. He said: May it be His will that you reach half my days. [R. Yehudah was taken aback and asked:] Not to all of them [i.e., do you begrudge me that I live as long as you]! He answered: Those who come after you — shall they tend flocks![678]

Avuha bar Ihi and Minyamin bar Ihi [were discussing their sources of merit]. One said: [Reward] will come to me because I did not look at gentiles. The other said: [Reward] will come to me because I did not form partnerships with gentiles.

R. Zeira's students asked him: How did you [merit to] live long?[679] He answered them: During my entire life I was never overly strict in my home, I never walked in front of one who was greater than me,[680] I never thought [about

---

678 - I.e., if you live as long as I have, your children and students will never have an opportunity to serve as leaders and teachers.

679 - I.e., what were the acts of piety that brought you long life. As we have already seen, all of those asked this question pointed to types of behavior that went beyond the requirements of *halachah*.

680 - *Maharsha* points out that even though this is a halachic requirement and not an act of piety, R. Zeira was careful when walking at the side of his teacher or someone greater than he not to step in front of him even though this would not be considered walking in front of him.

Torah] in the alleyways that were filthy [with sewage],[681] I never walked four
amos without [thinking about] Torah and without [wearing] *tefillin*, I never slept
in the study hall — neither for a regular sleep nor for a short nap, I never found
joy in my friend's mistakes[682] and I never called a friend by his childhood
nickname. Some say by his family nickname.

TALMUD

מִשְׁנָה. וְעוֹד אָמַר רַבִּי יְהוּדָה: בֵּית הַכְּנֶסֶת שֶׁחָרַב, אֵין מַסְפִּידִין בְּתוֹכוֹ וכו',
וְאֵין עוֹשִׂין אוֹתוֹ קַפַּנְדַּרְיָא, שֶׁנֶּאֱמַר: "וַהֲשִׁמּוֹתִי אֶת מִקְדְּשֵׁיכֶם" – קְדֻשָּׁתָן
אַף כְּשֶׁהֵן שׁוֹמֵמִין וכו'.

גְּמָרָא. תָּנוּ רַבָּנָן: בָּתֵּי כְנֵסִיּוֹת, אֵין נוֹהֲגִין בָּהֶן קַלּוּת רֹאשׁ: אֵין אוֹכְלִין בָּהֶן.
וְאֵין שׁוֹתִין בָּהֶן. וְאֵין נֵאוֹתִין בָּהֶן. וְאֵין מְטַיְּלִין בָּהֶן. וְאֵין נִכְנָסִין בָּהֶן, בַּחַמָּה
מִפְּנֵי הַחַמָּה, וּבַגְּשָׁמִים מִפְּנֵי הַגְּשָׁמִים. וְאֵין מַסְפִּידִין בָּהֶן הֶסְפֵּד שֶׁל יָחִיד.
אֲבָל קוֹרִין בָּהֶן, וְשׁוֹנִין בָּהֶן, וּמַסְפִּידִין בָּהֶן הֶסְפֵּד שֶׁל רַבִּים.

TRANSLATION

MISHNAH: R. Yehudah also taught: A synagogue that is desolate — we do
not eulogize in it and we do not make it into a shortcut,[683] for the verse
(*Vayikra* 26:31) states: *And I shall make desolate your Sanctuaries* — even when
they are desolate they are [still] sanctified.[684]

TALMUD: The Sages taught: Synagogues — one may not act lightheadedly
inside them. One may not eat inside them, one may not drink inside them,
[28b] one may not prettify himself inside them, one may not walk inside
them,[685] one may not enter them [to use them as shelter] in the summer because
of the sun or in the winter because of the rain and one may not deliver a eulogy

---

681 - *Maharsha* notes that this too is a halachic requirement and not an act of piety.
He explains that while one may not learn Torah in unsuitable places, R. Zeira's piety
was so refined that he was able to train himself to even refrain from thinking about
Torah in these places.

682 - *Maharsha* explains that R. Zeira even refrained from laughing when he saw
someone fall.

683 - See note 657.

684 - *Tosafos Yom Tov*, in his commentary to the *Mishnah*, explains that the
exegesis is based on the fact that the verse first states והשימותי — *I shall make
desolate* — and then states מקדשיכם — *your Sanctuaries*. Though God declares that He
will destroy them, they are still called *Sanctuaries* and thus retain their holiness.

685 - I.e., to walk so as to relax or exercise.

for an individual inside them. But one may read [Scripture] inside them, one may teach inside them and one may deliver eulogies for the community[686] inside them.

TALMUD

אָמַר רַבִּי יְהוּדָה: אֵימָתַי? בְּיִשׁוּבָן, אֲבָל בְּחֻרְבָּנָן, מַנִּיחִין אוֹתָן וְעוֹלִים בָּהֶן עֲשָׂבִים, וְלֹא יִתְלֹשׁ מִפְּנֵי עָגְמַת נֶפֶשׁ. ,עֲשָׂבִים', מָאן דְּכַר שְׁמַיְיהוּ? חַסּוֹרֵי מִחַסְּרָא, וְהָכֵי קָתְנֵי: וּמְכַבְּדִין אוֹתָן, וּמְרַבְּצִין אוֹתָן, כְּדֵי שֶׁלֹּא יַעֲלוּ בָהֶן עֲשָׂבִים. אָמַר רַבִּי יְהוּדָה: אֵימָתַי? בְּיִשׁוּבָן, אֲבָל בְּחֻרְבָּנָן, מַנִּיחִין אוֹתָן לַעֲלוֹת. עָלוּ בָהֶם עֲשָׂבִים, לֹא יִתְלֹשׁ, מִפְּנֵי עָגְמַת נֶפֶשׁ.

אָמַר רַבִּי אַסִּי: בָּתֵּי כְנֵסִיּוֹת שֶׁבְּבָבֶל, עַל תְּנַאי הֵן עֲשׂוּיִין, וְאַף עַל פִּי כֵן אֵין נוֹהֲגִין בָּהֶן קַלּוּת רֹאשׁ, וּמַאי נִיהוּ? חֶשְׁבּוֹנוֹת.

אָמַר רַבִּי אַסִּי: בֵּית הַכְּנֶסֶת שֶׁמְּחַשְּׁבִין בּוֹ חֶשְׁבּוֹנוֹת, מַלִּינִין בּוֹ אֶת הַמֵּת. מַלִּינִין, סַלְקָא דַּעְתָּךְ?! לָא סַגְיָא דְּלָאו הָכֵי?! אֶלָּא לַסּוֹף שֶׁיָּלִינוּ בּוֹ מֵת־מִצְוָה.

TRANSLATION

R. Yehudah taught: When [is one permitted to use a synagogue for these purposes]? When they are in use. But when they are in ruins, they are to be left alone and weeds are allowed to grow inside them and one should not pick them [the weeds] so that there be anguish [that the synagogue is in ruins]. Weeds? Who was referring to them?[687] [The text that quotes the Sages] is deficient and this is what should be said. They should be swept and they should be cleaned so that weeds do not grow inside them. R. Yehudah taught: When [are they to be swept and cleaned of weeds]? When they are in use. But when they are in ruins, they are to be allowed to grow. If weeds grow, they are not to be picked so that there be anguish [that the synagogue is in ruins].

R. Asi taught: The synagogues of Bavel are constructed with a condition [that

---

686 - I.e., eulogies that the community is required to attend — e.g., when an important member of the community passes away.

687 - I.e., at first it seemed that R. Yehudah was making the use of a synagogue for purposes other than prayer conditional on their being functional. He then ruled that if they were in ruins one could not use them and could not pick the weeds. The Talmud points out that this statement has nothing to do with the previous one and therefore explains that the text is deficient — i.e., the *halachah* cited in R. Yehudah's name was referring to a different case.

they are permitted to be utilized for other purposes].[688] But even so it is forbidden to act lightheadedly inside of them. And what is this [i.e., what type of use is considered to be lightheaded and therefore forbidden]? [It is forbidden to enter them to] arrange accounts.

R. Asi taught: A synagogue that is used to arrange accounts is used to store the dead [until burial]. Would you think [that it is permitted] to store [the dead in the synagogue because it was used for arranging one's accounts]!? Is it not sufficient [i.e., has the synagogue not been degraded enough by being used improperly] without this [i.e., without also using it as a place to store the dead]!? Rather, in the end [since the synagogue was not treated with due respect] it will be used to store a *meis mitzvah* [as punishment for the disrespect shown].

TALMUD

רְבִינָא וְרַב אַדָּא בַּר מַתְנָא, הָוּ קָיְימֵי, וְשָׁאֲלוּ שְׁאֶלְתָּא מֵרָבָא, אָתָא זִילְחָא דְמִיטְרָא, עַיְילֵי לְבֵית הַכְּנֶסֶת, אָמְרֵי: הַאי דְּעַיְילִינָן לְבֵית הַכְּנֶסֶת, לָאו מִשּׁוּם מִיטְרָא, אֶלָּא מִשּׁוּם דִּשְׁמַעֲתָּא בָעְיָא צִילוּתָא כְּיוֹמָא דְאִסְתְּנָא.

וּמַסְפִּידִין בָּהֶן הֶסְפֵּד שֶׁל רַבִּים. הֵיכִי דָמֵי הֶסְפֵּידָא דְרַבִּים? מַחְוֵי רַב חִסְדָּא: כְּגוֹן הֶסְפֵּידָא דְקָאֵי בֵי רַב שֵׁשֶׁת. מַחְוֵי רַב שֵׁשֶׁת: כְּגוֹן הֶסְפֵּידָא דְקָאֵי בֵי רַב חִסְדָּא.

TRANSLATION

Ravina and R. Ada bar Masna were standing [in the courtyard of the synagogue] and were asking Rava a question. A rainstorm came and they went into the synagogue. They explained: That which [i.e., the reason why] we went into the synagogue was not because of the rain, but because [Torah] study requires clarity [of thought] like a bright day.[689]

---

688 - I.e., at the time of construction a stipulation can be made that the building will be used for other purposes as well. Note that this stipulation is only efficacious as regards the synagogues in Bavel (or elsewhere in the Diaspora). The pre-condition would be of no avail regarding synagogues built in *Eretz Yisrael* — see *Orach Chaim* 151:11 and *Mishnah Berurah* (ad loc.). *Tosafos* (ד"ה בתי כנסיות) explains that the sanctity of the synagogues in Bavel is only temporary, since they are destined to be relocated to *Eretz Yisrael*, whereas the sanctity of the synagogues in *Eretz Yisrael* is permanent.

689 - I.e., since the *beraisa* ruled that one may not enter a synagogue to escape the rain, there must have been another reason why Ravina and R. Ada entered the synagogue.

One may deliver eulogies for the community inside them — What is meant by eulogies for the community? R. Chisda offered an example: A eulogy where R. Sheshes is present. R. Sheshes offered an example: A eulogy where R. Chisda is present.[690]

TALMUD

רַפְרָם אַסְפְּדָהּ לְכַלָּתֵיהּ בְּבֵי כְנִישְׁתָּא, אֲמַר: מִשּׁוּם יְקָרָא דִּידִי וּדְמִיתָא, אֲתוּ כּוּלֵי עָלְמָא.

רַבִּי זֵירָא סַפְדֵיהּ לְהַהוּא מֵרַבָּנָן בְּבֵי כְנִישְׁתָּא, אֲמַר: אִי מִשּׁוּם יְקָרָא דִּידִי, אִי מִשּׁוּם יְקָרָא דִּידֵיהּ – דְּמִיתָא, אֲתוּ כּוּלֵי עָלְמָא.

רֵישׁ לָקִישׁ סַפְדֵיהּ לְהַהוּא צוּרְבָא מֵרַבָּנָן דִּשְׁכִיחַ בְּאַרְעָא דְיִשְׂרָאֵל, דַּהֲוֵי תָנֵי הִלְכְתָא בְּעֶשְׂרִים וְאַרְבַּע שׁוּרָתָא, אֲמַר: וַוי חָסְרָא אַרְעָא דְיִשְׂרָאֵל גַּבְרָא רַבָּה.

TRANSLATION

Rafram eulogized his daughter-in-law in the synagogue. He explained: In tribute to me and to her, the entire community came [and it was therefore permitted to eulogize her in the synagogue].

R. Zeira eulogized a certain rabbi in the synagogue. He explained: Either in tribute to me, or in tribute to him — the deceased — the entire community came [and it was therefore permitted to eulogize him in the synagogue].

Reish Lakish eulogized a certain student who often came to the Land of Israel [from Bavel in order to study Torah] and who learned *halachah*[691] [sitting] in the twenty-fourth row.[692] He said [in his eulogy]: Woe, for the Land of Israel now lacks a great man.

---

690 - *Maharsha* explains that if a person of the importance of R. Chisda or R. Sheshes saw fit to attend, that would be considered a public eulogy. *Rashi* explains that the reference is to a eulogy in the study hall of R. Chisda or R. Sheshes.

691 - It is clear from the context of the following statements that the Talmud uses *halachah* as a synonym for the *Mishnah* rather than in its contemporary context.

692 - The students would sit in a semi-circle around their teacher, the most scholarly sitting in the front while those less learned sat in the back. Thus, the student who Reish Lakish eulogized was not the most scholarly of men since he was seated in the twenty-fourth row. Nevertheless, Reish Lakish deemed it appropriate to eulogize him and refer to him as a great man.

TALMUD

הַהוּא דַּהֲנָה תָּנֵי הִלְכְתָא, סִיפְרָא, סִיפְרֵי, וְתוֹסֶפְתָּא, וְשָׁכִיב. אָתוּ וַאֲמַרוּ
לֵיה לְרַב נַחְמָן: לִיסְפְּדֵיה מָר. אָמַר: הֵיכֵי נִסְפְּדֵיה? הִי צָנֵי דְּמַלָא סִפְרֵי
דְּחָסֵר? תָּא חֲזִי – מַה בֵּין תַּקִּיפֵי דְּאַרְעָא דְיִשְׂרָאֵל, לַחֲסִידֵי דְּבָבֶל.

תְּנָן הָתָם: וּדְאִשְׁתַּמֵּשׁ בְּתָגָא – חֲלָף. תָּנָא רֵישׁ לָקִישׁ: זֶה הַמִּשְׁתַּמֵּשׁ בְּמִי
שֶׁשּׁוֹנֶה הֲלָכוֹת – כְּתָרָה שֶׁל תּוֹרָה. וַאֲמַר עוּלָא: לִישְׁתַּמֵּשׁ אִינִישׁ בְּמָאן דְּתָנֵי
אַרְבָּעָה, וְלָא לִישְׁתַּמֵּשׁ בְּמָאן דְּמַתְנֵי אַרְבָּעָה. כִּי הָא דְּרֵישׁ לָקִישׁ הֲוָה אָזִיל
בְּאוֹרְחָא, מָטָא עוּרְקְמָא דְּמַיָּא, אָתָא הַהוּא גַּבְרָא, אַרְכְּבֵיהּ אַכַּתְפֵּיהּ וְקָא
מְעַבַּר לֵיהּ. אֲמַר לֵיהּ: קָרִיתָ? אֲמַר לֵיהּ: קָרִינָא. תָּנִיתָ? תָּנֵינָא אַרְבָּעָה סִדְרֵי
מִשְׁנָה. אֲמַר לֵיהּ: פָּסַלְתְּ לָךְ אַרְבָּעָה טוּרֵי, וְטָעֲנַתְּ בַּר לָקִישׁ אַכַּתְפִּיד?! שָׁדֵי
בַּר לָקִישָׁא בְּמַיָּא. אֲמַר לֵיהּ: נִיחָא לִי דְּאַשְׁמְעֵיהּ לְמַר. אִי הָכֵי, גְּמוֹר מִינִי הָא
מִילְתָא דְּאָמַר רַבִּי זֵירָא: בְּנוֹת יִשְׂרָאֵל, הֵן הֶחְמִירוּ עַל עַצְמָן, שֶׁאֲפִלּוּ רוֹאוֹת
טִפַּת דָּם כְּחַרְדָּל, יוֹשְׁבוֹת עָלָיו שִׁבְעָה נְקִיִּים.

TRANSLATION

Once a person who studied *halachah*, *Sifra*, *Sifri*[693] and the *Tosefta* died. They [his fellow students] went and asked R. Nachman: "Master, will you eulogize him?" He responded: "How shall he be eulogized [i.e., what can I say]? Woe to the basket that is full of books and is now missing!?"[694] Come and see what is the difference between the sharp [students] of the Land of Israel[695] and the righteous people of Bavel.[696]

---

693 - The *Sifra* is the *Midrash halachah* to *Vayikra* — also known as *Toras Kohanim* — and the *Sifri* is the *Midrash halachah* to *Bamidbar* and *Devarim*.

694 - I.e., since the deceased did not put his knowledge to practical use, he is like a basket of books and the fact that he is no longer alive is either not a great enough loss to justify a eulogy in the synagogue or that one of R. Nachman's stature should eulogize him.

695 - The reference is to Reish Lakish who was considered to be a prototype of the sharp minded students of Israel — see *Yoma* 9a.

696 - The reference is to R. Nachman who was considered to be the prototype of the righteous sages of Bavel — see *Sotah* 49a. This statement would seem to be cynically contrasting the willingness of Reish Lakish to deliver a eulogy for a student of weak caliber to the refusal of R. Nachman to deliver a eulogy for a student who had mastered an enormous amount of material. See also *Sanhedrin* 24a where the Talmud refers to the scholars of *Eretz Yisrael* as a "pleasant staff" and the scholars of Bavel as a "rigid staff".

We learned in a *Mishnah*[697] there: One who utilizes the crown [of Torah improperly] will pass away. Reish Lakish taught: This refers to one who [accepts the service of one who] studies *halachah*, the crown of Torah. Ula taught: One may accept the service of one who studied four [of the six orders of the *Mishnah*], but one may not accept the service of one who taught four [of the six orders].[698] An example of this can be seen from Reish Lakish who was once walking on his way and came to a puddle of water. A man came and lifted him onto his shoulders and carried him across. Reish Lakish asked him: "Have you [learned] Scripture?" He answered him: "I have learned Scripture." "Have you studied *Mishnah*?" "I have studied four orders of the *Mishnah*." [Reish Lakish then said:] "You have excavated four mountains and you carry Lakish's son on your shoulders!? Throw Lakish's son into the water!" He responded: "I prefer to serve the master." [Reish Lakish thereupon said:] "If so,[699] learn from me this teaching that R. Zeira taught: The daughters of Israel were stringent with themselves. Even if they see a drop of blood the size of a mustard seed, they count seven clean days [before immersing themselves]."[700]

COMMENTARY

Why did Reish Lakish choose to quote this specific teaching to the student who sought to serve him? *Maharsha* explains that Reish Lakish wanted to show the student that learning *Mishnah* alone was not sufficient, for a *halachah* based on a self-accepted stringency like the one taught by R. Zeira would not be known if

697 - אבות א:יג.

698 - *Maharsha* explains that the Talmud differentiates between one who studied the orders of *Moed, Nashim, Nezikin* and *Kodshim* and between one who also studied *Zeraim* and *Taharos* since many of the laws brought in the latter two are not relevant outside Eretz Yisrael.

699 - I.e., since you wish to serve me, I must teach you something so that I might be worthy of your service.

700 - According to Torah law, a woman need only count seven clean days if she is a *zavah* — i.e., if she has a vaginal emission three times within an eleven day period between the end of one menstrual flow and the beginning of the next. At the beginning of a menstrual period, she can — by Torah law — immerse as soon as her flow stops. Because we are no longer familiar with the differences between the laws of a *zavah* and the laws of a menstruant, women accepted a stringency upon themselves and count seven clean days whenever they have a vaginal emission — either at the beginning or in the middle of the menstrual cycle.

one limited himself to studying *Mishnah*. Adherence to *halachah* and mastery of
the material that forms basic Jewish practice demands that one study the Talmud
as well, for it is only through the Talmud's discussions and explanations that
one can become aware of the law in its entirety.

Ben Ish Chai adds that Reish Lakish sought to teach the student another lesson
as well. Reish Lakish's refusal to allow the student to serve him was based on a
stringency that he accepted upon himself, for as Ula pointed out, one could take
advantage of the services of one who had only learned four orders of the
Mishnah. The student could have told Reish Lakish that he did not accept Reish
Lakish's stringency and was therefore permitted to serve him. Reish Lakish
therefore quoted the teaching of R. Zeira which shows that a self-accepted
stringency can apply to others as well. The practice of counting seven clean days
after seeing a drop of blood which is a stringency that women accepted affects
their husbands as well.

TALMUD

תָּנָא דְּבֵי אֵלִיָּהוּ: כָּל הַשּׁוֹנֶה הֲלָכוֹת מֻבְטָח לוֹ שֶׁהוּא בֶן עוֹלָם הַבָּא, שֶׁנֶּאֱמַר:
"הֲלִיכוֹת עוֹלָם לוֹ", אַל תִּקְרֵי "הֲלִיכוֹת", אֶלָּא "הֲלָכוֹת".

תָּנוּ רַבָּנָן: מְבַטְּלִין תַּלְמוּד תּוֹרָה לְהוֹצָאַת הַמֵּת, וּלְהַכְנָסַת כַּלָּה. אָמְרוּ עָלָיו
עַל רַבִּי יְהוּדָה בְּרַבִּי אִילְעָי: שֶׁהָיָה מְבַטֵּל תַּלְמוּד תּוֹרָה לְהוֹצָאַת הַמֵּת
וּלְהַכְנָסַת הַכַּלָּה. בַּמֶּה דְּבָרִים אֲמוּרִים? כְּשֶׁאֵין שָׁם כָּל צָרְכּוֹ, אֲבָל יֵשׁ שָׁם כָּל
צָרְכּוֹ, אֵין מְבַטְּלִין. וְכַמָּה "כָּל צָרְכּוֹ"? אָמַר רַב שְׁמוּאֵל בַּר אִינְיָא מִשְׁמֵיהּ
דְּרַב: תְּרֵיסַר אַלְפֵי גַבְרֵי, וְשִׁיתָּא אַלְפֵי שִׁיפוּרָא. וְאָמְרֵי לָהּ: תְּרֵיסַר אַלְפֵי
גַבְרֵי, וּמִינַיְיהוּ שִׁיתָּא אַלְפֵי שִׁיפוּרָא. עוּלָא אָמַר: כְּגוֹן דְּחָיְיצֵי גַבְרֵי מֵאַבּוּלָא
עַד סִיכְרָא. רַב שֵׁשֶׁת אָמַר: כִּנְתִינָתָהּ כָּךְ נְטִילָתָהּ, מַה נְּתִינָתָהּ בְּשִׁשִּׁים
רִבּוֹא, אַף נְטִילָתָהּ בְּשִׁשִּׁים רִבּוֹא. הַנֵּי מִילֵּי לְמַאן דְּקָרֵי וְתָנֵי, אֲבָל לְמַאן
דְּמַתְנֵי, לֵית לֵיהּ שִׁיעוּרָא.

TRANSLATION

We learned in the school of Eliyahu:[701] All who study *halachah* are assured of
entry into the World to Come, as the verse (*Chavakuk* 3:6) states: *The paths of*

---

701 - The Talmud records a number of cases where *tannaim* were visited by the
Prophet Eliyahu who taught them various *halachos*. Some of these teachings are
quoted in the Talmud while the great majority are recorded in a *midrash* known as
Tanna d'Vei Eliyahu of unknown authorship.

the world are his. Do not read הליכות — *paths* — rather הלכות — *halachos.*

The Sages taught: [29a] The study of Torah is interrupted to accompany the dead [i.e., to accompany a burial processional] and to bring a bride [to the marriage canopy].[702] It was told of R. Yehudah bar Ilai that he would interrupt his Torah study to accompany the dead and to bring a bride [to the marriage canopy]. When was this said [i.e., under what circumstances may Torah study be interrupted]? When all of his needs [i.e., people to accompany the deceased as a sign of respect] are not there [then Torah study is interrupted and one should accompany the deceased]. But if all his needs are there, [Torah study may] not be interrupted.[703] What constitutes all of his needs? R. Shmuel bar Inia taught in the name of Rav: Twelve thousand men and six thousand who sound shofars. Some say [that he taught]: Twelve thousand men of whom six thousand sound shofars. Ula taught: [All of his needs are considered to have been met if those accompanying him are] a number equal to [the number of] men [necessary to form a line that would] stretch from the gates of the city until the cemetery. R. Sheshes taught: [The number of men considered to meet the needs of the deceased is based on the following:] As it [the Torah] was given, so is it taken. Just as it was given [in the presence] of six hundred thousand, so too it [the Torah] is taken [when a person dies] in the presence of six hundred thousand [i.e., if there are six hundred thousand men present to accompany the corpse, the needs of the deceased are considered to have been met and Torah study may not be interrupted]. This [number] applies to one who learned Scripture and *Mishnah*, but [regarding] one who taught [others], there is no limit [i.e., no matter how many people are already accompanying the deceased, Torah study is still interrupted so that everyone can accompany the deceased].

---

702 - Torah study is of paramount importance; thus, one may not interrupt his study to perform another mitzvah if it can be performed by others. The mitzvos of bringing joy to a bride or accompanying a burial procession are deemed to be exceptions to this rule even though they can be performed by others since the joy of a bride and the honor paid to the deceased is greater if more people attend.

703 - The Talmud differentiates between accompanying a burial procession and accompanying a bride, establishing that the honor due the deceased can be quantified whereas the joy that one brings to a bride cannot be measured. Thus, R. Yehudah bar Ilai only established criteria for the former.

TALMUD

תַּנְיָא, רַבִּי שִׁמְעוֹן בֶּן יוֹחַאי אוֹמֵר: בֹּא וּרְאֵה, כַּמָּה חֲבִיבִין יִשְׂרָאֵל לִפְנֵי הַקָּדוֹשׁ בָּרוּךְ הוּא, שֶׁבְּכָל מָקוֹם שֶׁגָּלוּ, שְׁכִינָה עִמָּהֶם. גָּלוּ לְמִצְרַיִם, שְׁכִינָה עִמָּהֶם, שֶׁנֶּאֱמַר: "הֲנִגְלֹה נִגְלֵיתִי אֶל בֵּית אָבִיךָ בִּהְיוֹתָם בְּמִצְרַיִם" וְגוֹ'. וְגלו לעילם שכינה עמהם, שנאמר: "ושמתי כסאי בעילם"). גָּלוּ לְבָבֶל, שְׁכִינָה עִמָּהֶם, שֶׁנֶּאֱמַר: "לְמַעַנְכֶם שִׁלַּחְתִּי בָבֶלָה". וְגלו לאדום שכינה עמהם, שנאמר: "מי זה בא מאדום, חמוץ בגדים מבצרה" וגו'). וְאַף כְּשֶׁהֶם עֲתִידִין לִיגָּאֵל, שְׁכִינָה עִמָּהֶם, שֶׁנֶּאֱמַר: "וְשָׁב ה' אֱלֹהֶיךָ אֶת שְׁבוּתְךָ, וְרִחֲמֶךָ"; "וְהֵשִׁיב" לֹא נֶאֱמַר, אֶלָּא "וְשָׁב", מְלַמֵּד שֶׁהַקָּדוֹשׁ בָּרוּךְ הוּא שָׁב עִמָּהֶם מִבֵּין הַגָּלֻיּוֹת.

בְּבָבֶל הֵיכָא? אָמַר אַבַּיֵי: בְּבֵי כְנִישְׁתָּא דְהוּצָל, וּבְבֵי כְנִישְׁתָּא דְשָׁף וְיָתִיב בִּנְהַרְדְּעָא. וְלָא תֵימָא: הָכָא וְהָכָא, אֶלָּא זִמְנִין הָכָא וְזִמְנִין הָכָא.

TRANSLATION

We learned in a *beraisa*: R. Shimon bar Yochai taught: Come and see how beloved Israel is to the Holy One, blessed is He, for wherever they were exiled, the *Shechinah*[704] is with them. They were exiled to Egypt and the *Shechinah* was with them, as the verse (*Shmuel* I 2:27) states: *For I was surely revealed to your father's house when they were in Egypt.* They were exiled to Eilam and the *Shechinah* was with them, as the verse (*Yirmiyahu* 49:38) states: *and I shall place My throne in Eilam.* They were exiled to Bavel and the *Shechinah* was with them, as the verse (*Yeshayahu* 43:14) states: *for your sake I have sent it to Bavel.*[705] They were exiled to Edom and the *Shechinah* was with them, as the verse (ibid. 63:1) states: *who is this [redeemer — i.e., the Shechinah] that comes*

---

704 - The word *Shechinah* is usually translated as Divine presence. However, the translation does not really explain the nature of that presence or how it differs from God himself. While it is beyond the scope of this work to delve into the subject at length, the following remarks might prove useful to the reader.

Ramchal (דעת תבונות, ספר הכללים) explains that the term *Shechinah* is used to describe the link between the supernal and temporal worlds and the way through which God's providence is manifested in the latter. He adds that the nature of this Providence changes according to man's actions.

R. Chaim Volozhin (נפש החיים, שער ב' פרק י"ח) writes that the *Shechinah* is that place where God chooses to manifest himself; שכינה from the word שכן — *dwell*.

705 - See *Yalkut Shimoni* to *Shmuel* who explains that the word שלחתי — *I have sent it* (i.e., the *Shechinah*) — can be read as שולחתי — *I have been sent.*

from Edom, with clothing colored in Batzra. And when they are destined to be redeemed the *Shechinah* is [i.e., will be] with them, as the verse (*Devarim* 30:1-4) states: *and God, your Lord, shall return your remnant and have mercy upon you.* The verse does not state והשיב — *and He shall bring back* — rather ושב — *and He shall return.* This teaches us that the Holy One, blessed is He, shall return with them from their exiles.

Where was the *Shechinah* exiled in Bavel? Abbaye taught: In the synagogue of Hutzal and in the synagogue of Shaf veYasiv[706] in Nehardea. And do not think that it was in both places. Rather, at times it was here and at times it was here.

COMMENTARY

Ramchal[707] writes: *In the hidden manner through which God directs the world, and according to the spiritual repairs that He deems necessary for its continued viability, at times God chooses to manifest His Shechinah to a greater degree in some places. This is what the verse (Tehillim 104:32) is referring to when it states: He glances at the earth and it trembles — i.e., when God glances at the earth and manifests His attention on a specific place, that place trembles.*

TALMUD

אָמַר אַבַּיֵי: תֵּיתֵי לִי, דְּכִי מְרַחִיקְנָא פַּרְסָה, עָיַילְנָא וּמַצְלֵינָא בְּגַוַּה. אֲבוּהַ דִּשְׁמוּאֵל, וְלֵוִי, הֲווּ יָתְבֵי בְּבֵי כְנִישְׁתָּא דְּשַׁף וְיָתִיב בִּנְהַרְדְּעָא, אַתְיָא שְׁכִינָה, שָׁמְעוּ קָל רִגְשָׁא, קָמוּ נְפַקוּ.

רַב שֵׁשֶׁת הֲוָה יָתִיב בְּבֵי כְנִישְׁתָּא דְּשַׁף וְיָתִיב בִּנְהַרְדְּעָא, אַתְיָא שְׁכִינָה, וְלָא נְפַק. אֲתוּ מַלְאֲכֵי־הַשָּׁרֵת קָא מְבַעְתִין לֵיהּ. אָמַר לְפָנָיו: רִבּוֹנוֹ שֶׁל עוֹלָם, עָלוּב וְשֶׁאֵינוֹ עָלוּב, (וְיָכוֹל וְשֶׁאֵינוֹ יָכוֹל), מִי נִדְחָה מִפְּנֵי מִי? אֲמַר לְהוּ: שַׁבְקוּהוּ.

TRANSLATION

Abbaye taught: It should be a source of merit for me that when I was a distance of one *parsah* [from these synagogues], I would go [out of my way] and pray in them.

Shmuel's father and Levi were once sitting in the synagogue of Shaf veYasiv in

---

706 - According to tradition, the synagogue in Nehardea was built by Yechonyah, king of Yehudah. It was constructed with earth and stones that the exiles brought with them from Jerusalem and was therefore called Shaf veYasiv — *shaf* (Aramaic for זז) meaning moved and *yasiv* (Aramaic for ישב) meaning settled.

707 - ילקוט ידיעת האמת, חלק א׳.

Nehardea. The *Shechinah* came and they heard sounds of excitement. They got up and left.

R. Sheshes [who was blind[708]] was once sitting in the synagogue of Shaf veYasiv in Nehardea and the *Shechinah* came but he did not leave. The ministering angels came and began to frighten him and cause him anguish. He said to God: Master of the World! [There is one who is] pitiful [i.e., me] and [one who] is not pitiful [i.e., Your presence]. [There is one] who is capable [of foregoing honor — i.e., Your presence] and [one who] is incapable [i.e., me, for I am incapacitated]. Who shall move for whom? God said to them [the angels]: Leave him alone.

TALMUD

"וָאֱהִי לָהֶם לְמִקְדָּשׁ מְעַט, בָּאֲרָצוֹת אֲשֶׁר בָּאוּ שָׁם". אָמַר רַבִּי יִצְחָק: אֵלוּ בָּתֵּי כְנֵסִיּוֹת וּבָתֵּי מִדְרָשׁוֹת שֶׁבְּבָבֶל. וְרַבִּי אֶלְעָזָר אָמַר: זֶה בֵּית רַבֵּינוּ שֶׁבְּבָבֶל.

דָּרַשׁ רָבָא, מַאי דִּכְתִיב: "ה', מָעוֹן אַתָּה הָיִיתָ לָּנוּ", אֵלוּ בָּתֵּי כְנֵסִיּוֹת וּבָתֵּי מִדְרָשׁוֹת. אָמַר אַבַּיֵי: מֵרֵישׁ הֲוָה גָּרִיסְנָא בְּגוֹ בֵּיתָאי, וּמְצַלֵּינָא בְּבֵי כְנִישְׁתָּא. כֵּיוָן דִּשְׁמַעִית לְהָא דְקָאָמַר דָּוִד: "ה', אָהַבְתִּי מְעוֹן בֵּיתֶךָ", לָא גָּרִיסְנָא אֶלָּא בְּבֵי כְנִישְׁתָּא.

TRANSLATION

[What is the meaning of the verse (*Yechezkel* 11:16) that states:] *and I shall be for them a minor Sanctuary in the lands that they will enter?* R. Yitzchak explained: This refers to the synagogues and study halls of Bavel. R. Elazar explained: This refers to the house of our master[709] in Bavel.

Rava expounded: What is the meaning of the verse (*Tehillim* 90:1) that states: *God, You were a hospice for us*? This refers to the synagogues and study halls.

Abbaye taught: At first I studied inside my home and prayed in the synagogue. After I heard [Rava's interpretation of] that which David said: *God, You are a hospice*, I only study in the synagogue.[710]

---

708 - See *Rashi*, ד"ה רב ששת.

709 - R. Elazar's teacher, Rav, who came to Bavel after the death of R. Yehudah ha-Nasi.

710 - Some texts add: *where I pray.*

TALMUD

תַּנְיָא, רַבִּי אֶלְעָזָר הַקַּפָּר אוֹמֵר: עֲתִידִין בָּתֵּי כְנֵסִיּוֹת וּבָתֵּי מִדְרָשׁוֹת שֶׁבְּחוּץ
לָאָרֶץ, שֶׁיִּקָּבְעוּ בְּאֶרֶץ יִשְׂרָאֵל, שֶׁנֶּאֱמַר: "כִּי כְּתָבוֹר בֶּהָרִים, וּכְכַרְמֶל בַּיָּם
יָבֹא". וַהֲלֹא דְּבָרִים קַל וָחֹמֶר: וּמַה תָּבוֹר וְכַרְמֶל, שֶׁלֹּא בָאוּ אֶלָּא לִלְמוֹד
תּוֹרָה לְפִי שָׁעָה, נִקְבְּעוּ בְּאֶרֶץ יִשְׂרָאֵל, בָּתֵּי כְנֵסִיּוֹת וּבָתֵּי מִדְרָשׁוֹת שֶׁקּוֹרִין
בָּהֶם, וּמַרְבִּיצִין בָּהֶם אֶת הַתּוֹרָה עַל אַחַת כַּמָּה וְכַמָּה?

דָּרַשׁ בַּר קַפָּרָא, מַאי דִּכְתִיב: "לָמָּה תְּרַצְּדוּן הָרִים גַּבְנֻנִּים". יָצְתָה בַּת־קוֹל
וְאָמְרָה לָהֶם: לָמָּה תִּרְצוּ דִין עִם סִינַי? כֻּלְּכֶם בַּעֲלֵי מוּמִין אַתֶּם אֵצֶל סִינַי!
כְּתִיב הָכָא: "גַּבְנֻנִּים", וּכְתִיב הָתָם: "אוֹ גִבֵּן אוֹ דַק". אָמַר רַב אַשִׁי: שְׁמַע
מִינָהּ הַאי מָאן דְּיָהִיר - בַּעַל מוּם הוּא.

TRANSLATION

We learned in a *beraisa*: R. Eliezer ha-Kipur taught: The synagogues and study
halls of the Diaspora are destined to be [transported from their sites and] established in the Land of Israel, as the verse (*Yirmiyahu* 46:18) states: *for like Tavor
among mountains and like Carmel from the sea they shall come*. If Tavor and
Carmel, who only came [to Mt. Sinai] to learn Torah temporarily, were [rewarded
and] established in the Land of Israel,[711] the synagogues and study halls in
which Scripture is read and Torah is taught shall surely [be brought to the Land of
Israel].

Bar Kappara expounded: What is the meaning of the verse (*Tehillim* 68:17) that
states: *Why are you envious, oh mountains of peaks*? A heavenly voice issued
forth and said to them [to the mountains of the world]: Why do you seek to judge
Sinai?[712] Compared to Sinai you are all blemished. The verse states here

---

711 - The text is somewhat difficult to understand, for the implication is that Tavor
and Carmel were once located elsewhere and were relocated in *Eretz Yisrael* after the
Torah was given. In a parallel version in *Midrash Rabbah* to *Bereishis*, the text
states that Carmel was once in Spain (across the sea from *Eretz Yisrael* or to the west)
and Tavor was in Eilam. We might suggest that Carmel and Tavor were originally
meant to be located elsewhere, but since they desired to learn Torah, they were
rewarded and moved from their intended locations. This would be consistent with the
teaching of the Sages in *Rosh Hashanah* (11a) that all parts of Creation were created
according to the manner that they chose for themselves.

712 - What claim do you have against Sinai that was chosen by God as the place
where the Torah was to be given? The exegesis is based on explaining the word
תרצדון as תרצו דין — seek judgement.

גבנונים — peaks — and there (*Vayikra* 21:20) the verse states: או גבן או דק —
with bushy eyebrows or a cataract.[713] R. Ashi taught: From this we see that
one who is haughty is considered to have a physical imperfection.

TALMUD

אָמַר רַבִּי יוֹחָנָן: כָּל מָקוֹם שֶׁאַתָּה מוֹצֵא גְּבוּרָתוֹ שֶׁל הַקָּדוֹשׁ בָּרוּךְ הוּא, אַתָּה
מוֹצֵא עַנְוְתָנוּתוֹ. דָּבָר זֶה כָּתוּב בַּתּוֹרָה, וְשָׁנוּי בַּנְּבִיאִים, וּמְשֻׁלָּשׁ בַּכְּתוּבִים.
כָּתוּב בַּתּוֹרָה: "כִּי ה' אֱלֹהֵיכֶם הוּא אֱלֹהֵי הָאֱלֹהִים וַאֲדֹנֵי הָאֲדֹנִים", וּכְתִיב
בַּתְרֵיהּ: "עֹשֶׂה מִשְׁפַּט יָתוֹם וְאַלְמָנָה". שָׁנוּי בַּנְּבִיאִים: "כִּי כֹה אָמַר רָם וְנִשָּׂא
שֹׁכֵן עַד וְקָדוֹשׁ" וְגוֹ'. וּכְתִיב בַּתְרֵיהּ: "וְאֶת דַּכָּא וּשְׁפַל־רוּחַ". וּמְשֻׁלָּשׁ
בַּכְּתוּבִים, דִּכְתִיב: "סֹלּוּ לָרֹכֵב בָּעֲרָבוֹת בְּיָהּ שְׁמוֹ", וּכְתִיב בַּתְרֵיהּ: "אֲבִי
יְתוֹמִים וְדַיַּן אַלְמָנוֹת".

TRANSLATION

[31a] R. Yochanan taught: Every place where you find [an indication of] God's
might, you will [also] find [an indication of] His humility. This trait [of God]
can be found in the Torah, is repeated in the Prophets and is repeated a third time
in the Writings. The Torah states (*Devarim* 10:17): *For God, your Lord, is the
Lord of all lords and the Master of all masters* [which is an indication of His
might] and afterwards it states: *He does justice for orphans and widows.*[714] It is
repeated in the Prophets, [for the verse (*Yeshayahu* 57:15) states:] *For thus says
He who is uplifted and high, who dwells forever and is holy* [which is an
indication of His might] and afterwards it states: *[I dwell on high and in holiness]
and with he who is downtrodden and humbled* [which is an indication of God's
humility].[715] And it is repeated a third time, as the verse (*Tehillim* 68:5) states:
[Offer] praise [to] He who rides through the desert, whose name is God [which is

---

713 - The verse is referring to the physical imperfections that render a *kohen* unfit
for the Divine service. Our translation of גבן as bushy eyebrows and דק as a cataract is
based on *Bechoros* 43b-44a. Bar Kappara's explanation of the word גבנונים in
Tehillim as a blemish is based on the similarity between גבן and גבנונים.

714 - *Maharal* (נתיבות עולם, נתיב הענוה) explains that although God is supreme and
His might surpasses all that in this world, He still concerns Himself, as it were, with
the cases of orphans and widows and does not see intervening in their plight as being
demeaning.

715 - *Maharal* (ad loc.) explains that since God is not limited by space or any other
natural law, He can be both high and uplifted and still be with the downtrodden.

an indication of His might] and afterwards (ibid. :6) it states: *the father of orphans and the judge of widows* [which is an indication of God's humility].

TALMUD

אָמַר רַב הוּנָא: רֹאשׁ חֹדֶשׁ אָב שֶׁחָל לִהְיוֹת בְּשַׁבָּת, מַפְטִירִין: "חָדְשֵׁיכֶם וּמוֹעֲדֵיכֶם שָׂנְאָה נַפְשִׁי, הָיוּ עָלַי לָטֹרַח." מַאי "הָיוּ עָלַי לָטֹרַח"? אָמַר הַקָּדוֹשׁ בָּרוּךְ הוּא: לֹא דַיָּן לָהֶם לְיִשְׂרָאֵל שֶׁחוֹטְאִין לְפָנַי, אֶלָּא שֶׁמַּטְרִיחִין אוֹתִי לֵידַע אֵיזוֹ גְזֵרָה קָשָׁה אָבִיא עֲלֵיהֶם.

TRANSLATION

R. Huna taught: **[31b]** If *Rosh Chodesh* Av falls on Shabbos, the *haftarah*[716] is [read from the Prophetic section (*Yeshayahu* 1) that states (ibid. ::13-14)]: *My soul despises your months and holidays — they are a burden to Me.* What is [the meaning of the phrase] *they are a burden to Me*? The Holy One, blessed is He, declared: Is it not sufficient that Israel sins before Me, that they also burden Me to determine the harsh edicts that I bring upon them!?

COMMENTARY

Sin has two causes: uncontrolled desire or denial of God. Those who sin because of their inability to overcome their desires still believe that there is reward and punishment for their actions. Hence, when they are punished and examine their lives, they realize that their suffering is a result of their shortcomings and they are able to repent. To stir this self-examination, it is

---

716 - The custom of reading a portion from *Nevi'im* dates from the time of the Greek conquest of *Eretz Yisrael* when a decree was issued forbidding the public reading of the Torah. The Sages of that generation decided to circumvent that decree by introducing the public reading of a portion drawn from *Nevi'im* whose subject matter was thematically related either to the Torah portion that would have been read or to the special nature of the day. See *Orach Chaim* 274 and *Mishnah Berurah* ad loc.

Although the *haftarah* for *Shabbos Rosh Chodesh* is drawn from the 66th chapter of *Yeshayahu*, according to R. Huna, on *Shabbos Rosh Chodesh Av*, we read the first chapter of *Yeshayahu* instead, for its contents relate to both *Rosh Chodesh* and *Tisha b'Av*.

Tosafos notes that this is not our custom, for the first chapter of *Yeshayahu* is read on the Shabbos preceding *Tishah b'Av* (which can not fall on *Shabbos Rosh Chodesh Av*). He writes that on *Shabbos Rosh Chodesh Av* we read *Yirmiyahu* 2 — the regular *haftarah* — for we do not interrupt the three *haftaros* of bad tidings that are read before *Tishah b'Av*. See *Orach Chaim* 425:1.

sufficient for God, as it were, to punish them in a natural manner that is related to their sins, for they can then see the cause and effect relationship that exists between their actions and their suffering. Their transgressions do not force God to act in a supernatural manner by changing the pattern of Creation.[717]

The second category of sin includes those whose wickedness has led them to deny God's existence and His Torah. Though they know, deep within their hearts, that denial is no more than a means of giving their desires free reign,[718] their road to repentance is surely longer and more complicated than those in the first category. In order to bring people like this to repent, it is necessary to punish them in a way that they will make them recognize God's hand despite their denial of His existence. This is especially true given that most of these people do their utmost to explain supernatural events as pure happenstance.

When evil and denial of God become prevalent and people fail to see the spiritual causes of natural disasters, Providence is forced, as it were, to change the natural pattern of events so that the cause and effect relationship of sin and punishment is unequivocal. *Maharsha* explains that this form of Divine intervention is characterized by the Sages as a burden to God.

TALMUD

מִשְׁנָה. בְּתַעֲנִיּוֹת, בְּרָכוֹת וּקְלָלוֹת, וְאֵין מַפְסִיקִין בִּקְלָלוֹת.

גְּמָרָא. מְנָא הַנֵּי מִילֵּי? אָמַר רַבִּי חִיָּא בַּר גַּמְדָּא, אָמַר רַב אַסִּי: דְּאָמַר קְרָא: "מוּסַר ה', בְּנִי, אַל תִּמְאָס".

רֵישׁ לָקִישׁ אָמַר: לְפִי שֶׁאֵין אוֹמְרִים בְּרָכָה עַל הַפֻּרְעָנוּת. אֶלָּא הֵיכִי עָבִיד? תָּנָא: כְּשֶׁהוּא מַתְחִיל, מַתְחִיל בַּפָּסוּק שֶׁלְּפָנֵיהֶם. וּכְשֶׁהוּא מְסַיֵּם, מְסַיֵּם בַּפָּסוּק שֶׁלְּאַחֲרֵיהֶם.

TRANSLATION

[30b-31a] **MISHNAH:** On fast days[719] [we read the portion from the Torah that speaks of] the blessings and curses [that occur depending upon Israel's behavior]

---

717 - See *Rabbenu Yonah* (שערי תשובה, שער השני).

718 - See *Sanhedrin* 63b: *Israel only worshipped idols to permit herself immoral relations.*

719 - I.e., on fast days which are declared as a result of famine, plague et. al. as opposed to the five fasts that appear in the calendar.

and we do not interrupt [the reading of] the curses.[720]

[31b] **TALMUD:** From where do we derive this [practice of not interrupting the reading of the curses]? R. Chiya bar Gamda taught in the name of R. Asi: The verse (*Mishlei* 3:11) states: *My son, do not be repulsed by the remonstrations of God.*[721]

Reish Lakish explained [that the reason why we do not interrupt the reading of the curses is] because one does not recite a *berachah* over retribution.[722] What then should we do?[723] We learned in a *beraisa*: When he begins [the Torah reading that includes the portion of the curses], he begins from the verse that precedes and when he finishes, he finishes with the verse that follows [them so that his *berachos* are recited over verses that are not solely curses].

COMMENTARY

Reish Lakish's statement would seem to contradict that which we learned in a *Mishnah*:[724] *One is required to recite a berachah over evil [that occurs] just as one [is required] to recite a berachah over good [that occurs].* How could he have ruled that we do not interrupt the reading of the curses because we do not recite *berachos* over retribution?

The *Yerushalmi*[725] records that the reason why we do not interrupt the

---

720 - I.e., we do not interrupt the reading of the portion that contains the curses so as to call up another person to the Torah. Rather, the person called up reads the entire portion of the curses himself.

721 - *Rashi* (ד״ה אל תמאס) explains that were we to interrupt the reading of the curses which are, in fact, God's remonstrations, it could be construed as indicating that we are repulsed by them.

722 - I.e., were we to call up another person in the middle of the portion, he would recite the *berachah* that precedes the Torah reading and immediately begin reading a portion that speaks of bad things. It would seem that Reish Lakish's statement is the source for the mistaken custom of not reciting *birchas ha-Torah* on the portions of the remonstrations.

723 - I.e., if one does not recite a *berachah* over retribution, how does the person who is called up for the entire portion of the curses recite the *berachos* that precede and follow the Torah reading?

724 - ברכות ט:ה.

725 - מגילה ג:ז. Note that the *Yerushalmi* reverses the order of the third and fourth chapters of *Megillah* — an order followed also in most volumes of the *Mishnah* alone but not followed in the Talmud Bavli. See also *Soferim* 12:1.

reading of the curses for the *berachos* is because it is as if God says: It is not fitting that My children be cursed while I am blessed. This too would seem to stand in contradiction to the *Mishnah's* ruling — a ruling that is derived from a verse!

R. Yehudah di Modena[726] answers that it is possible that the Talmud differentiates between evil that transpires in the life of an individual — where one would be required to recite a *berachah* — and evil that affects an entire community — as in the case of the curses read from the Torah which apply to Israel as a whole — where no *berachah* would be recited. Alternatively, one might be required to recite a *berachah* over evil that has already occurred — the situation to which the *Mishnah* refers — but would not recite a *berachah* before reading about travail that will occur if one fails to fulfill the Torah as in the case of the curses read in *Vayikra* and *Devarim*.

TALMUD

אָמַר אַבַּיֵי: לֹא שָׁנוּ, אֶלָּא בְקְלָלוֹת שֶׁ"בְּתוֹרַת כֹּהֲנִים", אֲבָל קְלָלוֹת שֶׁ"בְּמִשְׁנֵה תוֹרָה", פּוֹסֵק. מַאי טַעְמָא? הַלָּלוּ בִּלְשׁוֹן רַבִּים אֲמוּרוֹת, וּמֹשֶׁה מִפִּי הַגְּבוּרָה אֲמָרָן. וְהַלָּלוּ בִּלְשׁוֹן יָחִיד אֲמוּרוֹת, וּמֹשֶׁה מִפִּי עַצְמוֹ אֲמָרָן.

TRANSLATION

Abbaye taught: This [that we do not interrupt the reading of the curses] was only taught regarding the curses in *Toras Kohanim* [*Vayikra*], but the curses in *Mishneh Torah* [*Devarim*] may be interrupted. What is the reason [why do we differentiate between the two portions]? Those [the verses in *Vayikra*] were said in plural and Moshe recited them as God told him, while those [the verses in *Devarim*] were said in singular and Moshe said them himself.

COMMENTARY

This last statement should not be construed in any way as implying that Moshe authored even a single word of the Torah, for it is a cardinal principle of Judaism that the entire Torah is the word of God.

Maharal[727] explains that there is a fundamental difference between the first four Books of the Torah and the Book of *Devarim*. The first four Books

---

726 - Italian scholar (1571-1648) who edited one of the first reprints of *Ein Yaakov*, incorporating a number of his own comments under the title *ha-Boneh*.

727 - תפארת ישראל פרק מ"יג. See also Commentary of the *Ramban* to *Vayikra* 26:16.

represent the word of God from God's perspective whereas the Book of *Devarim* represents the the word of God from the perspective of Israel. Thus, in the Book of *Devarim*, God changed, as it were, His style and dictated the verses to Moshe in a form that made it appear as if man was talking. This would also serve to explain why some of the subjects in *Devarim* that are repetitions of subjects that appear elsewhere are more detailed.

Based on this explanation, we can understand the following statement:[728] *R. Levi said: Come and see that God's traits are not like man's. God gave them [Israel] twenty-two berachos and eight curses whereas Moshe gave them twenty-two curses and eight berachos.* The Talmud does not mean to imply that Moshe said this portion on his own. Rather, as part of *Devarim,* God dictated it from man's persepective and the Torah thereby teaches us the fundamental difference between God's perspective, as it were, towards man where blessing is far more numerous than curses and man's perspective where the opposite is true.

TALMUD

תַּנְיָא: רַבִּי שִׁמְעוֹן בֶּן אֶלְעָזָר אוֹמֵר: עֶזְרָא תִּקֵּן לָהֶם לְיִשְׂרָאֵל שֶׁיְּהוּ קוֹרִין קְלָלוֹת שֶׁבְּתוֹרַת כֹּהֲנִים קֹדֶם עֲצֶרֶת. וְשֶׁבְּמִשְׁנֵה תוֹרָה קֹדֶם רֹאשׁ הַשָּׁנָה. מַאי טַעְמָא? אָמַר אַבַּיֵּי, וְאִי תֵּימָא רֵישׁ לָקִישׁ: כְּדֵי שֶׁתִּכְלֶה הַשָּׁנָה וְקִלְלוֹתֶיהָ. בִּשְׁלָמָא, שֶׁבְּמִשְׁנֵה תוֹרָה, אִיכָּא - כְּדֵי שֶׁתִּכְלֶה שָׁנָה וְקִלְלוֹתֶיהָ. אֶלָּא שֶׁבְּתוֹרַת כֹּהֲנִים, אַטּוּ "עֲצֶרֶת" רֹאשׁ הַשָּׁנָה הִיא?! אִין, עֲצֶרֶת נַמִי רֹאשׁ הַשָּׁנָה הִיא, דִּתְנָן: וּבַעֲצֶרֶת עַל פֵּירוֹת הָאִילָן.

TRANSLATION

We learned in a *beraisa*: R. Shimon ben Elazar taught: Ezra[729] ordained that the portion of the curses in *Toras Kohanim* be read before Shavuos and those in *Mishneh Torah* before Rosh Hashanah. What is the reason? Abbaye taught, and some say that it was Reish Lakish: So that the year and its curses might end together.[730] This is logical as regards [the curses in] *Mishneh Torah,* [for by

---

728 - .בבא בתרא פח:

729 - The original custom was to read the Torah over a three year period. When Ezra returned from Bavel, he introduced the practice of reading the entire Torah in the course of a year. He was thus able to ordain that specific *parshiyos* be read at specific times.

730 - I.e., we finish the portion of the curses before Rosh Hashanah so as not to read that portion at the beginning of a new year.

reading the portion before Rosh Hashanah] we fulfill that the year and its curses end together. But as regards [the curses brought in] *Toras Kohanim*, is Shavuos the beginning of a new year!? Yes! Shavuos is also the beginning of a new year, for we learned in a *Mishnah*:[731] [During four periods the world is judged ...] on Shavuos concerning the fruits of the trees.

TALMUD

אָמַר רַבִּי שְׁפַטְיָה, אָמַר רַבִּי יוֹחָנָן: עֲשָׂרָה שֶׁקָּרְאוּ בַּתּוֹרָה, הַגָּדוֹל שֶׁבָּהֶן גּוֹלֵל סֵפֶר תּוֹרָה. וְהַגּוֹלְלוֹ, נוֹטֵל שָׂכָר כֻּלָּן. דַּאֲמַר רַבִּי יְהוֹשֻׁעַ בֶּן לֵוִי: עֲשָׂרָה שֶׁקָּרְאוּ בַּתּוֹרָה, הַגּוֹלֵל סֵפֶר תּוֹרָה קִבֵּל שָׂכָר כֻּלָּן. שָׂכָר כֻּלָּן, סַלְקָא דַּעְתָּדְ?! אֶלָּא אֵימָא קִבֵּל שָׂכָר כְּנֶגֶד כֻּלָּן.

TRANSLATION

[32a] R. Shefatyah taught in the name of R. Yochanan: When ten people[732] read from the Torah, the most important among them wraps[733] the Torah scroll and the one who wraps the Torah scroll receives the reward of all of them. As R. Yehoshua ben Levi taught: When ten people read from the Torah, the one who wraps the Torah scroll receives the reward of all of them. Do you think that he receives the reward of all of them!? Rather, say that he receives reward that is equivalent to all of them.

---

731 - ראש השנה א:ב. *Tosafos Yom Tov* (ad loc.) explains that the judgement on Shavuos pertains to mankind in general, while on Rosh Hashannah each individual is judged as to how much he will receive.

732 - *Rashi* explains that the reference is to the public Torah readings when three to seven people are called. The Talmud uses the number ten, because the Torah is not read if there are less than ten people present.

733 - The Talmud uses the term גולל which means to *wrap* or *roll* the Torah scroll. The reference would seem to be to the one who lifts the Torah from the table where it is read — what Ashkenazic communities refer to today as הגבהה. The Torah scrolls used by Sefardic communities are read upright and are encased — thus, the גולל is the one who rolls the Torah scroll and holds it up before the congregation as in the Talmud's statement. The Ashkenazic custom of separating גלילה and הגבהה does not exist. Although we no longer give this honor to the most important member of the congregation, we do differentiate between wrapping the scroll and lifting it, for the former is given to minors while the latter is only given to adults. See *Mishnah Berurah, Orach Chaim* 147:8.

See also Commentary of *Ramban* to *Devarim* 27:26 and *Aruch ha-Shulchan, Orach Chaim* 147:8.

TALMUD

וְאָמַר רַבִּי שְׁפַטְיָה, אָמַר רַבִּי יוֹחָנָן: מִנַּיִן שֶׁמִּשְׁתַּמְּשִׁין בְּבַת־קוֹל? שֶׁנֶּאֱמַר:
"וְאָזְנֶיךָ תִּשְׁמַעְנָה דָּבָר מֵאַחֲרֶיךָ לֵאמֹר". וְהָנֵי מִילֵי דְּשָׁמַע קָל גַּבְרָא בְּמָתָא,
וְאִתְּתָא בְּדַבְרָא. וְהוּא דַּאֲמַר: ,הֵן', ,הֵן'. וְהוּא דַּאֲמַר: ,לָאו', ,לָאו'.

TRANSLATION

R. Shefatyah also taught in the name of R. Yochanan: From where [do we see]
that we use a Heavenly voice[734] [i.e., that we may act according to its advice]?
The verse (*Yeshayahu* 30:21) states: *And your ears shall hear that which is said
behind you.* This is true when he hears the voice of a man in the city or the
voice of a woman in the fields[735] and when the voice says "Yes, Yes" or the
voice says "No, No."[736]

COMMENTARY

It would seem that there are two forms of *bas kol*. The *Mishnah*[737] refers to
a *bas kol* that issues forth from Sinai every day and says: *Woe to the created
because of the shame of the Torah, for all who do not occupy themselves in the
Torah is called [one who is] rebuked. Maharal*[738] explains that though this *bas
kol* is not heard by man, his soul is aware of it. The Talmud's statement[739] that
we do not follow the ruling of a *bas kol* would seem to be referring to this type
of Divine voice.

The second type of *bas kol* is heard by man, but by virtue of the

---

734 - A בת קול — a Heavenly voice — is a lower level of Divine instruction than
other forms of prophecy — see *Rambam, Hilchos Yesodei ha-Torah* 7:2. *Tosafos*
(סנהדרין יא. ד״ה בת קול) explains that it is referred to as a בת קול — literally the
daughter of a Voice — because it is an echo rather than the voice itself. *Tosafos Yom
Tov*, in his commentary to *Yevamos* 15:6, explains that it is referred to as בת קול
because it is not directed towards the recepient and is fainter than direct prophecy.

735 - *Rashi* (ד״ה קל גברא) explains that it is unusual for a man to speak loudly in the
city and unusual for a woman's voice to be heard in the fields. Thus, the departure
from the usual can be taken as indication that the voice that one hears is a *bas kol*.

736 - *Ritva* explains that the repetition is indicative of the truth of the message
heard. Compare to *Shavuos* 36a.

737 - אבות ו:ג.

738 - דרך חיים שם. See also our comments on page - regarding the ability of the soul
to perceive things that are invisible to the body.

739 - בבא מציעא נט: ושי״נ.

circumstances in which it is issued, man understands that the sound that he hears is a Heavenly voice. This form of *bas kol* does not express God's opinion, as it were. Rather, it serves as a means of conveying God's advice to man as to how he should act. *Tosafos*[740] notes that although using methods of divination are generally forbidden, this method of determining how to act is permitted because it is no more than a sign. It is to this type of *bas kol* that R. Shefatyah referred.

TALMUD

וְאָמַר רַבִּי שְׁפַטְיָה, אָמַר רַבִּי יוֹחָנָן: כָּל הַקּוֹרֵא בְּלֹא נְעִימָה, וְשׁוֹנֶה בְּלֹא זִמְרָה, עָלָיו הַכָּתוּב אוֹמֵר: "וְגַם אֲנִי נָתַתִּי לָהֶם חֻקִּים לֹא טוֹבִים, וּמִשְׁפָּטִים לֹא יִחְיוּ בָּהֶם". מַתְקִיף לָהּ אַבַּיֵי: מִשּׁוּם דְּלֹא יָדַע לְבַסּוּמֵי קָלֵיהּ, כְּתִיב בֵּיהּ: "וּמִשְׁפָּטִים לֹא יִחְיוּ בָּהֶם"?! אֶלָּא כְּדְרַב מְשַׁרְשְׁיָא, דְּאָמַר: שְׁנֵי תַּלְמִידֵי חֲכָמִים שֶׁיּוֹשְׁבִים בְּעִיר אַחַת, וְאֵין נוֹחִין זֶה לָזֶה בַּהֲלָכָה, עֲלֵיהֶם הַכָּתוּב אוֹמֵר: "וּמִשְׁפָּטִים לֹא יִחְיוּ בָּהֶם".

"וַיְדַבֵּר מֹשֶׁה אֶת מֹעֲדֵי ה' אֶל בְּנֵי יִשְׂרָאֵל", מִצְוָתָן שֶׁיִּהְיוּ קוֹרִין אוֹתָן, כָּל אֶחָד וְאֶחָד בִּזְמַנּוֹ.

TRANSLATION

R. Shefatyah also taught in the name of R. Yochanan: One who reads Scripture without a melody and studies *Mishnah* without a song, regarding him the verse (*Yechezkel* 20:25) states: *And I have also given them rules that are not good and laws that they cannot live with*. Abbaye asked him: Because he does not know how to sing pleasantly, does the verse refer to him [as being the cause for God having given] *laws that they cannot live with*!? Rather, [the explanation of the verse is] like R. Mesharshiyah who taught: Two scholars who reside in the same city and are not respectful to each other in learning halachah [i.e., they do not study together so as to reach a mutual decision but constantly dispute each other's rulings], regarding them the verse states: *laws that they cannot live with*.

[The verse (*Vayikra* 23:44) states:] *And Moshe spoke all of the festivals of God to the children of Israel* — [this teaches us that] the mitzvah is to read them [from the Torah], each one at the appropriate time.

---

740 - ד״ה מנין שמשתמשין. See also *Rambam, Hilchos Avodas Kochavim* 11:5 and the glosses of *Ra'avad* (ad loc.).

Note: The bibliography includes works that form the basis for the material quoted in the commentary and footnotes.

AHAVAS EISAN — Glosses to EIN YAAKOV by R. Avraham Maskileison of Minsk (Russia, 1788-1848).

ANAF YOSEF — Commentary to MIDRASH RABBAH, MIDRASH TANCHUMA and EIN YAAKOV by R. Chanoch Zundel ben Yosef (Poland — d. 1867). ANAF YOSEF is a homiletical exposition on the material while EITZ YOSEF provides the simple meaning of the text.

BEIS YOSEF — Commentary to TUR SHULCHAN ARUCH by R. Yosef Karo, author of KESSEF MISHNAH to Rambam's YAD HA-CHAZAKAH (Spain, 1488 — Tzefas, 1575). Although, R. Yosef Karo is best known for his SHULCHAN ARUCH, his commentary to TUR is the basis for that work.

BEN ISH CHAI — Commentary to the Torah and *halachah* by R. Yosef Chaim of Baghdad (Iraq, 1835 — 1909). R. Yosef Chaim also wrote B'NAYAHU and BEN YEHOYADAH — a commentary to the *aagados* of the Talmud.

BI'UR HALACHAH — see CHAFETZ CHAIM.

BRAVDA, R. SHLOMO — Contemporary Israeli author and lecturer.

CHAFETZ CHAIM — Pen name of R. Yisroel Meir *ha-Kohen* of Radin (Poland, 1838 — 1933), author of MISHNAH BERURAH to SHULCHAN ARUCH ORACH CHAIM, BIUR HALACHAH in which he elaborates on many of the rulings as well as SHA'AR HA-TZIYUN in which he provides sources.

CHASAM SOFER — Pen name of R. Moshe Sofer (Germany, 1762 — Hungary, 1839), rabbi and *rosh yeshiva* in Pressburg, commentator to the Bible, the Talmud and SHULCHAN ARUCH. He was succeeded by his son, R. Avraham Shmuel (1815-1871) who authored a commentary to the Bible and a collection of responsa under the title KSAV SOFER.

CHAZON ISH — Halachic commentary and responsa to SHULCHAN ARUCH by R. Avrohom Yeshayahu Karelitz (Poland, 1878 — Bnei Brak, 1953). In 1933, he moved to *Eretz Yisrael* and though he held no official position, was considered to be one of the most important halachic authorities of the period, especially as concerned the *halachos* dependent upon the Land of Israel. His philisophical and ethical writings were published under the title EMUNAH U'BITACHON as well as in a collection of his letters entitled IGGEROS CHAZON ISH.

CHIDUSHEI GAONIM — Anthology of commentaries compiled by the publishers of the ROMM edition of EIN YAAKOV.

CHIDUSHEI HA-RIM — Commentary to the Bible and Talmud by R. Yitzchak Meir Alter of Gur (Poland, 1789 — 1866), founder of the Gur dynasty. Upon his death, leadership passed to R. Chanoch of Alexander who held the position in trust until R. Yehudah Aryeh Leib, the former's grandson, assumed leadership. R. Yehudah Aryeh Leib wrote major commentaries to the Torah and Talmud published under the title SFAS EMES.

CHOVAS HA-LEVAVOS — Philisophical work by R. Bachya Ibn Paquda (Spain — 11th century) in which he stresses that the conceptual mitzvos are as an important part of Judaism as are the practical mitzvos.

DESSLER, R. ELIYAHU ELIEZER — Leading scholar of the *mussar* movement (Lithuania, 1891 — Bnei Brak, 1954). Four volumes of his lectures, which are a rare blend of *mussar*, *chassidus* and philosophy, were published by his students under the title MICHTAV MI'ELIYAHU.

EIGER, R. AKIVA — Rabbi of Bohemia (1761-1837). His glosses to the *Mishnah,* Talmud and *Shulchan Aruch* are included in almost every edition of these works. He also authored a commentary to the Talmud as well as numerous halachic responsa.

EITZ YOSEF — See ANAF YOSEF.

EYBESCHUTZ, R. YONASAN — Rabbi of Prague and later of the three sister communities, Altona, Wannsbeck and Hamburg (Cracow, 1690 — Hamburg, 1764). R. Yonasan authored KRESI U'PLESI on YOREH DEAH, URIM VE-TUMIM on CHOSHEN MISHPAT as well as the homiletical works YA'AROS DEVASH and AHAVAS YEHONASAN.

GAON YAAKOV — Anonymous digest of commentaries to EIN YAAKOV included in the ROMM edition.

GRA — Acronym of R. Eliyahu of Vilna (1720-1797). So great was his expertise in every field of Jewish scholarship, that R. Eliyahu became widely known as the Vilna Gaon or simply as the Gaon. His writings and comments include works in every area of Jewish learning — including glosses of textual emendations to the MISHNAH and Talmud, a concise commentary to SHULCHAN ARUCH, a commentary to *Tanach* as well as numerous philisophical and ethical essays.

HAGAOS MAIMONIS — Compendium of sources and cross-references to

Rambam's YAD HA-CHAZAKAH by R. Meir *ha-Kohen* of Rutenberg (France, 13th century).

HA-KOHEN, R. TZADDOK OF LUBLIN — (Latvia, 1823 — Lublin, 1900). Leader of the chassidim of Izbica after the death of R. Leibele Eiger and R. Mordechai Yosef, author of a commentary to the Torah entitled PRI TZADDIK as well as numerous philisophical and ethical works.

HIRSCH, R. SAMSON RAFAEL — (Germany, 1808 — 1888). Chief Rabbi of Moravia and Bohemia, R. Hirsch left his position to assume leadership of the tiny Orthodox community in Frankfurt. He authored a major commentary to the Torah as well as philisophical works — CHOREV — and numerous essays and polemics on a wide variety of subjects.

IYUN YAAKOV — Commentary to EIN YAAKOV by R. Yaakov Reicher (Poland, 18th century), author of the halachic responsa SHEVUS YAAKOV.

JOSEPHUS — Historical work by Josephus Flavius [Yosef ben Gurion *ha-Kohen* (*Eretz Yisrael* — 1st century C.E.)], commander of the Jewish forces in the Galilee at the time of the rebellion against Roman rule. It is not clear whether Josephus is identical to the SEFER YOSSIPON quoted by *Rashi* and other *rishonim*, or if it is an earlier record.

KORBAN EDAH — Explanatory commentary to Talmud *Yerushalmi* by R. Dovid Frankl (Germany, 1707—1762), rabbi of Dessau.

KSAV SOFER — See CHASAM SOFER.

KUZARI — Philisophical work by R. Yehudah ha-Levi, a disciple of R. Yitzchok Elfassi (Spain, 1075 — *Eretz Yisrael*, 1140). Written as a dialogue between a rabbi and a king who had summoned the former to teach him about Judaism, KUZARI is based on the historical conversion of King Bulan of Khazar and his people in the eighth century.

MAGEN AVRAHAM — Commentary to SHULCHAN ARUCH ORACH CHAIM by R. Avraham Abeli Gombiner (Poland, 1637 — 1683), head of the yeshiva in Kalisz and author of ZAYIS RA'ANAN to YALKUT SHIMONI.

MAHARAL — Acronym of R. Yehudah Loew ben Betzalel of Prague (Posen, 1525 — Prague, 1609). His CHIDUSHEI AGGADOS is one of the most important commentaries written to the *aggados* of the Talmud together with the commentary of *Maharsha*. References that do not specify the work are from his commentary to *Megillas Esther* — OR CHADASH.

MAHARITZ CHAYES — Acronym of R. Tzvi Hirsch Chayes (Poland, 1805-

1855). His notes and suggestions for textual emendations are included in the ROMM edition of the Talmud. He also wrote a number of scholarly articles and essays — collected under the title KOL KISVEI MAHARITZ CHAYES — which explain the nature of the *mesorah* process.

MAHARSHA — Textual emendations and Talmudic commentary by R. Shmuel Eidels (Poland, 1555-1631), rabbi of Chelm, Lublin and Ostrow. Maharsha included comments to the *aggadic* portions of the text and explains terminology, symbolism and the meaning of many passages.

MALBIM — R. Meir Loeb ben Yechiel (Poland, 1809 — Kiev, 1879). Malbim wrote a commentary to the Torah entitled HA-TORAH VEHA-MITZVAH as well as commentaries to all of *Nach*. An expert in philology, he also authored AYELES HA-SHACHAR and HA-KARMEL.

ME'IRI — Summary of Talmudic commentary by R. Menachem ben Shlomo Meiri (Southern France, 1249-1306).

MENOS HA-LEVI — Commentary to *Megillas Esther* by R. Shlomo Alkabetz (1505-1584), author of the liturgical poem *Lecha Dodi* and a colleague of R. Yosef Karo and R. Yitzchok Luria (the *Ari ha-Kadosh*).

METZUDOS DAVID AND TZION — Commentary to *Tanach* begun by R. David Altschuller (d. 1753) and completed by his son, R. Yechiel Hillel. The work was divided into two parts: METZUDAS TZION provides explanations for individual words while METZUDAS DAVID provides a phraseological explanation of the text.

MICHTAV MI'ELIYAHU — See DESSLER, R. ELIYAHU ELIEZER.

MIDRASH — When cited alone, the reference is to MIDRASH RABBAH, the main collection of *aggados* on the Torah and the Five *Megillos*. Much of the material cited in MIDRASH RABBAH is quoted in the Talmud, although there are numerous variances in both content and ascription of source. MIDRASH TANCHUMA is a collection of *aggados* arranged according to the order of the Torah ascribed to the *amora*, R. Tanchuma.

NEFESH HA-CHAIM — Philisophical work by R. Chaim of Volozhin (Poland, 1749 — 1821), disciple of the GRA and founder of the yeshiva movement.

NETZIV — Acronym of R. Naftali Tzvi Yehudah Berlin (1817-1893), *rosh yeshiva* of Volozhin and author of the Biblical commentary HA'AMEK DAVAR, RINAH SHEL TORAH to SHIR HA-SHIRIM, HA'AMEK SHEILAH to the SHEILTOS of *Rav Achai* and MEISHIV DAVAR — halachic responsa.

OHR SOMAYACH — Commentary to Rambam's YAD HA-CHAZAKAH by R. Meir Simchah of Dvinsk (d. 1926), author of the commentary MESHECH CHOCHMAH to the Torah.

OTZAR HA-TEFILLOS — Two volume *siddur* with an anthology of commentaries, first published in 1915 with the notes of R. Chanoch Zundel ben Yosef [see ANAF YOSEF] and R. Aryeh Leib Gordon of Jerusalem [author of BINAS HA-MIKRA].

OTZAR YISRAEL — Multi-volume Hebrew encyclopedia of Jews and Judaism, edited by J. D. Eisenstein.

PIRKEI D'REBBI ELIEZER — *Midrash aggadah* ascribed to the *tanna*, R. Eliezer ben Hurkanus, that follows a chronological order beginning from Creation.

PESIKTA D'RAV KAHANA — *Midrash aggadah* ascribed to the *amora*, R. Kahana. The PESIKTA is arranged according to the Torah portions read on festivals, holidays and the four special Shabbosos.

RA'AVAD — Acronym of R. Avraham ben David of Posquires (France, 1120-1198). He wrote concise, critical glosses to the *Rambam* as well as to the *Rif*.

RABBENU YONAH — (Spain, 1200-1263). Head of the rabbinical court in Gerona, author of the ethical treatise SHA'AREI TESHUVAH.

RAMA — Acronym of R. Moshe Isserles (Poland, 1525-1572). R. Moshe's short notes to SHULCHAN ARUCH indicate Ashkenazic practice whenever it differs from the Sephardic custom followed by BEIS YOSEF. He also wrote extensive glosses to TUR SHULCHAN ARUCH entitled DARKEI MOSHE

RAMBAM — Acronym of R. Moshe ben Maimon (Spain, 1135 — Egypt, 1204). His YAD HA-CHAZAKAH was the first work to cover the entire body of *halachah*. He also wrote a commentary to the *Mishnah*, works on philosophy [MOREH NEVUCHIM], responsa, and numerous essays on topical subjects [e.g., IGGERES TEIMAN].

RAMBAN — Acronym of R. Moshe ben Nachman (Spain, 1194 — *Eretz Yisrael*, 1270). R. Moshe wrote on almost every facet of Jewish learning, including a commentary to the Torah, to the Talmud, critical glosses to Rambam's SEFER HA-MITZVOS, a commentary to the *Rif* entitled MILCHEMES HASHEM as well as numerous halachic and topical essays.

RAMCHAL — Acronym of R. Moshe Chaim Luzatto (d. 1741), author of MESILAS YESHARIM, DERECH HASHEM, and DA'AS TEVUNOS.

RASHBA — Acronym of R. Shlomo ben Aderes (Spain, 1235-1310), author of a commentary to the Talmud as well as responsa and halachic essays.

RASHI — Acronym of R. Shlomo ben Yitzchak (France, 1040-1105). His commentaries to *Tanach* and the Talmud are the very basis for our understanding of Jewish learning. The commentary of Rashi printed in the ROMM edition of EIN YAAKOV differs slightly from that which appears in the Talmud and may be based on earlier editions.

RIAF — Commentary to EIN YAAKOV by R. Yoshiyahu ben R. Yosef Pinto (Damascus, 1565-1648).

RITVA — Commentary to the Talmud by R. Yom Tov ben Avraham of Seville (Spain, 1250-1330).

ROSH — Acronym of Rabbenu Asher ben Yechiel (Germany, 1250 — Spain, 1327). He wrote a halachic commentary to the Talmud which is the basis for Ashkenazic practice and was one of the three sources (along with YAD HA-CHAZAKAH and RIF) on which R. Yosef Karo based his rulings.

SCHORR, R. GEDALIAH — *Rosh yeshiva* of *Mesifta Torah ve-Daath* in Brooklyn and *Beis Midrash Elyon* in Spring Valley, N.Y. His lectures on the Torah and the Festivals were published under the title OHR GEDALYAHU.

SEFER HA-CHINUCH — Compilation of the 613 mitzvos of uncertain authorship — some ascribe it to R. Aharon ha-Levi of Barcelona (1235-1300).

SFAS EMES — See CHIDUSHEI HA-RIM.

S'FORNO — Biblical commentary by R. Ovadiah Siforno (Italy, 1470 — 1550).

SHA'AREI KEDUSHAH — Ethical work by R. Chaim Vital (*Eretz Yisrael*, 1542 — 1620), disciple of the *Ari ha-Kadosh*.

SHA'AREI TESHUVAH — See RABBENU YONAH.

TARGUM SHENI — *Targum* to *Megillas Esther* of unknown authorship.

TOSAFOS — Commentary to the Talmud compiled and edited in the yeshivos of France and Germany by a group of scholars over a period of some 200 years. The *Tosafos* schools began with *Rashi's* sons-in-law — R. Yehudah ben Nasan and R. Meir ben Shmuel — and were continued by his grandchildren — R. Meir ben Shmuel (Rashbam) and R. Yaakov ben Meir (Rabbenu Tam) — and greatgrandchildren — R. Yitzchak of Dampierre (Ri ha-Zaken). Among the other famous members of the schools of the *Tosafos* are R. Meir of Ruttenberg (Maharam Ruttenberg), R. Moshe of Coucy (author of SEMAG) and R. Shimon of Sens. The commentary of

Tosafos printed in our editions of the Talmud is referred to as *Tosafos Tuch* after the French city Touques where they were edited.

TOSAFOS HA-ROSH — Commentary to the Talmud in the style of the *Tosafos* by R. Asher ben Yechiel — see ROSH.

TOSAFOS RID — Commentary to the Talmud in the style of the *Tosafos* by R. Yeshayah di-Trani (Italy, 13th century).

TOSAFOS YOM TOV — Commentary to the *Mishnah* by R. Yom Tov Lipman Heller (Bavaria, 1579 — Cracow, 1654), a disciple of MAHARAL.

TUREI EVEN — Commentary to the Talmud by R. Aryeh Leib Ginzburg (Poland, 1695 — 1785), rabbi of Volozhin and author of the responsa, SHA'AGAS ARYEH.

VILNA GAON — See GRA.

VOLBE, R. SHLOMO — Contemporary Israeli author and lecturer, author of ALEI SHUR.

YA'AROS DEVASH — See EYBESCHUTZ, R. YONASAN.

YEFEH MAR'EH — Commentary to the Talmud by R. Aryeh Loeb Yellin, rabbi of Bielsk (Poland, 1820-1886). The author's major work, YAFEH EINAYIM in which he provides cross references between the *aggados* brought in the Talmud and those cited in the various *midrashim*, is included in most editions of the Vilna Talmud.

YALKUT SHIMONI — Collection of *aggados* on the entire *Tanach* compiled by R. Shimon *ha-Darshan* of Frankfurt (Germany — 13th century). While much of the material is also found in *Midrash Rabbah* and in the Talmud, the author also quotes numerous other *midrashim* that are no longer extant.

YOSEF LEKACH — Commentary to *Megillas Esther* by R. Eliezer ben R. Eliyahu *ha-Rofeh* (1613-1686), printed in *Mikraos Gedolos* editions of *Tanach*.